THE UNIVERSITY OF WINCHESTER

Martial Rose Library
Tel: 01962 827306

ILL

1 9 SEP 2014

2930701

1 9 JAN 2015

WITHDRAWN FROM THE LIBRARY

UNIVERSITY OF WINCHESTER

To be returned on or before the day marked above, subject to recall.

Also by Christos Yannaras

Elements of Faith
On the Absence and Unknowability of God
Orthodoxy and the West
Postmodern Metaphysics
The Freedom of Morality
Variations on the Song of Songs

CHRISTOS YANNARAS

PERSON AND EROS

Translated
by
Norman Russell

Holy Cross Orthodox Press
Brookline, Massachusetts

Original Title in Greek: *To prosopo kai o eros*
Published in Athens in 1987

© 2007 Holy Cross Orthodox Press

Published by Holy Cross Orthodox Press
50 Goddard Avenue
Brookline, Massachusetts 02445

On the cover: George Kordis, *Shining stars have brought the silence,* painting inspired by the poetry of Odysseas Elitis, 1998.

ISBN-10: 1-885652-88-7
ISBN-13: 978-1-885652-88-1

LIBRARY OF CONGRESS CATALOGING–IN–PUBLICATION DATA

Giannaras, Chrestos, 1935-
[To prosopo kai ho eros. English]
Person and eros / Christos Yannaras ; translated by Norman Russell.
    p. cm.
Includes index.
ISBN 1-885652-88-7 (pbk. : alk. paper)
1. Philosophical anthropology—History. 2. Ontology—History. 3. Fathers of the church, Greek. I. Title.
BD450.G47513 2007
126--dc22

                                                        2007036778

To Dimitri Mavropoulos

Close companion on the journey

CONTENTS

Part One
The Personal "Mode of Existence"

Chapter One
The Ecstatic Character of Personhood

Chapter Two
The Universality of the Person

Chapter Three
The Unity of the Person

Part Two
The Cosmic Dimensions of the Person

Chapter One
The Personal Aspect of the World

Part Three
The "Semantics" of Personal Disclosure

Chapter One
The Logos as Disclosure of the Person

Chapter Two
The Image as "Signifier" of Non-conventional Logos

Chapter Two
The Personal Dimension of Nothingness

Chapter Three
The Moral Dimension of Nothingness

Preface to the Fourth Edition

In this book I have attempted to set out in a contemporary manner (using a rational method and order) a personal response to the ontological question as I have understood it in the Greek philosophical literature of the early Christian and medieval periods.

The "ontological question" or the "problem of being" are verbal expressions of a later date which nevertheless draw attention to one of the starting-points of philosophical thought: our reference to the reality of being, i.e., to that which exists, with regard specifically to the attribute of existence. What does it mean to exist, before any other defining characteristic? We call the ontological question our perplexity about the reality or fact of being, about participation in existence (beyond the mere phenomenicity of that which exists). It is a question about existence as the common constitutive element or presupposition of that which exists (Being in itself, apart from the limitations of space, time, decay and death).

The replies given to the ontological question, as I have identified them in the particular philosophical tradition that I have studied, may be summarized under two basic terms: *person* and *eros*. In the Greek philosophical literature of the early Christian and medieval periods, the starting-point for approaching the fact of existence in itself is the reality of the *person*. And the mode of this approach which makes the person accessible to knowledge is *eros*.

Both the starting-point and the mode of the approach presuppose an empirical investigation. And the experience is not exhausted in what is affirmed by the senses. Nor is it sim-

xiii

ply an intellectual fact – a coincidence of meaning with the object of thought. Nor is it even an escape into a nebulous "mysticism," into individual existential "experiences" beyond any social verification. By the word *experience* I mean here the totality of the multifaceted fact of the *relation* of the subject with other subjects, as also the relation of the subject with the objective givens of the reality surrounding us.

Experience finds in intellectual expression only an outer dress for its social transmission – or only the boundaries protecting it. To approach the ontological question (the reality of beings and the knowledge of Being) presupposes – for Greek philosophical thought in the early Christian and medieval periods – experience as a multiplicity and unity of cognitive possibilities. It presupposes the existential wholeness (integrity, not division) of the human person – a unity of mind and heart, of word and deed, of morality and being.

This integral experiential approach to the ontological question receives its primary expression (or intellectual dress) in the distinctions between nature or essence and *persons*, nature or essence and *energies*. These distinctions do not refer exclusively to the study of human existence. They reveal and recapitulate the entire existential fact, the "mode of existence in its entirety." And this mode, in the perspective of the responses which I study here, is the *person,* in terms of existential otherness as against the common marks of the *essence*, and in terms of beings as "things" – deeds of a creator person, the results of the energies of the essence, which are always personal.

Personal otherness (otherness of existence and energies or "deeds" of the energy), as the starting-point and recapitulation of an integral mode of existence, precedes any intellectual definition of essences or of phenomenal onticities. It reveals the priority of the person (and the personal character of "things") as against that of the essence or nature, the priority which *existence* has with regard to the *understand-*

ing of objective essences. And the priority of the person is revealed (becomes understandable as a fact) by reference to the ecstasy [*ek-stasis* or "standing-out-from"] of the subject, to the ecstatic character of cognitive experience, to the dynamic transcendence of atomic existence with a view to achieving an experiential knowledge of that which exists.

This ecstatic self-transcendence is necessarily referential, a fact of relation and communion. It is *eros* as a voluntary ascetic renunciation of atomic (existential and intellectual) self-sufficiency, as a complete loving self-offering, which is always revelatory of the uniqueness and dissimilarity of the terms of a personal relation.

Nevertheless, in spite of relying on the written sources of Greek philosophical thought in the early Christian and medieval periods, this is not a historical study. A more "personal" quest underlies my appeal to history: whether in writing this book I can test the possibilities suggested by the terminology and problematics of modern philosophy within the context of an ontology founded on the terms *person* and *eros*.

And more specifically: whether this study can examine a fundamental social presupposition which seems to exist (along with equally fundamental differences) both in the ontological perceptions of Hellenism's early Christian centuries and in today's ontological inquiries, chiefly those of the phenomenological school and especially of the existentialist philosophers: refusal to define essence in ontic categories, a refusal to identify essence with the idea or concept of onticity as a whole. It was mainly Heidegger's turning to the Presocratic Greek philosophers, and the new (for the West) reading of Plato and Aristotle that he attempted that contributed decisively to the liberating of Western European philosophical thought from the impasse created by the objectification of truth in intellectual terms, the *adaequatio rei et intellectus*.

To be sure, Heidegger's attempt (that of the West's last "essence mystic") did not succeed in approaching the Greek understanding of truth as *relation* – the cognitive priority which the experience of erotic "surprise" has, the revelation of truth as personal immediacy – an understanding which became the foundation for the whole of the *apophatic* ontology of Hellenism's early Christian centuries. And it was inevitable that in the place of the object which had been demolished what should have appeared inexorably as an ontological reality was *nothingness* – the other "aspect" of ontic disclosure – since it was ruled out that the subject should be studied as *person* and experience of *relations* which destroy ontic objectivity but only to reveal truth (*a-lêtheia*) as immediacy of relation, or oblivion (*lêthê*) as absence of relation.

It is from such considerations as these that the aim of the present study has taken shape. I have sought to bring out the implications of the ontology of Greek thinkers of the early Christian and medieval periods, that is to say, the responses which their ontology might give to the questions raised by modern ontological research. I am not concerned with abstract issues unrelated to human life. I am, rather, anxiously questioning the judgment of a whole modern culture based on the "objectivity" and usefulness of truth, on the ongoing subjection of humanity to this usefulness.

The investigation of the themes brought together in this book has passed through many stages or phases since it began in about 1966. Nor could I say that the pages now before the reader represent a final expression. Once one begins to be preoccupied with the ontological problem, it inevitably becomes the central theme of one's life – a thirst or hope for the gift of abiding permanently in the ceaseless motion of the soul "around that which is the same and one and alone."

Christos Yannaras
Athens, 1987

Abbreviations

ANF	Ante-Nicene Fathers
Blackfriars trans.	*St Thomas Aquinas: Summa Theologiae*, Latin text and English trans. by Thomas Gilby, OP, *et al.*, 60 vols., London, 1964-73
CC	Corpus Christianorum
CWS	The Classics of Western Spirituality
Diels	H. Diels, *Die Fragmente der Vorsokratiker*, 6th ed., Berlin, 1952
ET	English translation
FT	French translation
Hamilton-Cairns	E. Hamilton and H. Cairns (eds.), *The Collected Dialogues of Plato including the Letters*, Princeton, 1961
Kirk-Raven-Schofield	G. S. Kirk, J. E. Raven and M. Schofield, *The Presocratic Philosophers*, 2nd ed., Cambridge, 1983
LCL	Loeb Classical Library
Louth	A. Louth, *Maximus the Confessor*, London and New York, 1996
Macquarrie-Robinson	M. Heidegger, *Being and Time*, trans. by J. Macquarrie and E. Robinson, Oxford, 1967
NPNF	Nicene and Post-Nicene Fathers
OECT	Oxford Early Christian Texts

Oxford trans.	*The Complete Works of Aristotle: The Revised Oxford Translation*, ed. J. Barnes, 2 vols., Princeton, 1984
Palmer-Sherrard-Ware	*The Philokalia: The Complete Text compiled by St. Nikodimos of the Holy Mountain and St. Makarios of Corinth,* trans. and ed. G. E. H. Palmer, P. Sherrard and K. Ware, London, 1979 ff.
Pears-McGuiness	L. Wittgenstein, *Tractatus Logico-Philosophicus*, trans. D. F. Pears and B. F. McGuiness, London and New York, 1974
PG	J. P. Migne (ed.), *Patrologia Graeca*, Paris, 1857-66
RSV	Revised Standard Version
SC	Sources Chrétiennes
ThWNT	*Theologische Wörterbuch zum Neuen Testament*, ed. G. Kittel, Stuttgart, 1933 ff. (ET ed. G. W. Bromiley, Grand Rapids, 1963 ff.)
Wheelwright	P. Wheelwright, *Heraclitus*, Oxford, 1959

Translator's Note

This book was originally published in Greek in 1970 under the title *The Ontological Content of the Theological Concept of the Person*. On the appearance of the second edition in 1974, it was given a new title: *Person and Eros*. The present translation is based on the greatly expanded fourth edition of 1987. I have attempted to render the Greek as faithfully as possible, enclosing any additional material in square brackets. The English translation of patristic texts not otherwise attributed is my own.

Norman Russell

PERSON AND EROS

PART ONE

The Personal "Mode of Existence"

Chapter One

The Ecstatic Character of Personhood

§1 *The fact of "relation" as the initial assumption of the ontological question, and the "person" as the sole existential possibility of relation*

By the word *prosôpon* ("person") we define a referential reality. The referential character of the term is revealed fundamentally by its primitive use, that is, by its grammatical construction and etymology. The preposition *pros* ("towards") together with the noun *ôps* (*ôpos* in the genitive), which means "eye," "face," "countenance,"[1] form the composite word *pros-ôpon*: I have my face turned towards someone or something; I am opposite someone or something. The word thus functioned initially as a term indicating an immediate reference, a relationship.

Prosôpon, or person, is defined as reference and relation and itself defines a reference and relation. The word's primordial semantic content does not allow us to interpret personhood simply as individuality outside the field of relation. The sense which the term "relation" acquires with regard to the person will be clarified gradually in what follows. At all events, it points not to an abstract analogy or comparison but to the fact of "being-opposite-someone/something." That which is "opposite-someone/something," i.e., the person, certainly represents an individual, but an individual in relation, a dynamic actualization of relationship. The relation is

5

the "specific differentia" of the person, the definition of the person, the radical differentiation of personhood from the sense of static individuality.

Personhood is fundamentally the only possible relationship with beings. Beings (*ta onta*) exist only as *anti-keimena*, as "things-set-opposite";[2] that is to say, they manifest being (*to einai*) only in relation to the person. This reference defines the existential character of beings as *phenomena* – beings appear (*phainontai*), are disclosed as that which is, only according to the principle, or *logos*, of their relation to the person. Our attempt to define beings as they are in themselves, without reference to their relation to whoever is defining them, is an instance of a definition that arbitrarily presupposes relation to be non-relation. This is a conventional intellectual construct, a denial of the only possible experience that confirms the existence of beings – the experience of things-set-opposite. It is a conventional intellectual construct because beings "in themselves" as a "synthesis of *being-for-itself* and *being-in-itself*" (Sartre),[3] are no longer the disclosed objects [or "things-set-opposite"] of ontological reality, but only the ideas or concepts of beings. Beings *are* (*einai*) only as phenomena, only insofar as they become accessible to a referential relation of disclosure. We cannot speak of the *being-in-itself* of beings; we can speak only of *being-there* or *being-present* (*par-einai*), of co-existence with the possibility of their disclosure. We know beings as presence (*par-ousia*), not as essence (*ousia*).

§2   *The ontological priority of personal relation with regard to consciousness*

This referential relation is expressed directly as the consciousness (*syn-eidêsis*) of persons, as a universal conception and synthesis of items of knowledge (*eidêseis*) concerning the world, of the evidence supplied by objects. Consciousness appears first of all as a necessary and sufficient condition of the phenomenicity of phenomena – the definition of beings as "phenomena" presupposes the fact of their disclosure, a fact of relation. And relation is an exclusive potentiality of persons, which is expressed first of all by the function of consciousness. The function of consciousness is necessarily referential, a function of relation. Husserl showed that consciousness is always "consciousness of something." There is no consciousness without reference to some content ("Intentionalität"). Consciousness signifies an *a priori* relationship with objects. We say at this point: consciousness is a "personal" property.

In defining consciousness as a personal *property*, we mean that the reference of consciousness to some content does not exhaust the reality of the *relation* between the person and beings. The capacity for consciousness alone is not sufficient to explain the universality or principle (*logos*) of the relationship of beings to the person. Consciousness belongs to the referential character of the person, but does not exhaust it. We may express the primary distinction between the universal reality of the person and the fact of consciousness by drawing on Husserl's account of the real difference between the subjectivity of cognition ("die Subjektivität des Erkennens") and the objectivity of the content of cognition ("die Objektivität des Erkenntnisinhaltes").[4] I am aware of objects, and with the help of the "semantics" which language offers me, I define a stone, a river, or a child, and yet the information or sense arising from consciousness which makes the content of cognition common knowledge has its origin in my "personal" cognition (or experience) of these common objects. That is to say, cognition differs from one human being to another. The objectivity[5] of the cognitive content of consciousness is not primordial. It is defined and formed by the "semantics" of language, that is, by the association of subjective experience with the "acoustic images" imposed on us by the common language we speak.[6] Subjective experience, that is, the differentiation from one human being to another of the initial conscious cognition, remains a "personal" fact in spite of the automatic association with acoustic images which our language imposes on us. And this "personal" fact is very vivid and immediately accessible when it concerns concepts or sensory perceptions that are ethical or religious: beauty, obligation and metaphysical faith, as contents of consciousness, confirm very directly the "personal" character of cognition. They reveal the reality of the person *beyond* consciousness, the universality of the person in relation to consciousness.

The difference, then, between the subjectivity of knowledge and the objectivity of the conscious content of knowledge is not theoretical. It does not refer to some kind of psychological idealism, but is real and defines the *reality* of the person, that is, the priority of personhood with regard to consciousness. Being-as-person signifies a cognitive power before any "semantic" shaping of the content of consciousness. It signifies the existential space of the primary *disclosure* of beings. This transcendence of the priority of the "semantic" (intellectual) shaping of the content of consciousness prevents us from identifying human existence purely and simply with *thinking* (*noeô/cogito*). Since the *mode* by which human beings *are* (as persons) in relation to what exists is not restricted to the semantic-intellectual definition of their temporal and spatial (dimensional) presence but the reality of the person is prior to any intellectual-objective definition, it follows that the starting-point of the ontological question (the question about beings and Being, their relation and their difference) is not humanity's power of rational thought but the much more universal reality of the person itself.

§3   *A void in ontology as such*

The understanding of the human being purely in terms of

its capacity for rational thought, as a *zôon logon echon* or an "animal rationale," was strongly challenged by Heidegger. He demonstrated that it was far removed from the core of the ontological problem, and transferred the problem to the realm of value judgments, making it the starting-point of an axiological metaphysics.[7] The exclusive priority given to the faculty of reason, the identification of existence with *thinking* ("cogito ergo sum"), lays the foundations for an axiological (and consequently conventional) metaphysics, because then the causal connection between beings and Being is always logically more consistent. The ontological problem is posed as an *a priori* etiological question: What is that which makes beings *be*? Being is presupposed as the cause of beings (axiologically superior to that which is caused), and at the same time its interpretation within the context of the etiological question is necessarily ontic. That is, the interpretation of onticity is predetermined by the reasons which make it the cause of beings.

Western metaphysics borrowed elements from Aristotle to give axiological expression to the way the ontological interpretation of Being differs from the reality of beings in the world. The Scholastics based their definition of the difference on the method of *analogy* and *eminence* ("analogia entis," "via eminentiae"). This differentiation was understood in terms of a scale of magnitude, that is, in the context of the antithesis between absolute and relative, or infinite and finite. Being (*Einai*) was defined unavoidably as "a consummate, divine being – a most honorable species," self-caused and the cause of other beings, an ascent to the absolute ("regressus in infinitum") of ontic individuality. Being summarizes the eternal causes or principles of beings. The existence of beings is identified purely and simply with the correspondence of objects to their eternal principles (*logoi*), to their absolute concepts. Truth is defined as the coincidence of meaning with the mind's object of thought ("adaequatio rei et intellectus").[8]

This coincidence is realized and manifested in rational judgment, that is, in the context of the faculty of reason. That is why to define existence is to identify it with *thinking*.

This axiological and rationalistic understanding of ontology was originally challenged by Kant. He was the first to deny the exclusive primacy of the faculty of reason, to distinguish thought from existence, to reject the identification of the meaning of being with the *Being* of being, and thus to mark the end of scholastic ontology. But Kant harmonized intellect with existence on the level of the subject's critical faculty, transposing the ontological problem to the question of the acquisition of cognitive experience and so inaugurating the individualist subjectivism of modern "metaphysics."

Hegel went one step further, and in the terminology of an early phenomenology defined the essential estrangement of the intellect from material things:[9] We know beings only on the phenomenal level, not on the level of essence, and phenomenal means that which is apparent, that which is disclosed (*phainetai*), independently of that which a being *is* in its essence.[10] For Hegel the only possibility of overcoming this estrangement is history. History makes *being* accessible as *fact*. But it is evident that the leap made by Kant and Hegel does not transcend the limits of the subject, the limits of individuality. "A valid description of Hegel's metaphysics might be: a metaphysics of absolute subjectivism."[11] The exclusive priority of the rational faculty is overthrown, only to be replaced by the priority of the self-awareness of the human subject – the priority of the activity of the spirit that produces, directs and gives purpose and meaning to universal becoming, to the rational historical existence of subjects. The "modern age" is characterized by humanity's imprisonment in complete subjectivity and at the same time by its effort to attain absolute objectivity, centered, in both cases, on the individual.

Not only the most indicative but also the most interesting expression of this imprisonment is the "great moment" of modern philosophy, the "new ontology" of Martin Heidegger – his attempt to formulate a non-metaphysical ontology, to transcend, by the phenomenological method, the absolute and ontic or the mystical definition of Being, as well as the subjectivity and rationalism imposed on the phenomenological method by the positing of consciousness as the exclusive field of the interpretation of *being*.

Heidegger rejects any definition of *Being*, regarding the power to define as inescapably bound up with ontic categories. That is why he also rejects the etiological formulation of the ontological problem, as a question about the *relation* of beings to Being, the interpretation of Being as the cause of beings. He transfers the ontological question from the relation to the *difference* between beings and Being. The difference lies in the fact that beings are disclosed (*phainontai*), they are *phenomena*, while Being, or essence, "loves to hide."[12] We do not know the essence, the Being of beings (*to Einai tôn ontôn*); we only know the *mode* by which they *are*, and this mode is the fact of disclosure.

Heidegger accepts as a starting-point for the understanding of the Being of beings (the mode by which it is what it is) an interpretation of truth as disclosure, as rising up out of oblivion: the Being of beings is not identified with their reality "in itself," that is, with a given "essence," but is understood as energy, as the specific fact of "coming into light" ("ans Licht kommen"), as rising up from oblivion (*lêthe*) into non-oblivion, or truth (*a-lêtheia*), from absence (*ap-ousia*) to presence (*par-ousia*). Consequently, what belongs to the *mode* by which beings *are* is not only the reality of their disclosure, the dimension of their presence, but also their constant rising up from oblivion. Beings are *disclosed* (*phainontai*) as presence and *are* (*einai*) as both absence and presence. This constant rising up from absence defines the dimension of the temporality of the *being* of beings. *Time* is a presupposition for the understanding of the truth (the *a-lêtheia*) of beings, their rising up from absence to presence. It is the "horizon" where beings are understood as that which they *are*.

The *mode* by which beings *are* therefore not only presupposes but also determines their disclosure as temporality, as emergence from absence. Thus our understanding of the *being* of beings proves to be necessarily phenomenal. Our knowledge of beings is exhausted in their temporal emergence from oblivion, in the distinction between presence (*par-ousia*) and absence (*ap-ousia*), that is, in the disclosure of our cognitive distance from essence (*ousia*). Knowledge is not the ascent of the phenomenon to the universal "idea," or an intellectual conception of its essence. It is the cognition of disclosure or of oblivion as the *mode* by which it may be what it is. It is the understanding of the *fact* of disclosure as a definition of time – the only "horizon" where that which *is* comes into the light, is *disclosed*.

This understanding of ontology prevents us from remaining satisfied with a simplistic version of the problem of truth that defines truth as the coincidence of meaning with the mentally conceived object, limiting essence to the idea or concept. In Heidegger the understanding of truth is cognition or experience of distance from essence, of possible presence or absence. It is a restriction of the knowledge of beings to the *mode* by which these are *disclosed*. That is to say, it is not nothingness. Knowledge is no longer an objectively complete intellectual certainty, but a cognition of relativity with regard to the hidden essence – in sum, an anxiety in the face of oblivion or nothingness, an awareness that oblivion or nothingness is the other side of temporal disclosure.

The understanding or experience of the distance from essence, that is, knowledge of beings as *phenomena*, ends up by being experience of the existential distance between humanity and objective beings in their inaccessible essence. Humanity understands the *mode* in which beings *are* – the truth (*a-lêtheia*) of beings as disclosure and disclosure as temporality – but the understanding of disclosure, that is, the consciousness of time as an exclusively human property, is only a necessary and sufficient condition of the phenomenicity of phenomena. It does not abrogate the self-hiddenness of essence, the distantiality between humanity and the hidden essence of beings. The experience of this distantiality is an experience of estrangement ("Entfremdung"), the anxiety of not-being-at-home, which Heidegger calls "die Unheimlichkeit des Daseins," "das Un-zuhause."[13] Humanity is "thrown into a world" where the phenomenicity of phenomena discloses the ontological reality of nothingness. Humanity's relationship with the world is only the anguish of being faced with nothingness.[14]

The existential experience of the phenomenicity of phenomena, as anxiety in the face of nothingness, although representing a radical relation to the Cartesian *cogito*, nevertheless does not differ essentially from the presuppositions of ontic individuality, on which Cartesian ontology is based. We have noted that according to Heidegger beings are *disclosed* as presence and *are* as presence and absence. As presence, beings are conceived of as *phenomena*. As presence-absence, beings *are*, conceived of through intellect and word. The separation of presence from absence lies in the understanding of beings as that which they *are*, that is, it lies in *intellection* (*noein*). *Intellection*, as a presupposition of conceiving of the *Being* of beings as presence and absence, proves also to be a presupposition of the separation of absence from presence, that is, a presupposition of the definition of the onticity of beings, of the conception of beings as individual things. Phenomenology insists that this individuality is phenomenal; it must be understood as *energeia*,[15] as the emergence from absence into presence, that is, as temporality. But temporality implies the *understanding* of Being as emergence from absence into presence, and this understanding is concomitant to the separation of presence from absence, and consequently to a determination of temporal disclosure as ontic individuality. Even as the *energeia* of temporal disclosure, individuality remains ontic, since beings (*onta*) are *disclosed* (*phainontai*) only as objects, only in the distantiality of ontic individuality.

But if we accept temporal disclosure as ontic individuality, we leave its other aspect, forgetfulness or nothingness, in an almost mystical state of indetermination. Being, or essence, self-conceals itself as presence and absence, as disclosure but also as constant emergence from forgetfulness. This self-concealment, however, cannot be conceived of in both ontic and non-ontic categories. When ontic categories are observed in one phase of the self-concealment of essence, that of presence, but are replaced in the second phase, that of absence, by the non-ontic categories of forgetfulness or nothingness, then the problem of essence, the problem of Being – the ontological problem – remains philosophically in suspension. It is not possible for presence, one of the aspects of the problem of essence, to be conceived of as temporal disclosure, using ontic categories, and for the other aspect alone, that of absence, the eventuality of non-disclosure, to remain as the basis for the difference of beings from essence, from essence, that is, as self-concealment.

We can accept that temporal disclosure does not exhaust the truth of a being (*a-lêtheia tou ontos*), that truth is not an ontic category, that it is the emergence from forgetfulness, the *energeia* of disclosure. But although the rising up, the *energeia*, of disclosure is understood as time – and time proves to be a presupposition of the phenomenicity of phenomena – the phenomena themselves can be conceived of only as ontic individualities if they are to be distinguished from non-disclosure. However much forgetfulness or nothingness is emphasized by phenomenology as the other side of the phenomenicity of phenomena, the ontic individuality

of phenomena is not impaired. The transition from absence
to presence, the separation into the two, even if interpreted
exclusively as temporal phenomenicity, does not cease to define objects in terms of the distantiality of individuality. And
individuality exhausts only one side of the problem of essence, leaving the other side suspended in an arbitrary identification with forgetfulness or nothingness, leaving, that is to
say, a void in ontology as such. Heidegger was aware of this
void. It is well known that in *Sein und Zeit* he confined himself to the interpretation of humanity's *being* (*einai*), which
represents the unique possibility of understanding time, that
is, the *mode* by which it is what it is. He did, however, prom-
ise a sequel on ontology itself (*Zeit und Sein*), in which the
problem was not to be humanity's *being* but Being in itself,
an ontology interpretative of Being as Being. But he never
wrote it.

§4   *The ontological priority of personal relation with
        regard to the capacity for rational thought*

   In the context of the ontological problem the term *person*
(*prosôpon*) first appears in the Greek East, in the fourth-
century theologian Gregory of Nyssa (d. 394).[16] In their attempt to determine the ecclesiastical experience of the truth
of the Triadic God, that is, the mode of divine existence as
revealed in history, and distinguish this truth from its heretical variants (Arianism, Sabellianism, Eunomianism,
Apollinarianism), the ecclesiastical writers of the early
Christian centuries sought to clarify two terms drawn from
Neoplatonic ontology,[17] *ousia* ("essence" or "substance") and
hypostasis ("substantive existence" or "existence instantiated
in an individual"), with reference to the divine essence and the
three divine hypostases. They needed to show how the three
hypostases were differentiated without impairing the unity of
the One Godhead, the *homoousion* of the hypostases.

In the age of the Cappadocian Fathers, however – Basil the Great (d. 379), Gregory of Nazianzus (d. 390) and Gregory of Nyssa – the two terms, essence and hypostasis, had not yet been fully distinguished from each other and are often confused or identified.[18] It is characteristic that even the First Ecumenical Council (325) took the term *homoousios* to mean *one essence and hypostasis*. The Cappadocians were the first to separate the terms *ousia* and *hypostasis* and distinguish clearly between them on the basis of the Aristotelian distinction between primary and secondary substances (*ousia prôtê* and *ousia deutera*).[19] Hypostasis acquires the sense of the Aristotelian "primary substance" and in Gregory of Nyssa becomes synonymous with "person." Person or hypostasis is distinguished from essence or nature on the basis of the uniqueness and dissimilarity of the properties. It is "that which makes distinctive" (*to idiazon*), or "otherness." It is defined as "the concurrence of the characteristic features around each … The distinguishing sign of the existence of each,"[20] "the concept which by the characteristic features that appear restrict the common and uncircumscribed in a particular thing."[21] Although essence is the general, the species, the community of recognizable signs, "essence … is not distributed to produce any difference of nature,"[22] "it has been demonstrated with regard to the essence by those who know how to discuss such matters in a philosophical manner that no difference can be conceived of if one pares it down and strips it of the qualities and characteristics considered to be in it and examines it as it is in itself, according to the principle of being."[23]

The development and interpretation of the two terms by the later Fathers of the Greek East will be examined to some extent below. Here what principally interests us is this first appearance of the term *person* in ontological discussion, its initial definition as "the distinguishing sign of the existence of each" – the "uncircumscribed" aspect of the person, its absolute otherness. The ontological meaning which Greek patristic literature gave to the term is precisely absolute otherness as its existential difference from essence. We conceive of essence as the fact of the universal, as species, as a community of recognizable signs, but in the case of God and humanity essence *exists* only "in persons," and the person is the absolute otherness with regard to the common characteristics of essence. Personhood is differentiated from essence or nature on the basis of the "distinctive" (*idiazonta*) and uncircumscribed character of the *mode* in which it embodies the common existential marks of the essence – that is, it is differentiated from whatever is conceived of as being (*on*) in itself, as a community of recognizable signs, as a general species.

Finally, the difference is between the *mode of existence*, that is, the person as absolute otherness, and the intellectual conception of essence, that is, of being as a universal, as a community of objective recognizable signs. This implies that the ontological problem, the question concerning the *mode* by which whatever is *is*, can only be posited within the context of the reality of the person, on the basis of the priority of the person with regard to essence, the priority which *existence* has in relation to the *understanding* of objective essences.

§5   *Personal relation as an ontological presupposition to the disclosure of the general "mode of existence"*

The person, as absolute otherness, is differentiated from anything conceived of by the intellect as a genuine being, as a community of recognizable signs. That is why every person's mode of existence is objectively indeterminable, unique, dissimilar and unrepeatable, since every precise determination and every predication necessarily represents a community of recognizable signs. That which makes a person distinctive – *to idiazon*, his or her otherness – cannot be defined but can only be experienced as *fact*, that is, as unique, dissimilar and unrepeatable *relation*. Otherness is by definition referential. It is always defined "relatively" (*en schesei*), and absolute otherness can only be experienced as unique, dissimilar and unrepeatable relation. This means that in the case of the person, reference or relation is not simply a matter of comparison. It is not just a way of understanding otherness as the differentiation of ontic individualities. It is that mode of existence which is *actualized* as relation, not merely *disclosed* as relation. The person *is* only as dynamic reference, only as "opposite-something," only as unique, dissimilar and unrepeatable relation. Within the fact of this relation, the "towards-something" (*pros ti*) of personal reference appears as an occasion for the disclosure of the person's otherness (the existential *how* or *mode of existence*) and at the same time is defined with regard to the otherness. It *is disclosed* (*phainetai*) as that which it *is* only in the fact of the relation that reveals the otherness of the person.

Consequently, in the ontological perspective that the priority of the person defines, the definition of beings as *phenomena* acquires a sense of pre-conscious cognition: beings *are disclosed* not simply as temporality in the distantiality of ontic individuality, but in the dynamic of a personal *fact*, which precedes any conscious-intellectual determination. And this fact is the *relation*, which is revelatory of the otherness of the person and of the *mode* by which beings *are*. Of course, the actualization of personal relation is made complete (as we shall see below) only in the fact of interpersonal communion, only with reference to supreme (that is, *essential*) otherness. Yet it finds its dynamic starting-point in the fact of the *disclosure* of beings in the "horizon" of personal cognition-relation, that is, in the transcending of the *understanding* of objective essences. Thus the disclosure of beings represents a fact of *invitation* (*klêsis*) to reveal the person, and the person represents the unique power of approaching the *mode* of existence of beings, beyond any objective, i.e., conventional, determination.

§6   *Personal relation as existential ek-stasis*

It is evident, even from these introductory remarks, that here we are very far from any kind of objectified subjectivism, any kind of axiologically determined priority of the subject as the capacity for consciousness and intellectuality. The person, as a power of the disclosure of beings, does not mean that a human being is primarily a given conscious-intellectual capacity and that what it conceives of intellectually coincides with the hypostasis or temporality of the object. It is not confined to the priority of the functioning of consciousness, which has an axiological character because it "judges," because it endows the object formed in the mind with sense (gives assurance of the bulk, weight, form, color, cause and aim of beings). The meaning it has is this: whatever *is* becomes apparent only with reference to the person, is disclosed only within the terms of the *relation* which reveals the otherness of the person. In other words, person and beings are the terms of a *relation*, and this relation poses the ontological question. Beings *are* as the principle (*logos*) of relationship with the person. The truth (*a-lêtheia*) or oblivion (*lêthe*) of beings is identified with their reference or non-reference to the person.

The initial question of ontology, the question about beings and Being, about the *mode* in which anything *is* what it is, is consequently identified with the question about the person, with the investigation of the existential fact of personal relation. The *logos* of the otherness of the person responds to the question about Being, no longer as Being-in-itself, as an intellectual conception or undetermined revelation and temporal disclosure, but as *mode of existence*. The human person participates in the question as one questioned, as a unique ability for experiential response, as a term of a "personal" relation. Being-as-person signifies the change of the thinking subject into a term of a universal-existential rela-

tion, into a fact of *ek-stasis* from the objectiveness of understanding to a universal-existential relation.

This movement from noetic-conscious stationariness (*stasis*) to universal *relation* is also a transition from the ontic-
individual perception of human existence to its ecstatic determination. And here *ek-stasis* (from *exo-istamai*, "stand
outside") is not confined to humanity's ability to "stand
outside" its natural identity, to wonder at its *being*, to conceive – alone amongst beings – of disclosure as temporality.[24] *Ek-stasis* here is identified with the actualization of the
person's otherness, that is, with the existential presupposition itself of the person, which is also a unique ability to
approach the *mode* of the existence of beings. *Ek-stasis*, or
ecstasy, signifies self-transference from the naturally given
capacity for intellectualization to the otherness of its personal actualization, from the self-evidentness of noetic-
conscious conceptualization of objective conventionality
and the naturally given common understanding of objective
essences to universal existential relation.

The dynamic and always unachieved consummation of this
relation is the *eros* of the Greek Church Fathers, the loving
impetus and movement of exodus from individualized existence in the realm of objects, for the sake of the actualization of *relation* in the highest sense. Eros is the dynamics of
ecstasy, which finds its consummation as personal reference
to supreme Otherness: "divine eros is also ecstatic, so that
the lovers belong not to themselves but to the beloved."[25]

§7   *Apophaticism at the boundaries of the ontological
      problem: apophaticism of essence and apophaticism
      of person*

The ontological meaning which Greek patristic literature
of the Byzantine period gave to the term *prosôpon* ("person") became the occasion of an ontology radically different

from that which the Western theological and philosophical tradition represents in the course of its historical development. The West was trapped in a polarized view of Being as either analogically absolute and ontic or else mystical. This came about as the inevitable consequence of the priority Westerners gave, even in the first Christian centuries, to the intellectual definition of essence over the historical and existential experience of personhood – in contrast to the Greek East, which always relied for its starting-point on the priority of person over essence.[26]

The priority of the need to define essence within the context of the ontological question requires the objective definition of the existence of beings and an intellectualist (analogical-ontic) and etiological explanation of Being. The Scholastics established the threefold way ("via triplex") in the West of the analogical cognition of Being: the way of negation ("via negationis"), the way of eminence ("via eminentiae"), and the way of causality ("via causalitatis").[27]

In contradictory but historical conjunction with its cataphatic-analogical determination of Being, the West was also preoccupied with the *apophaticism* of Being, with the impossibility of the human intellect to exhaust the truth of Being by means of definitions. Apophaticism in the West arose from the need to protect the mystery of the divine essence. That is to say, it is always an *apophaticism of essence*. It is characteristic that the two thinkers who did most to shape the positive-analogical approach to the knowledge of God, Anselm of Canterbury (d. 1109) and Thomas Aquinas (d. 1274), at the same time proclaim the apophatic nature of this knowledge, the essential unknowability of God, the inaccessibility of Being.[28] And we find following this line on the apophaticism of essence not only the leading Scholastics but also the great mystics of the Middle Ages – Peter Abelard (d. 1142), Albert the Great (d. 1280) and John Duns Scotus (d. 1308), as well as Meister Eckhart (d. 1327) and Nicholas of Cusa (d. 1464).

But it is impossible for the apophaticism of essence to confront the ontological problem as an existential problem, as
a question about the *mode* by which whatever *is* is, about
the "mode of existence."[29] The absolutizing of the existential
fact by the Scholastics, with regard to God, who is defined
as "pure act" ("actus purus" [in Greek *katharê energeia tou
hyparchein*]), interprets the *mode* in which the essence *is* and
this mode is to *exist* ("essentia est id cuius actus est esse").[30]
But it does not touch upon the *mode of existing* (*tropos tou
hyparchein*), and consequently it continues to limit the ontological problem to the field of abstract definitions.

By contrast, Eastern theology had always rejected any polarization between the analogical-ontological and the mystical determinations of Being. The ontology of the Easterners
was primarily existential because its basis and starting-point
is the *apophaticism of the person*, not the apophaticism of
essence.

> In the tradition of the Eastern Church there is no place for
> a theology, and even less for a mysticism, of the divine es-
> sence …. If one speaks of God it is always, for the Eastern
> Church, in the concrete: "the God of Abraham, of Isaac and
> of Jacob; the God of Jesus Christ." It is always the Trinity:
> Father, Son and Holy Ghost. When, on the contrary, the
> common nature assumes the first place in our conception
> of trinitarian dogma the religious reality of God in Trinity
> is inevitably obscured in some measure and gives place to
> a certain philosophy of essence …. Indeed, in the doctri-
> nal conditions peculiar to the West all properly theocentric
> speculation runs the risk of considering the nature before the
> persons and becoming a mysticism of "the divine abyss,"
> as in the *Gottheit* of Meister Eckhart; of becoming an im-
> personal apophaticism of the divine nothingness prior to
> the Trinity. Thus by a paradoxical circuit we return through
> Christianity to the mysticism of the neo-platonists.[31]

The distinction between the apophaticism of the person and
the apophaticism of the essence cannot be fully accounted

for as a theoretical difference. It represents and constitutes two diametrically opposed spiritual attitudes, two modes of life, in short, two different cultures. On the one side, life is based on truth as *relation* and as existential experience; truth is actualized as life's social dynamics and life is justified as the identification of being true with being in communion. On the other side, truth is identified with intellectual definitions; it is objectivized and subordinated to usefulness. And truth as usefulness objectivizes life itself; it comes to be translated into technological hype, into the tormenting and alienation of humanity.

But the historical and cultural consequences arising from the differences between East and West in the realm of ontology must remain the subject for another book.[32] Here I simply draw attention to the brilliant formulation by Martin Heidegger (perhaps the last "essence mystic" in the West) of the quandary created by the priority of the apophaticism of essence.[33] Heidegger's approach showed clearly how the apophaticism of essence defines and respects the limits of thought, and consequently the limits of metaphysics or of the ineffable, but leaves the problem of ontic individuality on the borders of a possible nihilism, reveals Nothingness as an eventuality as equally possible as Being, and transposes the ontological question to the dilemma between being and Nothingness: "warum ist überhaupt Seiendes und nicht vielmehr Nichts?"[34] With Heidegger the apophaticism of essence proves to be as much a possibility of ontological and theological nihilism as an ontic-intellectual definition of essence. We shall return to this theme in a later chapter.

Chapter Two

The Universality of the Person

§8   *Personal otherness as existential actualization of "nature in general"*

The universality of the person is determined by its ecstatic character. In its ecstatic reference, that is, in its otherness, the person is differentiated from the referential presence of beings by the measure in which its universality is differentiated: the principle of the otherness of the person recapitulates the *mode* in which human existence *is*, the "universal"[1] mode of existence. Although the referential presence of beings is restricted to the principle of their relation to the person, it defines beings as *phenomena*, as individual entities disclosed by the fact of personal *relation*. A being, as referential presence, is the particular, the partial, the phenomenal (through relation) individual. A person, as possibility of relation, that is, as a presupposition of the disclosure of beings, is the whole, the universal. Every human person is the possibility of the universal disclosure of the *mode* in which human existence *is* and, at the same time, the presupposition of universal *relation*, in the context of which beings become true (*a-lêtheuousi*), that is, they are *disclosed* as that which they *are*.

Using this definition of the universality of the person, we can reply to the question about the *essence* or *nature*[2] of humanity. We have said that the person in its ecstatic reference – that is, in its otherness – transcends the objective properties and common signs of recognition of the form, and consequently is not defined by its nature. On the contrary, it defines its nature or essence.[3] The ec-stasy of the person, the actualization of otherness, is the *mode* by which humanity *is* as a "universal."

But in this last phrase there is a fundamental logical contradiction: We speak of the "actualization" of otherness, while at the same time we define otherness as the *mode* by which humanity *is* a "universal." This simultaneous reference to otherness as a definition and as a dynamic actualization is a vital theme which will be discussed at greater length in the next chapter. Here we shall confine ourselves to the indicative character of this fundamental logical contradiction: it indicates the transcendence of schematic-ontic definitions; it marks off otherness as a definition, and at the same time as a term of an existential fact. The fundamental contradiction confirms the existential and not only the theoretical character both of the otherness of the person and of the common properties of the nature in relation to which otherness is defined. The ecstasy of the person, its differentiation from the common properties of the nature, cannot be conceived of in a purely intellectual manner. It not only *defines* the otherness, but also *is defined* as an existential fact, that is, as a pragmatic reality which is only capable of being known dynamically – as a possibility. Personal otherness *is* as a definition, but it is also *constituted* dynamically as an existential fact within the terms of natural individuality.

This means that the objective properties of the nature are construed here not simply as the theoretical and abstract recognizable signs of form, but also as individual properties of existence, as recognizable existential signs of natural individuality. The person in any event represents a primarily natural individual. The fundamental approach to the person is realized by starting from the natural individuality with regard to which otherness is defined.[4] Consequently, the fundamental approach to nature can be realized by starting from the level of personal existence, whereupon nature not only simply *defines* the intellectual conception of the "universal," but also *is defined* as existential reality on the boundaries of the *fact* of otherness.[5] The person "supports" (*hyphistatai*) that which occurs in nature[6] – the "accidents" of nature are the "passions" of the person[7] – and at the same time the person *is* as otherness with regard to nature and the "accidents" of nature. The transcendence of objective properties – of the "accidents" of nature – the actualization of otherness is an existential fact which is constituted within the similarly existential boundaries of natural individuality – and consequently otherness does not refer only to objective beings and other persons, but is also actualized principally with regard to the natural individuality of personal existence.

Dynamic otherness with regard to the individual "passions," which are the "accidents" of nature, determines the *ecstatic* character of personal existence – ecstasy (*ek-stasis*) meaning the dynamic self-transcendence of natural individuality, its freedom from the very things that naturally predetermine it. Ecstasy as self-transcendence recapitulates, that is, determines, personal otherness and at the same time presupposes, that is, "contains," universal nature as an existential reality. This means that the human person is not a part or portion of humanity's being, human essence or nature, but is the *existence* of that nature[8] – since otherness recapitulates nature in the fact of its ecstatic self-transcendence: human nature exists only "in persons,"[9] only as ecstatic otherness with regard to its very self; nature is the *content* of the person. Since personal otherness constitutes nature's *mode of existence* and every person defines the universal otherness it follows that every human person in its ecstatic otherness "contains" the universal nature,[10] recapitulates the nature in the fact of the dynamic reference "outside" (*ektos*) nature (within the lim-

its of personal ecstasy) – that is, every human person is the
dynamic recapitulation of universal humanity.

   This ascent to universal humanity could form the basis of
an intellectual schema – the unity of all human persons is a
fundamental intellectual definition of the "universal" ("that
which is true of a whole class and is said to hold good as a
whole is true of a whole in the sense that it contains many
things by being predicated of each, and that each and all of
them are one" – Aristotle)[11] The ecstasy, however, of the person, as a recapitulation of essence or nature in the *fact* of its
self-transcendence, corresponds not to the intellectual-semi-
ological (and consequently ontic) definition of "universal"
but to its existential-ontological sense. It is nature in general
which "stands out" (*ex-istatai*) in the existential fact of personal otherness, both as self-transcendence and as *relation*
with beings – an existential presupposition of the general
disclosure of beings.

   Consequently, the universality of the person demands an
understanding of essence or nature very different from the
intellectual ascent to a "whole of the same form." In its ecstatic otherness the person remains a *fact* of recapitulation
of human nature – a determining of the uniformity of human nature. But here the recapitulation and the determining
presuppose the existential reality of ecstasy, that is, the ontological-existential, not the noetic-ontic version of essence
or nature.[12]

§9   *The ontological, as distinct from the ontic, interpre-*
      tation of essence or nature

The ontic version of essence in the Western metaphysical
tradition, the intellectual conception of Being as an existential "universal," as an intellectual definition of the unity of
being ("Sedes ipsius esse in uno est, in uno semper sedet
esse" – Meister Eckhart), introduces the relation of abstract

and concrete into the fact of existence as a relation of essence and person,[13] that is, it leads unavoidably to the understanding even of the person as an ontic unit, as a division or portion of the universal nature, and finally to the understanding of the person as an *individual* (Thomas Aquinas interprets "substantia" as "natura rei, per se esse").[14]

By contrast, the ontological-existential interpretation of nature or essence corresponds to the understanding of the person as an existential fact of ecstatic otherness. Personhood is the unique possibility of "being-opposite" in respect of beings and also in respect of its nature itself – not just as fundamentally a conscious capacity for an objective determination of the dimensional presence of beings and an intellectual conception of the "universality" of its nature, but as a universal existential *relation* with objective (*anti-keimena*) beings and their underlying (*hypo-keimenê*) nature, a relation which recapitulates Being as *fact*, that is, as *mode of existence*. Within the bounds of an ontology which the priority of the person defines, we "recognize" Being as the *mode* by which it *is* what it is: human nature as personal ec-stasy, the essence (*ousia*) of beings as presence (*par-ousia*) referring to the person.

Nature is the first onomastic expression for Being;[15] it is the principle (*logos*) of Being.[16] The principle signifies the disclosure, the possibility of knowledge. Being is disclosed, that is, is recognized as essence or nature: nature is not the general intellectual conception of being or the semantic definition of Being as an existential "universal," but the existential reality – that is, the mode of existence – which makes Being known, the real possibility of the principle of Being. I say "possibility" (*dynatotês*) not to suggest the distinction of disclosure from some possible "concealment" in an intellectual fashion, but because nature as an existential reality represents only a cognitive potentiality, a possibility of knowledge: the disclosure of Being presupposes a "horizon" of disclosure; the principle of Being presupposes the possibility of its acceptation, that is, dia-logue, ec-stasy, a *personal* approach to Being.

Consequently, the question about Being is recapitulated in the determination of an ontological-existential reality, which represents the principle of Being as a cognitive possibility. And essence or nature is such a reality only and exclusively as a fact of existence that is, as personal ecstasy or as presence of beings with reference to the person. This means that essence or nature is the unique possibility of the general disclosure of Being only as the content of the person. Nature is the principle of Being only as a dynamic-existential fact, only as personal ecstasy or as presence (of beings) with reference to the person. Every person is the potentiality for a general disclosure of the principle of Being.

§10   *The priority of the person with regard to nature or essence. The problem of essence in Heidegger's ontology*

Up to this point I have used two basic approaches to, or definitions of, essence or nature and the relation which exists between nature and person. In accordance with the first approach, nature is an existential reality which is defined as a *fact* (with "passions" and "accidents") within the limits of personal existence and "opposite" which the otherness of the person is realized. And by the second approach I defined nature as the principle of Being, as again an existential reality, which represents the unique possibility of the disclosure or cognition of Being – as a reality of personal ecstasy or of presence of beings with reference to the person.

This attempt at an initial definition of the relationship between nature or essence and the person, even if it presupposes the person as an exclusive way of approaching essence or nature, as the mode of its existence, does not coincide with deciding on a methodological priority of the person in relation to nature. The person does not "precede nature" as the subjective determinative principle of objective universality, as Western metaphysics would have it from the time of Descartes onwards. Moreover, the person does not "precede nature" in the way Sartre declares that "existence precedes essence."[17] The person is not just a self-awareness which is self-determined before it can be determined by any universal concept, that is, by any universal nature or essence.[18] Both the priority of the subject (as the bearer of the capacity for thought or of moral and historical experience) and the priority of existential self-awareness (as "apostasy" of the self from its being or nature, an apostasy which consciousness creates by "secreting" the nothingness of its being, projecting itself on to that which it intends to be, as a ceaseless and undetermined refutation of being-in-itself), presuppose the sense of the noetic-ontic understanding of essence or Being, the noetic-objective definition of the "universal," even though this definition follows rather than precedes existence. When the relation of essence to existence is posited as a problem of the priority to be given to definitions, then the question about Being as an existential question is circumvented, that is, as transcendence of the definitions and reference to the *fact* of Being, to the *mode* by which it *is* what it is. Heidegger showed that the converse of the metaphysical proposition "essence precedes existence" does not detach it from metaphysics. The converse of a metaphysical principle still remains a metaphysical principle.[19] The truth of humankind (even if as a definition it follows rather than precedes existence) is exhausted, as is the truth of every being, in its coincidence with the corresponding sense which is contained in the understanding. Imprisonment in the medieval objectification of man as "an animal that possesses reason" ("animal rationale") is not transcended.[20]

Nevertheless, by defining nature as the content of the person, and the person as the existence of nature, we find ourselves beyond even the transcending of the defining priority of essence with regard to existence, or of existential self-awareness with regard to essence, achieved by Heidegger. In accordance with Heidegger's perception, the distinction of essence from existence – a distinction which dominates the spiritual history of the West[21] – is refuted by the understanding of the human presence ("Da-sein") as ec-static fact.[22] Here ecstasy ("Ek-sistenz," as Heidegger has it) means rising up into the truth of Being,[23] and the truth (*a-lêtheia*) of Being, that is, the possibility of beings to *be disclosed* as that which they are, is time.[24] Temporality signifies the *understanding* of Being as a fact of rising up to presence. Without time nothing *is disclosed* as that which it *is*. The human person is the only being which understands Being as temporality, as a rising up to presence, and this means that the human person is the only being which "stands out" (*ex-istatai*), which can "stand outside" its *being*, that is, which can understand its *being*, as presence, as temporal "nowness."[25]

Consequently, "Ek-sistenz" differs essentially from "Existenz" ("existentia"), the term established by Western existentialists for distinguishing reality from essence, that is, from possibility.[26] Even for Sartre, "existence" means the reality of being as distinct from the simple possibility of the idea,[27] while "Ek-sistenz" defines an activity, the fact of Being's rising up into truth, and this truth (*a-lêtheia*) is understood only as temporality.

Heidegger's statement that humanity's "essence" is defined by the ecstatic character of its existence,[28] nevertheless summarizes what distinguishes Heideggerian ontology from the ontology of the ontic-noetic categories of the Western philosophical tradition. But in spite of the denial of an *a priori* intellectual objectivization ("Verdinglichung"), Heidegger's interpretation of "essence" is very far removed from the ontological understanding of the Greek East. There is in Greek thought a common assumption which is precisely the denial that the truth of being can be exhausted in the coincidence

of sense with what is conceived ("adaequatio rei et intellectus"). Heidegger can thus provide the Western thinker with
a very good starting-point for entering into the Greek East's
understanding of essence or nature. His iconoclastic attitude
(his denial of "intellectual idols"[29]) strips Western subjectivism of the illusion of certainty provided by the common
understanding of objective syllogisms. Stripped of the metaphysical props of logical necessity, props founded on the
syllogistic capability of the subject or on his or her *a priori*
moral judgments, ontology reveals the threatening ("das
bedrohende") void of absence as an ontological presupposition of the phenomenicity of phenomena, nothingness as the
hidden essence of every being.[30]

The ec-static character of human presence is restricted by
Heidegger to the *understanding* ("Verständnis") of being as
temporality, that is, as presence or absence, in the event of
the disclosure or annihilation of any being. This ec-static
"understanding" is an existential fact. It is defined by the existential consciousness of being in the world ("In-der-Welt-
sein") and is actualized as *anxiety* or *anguish* ("Angst") in
the face of Being as nothingness or disclosure.[31] The world,
beings, the human presence are all "suspended" ("schwe-
ben") – they are phenomena hanging in the void – within
the ontological reality of Nothing. Finally, the ec-static character of the human "essence" proves, within the framework
of Heidegger's ontology, to be a possibility of "rising up"
to cognition of Nothing, that is, the *anguish* of existential
confrontation with Nothing.[32] Essence is no longer either the
a priori noetic-conscious definition of being or the becoming of being, the principle of the dynamic of Being. Essence
is the space of both Being and Nothingness,[33] the reality of
their co-existence,[34] the disclosure of the "abyss-like foundation" or "groundless ground" ("abgründiger Grund") of
beings and existence.

The transcendence of the exclusivity of syllogistic thought

within the framework of Heidegger's ontology, the denial
of the intellectual certitude offered by objectively obligatory
syllogisms, certainly marks a radical change in the historical development of the West's ontological understanding.
Nevertheless, Heidegger's ontology does not thereby cease
from being a typical consequence of this historical development. Both the intellectual confirmation of Being and the
existential anxiety of the experience of Nothing represent a
common attitude (*stasis*) towards the ontological problem,
an attitude which is defined by the subjectivity of a cognitive
self-confirmation, the absence of understanding or experience of the fact of *relation*, that is, of the ontological priority
of the person.[35] But in spite of all this, many of Heidegger's
ontological discussions are particularly valuable today if we
are to rediscover a correct understanding of the ontological
categories of the Christian East, that is, if we are to detach
ourselves from what in our own time (within the limits of
Western culture) is the self-evident ontic-noetic content
which the Western Middle Ages gave to the basic common
categories of Christian ontology.

§11   *Truth as relation*

With regard to the problem of essence or Being, we could
perhaps make use of the way Heidegger speaks of *disclosure*
and *nothingness* as the unique modes by which we understand Being in its temporality in order to show how we can
transcend ontic-noetic definitions. But with the ontological
presuppositions of the Christian East we should understand
disclosure as personal relation and *nothingness* as the absence of relation, whereupon it is no longer *temporality* but
relation which defines the unique possibility of understanding Being as presence and absence. (We shall see in a later
chapter how even temporality is a connection of personal relationship, the *measure* of relation). Being or nothingness,

the truth or forgetfulness of being, is the reference or non-reference to the person, the revealing or the hiding of the principle of Being as content of the person. Beings *are*, exist not as intellectual, conscious or *a priori* empirical (always objective) confirmation, nor as calm identity with their being, with the structured coherence of their properties (that is, as beings in themselves), nor even as not-nothing ("nicht Nichts"), that is, as "disclosure" in temporality, but only as a fact of reference to the person, as presence (*par-eimi*). We shall see in what follows that the person itself exists only as presence, but in the case of the referential presence of the person, the reference is actualized (ontologically – "constitutively," not simply "functionally") with regard to another not only personal but also "essential" otherness.

Yet even though I am urging here an understanding of the presence of beings as referential to the person, we must define this understanding as fundamentally a cognitive possibility, not as an objective necessity. The reference of beings to the person is their rising up from the oblivion of non-relation. The truth of beings is the principle (*logos*) of Being within the bounds of the dialogue (*dia-logos*) of personal relation. Beings do not contain Being. Being is not their very self, the structured coherence of their properties. Beings *witness to Being* when they rise up in the space of personal relation. They refer to being as the content of the person. Consequently, we cannot separate the existence of beings from the *mode* by which they *are* what they are, i.e., from personal reference. The person is in relation to beings with regard to the principle of essence (*ousia*) as presence (*par-ousia*). Person and beings compose the ontological, revelatory relation of Being.

§12   *Beings as "things"*

The truth of beings, as a rising up into the space of personal relation, corresponds to the definition of beings as *things*

(*pragmata*), as those things which have been accomplished
(*pepragmena*), as the products of a personal act (*praxis*),
as the principle of personal existence.[36] Beings as "things"
constitute a principle of personal uniqueness and dissimilarity, that is, the principle of Being as content of the person,
the disclosure of essence as personal ecstasy – they reveal
the "mode of existence" as personal otherness. Accordingly,
they define a *possibility* rather than a reality.[37]

We can gain a more immediate understanding of this chink
of possibility in phenomenal reality – the character of beings
as "things" (the rising up of beings into personal *relation*) –
most of all when we are considering art objects. A painting, e.g., by van Gogh, is fundamentally a composite whole
made up of neutral materials (canvas and pigments) without
these *in themselves*, as material objects, possessing any fundamental qualitative-objective difference from other similar
materials (many other pieces of canvas and the same colors).
But a painting by van Gogh is, at the same time, something
essentially different from the dimensional-qualitative objectivity of the materials which compose it. It is a *thing*, a *pragma*, a personal act. It testifies to the person of van Gogh. It
is van Gogh. When we have "recognized" the unlike, unique
and unrepeatable character of the extraordinary creative genius of van Gogh and meet with another expression of this
genius which is new to us – when we find ourselves in front
of another of his paintings – then we say: this *is* van Gogh.

Beings as "things," that is, as things that have risen up into
personal *relation*, witness to the person, which means, they
reveal the unlike, unique and unrepeatable character of both
terms of the relation: not only of the personal transaction,
of which they are consequences as things-accomplished,
but also of the pre-semantic cognition which recognizes the
character of a being as a "thing." Accordingly, the character
of beings as "things" confirms the personal otherness as the
universal *mode of existence* of the essence of every being:

otherness as the unlike, unique and unrepeatable principle of a personal-creative act, and as the personal expression-cognition of this principle. (Except that when the productive act ceases to be personal – and this happens only with the intervention of the impersonal agency of a machine – the objects produced are neutralized in the forms of a standardized uniformity. They are no longer "things" [*pragmata*] but "goods" [*chrêmata*], objects of use, not relation. Accordingly, the machine, at least as we know it today in terms of Western technology, represents the most radical undermining of the personal truth of the person and of the world, the denial of the ontological character of existential otherness, in the degree in which it gives material form to that human attitude towards the world which does not aim at relation but only at the subjection of the world – subjection to impersonal individualistic need and desire.)

Yet "things," as the principle of the personal act which constitutes their cause, witness to the person without exhausting the definition of the person. The person as witnessed to by "things" is defined without being determined either according to essence or according to dimensional presence – it is the nearest and the farthest.[38] The reference of beings to the person is the presupposition of their truth. Beings *are* as "things" with reference to the person – they manifest the principle of their essence as a presence that refers to the person.

But although the presence of "things" witnesses to the person, it does not interpret the person except as absence. A painting of van Gogh is the principle of the person of van Gogh, but only as the principle of his dimensional absence. On the basis of beings as "things" we recognize the person fundamentally as a *summons* or *invitation* to a relation which transcends the limitations of space and time. We recognize, too, the character of the relation, which escapes semantic-objective determination and is unique and unrepeatable. But the truth of the person is not exhausted only as an *invita-*

tion to an exclusive relation through "things" as the principle of its absence. "Knowledge" of the person presupposes the actualization of the exclusive relation in the context of immediate personal communion, which is a fact of ecstatic reciprocity, that is, of a reciprocal, loving self-offering. This ecstatic reciprocity, the fact of the "personal" knowledge of the person, is *eros*.

Without at this point analyzing this possibility of the "erotic" knowledge of the human person and of the "person" of the world any further, we can, in summary of what we have said above, say that personal otherness, as the *mode of existence* to which every essence in the world refers, represents the only possibility for a cognitive approach to Being. We know Being only in the *mode* by which it *is* what it is, and this mode is personal otherness as an invitation to relation and as the actualization of the relation. The distinguishing of the partial essences on the basis of the common and uniform marks of recognition constitutes, no doubt, an initial "semantics" for cognitive access to the "rational" otherness of beings. It also constitutes, however, a possible conventional objectivization, a transformation of essences into semantic "signs." And this objectivization precludes an existential approach to Being. Only when the essence of a being is understood as simply a basically semantic definition of its otherness, only then does the problem of Being remain open as an existential possibility. And only then is the universality of Being not exhausted in the intellectual conception of the universal, as an intellectual definition of the unity of a being, but is identified with the existential experience of the universality of the person, with the possibility for it to "be-opposite" the "rational" otherness of beings as a whole. The person recapitulates the possibilities of Being. Being can be "known" only as the content of the person, only as the ecstatic impulse of *relation* and the "rational" invitation to *relation*, that is, as loving-erotic self-transcendence.

But the person recapitulates Being without ever exhausting it. Being as the content of the person, as a fact of universal ecstatic reference, is defined without being determined, is also the nearest and the farthest.[39] Every person recapitulates the possibilities of Being without exhausting Being, either as the assumption of the principle of a universal disclosure of the referential presence of objects, or even as a fact of ecstatic self-transcendence of nature within the boundaries of the *relation* of love. Every person recapitulates the universality of Being as an endless existential possibility, not simply as conscious information about the *universal* as an intellectual determination of the unity of the species. To return, then, to our original definition, we must say that nature or essence is the first name given to Being as "signifying" otherness, that is to say, as signifying the *possibilities of personal relation.*

§13   *The truth of Being as experience of personal universality*

The transition from the conventional marking of the phenomenicity of phenomena to the cognition of the "logic" of otherness, as also the transition from the sense of essence as an intelligible *universality* to the existential experience of Being as content of the person, can itself be taken only as a syllogistic formulation, only as an intellectual construct expressed in a poetic or "mystical" way. Nevertheless, it does not cease to be the determination of a possibility that is actually felt, the "semantic" term of an experience. But this possibility of actual experience – the transcendence of the abstract formulations and the entry into the realm of existential truth – necessarily presupposes the fact of personal relation: the meeting of the person with the personal principle of "things" in the world, that is, the entry of a personal God within what is bounded by humanity's personal experience.

The phenomenal beings of the world as a whole, having risen up to a personal relation as "things," have reference to the universal "act" of the actuality of nature, that is, to "Creation," to the unified principle (*logos*) of the Person, whose things-acts are the beings.[40] The transition from beings to Being is a transition from "things" to Person, and as an existential possibility it defines a possible eventuality, not an intellectual certainty. The principle of the presence of "things," a principle of personal act (*praxis*) which constitutes their cause, witnesses to the Person of God without exhausting the determination of the divine Person. In the way that "every house" testifies to its having been "built by someone,"[41] to the wisdom and skill of the builder, to his aesthetic sense and love, his intelligence and ability – that is, it reveals the "personal" qualities of an artist and poet, but does not replace the fullness of the knowledge of his person, which is provided only by immediate communion with him – in the same way beings witness to the Creator God. On the basis of the principle (*logos*) of "things" as invitation or summons (*klêsis*) to a relation which transcends the limitations of space and time and evades semantic-objective determination, since it is unique and unrepeatable, that is to say, *personal*, we recognize fundamentally the existence of a personal God-Logos. But "knowledge" of the Person of the Logos presupposes, by means of the *summons*, the actualization of an exclusive relation, of an immediate communion, which is an event of ecstatic reciprocity, that is, of reciprocal loving-erotic self-offering.

Consequently, within the context of humanity's personal encounter with the personal principle (*logos*) of the "things" in the world, the problem of Being is no longer posited as a question requiring analysis by syllogistic reasoning, an etiological ascent from beings to Being or explanation of their "existential" difference. Being does not simply represent the etiological First Cause ("causa prima") of beings, nor simply the *mode* by which that which is *is disclosed* as it rises up to the horizon of time. In the context of relation with the world's personal Logos, the truth of Being is identified with the experience of personal universality – an experience of ecstatic-erotic self-transcendence. Knowledge of Being constitutes a "moral" achievement of actualization of erotic self-transcendence, an entry into that realm of life which is revelatory of beings as "things," of matter as personal Energy, of the Person of God and of the person of humanity "beyond" any ontic essence.

The first move towards the actualization of this cognitive-revelatory relation of humanity with God is made on the part of God. The Christian theology of the Greek East refers to the *ecstatic* existence of God, to the erotic will of the divine supraessential essence to offer himself as a relation of personal communion. "The very cause of all things," note the Areopagitical writings, "through a superabundance of erotic goodness comes to be outside of himself ... and is, as it were, beguiled by goodness and love and eros. And from being exalted over all things and beyond all things he is drawn down to being in all things by an ecstatic supraessential power which does not depart from itself."[42] The ecstatic "movement" of the divine supraessential essence is also the presupposition that founds and constitutes the human person: "for the beneficent eros moved the divine to providence for us to be constituted," writes Maximus the Confessor.[43] Moreover, the human person becomes an "image" and disclosure of God precisely in its self-offering. And elsewhere Maximus writes: "Since the divine exists as *eros* and moves as *agapê*, it draws towards itself as the objects of its *eros* and *agapê* those things that are receptive of *eros* and *agapê*. And now to speak even more clearly: on the one hand it moves as creating a deep-seated relation of *eros* and *agapê* in those receptive of it, and on the other it draws as attracting by nature the desire of those that are drawn to it."[44]

When Christian theology refers to God, it refers specifically to the God of personal reference and historical experience, to the God of Abraham, Isaac and Jacob, to the God and Father of the Lord Jesus Christ.

Chapter Three

The Unity of the Person

§14   *The unitary character of the person as a prerequisite of ecstatic otherness*

The ontological content which Christian Greek literature gave to the term *person* defines a unified existential reality. The disclosure of the ontological priority of the person, its rising up to a fundamental existential truth, presupposes its primordial *unity*. The person is primordially unified: as a pre-conscious power of "being-opposite" beings, as a unique existential presupposition of disclosure of the principle of Being, but also in its ecstatic otherness with regard to the common recognizable signs of the essence, the person is incomparably unified – "there is nothing more unitary"[1] than the person. In locating the fundamental recapitulation of the powers of Being in the dimension of the universality of the person, we are referring to the single and unique presupposition of the appearance of the principle of Being, before any "semantic" definition, in a single and uniform – not composite – "horizon" of disclosure. The unity of the person is the real presupposition of pre-conscious reference and ecstatic otherness, the existentially necessary and sufficient condition of the unique, dissimilar and unrepeatable character of personal relation: the real presupposition for approaching the *mode of existence* at all.

43

§15 *The dual character of nature and the unitary character of personal existence*

Philosophical anthropology's attempt to define human existence as a composite – and specifically as a dual – reality
by distinguishing soul from body, or matter from spirit, was
accepted by Christian theology with exclusive reference to
the *nature* of humanity, or as a schematic expression of the
ontological distinction between person and nature. The reference of this duality to human *nature* was expressed clearly
by the Fourth Ecumenical Council (451) when it pronounced
the incarnate God "truly God and truly man the same [con-
sisting] of a *rational soul and a body*."[2] This reference finds
support in the Bible as well as in patristic texts.[3] But the
terms "soul" and "body" are always used loosely with a kind
of "perichoresis,"[4] without their precise difference ever being defined objectively or being identified with a dualistic-
axiological antithesis of matter and spirit.

There are nevertheless patristic expressions which attribute two "essences" to human nature, the "incorporeal essence of the soul" and the "irrational essence of the body."[5]
But the soul does not simply represent the "intellectual" and
"rational" element of human nature. It also represents the
"sensible,"[6] being "mingled with the material nature through
the senses."[7] There are Fathers who speak of the "somatic"[8]
or "animal"[9] soul, and others who distinguish "parts" of
the soul, the "rational," the "incensive" and the "appetitive" elements.[10] The soul is "heavenly"[11] and "deiform,"[12]
"rational and contemplative of beings."[13] But there is also
an "impassioned and irrational" part of the soul.[14] The soul
is "possessed of free will" (*autexousios*)[15] but is also "en-
amored of material things" (*philoylos*),[16] "since it has the
passions dwelling within it."[17] From the great variety of patristic expressions, the relationship between the material and
the spiritual within the terms of human *nature* is revealed in

the end to be an existential human "mystery," the *mystery of mingling*, of which the unitary personality of every person is conscious and has experience,[18] and thanks to which human nature can become receptive to uncreated grace, that is, to the life of God.[19]

The existential "mystery" of the composite human being does not in any way affect the unicity of human personal existence. We could perhaps say that Gregory of Nyssa sums up the tradition by defining man as "a single being composed of soul and body."[20] At the same time one could express the view – while avoiding any kind of definition – that in the terminology of both the Bible and the Fathers the distinction between body and soul often appears to adumbrate the ontological distinction between person and nature. The *soul* (the Hebrew *nephesh* of the Old Testament, the result of the *breath* which God breathed into the man of dust)[21] is not confined to one sector or part of human existence – to the spiritual as opposed to the material – but signifies the "particular property" (*to idiazon*) of the human being (an effect of God's particular creative energy),[22] the vivification and transmission of personal faculties to the earth-born essence of man.[23] In other words, the soul signifies the entire human being as a unitary living personal hypostasis. It is the personality in the strict sense, what we have called here the human *person*,[24] which is the image and "glory" (i.e., "disclosure") of a personal God.[25] And the body is the *nature*, the material reality which constitutes the worldly dimension of the person, humanity's participation in the world's material nature, the summing up of the material world in the human person.[26]

The relation of soul and body within the limits of human existence is something more than the mutual indwelling of two ontological realities. It is a unitary *blending* (*sygkrasis*) and *yoking* (*zeuxis*), in the words of John Climacus.[27] The principle of this commingling is inexpressible, according to

Gregory of Nyssa, and its mode is inexplicable and incomprehensible.[28] Humanity's earthly nature is the only product in God's material creation in which the "supramundane nature" of the soul is "implanted," "permeating each part equally," to mark it out for personal existence, to imprint on the body the image of the personal God "as in the impression of a seal." And it is precisely this blending of soul and body, the "highest union" (*akra henôsis*) in the words of Maximus,[29] which defines without determining the ineffable mystery of humanity's simultaneous identity and difference. The simultaneous identity and difference of the one human existence, the "highest union," confirms both the person's unitary "principle" and its essential-natural constitution "from soul and body." It conveys both the ontological distinction of person and nature and the existential mystery of humanity's twofold nature.

Even though the two distinctions – soul and body, person and nature – mutually coinhere in existential terms, it is nevertheless impossible for them to be identified without destroying, through an intellectual objectification, the real and ineffable unity of all the "levels" of human existence in the fact of personal ecstasy, the "enhypostatic communion"[30] of corporeal and psychical, of personal and natural, distinctive properties.

§16 *The distinction between soul and body as an important differentiation of natural energy*

The reverence of the Greek Fathers for the existential mystery of the human composite being – a reverence expressed in the avoidance of any definition or any objectification of existential distinctions – was not maintained by later "systematic" theology. It was specifically the need of the Scholastics for rationalistic clarifications and comprehensive definitions, for the intellectualist objectification of the existential fact,[31] that led unavoidably to a schematization of the existential mystery of humanity's composite nature, to an antithetical-pragmatic separation of soul and body, matter and spirit.[32] This separation is a typical consequence of accepting a definition of man as "an animal possessing reason" ("animal rationale"), as fundamentally a biological being, subsequently endowed with a soul or with a soul and spirit.

We have already seen[33] that this definition refers to an axiological metaphysics, not to an ontology of existential experience. It presupposes ontic-intellectual rather than ontological-existential categories. And it ignores the question of the difference between beings and Being, between nature and person.[34] On the basis of the objective definitions of scholastic anthropology,[35] the Roman Catholic Church at the Council of Vienne (1311-12) raised Aristotle's teaching on the soul as the entelechy of the body to dogmatic status.[36] It would belong to a different chapter to show how the reception of this objectified Aristotelian *hylomorphism* led the Westerners inevitably to an external and schematic understanding of the moral life – and finally to the juridical moralism of the Roman Catholic Church and the pietism and puritanism of the Protestants.[37]

In the Christian thinking of the Greek East it is not possible for the elements making up the human composite being – soul and body – to correspond to ontological definitions. These elements do not determine the *mode* by which the human person *is*, but are determined and marked (always in a relative or conventional way) as differentiations of the result of natural energy. I am speaking here of corporeal, psychical or spiritual manifestations, marking objectively (and therefore conventionally) the manifest result of natural energy, that is, of the universal-ecstatic reference of the bicomposite essence or nature. The ecstatic reference presupposes, i.e., "contains," the bicomposite nature as an existential reality. But it is accomplished only within the conditions of the unitary fact of personal existence: it is defined with regard to personal otherness or it defines personal otherness.

Consequently, psychical or corporeal energy has an ontological content. That is, it constitutes an existential fact only as psychical energy "over against" personal (or, as Maximus calls it, "gnomic")[38] energy – in opposition to, or in coordination with, the will or energy of the person. In other words, the distinction between soul and body does not refer to the *mode* by which humanity *is* (as nature and person), but to the semantic differentiation of the result of natural energy.

The immediate experience of relation confirms the relative or even conventional character of the semantic differentiations of the natural energy: the human glance, the expression of the face, the gesture, the articulated thought, the manifestation of love – are these expressions of the soul or body? Modern depth psychology ("Tiefenpsychologie") has shown experimentally how difficult it is to make real distinctions between different areas of experience and has demonstrated the non-existence of unmixed manifestations of the body, the soul or the spirit.[39] But even the pragmatic ontology of the existential philosophers, based precisely on an empirical interpretation of the reality of humanity in the world, its being-there ("Da-sein"), refers the body to the *essence* of humanity, and determines the *essential* difference between the human body and the animal organism (Heidegger),[40] the body as furnishing the immediate presence of soulness (Sartre).[41]

§17   *The reference of "in the image" to the uniformity* (henoeidia) *of existence*

The semantic-objective distinction of partial areas of existence, that is, the presuppositional definition of man as "an animal possessing reason," is also the basis for the attempt of scholastic theology to interpret God's "image" in humanity by attributing the elements appertaining to "in the image" to the objectified result of the natural energy, that is, to objective properties of ontic individuality – to one of the two conventional "parts" of ontic nature, humanity's "spirit"-intelligence.[42] Existential predicates which were used by the Greek Fathers as indicators of the ontological difference between person and nature (predicates revelatory of personal universality and dissimilarity), such as "rationality," "self-determination" and "sovereignty,"[43] are interpreted by the theology of objective categories as individual properties (universals)[44] of humanity's "spiritual" nature: individual properties are referred to an analogical and comparative interpretation of the phrase "in the image," which is exhausted in the phenomenology of ontic individuality and cannot interpret the ontological reality of the difference between person and nature, humanity's "mode of existence." The image of God in humanity defines an analogical ascent,[45] that is, a rationalistic reference of ontic predicates to God and to humanity. The image of God is not referred to humanity's *being*, to the *mode* in which human existence *is*. Humanity does not image God existentially and ontologically, that is, as personal uniqueness and dissimilarity, as "mode of existence" which allows humanity a loving relation and communion with God, its assimilation to the divine archetype. Instead, defined as the absolutely rational, self-determining and sovereign being, God images humanity analogically and anagogically.[46]

In contrast to scholastic objectification, when the Greek East interpreted the image of God in humanity, it sought to protect the mystery of the mode of divine existence, and its imprint in human existence, from the danger of intellectual schematizations. As in their distinction of soul and body, so too in their interpretation of "in the image" the Greek Fathers rejected any objective definition – dualistic or monistic – and any subjection of existential truth to *a priori* conceptual definitions. They confined themselves to a semantic outline of the existential mystery of the difference between person and nature, preserving the unitary character of the person, the priority of the person over nature (the power of the person to determine its nature and not to be determined by it – dynamically to make its nature become like the divine archetype).

Of course there were writers (mainly in the Early Christian period, in a historical environment still dominated by paganism) who denied the relationship of the image of God to the human body, ostensibly to safeguard the truth of God from any analogy fitted to the body and human passions.[47] There were also others who strongly emphasized the reference of the image of God to the psychosomatic wholeness and unity of man.[48] But more often the patristic interpretations sum up the truth of the words "in the image" in the triadic character of the personal energies (mind, reason, spirit)[49] or in the "sovereignty"[50] and "self-determination"[51] which sum up perfectly the ontological differentiation of the person with regard to nature.

§18   *The formal definition of the unity* (henotês) *of the subject and the unitary* (henikê) *otherness of the person*

Thus the unity of the person refers to a pragmatic-existential rather than intellectual-semantic definition, just as the universality does. The intellectual is always exhausted in the ontic definition: it defines a being in itself, its onticity and manifold senses – "now 'being' and 'unity' have an equal number of senses"[52] / "there are many senses in which a thing may be said to 'be,' but they are related to one thing and one nature"[53] / "all refer to one starting-point"[54] – it identifies the semantics of being with the *Being* of being, it refers to Being as a being, never adverting to their difference.[55] And the pragmatic corresponds to the ontological definition: it refers to the *mode* by which being *is*, to the difference between beings and Being – to Being as the possibility and fact of relation, to beings as the word or principle (*logos*) of Being.

The distinction between an ontic definition and an ontological one also clarifies the difference between the objec-
tive-semantic interpretations of the unity of the being and
the unitary otherness of the person. If we wish to define the
unity of a being in the language of Aristotelian ontology, that
is, if we wish to speak of an ontic definition of unity, we
refer to the *matter* (*hylê,* substratum) and the *shape* (*morphê,* form) and the "third which arises from these." ("By the
matter I mean, for instance, the bronze, by the shape, the
plan of its form, and by the compound of these [the totality]
the statue.")[56] The Aristotelian *form* defines the unity of the
"whole" insofar as it manifests the "form-giving" character of the "universal" – "the universal is predicable of some
subject always."[57] The "form-giving" character of the "universal," the Aristotelian "form," this given that unifies the
multiplicity of substrata, in its various "total" manifestations
refers to that which can "see," that is, so that the intellect
may define, and consequently refers to the phenomenon and
to the "semantics" or to the principle (*logos*) of the phenomenon[58] – it is exhausted in the "definition," in the coincidence
of the sense with the thing thought of as a "universal": "for
definition is of the universal and of the form."[59] Thus the
"third" "from both"[60] (shape and matter) is defined as unitary
thanks to the *form* (*eidos*), which precedes both the matter
and the "from both":[61] "they are parts of the totality, but not
of the form and its principle"[62] – where the principle (*logos*)
carries the sense of the definition ("the principle we say is a
definition").[63]

Consequently, this definition of the unity of every "total"
substratum with reference to the form-giving character of the
universal cannot interpret the existential fact of the unitary
human hypostasis, since the difference between the "universal" and the "particular" only pertains to the theory of forms:
a difference "according to principle" and "according to sense-
perception" ("the universal is knowable according to the

principle, the particular according to sense-perception; for the principle has to do with the universal, sense-perception with the particular").[64] The intellectual and sensory (according to the perception of the senses) conception of being as "universal" and "particular" simply *defines*, that is, formally marks, the "total" – simultaneously composite and unitary – hypostasis of the human subject: "It is clear also that the soul is the primary substance [the shape-*morphê*] and the body is matter, and man or animal is the compound of both taken universally."[65]

Thus the *mode* by which the human subject *is* as an existential unity and identity, as a fact which is the ground of every definition of identity and otherness, is not affected by Aristotelian metaphysics. In Aristotle the unity is a formal-semantic rather than ontological-existential category. It arises from the difference between "total" and "whole," and refers to the non-categorical character of the subject ("the subject is that of which the other things are predicated, while in itself it is not predicated of anything").[66] The same subject taken as a "totality" (*synolon*) has discrete parts, while taken as a "whole" (*katholou*) it is unitary and without parts: "the bronze is a part of the total statue, but not of the statue regarded as form."[67] It is evident that the formal-ontic definition of the unity of the human subject does not affect the existential problem of the unitary ecstatic otherness of the person.

§19   *The distinction between nature and energies in terms of the unitary mode of existence*

Concerning the person, I affirm its unity by referring not to an intellectual-objective definition but to the universal-existential experience of *relation*. In the fact of *relation* we confirm the unity of the person as fundamental uniqueness and dissimilarity of pre-conscious cognition and as ecstatic otherness of the person with regard to nature. Certainly, both the pre-conscious relation with the personal principle (*logos*) of "things" and the ec-static relation of the person with regard to nature cannot in the end be expressed except through thoughts – by means of intellection. There is, however, a very great difference between intellectual definition, which exhausts the truth in conceiving and formally describing its meaning, and using thoughts as symbols or images of the terms, simply, of the existential fact, which presents truth as the possibility of universal participation in living experience, that is, as "moral" achievement. The sense of the "whole" unity of the elements of the human composition does not affect the existential-ontological problem of the *mode* by which this bi-composite human nature *is* as a single human existence. The formal unity does not cover the ontological reality of personal reference and ecstatic otherness. It ignores the existential relation of person to nature: the person as a referential summing up of nature, nature as the content of the person.

By defining the person as an existential-referential summing up of nature, I do not of course deny the form-generating character of nature or essence. I am simply interpreting it ontologically, not ontically (as a cognitive *power*, not as phenomenological objectivity). The form-generating character of nature, as existential fact, is what I called earlier "manifested result of natural energy" within the terms of personal otherness.[68] It is precisely the ecstatic reference of essence or nature, as a fact of interpersonal relation and as a unique and dissimilar pre-conscious cognition, that reveals the form-generating character of the nature and witnesses to the essence (*ousia*) as presence (*par-ousia*). Thus even the "corporeal nature" of humanity is not simply the "material cause" ("causa materialis") of human existence, the *matter* (*hylê*) with the sense of the substratum in its relation to the shape (*morphê*).[69] It is the natural power of disclosure of the otherness of the person, of the actualization of the ecstatic reference of nature *outside* nature, the manifested result of nature's energies in the fact of personal otherness.

We therefore find ourselves in the area of a second ontological distinction, parallel with the distinction between nature and persons: We distinguish the universal nature or essence from its form-generating character, that is, from the manifested result of natural energy in the fact of personal otherness – in the end we distinguish *nature* from natural *energy*. The distinction is a real one, not simply a matter of semantics, since our only way of knowing nature is through the manifested energies which "formalize" (give form to) nature without being identified with it. "If anything operates like fire, and shines and warms in the same way, it is assuredly fire," says Gregory of Nyssa. Consequently the identity of the common nature "is conveyed by the identity of the operations."[70]

But if identity of operations discloses identity of nature, the nature is nevertheless not identified with the operations, just as the cause is not identified with the result. The products of causes make known and "image" causes, but are not identified with, the causes themselves. "There is no exact likeness between caused and cause," says Dionysius, "for the caused carry within themselves only such images of their originating sources as are possible for them, whereas the causes themselves are located in a realm transcending the caused, according to the argument regarding their source. Take a familiar example. Joys and woes are said to be the cause in us of joy and woe without themselves being the possessors of such feelings. The fire which warms and burns is never said itself to be burnt and warmed ... caused things preexist more fully and more truly in the causes."[71] We have here yet another existential confliction of identity and otherness: it is in practice impossible for us to separate nature from energy, to contemplate nature without energy or energy without nature,[72] and at the same time it is impossible for us to identify nature with the energy of nature.[73]

§20   *The rationalistic ascent to the operative First Cause and the existential experience of the personal expression of the natural energies*

Aristotle identified the *energy* with the *form*, and this phenomenological assertion was perhaps his most vital contribution to the development of philosophical metaphysics. Aristotle distinguished between *being in potentiality*, which is matter (the material, which has the power or the possibility to *be* something), and *being in act*, which is the form (the *mode* by which being *is*).[74] For *being in potentiality* to be activated, there must be movement, and movement is the transition from *being in potentiality* to *being in act*. But movement always has some initial impetus or beginning ("everything that is in motion must be moved by something").[75] *Being in potentiality* must be moved by some *being in act*, otherwise movement does not exist: "But if there is something which is capable of moving things or acting on them, but is not actually doing so, there will not be movement; for that which has a capacity need not exercise it."[76] Thomas Aquinas adds a specific example: "That which is actually hot, as fire, makes wood, which is potentially hot, to be actually hot, and thereby moves and changes it ... It is therefore impossible that in the same respect and in the same way a thing should be both mover and moved, i.e., that it should move itself."[77]

It is evident that the backwards sequence of mover and moved leads unavoidably to the metaphysical necessity of a first beginning of movement, the *first mover*.[78] The *first mover* cannot simply have a power of moving, because that which only has a power might not exercise it – "it is possible for that which has the power not to be in act." We therefore gain nothing by creating eternal essences, like the Platonic *Ideas*, if there is not in these essences a principle capable of evoking change and, consequently, movement ("nothing, then, is gained even if we suppose eternal substances, as the

believers in the Forms do, unless there is to be in them some
principle which can cause movement").[79] And for the principle of movement to be only active, since a transition from
in potentiality to *in act* is inadmissable for the first mover,
which no one has set in motion, its essence must be energy
alone: "there must be such a principle whose very essence is
actuality [*energeia*]."[80] And since movement is the transition
from *potentiality* (*dynamei*) to *actuality* (*energeia*), and this
transition is inadmissable for the first mover, the first mover,
as pure actuality, is itself unmoved.[81]

At the same time, since the first mover can only be *in actuality* and in no circumstances *in potentiality*, and since a
being that is *in potentiality* is matter, it is evident that the
first mover is immaterial and incorporeal. And since movement is neither begotten nor corrupts, but always *is*, at least
as a temporal transition from *prior* to *posterior* ("for it was
always"), and without temporal change nature does not exist, it follows that movement is eternal, just as time is eternal
and the first mover is eternal actuality (*energeia*).[82]

The Aristotelian interpretation of *energeia* was transferred
intact by Thomas Aquinas into the realm of Christian theology.[83] But the logical ascent to the first mover, which according to our reasoning must be, as regards its essence, eternal
energy, pure and immaterial, entirely ignores the *personal*
mode of existence of the Deity as he reveals himself as a
fact in the historical experience of the Church. The question of *energy* interests Aquinas in the objective context of a
rational-apodictic procedure which exhausts the mystery of
the divine existence in the logically obligatory concept of a
productive and motive cause of creation. That is why there
is no reference in the *Summa Theologiae* to the personal God
of existential relation: there God is the object[84] of rational
inquiry, an abstract intellectual certainty, an ontic essence
absolutely in actuality, an impersonal and existentially inaccessible motive cause.

By contrast, in the Greek East the question of the *energies* is posed exclusively within the context of existential experience. The Church's experience is the *knowledge* of God as a fact of personal relation, and the question that is posed concerns the witness to this fact and the defense of it, the question "how we know God not as an object of the mind, or of the senses, or anything at all that belongs among beings."[85] The *knowledge* of God, as a fact of personal relation, discloses the priority of the truth of the person in the field of theological epistemology. There is no margin for us to sidestep the person by making a direct intellectual leap of reference to the essence – "as if the truth were in things for us and not in names."[86] The unity of the person, its oneness, recapitulates the *mode of existence*, and consequently every possibility of approaching the existential content of the ontological distinctions between nature and person, nature and energies. We know the essence or nature only as the content of the person, and this unique power of knowing the nature signifies its ecstatic recapitulation in the fact of personal reference, the nature's power of "standing-outside-itself," and becoming accessible and participable not as concept, but as personal uniqueness and dissimilarity. The nature's ecstasy, however, cannot be identified with the nature, since the very experience of relation itself is an experience of non-identification. The ecstasy is the *mode* by which the nature becomes accessible and known in the fact of personal otherness. It is the *energy* of the nature,[87] which is not identified either with its bearer or its result: "The energy is neither the one operating, nor what is operated."[88]

It is not of course possible for us to know the energy except through the one operating, and even the one operating can only be known by us through the natural energy both as personal otherness and as nature or essence. The will, for example, is an energy of our nature, yet is accessible only through its personal bearer. We refer to the *what* of the will only because we know the *how* of its personal expression.[89]

The *what* of the will makes known to us the nature which has the power of willing, while the *how* of the will reveals the personal otherness of its bearer.[90] The will, however, is identified neither with the nature, which has the power of willing, nor even with the person, which always wills in a unique, dissimilar and unrepeatable way. That is why we recognize in the will an *energy* of the nature ontologically distinct from both the nature and the person.

Even though we distinguish energy from nature and nature from persons, we do not attribute any composite character to the nature itself. That is to say, we do not divide up and apportion nature to persons and energies. Persons and energies are not "parts," or "constituents," or "passions," or "accidents" of the nature, but the nature's *mode of existence*. The personal expression of every energy recapitulates "without parts" and "in the form of unity" the whole natural energy, just as the person recapitulates the whole nature and is the existence of the nature. The *how* of volitional energy (or of creative or loving or whatever other energy) recapitulates the *what* of the natural volitional energy. The nature's power of willing exists and is manifested only through the otherness of the personal will. Music, painting and sculpture are creative energies of human nature. But they do not exist except as disclosures of personal otherness: as the music of Mozart, the painting of van Gogh, the sculpture of Rodin, etc. But nor does any other mode of disclosure and definition of essence or nature exist outside the operation of ec-stasy in the fact of personal otherness. The only way we have of naming the nature is the personally manifested energy of the nature. The principle of the energy "signifies" the nature – "both the essence and the energy admit of the same principle."[91]

Thus every formal predicate of the human essence or nature (rationality, free will, sovereignty) is a subsequent characterization of the essence, an objective determination of the manifestations which refer to the energies, that is, to the universal nature as the content of the person. But even "God has his divine names from the energies, for his supra-essentiality is nameless."[92] That which we call God's uncreated "essence" transcends all human powers of knowledge, or determination, or even of relative comparison, and for that reason the divine essence is also "beyond apprehension," "unevocable," "above every name," "and eludes every perception, imagination, opinion, name, word, contact or cognition."[93]

Consequently, the names we give God only refer to his energies, by which the divine nature becomes accessible, knowable and participable. In its essence it remains inaccessible, unknowable and non-participable. And so, "if we give the name 'God,' or 'life,' or 'essence,' or 'light,' or 'word' to the transcendent hiddenness, what we conceive of mentally is nothing other than the powers which reach out from it towards us and deify, create substance, generate life, or bestow wisdom."[94] The very divinity of God reveals the divine energy rather than the divine essence:

> The holy Fathers affirm unanimously that it is impossible to find a name to manifest the nature of the uncreated Trinity, but that the names belong to the energies. "The divinity" also designates an energy, that of moving or contemplating or burning, or else it indicates the "deification-in-itself." But he who is beyond every name is not identical with what he is named; for the essence and energy of God are not identical ... the divinity of God designates the divine energy *par excellence*.[95]

§21   *The nature participable through the energies. The energies homogeneous and heterogeneous with regard to the nature*

But the energies are not solely and exclusively the mode by which we name the nature, by which we "signify" the *operator* by means of his *operations*. The natural energy personally revealed represents that power of experiential knowledge which derives from personal "sharing" and "participation" in the essence or nature, without the participation also signifying identification with the nature. The Dionysian corpus uses as an image and example of such sharing the human voice, which "being one and the same, is shared in by many hearers as if it were just one."[96]

If we treat this image schematically and arbitrarily regard the word as an essence in itself, then the voice represents the energy of the word's essence. It represents the power we have of sharing in the word's essence as the voice makes it known and participable – the power all of us who hear the same voice have of sharing the same essence of the one word, without participation also signifying our identification with the essence of the word or the division of the essence into as many parts as there are participants in the word through the voice. Although uttered in a personal manner, the word remains formally one and undivided, while at the same time "it is participated in individually by all."

If we dwell a little longer on this schematic paradigm of the voice (*phônê*) and the word (*logos*), we can shed some further light on another assertion relating to the possibilities of sharing in the essence by means of the energy. Certainly the voice represents a disclosure of the word's energy "homogeneous" with the word's essence, which makes the immediate participation in the word possible. But a disclosure of the word's energy can also come to exist through essences "heterogeneous" to the word – the possibility that other "essences" can be formed as a word, such as writing, color, music or marble.

The paradigm implies that we can speak of two forms of energy of the same essence or nature: one "homogeneous," as we have called it, with the nature of the energy's operator (what we described above as an ecstatic self-offering of nature within the context of the fact of personal otherness);

and another energy which is disclosed through essences that are "heterogeneous" with regard to the nature of the operator, "productive of external things, according to which one constructs something different from some pre-existing matter."[97]

With regard to God, the "homogeneous" energy interprets the Church's experience of divine grace (the gift of true life) which is *uncreated*[98] ("heterogeneous" with respect to creatures and "homogeneous" with respect to God), through which God is "wholly participated in"[99] and "shared individually by all,"[100] while remaining simple and undivided, offering to the participant that which he has "by nature" except "identity according to essence,"[101] and proving the human being, according to the word of Scripture, to be "a partaker of divine nature" (2 Pet 1:4). And the disclosure of God's energy through essences "heterogeneous" to him interprets the character of beings as "things" – products of the divine energy: The personal principle of "things" (a principle of power and wisdom and skill),[102] although "belonging properly" (*idiazôn*) to each being within the limits of the infinite variety of essences, makes known the "single wholeness" of the one divine energy, and witnesses to the one simple and indivisible God.[103]

And with regard to man, we could say that the "homogeneous" energy refers to the power of love and erotic ecstatic self-offering, by means of which the existential truth of humanity, the mystery of nature and person as a single otherness, is "recognized" and becomes participable – when man "becomes wholly in the whole of the lover and is voluntarily embraced by the whole."[104] But the "homogeneous" energy also interprets the reality of the human body as an expression and disclosure of the separate otherness of the person – the body as the supreme personal differentiation of the natural energies[105] and the power of the meeting and communion of the created energy of the human essence with the uncreated

energy of the grace of God.[106] As for the disclosure of the
energy of humanity through humanity's "heterogeneous" essences, this interprets the preserving and making known of
personal otherness in the various human "creations,"[107] in
humanity's works of art, wisdom and power.

The basic assertion which is maintained and confirmed by
the distinction between the "homogeneous" energy of the essence or nature and its "heterogeneous" disclosure is that
both these forms of the manifestation of the energy always
reveal the nature or essence in a "single" fashion (*henikôs*),
always as the "uniform" (*henoeides*) content of the person.
The personal differentiation of the natural energies (the
uniqueness and dissimilarity of every human body, as well
as the absolute otherness of every erotic fact, and the differentiation of "creative" expression – the differentiation, for
example, of Bach from Mozart or of van Gogh from Goya)
distinguishes nature without dividing it, reveals the *mode* by
which nature *is* – and this mode is personal oneness and otherness. To the energies of distinctions of the nature belongs
everything that discloses and reveals the universal nature as
the content of the person.

§22   *The consequences of accepting or rejecting the dis-
       tinction between essence and energies*

To summarize the earlier part of this chapter, we may now
say that in distinguishing between nature and energies we
rely on an interpretation of the existential fact as the *unity* of
the person.

On the basis of this distinction we may (i) define the human body not as a part or a division of humanity's personal
existence, but as the supreme personal differentiation of the
energies of humanity's "bicomposite" – material and spiritual – nature (which are "created" energies of a "created"
nature,[108] in contrast with the uncreated divine energies), and

(ii) interpret the body as the immediate manifestation and accessibility of the recapitulation of the natural energies in the fact of personal otherness.

We have also seen that Greek patristic writers rely on the same distinction between nature and energies for the pre-suppositions and power of the knowledge of God by human beings. One might say that the linking of the interpretation of the human body with the definition of the possibility of knowing God, the reference to the same ontological pre-supposition, did not come about by chance. If knowledge of the personal God by human beings is possible, it must be as real as the experiential reality of the recapitulation of the natural energies in the personal otherness of the human body. Transferring the knowledge of God from the realm of immediate personal disclosure, through the natural energies, to the level of an intellectual and rationalistic approach, the restriction of the possibilities of the knowledge of God to the particular abilities of the human mind,[109] unavoidably exhausts the truth of God in abstract intellectual forms and etiological deductions,[110] that is to say, it destroys the very reality of divine personal existence.[111]

It is evident that the problem of the knowledge not only of God but also of humanity and the world – knowledge as immediate personal *relation* and existential experience, or as an abstract intellectual approach – is judged by the acceptance or rejection of the essence-energies distinction. The acceptance or rejection of this distinction represents two radically different concepts of reality, two incompatible "ontologies." This does not simply mean two different theoretical views or interpretations. It means two diametrically opposed *attitudes* to life, with specific spiritual, historical and cultural consequences.

The acceptance of the distinction means the recognition of truth as a personal *relation*, and of knowledge as *participation* in truth, not simply as the understanding of concepts arising from abstract thought. It therefore means the priority of the reality of the person and of interpersonal relationship over any intellectual definition. Within the unrestricted terms of this priority, God is known and participated through his uncreated energies, which are beyond the reach of the intellect, while in his essence he remains unknown and unparticipated. That is to say, God is known only as personal disclosure, as a triadic communion of persons, as an ecstatic self-offering of erotic goodness. And the world is the consequence of God's personal energies, a "product" revelatory of the Person of the Word, who witnesses to the Father by means of the grace of the Spirit – the "essentialized" invitation of God to relation and communion, an invitation which is personal and yet also "essentialized" in a manner differentiated according to essence.[112]

By contrast, the rejection of the distinction between essence and energies means the exclusion of universal-personal experience and the priority of the individual intellect as the path to knowledge. It means that truth is exhausted in the coincidence of meaning with concept, in the understanding of nature and person as determinations arising from intellectual abstraction: persons have the character of the relations of essences; relations do not characterize persons, but are identified with persons, with a view to supporting the logical necessity of the simplicity of essence. Finally, God becomes accessible only as essence, that is, only as an object of rational inquiry, as the necessary "first mover" who is himself "unmoved," that is, as "pure act," and whose existence must be identified with the self-actualization of his essence. And the world is the "effect" of the "first mover," just as God's grace is the "effect" of the divine essence ("supernatural" but created). The only relation of the world to God is the intellectual connection of cause and effect, a "connection" which detaches God organically from the world – the world is made autonomous and is subordinated to intellectual objectification and to a utilitarian intentionality.[113]

The problem of the essence-energies distinction set the seal on the differentiation of the Latin West from the Greek East. The West denied the distinction, wishing to safeguard the simplicity of the divine essence, since rational thought cannot tolerate the conflict between existential identity and otherness, a distinction not entailing division or separation.[114] In the West's understanding, God is defined only by his essence. What is not essence does not belong to God; it is a creation of God. Consequently, the energies of God are either identified with the essence as "pure act," or any external manifestation of them is necessarily of a different essence, that is, a created effect of the divine cause.[115]

But this means that *theosis*, the participation of human beings in the divine life,[116] is ultimately impossible, since the grace that deifies the saints, even if "supernatural," according to the arbitrary definition given to it by Western theologians from as early as the ninth century,[117] remains without any real explanation. And it was precisely the defense of the fact of the theosis of human beings, the participation of the hesychasts in the sensory experience of the *mode* of the divine life (in the uncreated light of God's glory), that led the Orthodox Church in the synods of the fourteenth century (1341, 1347, 1351 and 1368) to define the essence-energies distinction as the formal difference distinguishing the Orthodox East from the Latin West and to see summarized under the heading of the knowledge of God the heretical deviations of the Roman Church.[118]

In the following centuries the Eastern theologians were vindicated historically by the tragic dimensions of the impasse in which metaphysics found itself in the West. The transference of the knowledge of God from the realm of direct personal disclosure, through the natural energies, to that of an intellectual and rationalist approach had as an inevitable consequence the driving of a wedge between the transcendent and the immanent, the "exiling" of God to the realm of the experientially inaccessible, the separating of religion from life and restricting it to credal statements, the technological violating of natural and historical reality and subjecting it to the demands of individualistic comfortable living – ending up finally in the "death of God" of the Western metaphysical tradition and the emergence of *nothingness* and *the absurd* as Western man's fundamental existential categories.

§23   *The distinction between nature and energies as a presupposition of the powers of knowing unitary personal otherness*

We saw in the previous chapter[119] that within the limits of existential experience the person's power of "knowledge" refers either to an *invitation* to an exclusive relation through "things," which is not only the principle of the person but also the principle of its distinct absence, or to immediate interpersonal communion, which is a fact of ecstatic reciprocity, that is, of reciprocal *erotic* self-offering. The distinction between essence and energies clarifies these powers, especially with regard to the knowledge of God. We saw that nature or essence in itself remains unrecognizable and inaccessible – it is both the nearest and the farthest. Only through the natural energies is the *mode* revealed by which essence or nature *is*, and this mode is personal otherness. Personal otherness is disclosed within the context of experiential reality either as the "real" principle of its distinct absence or as the realization of erotic relation.

These powers of the person's "knowledge" refer both to the interpretation of humanity's *being* and to the revelation of a personal God. A work of art witnesses to the person of its creator; it is the personal disclosure of human creative energy; it makes known the *mode* by which human nature *is* as personal otherness. Yet the person itself of the creator is revealed only as distinct absence. At the same time the knowledge of the person which is attained in the erotic relation, in the relation of universal ecstatic reciprocity, cannot be made known objectively or be defined or described in individual categories (i.e., categories of the individual nature). The *mode* by which the person *is*, revealed in the erotic ecstatic relation, is a primordial epistemic certainty, but a certainty which is defined only as a possibility.

To these two givens of experiential reality relating to the knowledge of the human person (the givens of "real" absence and erotic certainty) there correspond, respectively, the basic positions of the Eastern Orthodox on the "knowledge" of God: God becomes "known" either through the "things" of the reality of the world as distinct absence, or as erotic certainty within the context of a reciprocal ec-static relation. And here ec-stasy finds its most complete meaning, since the relation is realized within the limits not only of personal but also of natural or essential otherness. We call *grace* (*charis*) the fact that God *gives himself* (*charizetai*) in his erotic ec-static self-offering. Unknowable and inaccessible as a whole in his essence – "which is beyond all things and transcends all things" – he is revealed as self-offering love for every human person – "condescends to abide in all things" – as passion for erotic goodness, as zeal for an exclusive personal relation. God "goes out of himself," "by virtue of his supernatural and ecstatic capacity to remain nevertheless, within himself."[120] He actualizes "outside" his nature the ineffable power of personal relation, communion and participation. That is why our knowledge of God also transcends every objective cognitive approach. It is an experiential fact of dynamic recognition and affirmation of God's erotic ecstasy – a fact of participation in another mode of existence, in the true life of the Uncreated. The knowledge of God does not refer to the realm of our objective inquiries. It refers to our inward, personal discovery and certainty that God's erotic ecstasy (the gift of life) is directed exclusively towards us, that we are *known* and loved by God and consequently all we have to do is to respond positively to this erotic invitation, with the aim of "knowing" the Person of our Bridegroom and Lover: "having come to know God, or rather to be known by God" (Gal 4:9).

Of course, the objects of natural reality remain primary data in the realm of objective inquiries directed towards the knowledge of God. For they rise up in the personal relation as "things" (acts – products of a Creator Person) – that is, the results of the energies of the unknowable, inaccessible and incomprehensible divine essence or nature, its external manifestations which make known the mode of existence of the Godhead, its personal character. Through the "things" the Person of the Creator God is witnessed to and made known as existential immediacy of personal relation, and simultaneously as distinct absence. In our personal relation to the world, beings as "things" reveal the existence of a personal God, the personal Word of the Creator God, the Person of God the Word, yet inevitably also the distinct absence of the Person. Outside the realm of reciprocal erotic relation, God is absence. The Church's theology of experience could justify Sartre's expression summarizing the tragic experiential search for God by Western man after the "death of God," the God of ontic categories: "the absence is God."[121] Yes, but a "personal" absence, which means a fact and an experience of certainty about the existence of God. Only within the bounds of personal relation is the experience of absence possible. The absence is always experience of the privation of a personal immediacy, which presupposes the reality or the possibility of the relation.

This experiential sense of loss of personal immediacy, the pain of the personal absence of God, sometimes shows through in Sartre's writings,[122] as in the works of other contemporary Westerners who refuse to exhaust the truth about

God simply in intellectual constructs.[123] Sometimes the sense of personal absence can even arrive at the immediacy of an erotic fact. Sartre says: "Let him condemn me to hell a hundred, a thousand, times, only let him exist!"[124] Only a privation of love can be indifferent to any benefit, provided the pain of absence can be exchanged for the certainty and immediacy of personal presence.

Of course, for this pain at the loss of God to be an erotic pain, a previous knowledge and sense of his Person is implied. "For if one has mind and senses," says John Chrysostom, "one already experiences hell when one is cut off from the face of God."[125] In the language of the Church's experience we speak in these circumstances of a "divine eros," drawing on the "mourning" of the monks at the loss of the divine Person. "Mourning which is according to God," says John Climacus, "is a melancholy of the soul, a disposition of an anguished heart that passionately seeks what it thirsts for, and when it fails to attain it, pursues it diligently and follows behind it lamenting bitterly."[126] And Symeon the New Theologian calls on the "unknowable person," "the hidden mystery," to disclose himself and manifest his immediate presence. "Come," he says, "invisible one, wholly intangible and impalpable ... Come, thou name so greatly desired and constantly proclaimed ... Come, thou who thyself art become desire in me, who hast willed that I should desire thee, thou, absolutely inaccessible."[127] Doubtless this "mourning" for the absence of "sensible" immediacy is not only painful but is also the prerequisite for erotic relationship and communion, and for that reason is in the end "mourning bringing joy" and "a blessed madness,"[128] a prerequisite of apophatic-experiential theological knowledge. The cognitive aspects of erotic absence, however, must await discussion in a later chapter.

By this point it should have become evident that the unity of the person presupposes, as an existential fact, the distinction between nature and energies, that is, the possibility of summing up nature in ecstatic personal unicity – which is witnessed to and made known through the actions (*energê-mata*) of the nature which are "products" (*poiêmata*) of the person, or are experienced in terms of erotic immediacy.

PART TWO

The Cosmic Dimensions of the Person

Chapter One

The Personal Aspect of the World

§24   *The "world" as "mode of disclosure" of physical reality*

Being as "things," as that which rises up into personal relationship, define physical reality as personal disclosure. The very word "world" (in Greek: *kosmos* – "order" or "ornament") determines the *mode* by which physical reality *is*, the *how* rather than the *what* of the physical Creation. World (*kosmos*) is the ordered (*kata kosmon*) disclosure of beings. It is a category of beauty, and beauty implies personal differentiation, which is affirmed only within the terms of relation.

Presocratic writers used the word *kosmos* to determine the *how*, the *harmony* and *order*, of physical reality. Aetius mentions that "Pythagoras was the first to call the mass of the whole a *kosmos* because of the order therein."[1] The objective "all" or "whole" of human experience appears as "most beautiful," that is, "a cosmos, for it is a product of God" (Thales),[2] since it is an organized and indivisible unity ("the things in the one cosmos are not separated from each other" – Anaxagoras)[3] harmoniously put together from infinite and finite quantities ("harmonized from both unlimiteds and limiters" – Philolaus),[4] a unity which can neither perish nor be developed further, nor lose its harmony and orderedness ("it will not lose anything nor become larger nor be rearranged" – Melissus).[5]

73

More specifically, Anaximander says that the order and harmony of the world are not a mechanical necessity but a moral one which has its counterpart in the laws of human society, in "the public social order."[6] Anaximander says: "And the source of coming-to-be for existing things is that into which destruction, too, happens 'according to necessity. For they pay penalty and retribution to each other for their injustice according to the order of time.'"[7] There is a common starting-point both for the genesis and the destruction of beings, a necessity which keeps beings in a harmony and order which we must suppose to be moral, since it is analogous to the relationship between punishment and retribution, with time as an objective organizer.

These Presocratic insights were incorporated by Plato into his view of the world as an ensouled unity – "a living creature endowed with soul and intelligence"[8] – of a living totality of the animate and the inanimate, of gods and men: "Wise men ... say that the heavens and the earth, gods and men, are bound together by fellowship and friendship, and order and temperance and justice, and for this reason they call the sum of things the 'ordered' universe ... not the world of disorder or riot."[9] The banishment of disorder and riot is the disclosure of life, and for that reason the world is revealed as a living whole, as a "visible living creature": "The world has received animals, mortal and immortal, and has been filled with them, and become a visible animal containing the visible – a sensible god who is the image of the intellectual, the greatest, best, fairest, most perfect."[10]

But life implies soul, and that is why the "body" of the world is *ensouled*.[11] The world's beauty is revealed as a living and therefore ensouled organism, a god perceptible by the senses, a "perfect animal from perfect parts."[12] And the soul is not irrational but *intellectual* – the order, division, harmony and proportion which manifest the beauty of the world[13] betray the existence of mind, and therefore the beauty of the world is endowed not only with soul but also with mind.[14] The beauty reveals the mode by which the world *is*, the *how,* not the *what,* of natural reality, the world as "a living creature endowed with soul and intelligence."[15]

It is clear, however, that in Platonic thought the categories of beauty are revelatory of life rather than of a personal presence. The world as a whole is a living subject, not an objective disclosure of a personal energy that is outside the world. Plato nevertheless also proceeds to raise the beautiful to the level of *good.* Beauty, together with proportion and truth, defines the idea of the good.[16] And since the good (whether divine or human) is necessarily dependent on God[17] and beauty is "mingled" with the good, the world's beauty is shown to have a divine quality.[18] Thus from the world's beauty we can be led up to the goodness of the creator God.[19] Only that the creativity of God refers not to creation "ex nihilo" but to the *arrangement* of the world,[20] to its dynamic transference from disorder to order,[21] in short, to its endowment with life.

This interpretation of the cosmic whole on the basis of the category of beauty, the treatment of the world as "a most beautiful work," as a living creature endowed with soul and intelligence, keeps human knowledge of the world within the bounds of an experiential relationship with the objective whole or totality of physical reality. It does not permit a rationalistic approach to causality, that is, neutering the world within an abstract intellectual framework. The category of beauty presupposes the experiential cognition and valuation of the *mode* by which the reality of the world exists. The experiential confirmation of the world's beauty (as indeed of any beauty) is realized only in the context of a direct relation and cannot be imposed objectively by using the methods of abstract proof.

§25   *The world as the noetic conception of ontic universal-*
       ity. Materialist, pantheist and theocentric approaches

Parallel to the experiential reference to the *how* of the cosmic
whole, we also find in the Greek philosophers a rationalistic
objectification and abstract approach to the causality of physical reality, the reduction of the world to a *what* in the neuter
gender susceptible of intellectual investigation. We may distinguish (in a completely schematic way without exhausting
the information conveyed by the texts) three different modes
of interpreting the reality of the world within the context of
the rationalistic objectivizing of nature as a totality.

The first mode explains the world's cause by adopting the
idea of its complete self-containedness. It accepts the eternity,
self-existence and autonomy of the world and is summarized
characteristically in Heraclitus' saying: "This universe, which
is the same for all, has not been made by any god or man,
but it always has been, is, and will be – an ever-living fire,
kindling itself by regular measures and going out by regular
measures."[22]

The second interpretation similarly does not locate the
world's cause outside the cosmic whole. Instead it deifies the
elements themselves that make up physical reality. This reflects essentially the same understanding of the world's self-
existence, autonomy and completion. It attributes properties
to the world which, in contrast to humanity's mortality and
corruptibility, are described as divine. It is a primordial human attitude towards the world, an attitude which Plato attributes equally to uneducated barbarians and educated Greeks:
"Why, to begin with, think of the earth, and sun, and planets,
and everything! And the wonderful and beautiful order of the
seasons with its distinctions of years and months! Besides,
there is the fact that all mankind, Greeks and non-Greeks
alike, believe in the existence of the gods."[23]

The third interpretation is determined by the rationalistic attribution of the world's cause to a supreme divine principle, to a demiurgic god experientially inaccessible and summarized by Aristotle as follows: "And from the heavenly bodies too: seeing by day the revolution of the sun and by night the well-ordered movement of the other stars, they came to think that there was a god who is the cause of such movement and order."[24]

These three theories of cosmic reality, positing the world as self-existent and autonomous, or deifying the elements and laws of the physical universe, or attributing the world's cause to some god, may perhaps serve as headings that subsume all the later theories – all of them being of a materialistic, pantheistic, or theocentric-etiological type. For they all have a common presupposition which unites them in a uniform attitude towards the world: all three fundamentally objectify the world in a rationalist manner, adopt an abstract etiological approach to the reality of nature, and turn the dimensions of ontological self-completion – whether deified or not – into absolute intellectual categories, such as the measurable analogy of sizes, the smooth succession of temporal movement with respect to before and after, the spatial organization of movement, i.e., orderliness, and so on.

But this raising of intellectual categories to cosmological theory implies the priority of the reasoning capacity of the human subject over the objective world. Physical reality is interpreted according to its coincidence with our noetic conception of the composite unity of the cosmic whole, the "universitas creaturarum." The world does not disclose the *mode* by which physical reality *is*, preserving the truth of Being as a power of relation and participation. It objectifies Being as ontic universality, identifies Being with the ontic-noetic conception of essence.[25] Thus the world is held up as a fundamental metaphysical category,[26] as a presupposition of the entire intellectual structure of an objectified metaphysics: Being as ontic universality becomes the measure of working back to the absolute ontic essence of the deity: the world, as the direct experience of truth, is offered to us with the intention that it should be traced back etiologically to the truth of the deity. It becomes the measure of the differentiation of the relative from the absolute, of the moved from the unmoved, of the composite from the simple, of the "third term of the comparison" ("tertium comparationis") between man and God.

All this happens when our image of the world is theocentric, that is, when the God-cause is set in contradistinction to the neuter *what* of the cosmic whole, of the "universitas creaturarum." But the world also remains a fundamental category of Metaphysics in the case of a non-theocentric image of the world, that is, when it is made autonomous as an objective ontic universality or even as the "horizon" of existential experience. In reality, the world is made autonomous as an ontic-noetic conception of the physical "whole" both with the theocentric and the non-theocentric world-images: When God as *first cause* ("causa prima") is set against the neuter *what* of the cosmic whole, this creates a very sharp antithesis between the transcendent and the immanent – the transcendent onticity of God is distinguished to an infinite degree from the relative and perceptible onticity of the world.

An immediate consequence of this is the "exile" – as it has aptly been called – of God from the world, his transference to "heaven," to a realm different from that which is accessible to human experience. This Being, which is God, is separated from the reality of the world by the boundary which distinguishes the known from the unknown, the experientially existent from the experientially non-existent, sensible reality from intellectual conception. The field is left clear for humankind to exercise its sovereignty over nature and over history. Humanity interprets and subjects the reality of the world to its individual intellectual capacity. The objective *what* of the world and of history is organized rationally to serve the autonomy of human needs and desires. The whole phenomenon of modern technology is founded very clearly on this attitude.

§26   *The scientific indeterminacy of cosmic harmony*

This autonomized objectivity of physical reality and its rationalistic interpretation, however, appear to be opposed today, before any other objection, by developments in modern physics, that is, by the very conclusions themselves of the rationalistic processing of the reality of the physical world.[27] The objectivizing of matter and of the "principles" and "laws" in accordance with which physical reality is articulated were always based on the intellectual processing of the material provided by observation and experiment, that is, on the objectivized and measured experience of the senses, and also on arithmetical-quantitative relations as the absolute and unique possibility of knowledge of the world.[28] But even from the beginning of the twentieth century the neuter *what* of the world's reality began to be revealed in the light of scientific observation itself more and more as a multiform *how* of an infinity of undetermined differentiations.

One could mention purely by way of example, without wishing to trespass on the territory of other scientific disciplines, that the first crack in the intellectual certainty of objective measurements was the theory of relativity, which showed that on the planetary level observation always involves the position and movement of the observer. And later, Heisenberg's uncertainty principle ("Unbestimmtheitsrelations") precluded prediction in the field of physical becoming and linked the result or conclusion of observation not simply with the aspect of the "observer," but also with the very fact of observation, with the *relation* between the observer and what is observed. Then there were the radical observations of Niels Bohr on the property of the electron to appear either as a particle or as a wave, without its being in itself either one or the other but something that implies both; the acceptance that energy in nuclear physics is not only kinetic but also identified with mass and increases with movement; the belief that "anti-matter" exists, or the theory of the continuing "generation" of matter and asteroids in the universe; and a host of further conclusions both on the microphysical and the macrophysical levels which have shaken faith in the objective and mechanical nature of the laws governing the universe.[29]

These conclusions in the end present the distinction between truth and error as methodologically unhelpful, so that it is only on a scale between these two poles of knowledge that scientific research can make any progress. The harmony and order of the world is revealed more and more as scientific indeterminacy and asymmetry: "The scientific conception of the world of physics ceases to be of a purely scientific nature."[30] But the indeterminacy and asymmetry are categories that refer preeminently to the realm of personal uniqueness and dissimilarity. The scientific conclusions of modern physics can be starting-points for the understanding of the world not as a mechanical system organized deterministically, but as a universal harmony of infinite and indeterminate differentiations of a personal energy.[31]

§27   *The personal logos of the world's decorum*

Ultimately the transcendence of arithmetical-quantitative relations as the absolute and unique power of cognition of the world, that is, the denial of the ontic-noetic determination of the truth of the reality of the world (the world as a coincidence of phenomenal objectivity with its determination by the intellect) becomes possible only on the basis of the ontological distinction, the distinction between a being (*to on*) and Being (*Einai*). And this means: only under the aspect of an event of "disclosure" of Being within the context of personal *relation*, and not in the dimensions of its

ontic-objective sense. Within the context of personal relation with the reality of the world we recognize Being not
as a being, not as an ontic universality arithmetically and
quantitatively measurable, not as nature or essence, but as an
infinite indeterminacy of ontic differentiations, that is, as the
mode by which beings *are* in their unique and incomparable
dissimilarity, in their "personal" uniqueness. This mode of
the "personal" uniqueness of beings is beauty, is the reality
of nature as "cosmos." Within the context of the whole of
physical reality, ontological difference, the difference of beings from Being, appears as a distinction between the noetic-
ontic conception of beings – their conventional denotation
on the basis of arithmetical-quantitative relations – and the
mode by which beings *are*, that is, the "personal" differentiation of beings, the truth (*a-lêtheia*) of beings, their rising up
into personal relation, their beauty. "Cosmos," then, is the
apearance of the personal universality of Being, of the mode
by which beings are as disclosures of a personal uniqueness
and decorum, as presences of beauty. The truth of beings is
witnessed to as beauty, as the principle of a personal uniqueness and dissimilarity, which presupposes and discloses a
personal creative presence and energy.

This cosmopoeic personal energy, the principle of the
world's decorum (*kosmiotês*), beauty as the truth of beings,
is not exhausted cognitively by a "semantic" definition (arithmetical and quantitative) arising from human reason, but
is encountered by human reason (*logos*) within the context
of a personal dialogue (*dia-logos*), a fact of personal relation. And it is this relation which defines the possibility of
knowledge of the world, the unique possibility of the disclosure of Being. We recognize the world as the appearance and
disclosure of Being[32] in the measure in which we recognize it
personally (through the experience of *relation*) as "cosmos"-
adornment (*kosmos-kosmêma*), as personal uniqueness and
decorum (*kosmiotês*) within the context of the undetermined

differentiation which represents the beauty, the "personal" dissimilarity of beings. We recognize Being as the mode of personal uniqueness and dissimilarity, as the dissimilar and unique *how* of personal disclosure, in short, as the content of personhood.

To return to the example of a work of art, we can determine the disclosure of personal uniqueness and dissimilarity more directly and with greater precision through the beauty of personal creative energy: The dissimilar and unrepeatable character of artistic expression is not the exactness of a programmed uniqueness arranged with quantitative relations but the universal ec-static energy which is always revelatory of the creative person, the principle-disclosure of a personal presence-absence. Similarly, the beauty of the entire reality of the universe does not refer to the arranged exactness of a mechanical orderliness, but is a personal principle or logos. It is the beauty of the revelation of a person, the *logos* of the person, the person of the logos.

§28   *The erotic dimensions of the world's beauty*

The beauty of the world, which shows beings to be the products and principles[33] of the divine creative presence, is not simply and solely an "aesthetic" beauty, that is, a subjective impression which is evoked by the pleasure of the individual senses. Of course, only the impressions of the senses represent a form of "knowledge" which transcends objective definitions, arithmetical-quantitative relations, *a priori* concepts and descriptions.[34] And it is not by chance that beauty becomes a springboard for love, that is, for that universal "knowledge" which tends towards completion in the fulfilling relation of bodily union and self-offering. Aesthetic beauty can lead to the objectively undetermined "wonder" which is introduced by the new and revelatory "knowledge" of erotic experience, beyond any conceptual definition or objective assessment.[35] Erotic "wonder" in the presence of the uniqueness of a physical beauty is always an invitation to communion and relation, an attraction which aims at union, at the satisfaction of the existential desire for communion. This attraction is not always tied to human bodily beauty. Sometimes the physical beauty of a place or a work of art can generate through wonder the same need for erotic fulfillment which is generated by the presence of a beloved person. The contemplation of natural beauty can be accompanied by the same physical demand for the fullness of pleasure within the "absolute" relation which the beauty of a human presence also evokes.

But it is precisely in its erotic dimension that beauty reveals the tragic nature of human insufficiency, humanity's weakness in responding to the call of beauty, to its essential "goal": To succeed in a fulfilling communion and relation with the world's personal principle or *logos*. Thus beauty appears as a tragic call to a fullness of life which proves unattainable. The more sensitive we are to the need for communion, the more the world's beauty torments us, a tragic unquenchable thirst. It is individual nature, the naturally egocentric human being, which cannot transcend itself to respond to the call of beauty. It cannot attain the self-offering which creates the fulfilling relation. Natural individuality – individual feelings, individual thoughts, individual impressions – are a closed circle of life which sets the call of beauty in the impasse of self-satisfaction. It receives the call of beauty as an invitation to seek its own pleasure, since individual nature always tends to exhaust life in terms of its own pleasure and self-sufficiency. The weakness of personal relation and self-offering transforms beauty into an agonizingly unattainable thirst for fulfillment. The beautiful proves to be a tragic impasse. One only need think of the erotic poetry of Baudelaire, Cavafy or Saint-John Perse to understand the agonizing character of physical beauty, the torment that accompanies the aesthetic experience of beauty.

§29   *Ascetic self-transcendence as a presupposition for knowledge of the truth of the world's beauty*

The way in which the Church Fathers speak of the world's beauty suggests that they assume a moral effort. Any truth that becomes an object to be subjected to the individual's understanding or the individual's feeling or the individual's psychological experience is only a shadow of the truth, an image of reality produced in the imagination. For us to encounter the world's true beauty – "not the imaginary beauty of the flesh"[36] – we must draw back from the physical demand for pleasure which accompanies the vision of beauty. We must refuse to change the beautiful into a pleasurable "fantasy" of the flesh. And this means that we must deny our individualistic nature, mortify our individualistic desires which project onto the world's beauty the physical demands of pleasure and self-sufficiency.

Through the senses that bring us into contact with the world we are informed of the world and the world's beauty. But at the same time the senses express and make specific the irrational desires of biological individuality: the insatiable thirst of the senses for absolute pleasure is the rebellious tendency of physical individuality to be absolutized as an end in itself. Therefore the experience of the world and the world's beauty, which the senses provide us with, corresponds not to the truth of the world and its beauty, but to the senses' demands for pleasure. The world's beauty is changed into a delectable object of the individual's senses, serving individual self-containedness. The senses do not constitute and do not recognize the true beauty of the world; they constitute and recognize merely a "phantasm" of this beauty, the distorted image of a beauty subjected to individualistic demand. "The contemplation of creatures," says Isaac the Syrian, "even if it is sweet, is only a shadow of knowledge, and its sweetness is not set apart from the fantasy of dreams."[37]

We need to draw back from the physical demands of the senses if we are to know the true beauty of the world – the world's "personal" beauty. And this drawing back is the work of asceticism. Asceticism, as the Church's experience has established it in its specific practical and bodily forms, aims at the denial of individual desires so as to free our *personal* capabilities, our capabilities for communion and loving self-offering. Maximus says: "All phenomena need the cross."[38] All phenomena, everything that is accessible to us through the senses, must pass through the experience of the cross. We must come to know phenomena through the experience of the cross's self-denial, the experience of the mortification of the natural-individualistic will. A cross-like withdrawal from our natural will is the only possibility we have of discerning, beyond the fantasies of the phenomenal, the truth of things. The truth of things becomes knowable only within the terms of personal *relation*, which means: the possibility of ecstatic "standing outside" that closed circle of life which is physical individuality, a humble study of the *logos* of things, a loving reception of this *logos*. That is why the knowledge of the world, the knowledge of the truth of things, is a moral achievement which is realized within the context of asceticism. Bodily *askesis* is a way of knowledge, is the presupposition of cosmological truth, our only possibility of finding "the truly beautiful."

§30   *"Natural contemplation"*

In the patristic literature of the Byzantine period, we often find the path of knowledge expressed as three stages: *praxis – natural contemplation – theology*.[39] *Praxis* is the ascetic life, the specific bodily endeavor to mortify the individual desires, the denial of individual pleasure through the senses. Knowledge begins with this purification of our cognitive powers, which opens up the possibility of personal relationship. Thus the world, from being an object of the senses, an objective "phenomenon" and subjective impression, is transformed into the second term of a personal relationship.

Personal relationship with the world defines *natural contemplation*. Maximus the Confessor interprets "natural contemplation" as "the middle ground between types and truth."[40] Between the objective "semantics" of types (that is, of conventional definitions, of objectified impressions of phenomena) and the truth of theology (which is a transformation of the "heart" into "a place of the mysteries of the new world,"[41] the direct vision of God) lies natural contemplation, the personal discovery of and encounter with the *logos* of things,[42] the personal *logos* of the world, and the first experiential certainty of the presence of the personal God-Logos: "When we understand the spiritual *logoi* of visible things, we are taught that there is a maker of the phenomenal world, but we cannot attain to or examine the concept of who he is. For the visible creation clearly provides an understanding that there is a maker but not who that maker is."[43]

The Church's cosmology, that is to say, *natural contemplation*, begins with the personal discovery of the *logos* of things, with the revelation of matter as "logical" energy. Matter is not a reality which simply has its cause and first principle in God. Matter is the substantiation of the will of God, a result of God's personal energy, and remains active as the *logos* revelatory of the divine energy: "Beings as a whole were not brought into the phenomenal world from some underlying matter," says Gregory of Nyssa, "but the divine will became the matter and essence of what was created."[44] God is not simply the cause of the "forms" or "ideas" or "shapes" of matter, but matter itself, inseparably tied to the form or shape (that is, with the *logos* peculiar to each essence), constitutes the substantiation of the divine will. The form or shape, that is, the *logos* of matter,[45] is the disclosure of the personal energy of God which is substantiated in matter.

In the words of Basil the Great, God, "after having it in mind and determining to bring into being that which had no being, conceived of the world as it ought to be, and created matter in harmony with the world's form."[46] On the basis of this statement we could say that God's *mental concept* refers to the *form*, but the mental concept cannot be distinguished from the matter, that is, from its specific hypostatic realization, since "God creates by conceiving and the mental concepts subsist as the work."[47] There is no difference or distance between the concept, the will and the energy of God, and the substantiation of his *logos*: The will of God is a work and the work of God is his *logos* – "for with God his work is *logos*."[48] The word or *logos* of God, which expresses his will, is not like the uttered human word which passes without hypostasis; the word of God is substantiated "immediately" "as the hypostasis and shape of creation."[49] "The movement of God's will becomes – at any moment that he pleases – a fact, and the intention becomes at once realized in nature; for omnipotence does not leave the plans of its far-seeing skill in the state of unsubstantial wishes. And the actualizing of the wish is essence."[50]

§31   *The "logical" constitution of matter*

Matter, then, is the substantiation of the divine will. The *logoi* of matter, its "forms" or "shapes," reflect the creative *logoi* of the divine acts of thought and will.[51] In its very organic constitution matter is the result of the union of "logical" qualities, the conjunction and union of which defines the hypostasis of sensible things. "All the things through which matter is constituted," says Gregory of Nyssa, "lightness, heaviness, density, rarity, softness, hardness, wetness, dryness, cold, heat, color, form, outline, dimensions – all of them in themselves are bare concepts ... for none of these as such is matter, but when they come together with each other, matter comes into being."[52] The "logical" constitution of matter entirely refutes the ontic-objective character of things. Matter is not the *what* of physical reality, the material which assumes a "form" or "shape" in order to manifest the essence, but is the coming together of "logical" qualities (the energies of nuclear units, we might say today).[53] It is the coordination in the *how* of a unique harmony, which constitutes the "form" or "shape" of material things. The entire reality of the universe, the countless variety of the "forms"-essences, is not the *what* of objective observation and intellectual conception, but the *how* of the "personal" harmony of the "logical" qualities – "some musical harmony constituting the mingled and divinely sweet hymnody of the power that sustains the universe."[54]

This ceaselessly activated "personal" cosmic harmony constitutes the fundamental potentiality of humanity's personal relation with the world, the potentiality of a personal relation with the Creator through the *logos* of that which has been created. In other words, the connection of the world with God is for humankind not only a possibility of intellectual ascent of the caused to its cause. This connection should not be identified with the intellectual leap that traces the "ideas" or "forms" or "shapes" back to the archetypes conceived eternally by the divine Wisdom, to the eternal causes of created things which are included in the essence of God.[55] It means that the presence of God, as personal will and energy (not as essence), is immediate and active in the world – a ceaselessly active invitation to personal relation, through the *logos* of material things, with the personal God-Logos.

This active invitation is not identified *according to the essence* with the one who invites, nor with the energy of the one who invites. The *logos* and will of God are not identified with the creatures themselves,[56] just as the will of an artist is not identified with the work of art itself, with the result of the personal creative energy. The work of art is the substantiation and embodiment of the personal *logos* and will of the artist, the active invitation and potentiality of personal relation with the creator through the *logos* of what he or she has created. The work of art is different in essence and energy from the artist[57] ("the skill in the product of a craft" is one thing and "the skill in the person who takes up a craft" is another, according to Basil the Great).[58] Nevertheless, that which a work of art *is* discloses and reveals the unique, dissimilar and unrepeatable personal *logos* of the artist. And to refer again to the example used in the previous chapter, a painting by van Gogh is "according to the essence" a canvas with pigments, but this canvas with pigments testifies to the person of van Gogh; it is the substantiation of the personal *logos* of van Gogh. Outside the terms of the fact of personal relation, the personal reception of the *logos* which the work of art embodies, it remains an object made out of neutral materials: the artist's *logos* remains unapproachable, the truth of the "thing" uninterpreted, the experience of personal presence, the personal uniqueness and dissimilarity of the artist, inaccessible.

§32   *The "triadic adornment" of creation*

"For from the beauty of created things their creator is contemplated proportionately in the creation."[59] In terms of "natural contemplation," as expressed by the Byzantine Fathers, "proportionately" (*analogôs*) does not imply a rationalistic comparison of dimensions or qualities. It is more like a moral presupposition. Humanity reveals the true – that is to say, the personal – beauty of the world in proportion to the measure of the purification of its individual sense-organs. "The beauty which is true and most beloved can only be contemplated by one whose mind has been purified."[60] When the "unreal" (*phantasiôdês*) impressions of sensible beauty formed in the individual have been transcended through asceticism, beings are contemplated as "all of them very good,"[61] since they participate in the "beautifying" energy of the divine creative wisdom:

> We call "beautiful" (*kalon*) that which has a share in beauty (*kallos*), and we give the name of "beauty" to that which is the cause of beauty in everything. But the suprasubstantially beautiful (*kalon*) is called "beauty" (*kallos*) because of the beauty (*kallonên*) which is bestowed by it on all things, each in accordance with what it is, and because it is the cause of harmony and splendor ... and because beauty summons (*kaloun*) all things to itself (hence it is called "beauty" [*kallos*]) and gathers all things into itself.[62]

The ascent from the beauty of creatures to the personal presence of the creative God-Logos is a moral journey of participation in the "beautifying" personal divine energy, an acceptance of the *summons* or *invitation* which is embodied by the beauty of creatures – a moral journey of purification, of a progressive and dynamic clarifying of the mind, "of being astonished and comprehending ... raised up from knowledge to knowledge, and from contemplation to contemplation, and from comprehension to comprehension."[63]

The ever-inexhaustible goal of this dynamic contemplation of the world is the revelation, through beauty, of the triadic nature of the divine energy, "the triadic adornment of creation."[64] The beauty of created things is not the one-dimensional *logos* of a creative cause, but the disclosure of the single and at the same time triadic mode of the divine energy, which reflects the mystery of the single and at the same time triadic mode of the divine life. "From the wise contemplation of creation," says Maximus, "I mean of the things around the Holy Trinity, the Father, Son and Holy Spirit, we receive a *logos* ... Indeed creation cries out through the created things in it, and proclaims, as it were, to those who are able to hear spiritually the very cause that is celebrated triadically in hymns."[65]

This triadic witness to beauty is an experiential power of participation in the traces discernible in the world of the mode of the divine life, which can only be expressed in appropriate images and conventional concepts.[66] We venture to say that the Father "conceives" of the created world, the Son "actualizes" it, and the Holy Spirit "perfects" it.[67] Creation is the common work of the Trinity, but each of the three Persons is the cause of creatures in a different mode, even though the mode is unified.[68] The wisdom of the Father "exercises providential care over all things," is intellective before all ages, and wills and loves the world's created things. The world's true beauty reveals this providence and will and love of the Father. But this revelation is *logos*, the disclosure of the energy of the Son and Logos, "through whom all things were made." And the *logos* of created things is not simply their "mental representation," the "idea" of every being. It is the *being* of beings, revealed as "subsistent life and life-giving power,"[69] that is, as energy of the Holy Spirit. The beauty of created things (not the beauty arising through the senses and the imagination, but that which is revealed to the person who has been purified of individualistic-egocentric resistance, that is to say, the person who has been crucified) reflects the personal uniqueness of the divine energy, which is disclosed as triadic, and yet at the same time as single and undivided. "For the Father creates all things through the Logos in the Holy Spirit, since where the Logos is there the Spirit is too. And the things created through the Logos have from the Spirit by the Logos the strength of being. For thus it is written in the thirty-second psalm: 'By the word (*logos*) of the Lord the heavens were established, and all their strength by the breath (spirit) of his mouth.'"[70] All these expressions remain "bare" thoughts without a real correspondence in life and truth, outside the field of *natural contemplation*, which is a specific ascetic practice of purification and self-denial designed to effect a personal approach to the world's beauty, to bring about an immediate experience of the world's personal dimensions.

§33   *The human being as "microcosm" and "mediator"*

The idea of *natural contemplation*, the moral achievement of our personal *relation* with the world, also sheds light on the teaching of the Greek Fathers on man as a recapitulation of the created world, on man as *microcosm*[71] and the world as *macroanthropos*.[72] We also meet the idea of the world summed up in man in ancient Greek thought in the context of moral theory (as in Democritus[73]) or a theory of nature (as in Plato[74] and Aristotle[75]).

Patristic literature borrows this idea of the analogous relationship between man and the world: the world may be described "microscopically" in terms of a human being, just as a human being from a certain point of view may be described "macroscopically" in terms of the world. Nevertheless, the "differentia" in the patristic view is in fact the transcendence of the descriptive analogy, the dynamic character of the truth of humanity as *microcosm*, which we find chiefly in the teaching of Maximus the Confessor.

The human being, as a natural structure, summarizes the elements of the world as a whole, but these elements, after the Fall, humanity's "unnatural" estrangement, are found both within humanity and without in the outside world in a state of division and separation. But since the human being remains a *personal* existence even after the Fall, a rational psychosomatic hypostasis, it retains the power to realize the unity of the world dynamically in its person, to recapitulate the *logos* of the world in a *personal* response to God's invitation to communion and relation between the created and the uncreated – to disclose the universal *logos* of the world as a personal *logos* of praise of the creature for the Creator.

Maximus identifies five divisions, already apparent in the first chapter of Genesis, which must be transcended if humanity is to fulfill its natural destiny:[76] The first is the division between created and uncreated nature. Then follows the division of created nature into intelligible and sensible things. Sensible things again are divided into heaven and earth. The earth is divided into paradise and inhabited world. And finally, humanity itself is divided into male and female. From its very constitution humanity has the privilege of finding itself in the "mean point" of these divisions, as a *bond* and *mediator*, that is, as a personal power of uniting the opposites. That is the purpose for which humanity was created: "For this reason the human person was introduced last among beings, as a kind of natural bond mediating between the universal poles through their proper parts, and leading into unity in itself those things that are naturally set apart from one another by a great interval."[77] Maximus cites the soul as a specific example of humanity's existential *mediation*, for "the soul is a middle being between God and matter and has powers that can unite it with both, that is, it has a mind that links it with God and senses that link it with matter."[78]

Human beings must begin the work of unifying what is set apart within the bounds of their own nature, transcending the division into male and female, attaining, that is to say, a passionless personal unity according to the divine model. Next they must unite paradise with the inhabited world, that is to say, they must transform the whole earth into a paradise (must manifest the earth's beauty as God's constantly actualized blessing, which human beings receive within the context of a personal *relationship* with him, a sacramental eucharistic thanksgiving: must turn the whole earth into a paradise of the presence of God). Then they must go on to abolish the intervals that set apart, not only with regard to their souls, but also with regard to their bodies, uniting the earth with heaven, the totality of the sensory world.

> And then the human person unites what is perceived by the
> mind and what is perceived by the senses with each other by
> achieving equality with the angels in its manner of knowing,
> and thus makes the whole creation one single creation, no
> longer divided by what it can know and what it cannot know
> through its equality to the angels lacking nothing in their
> knowledge and understanding of the *logoi* in the things that
> exist, according to which the infinite pouring out of the gift
> of true wisdom inviolably and without intermediary furnish-
> es, so far as is permitted, to those who are worthy a concept
> of God beyond understanding or explanation. And finally,
> beyond all these, the human person unites the created nature
> with the uncreated through love ... showing them to be one
> and the same through the possession of grace, the whole
> [creation] wholly interpenetrated by God, and become com-
> pletely whatever God is, save at the level of being.[79]

This work, which has its starting-point in the human person's
natural capacity for existential *mediation* between God and
the world, and is completed by the deification of the human
person and the world, by the entire interpenetration of created
and uncreated, was not accomplished by the first Adam. But
it found its realization in the person of the second Adam, the
person of Christ, the progenitor of the "new creation."[80]

With the theory of the human person as *microcosm* and *mediator*, within the terms of a dynamic relationship which leads
towards the loving union of the created with the uncreated,
the truth of the personal dimensions of the world reaches its
fulfillment. The world becomes a personal *logos*-disclosure
of God, a *logos* which the human person receives and summarizes dynamically, to refer again to God from whom it
originated and to whom it finally returns.

The human person has been called to realize within the context of its personal freedom the dynamic recapitulation and
unification of the cause and end or *telos* of the *logos* of cre-

ated things, the "ultimate union" of the created and uncreated *logos* which is the complete interpenetration and identity "by grace" of beings in the world and the divine Being. Until the personal unification of the cause and *telos* of the *logos* of created things is effected by the human person, this *logos* will remain a dynamic energy and movement, that is, a polyphony of *logoi*, the "natural" monad of which is the human *logos*. The "myriad" of the polyphony "is known by the element of the monad alone ... as being identical as to its underlying reality with the monad, even though it admits of a conceptual difference alone ... For the end of the monad is the myriad, and the beginning of the myriad is the monad; or, to put it more precisely, the monad in motion is the myriad, and the motionless myriad is the monad."[81] The human person's natural capacity as *microcosm* and *mediator*, that is, its personal ability to turn the world into *logos*, is summarized in this relation of unmoved myriad and moved monad.

In the context, however, of humanity's failure and fall, the difference between the "monad" of the human *logos* and the polyphony of the *logos* of all created things is manifested as movement towards an unattainable goal, a movement which fails with regard to its *telos*, and therefore has the character of changing life. We perceive this movement producing change chiefly as a corrupting "mutation" of the world in the aspects both of temporal succession and of spatial distance as "a circumscribed fixed position." The renewal of nature by Christ lies in the restoration of the possibility of nature to be "united in an immediate fashion" with God, realizing in the fact of this "union" (*synapsis*) and relation the unification of the created with the uncreated *logos*, and manifesting the Incarnate Logos as the reality "of all things in all things." Maximus says:

> At such time when nature has passed through space and time both actively and conceptually, and has been united directly with providence, it finds providence a *logos* natu-

rally simple and stable (*stasimon*), not circumscribed in any
way, and therefore entirely without movement. But as nature exists in the world temporally, its movement is subject
to change because of the finite state (*stasis*) of the world
and the mutable decay of time. When it has come to be in
God through the natural monad of him in whom it has come
to be, it will possess an ever-moving state and a stable uniform movement which has come to be eternally around that
which is the same and one and alone.[82]

§34   *The use of the world. History and culture*

It is obvious that the cosmology of the Greek Fathers is not
exhausted by a single doctrine, that is, by a particular set of
views about the world. It represents a specific *attitude* to the
world, a *mode* of life and use of the world: the world is the
second term and *logos* of a dialogue (*dia-logos*), a personal
relation directed towards the realization and disclosure of
the onefold truth of Being.

Within the context of this *relation*, which refers to the basic requirements of human life (the taking of food, the use
of matter, art, technology and economics), the human person is in dialogue with the world, respecting, studying and
highlighting the *logos* of existing things. It does not subject
the world like an impersonal and non-rational object to its
individual understanding and technical ability – it does not
violate the *logos* of material things to serve the needs and
desires of its individual life purely on utilitarian principles.
For a use of the world which denies the *logos* of creation,
that is, which denies both the personal truth of the world and
the personal truth of the human person, mutilates nature and
even humanity itself, since it destroys the truth and "perfection" of life, the attainment of the "end" of creation: "For
nature does not produce perfection through art when it has
been mutilated," says Maximus, "and when what belongs to

it from God on account of the *logos* of creation is cynically disregarded."[83]

In other words, Byzantine cosmology, as a mode of life and of use of the world, represents the possibility of a specific cultural reality: a particular art, technology, economics and politics which respects, studies and highlights the personal *logos* of the world, and therefore preserves the truth of life, and life itself, as truth and perfection and serves it. This culture found its historical embodiment, roughly speaking, in the period we call Byzantine and post-Byzantine.[84] It is, of course, inappropriate to discuss here how art, technology, economics, culture and law expressed the basic attitude to life of Orthodox cosmology in the context of Byzantine life, how they preserved a liturgical understanding of the world and history, and the cosmopoeic principle of humanity's relation with things, a principle which arises when the arbitrary will of the individual is subjected to the cosmic harmony and wisdom.[85]

What interests us here is to note, even if briefly, the cultural expression of a different cosmology, equally theological but at the opposite pole to the Byzantine, which completely negated Byzantine culture as a mode of life and approach to using the world. This was the cosmology that arose from Western theology and was embodied historically in the technological culture of the West.

The development of a different cosmology in the West appears to be founded on the Byzantine teaching of the human person as a *microcosm*.[86] This teaching was transferred to the West in the ninth century through John Scotus Eriugena's Latin translations of Maximus the Confessor and Gregory of Nyssa.[87] But it only became widely disseminated in the first decades of the twelfth century, that is, with the renaissance of learning that accompanied the appearance of scholasticism in the West (the rediscovery of classical antiquity, the entry of Aristotelian epistemology into the field of theology, the rationalistic organization of human knowledge, and the utilitarian objectivizing of truth).[88] It is the century of the "awakening" of Western theologians to the potentiality of logic and of their appreciation of the first rationalistic conclusions of scientific observation and the systematic organization of knowledge.

Early scholastic thought set the doctrine of man-*microcosm* and world-*macroanthropos* in the context of the cognitive possibilities of the analogous syllogism, that is to say, it interpreted the microcosm-macrocosm relationship with the help of a rationalistic comparative epistemology.[89] The world was treated as an object along the lines of the human microcosm as mental concept, sensory observation and measurable size. Its objective truth was defined, measured and subjected by the human intellect and its material embodiment to human tools.[90]

Thus the doctrine of man as microcosm was developed in the West as a basis for the construction of an anthropocentric world-view, a *humanism*,[91] which saw in the human microcosm and its "interior life" the possibility of an intellectual and mechanical influence on the macrocosm.[92] Within the context of the mental concept, the sensory observation and the measurable relations, knowledge of the world becomes autonomous, is a knowledge with its own structure and organization, which is no longer expressed by the "semantic" terminology of aesthetic theory and personal relationship, but by an objectively articulated scientific method, which can predict events in nature and account for them causally.[93]

The objectivizing of the truth of the world and its subjection to the understanding of the individual, and also more generally the introduction of intellectualism into Western theology, is not an isolated symptom in the general development of Western Christianity. In the first place, one should note that in the context of historical phenomenology, the rationalistic structuring and systematization of knowledge in the

medieval West is drawn primarily from jurisprudence, and is
first introduced into theology, and then from there into cosmology and the natural sciences[94] – without in consequence
there failing to be a reverse influence: on theology from the
natural sciences.[95] But the historical causes which provoked
the generation of theological rationalism are much deeper,
and should rather be sought in the need for the objective imposition of the authority of the Roman Church on the peoples
of the West – a need which appears to have its roots not only
in purely historical and sociological[96] conditions but also in
the underlying monarchianism of Roman theology, from as
early as the time of Sabellius[97] and Augustine.[98]

The objective strengthening of truth, which a clear and
unambiguous authority lent to its institutional bearer, the
Church, led Western theologians to separate faith from theology[99] and to organize the latter as an independent science.[100]
This organization of theology as a science demands an apodictic methodology which objectifies the truth under examination and subjects it to the thinking and principles ("regulae,
axiomata, principia") of the human intellect.[101] An apodictic
theological methodology took shape largely in the second
half of the twelfth century, when the *logica nova*, the second part of the Aristotelian *Organon*,[102] appeared in the West.
This became the basis of a theory of knowledge and a technique of probability.[103]

The next step was the transfer of Aristotelian methodology from systematic theory to experiential reality, that is, to
cosmology and physics – and it seems to be the naturalist
doctor-philosophers of Toledo who led the way.[104] Science
thus opened up a path for the systematic organization of
knowledge in all fields of rational enquiry, that is, for the
restriction of knowledge to the bounds of mental conception
and intellectual expression, leading finally to the subjection
of truth to the human intellect, and consequently to the subjection of the world to human will and human desire.[105]

When theology, as an apodictic methodology, objectified knowledge, when it took truth to be an object of the intellect and excluded truth as a fact of personal relation, it also excluded the possibility of a personal approach to the world. It ruled out a personal relation with the *logos* of things, with the disclosure of God's personal energy in creation. (The rejection of the distinction between the essence and the energies of God by Western theologians in the fourteenth century was the formal consequence of an intellectualist theology and completed the exclusion of truth as personal relation.) And when knowledge of the world is not realized as personal relation, when it does not aim at the reception and study of the *logos* of things, the only motive that can stimulate human interest in knowledge of the world is its *usefulness*. And the criterion of usefulness implies the subjection of the world to humanity's will and desire.

Thus the knowledge of nature began to serve technology alone. The criterion of usefulness transformed the world into an impersonal object. It forced nature to subject it to human need and desire.[106] The world lost its personal dimension. The world's *logos* ceased to be the disclosure of God's personal energy. God was radically set apart from the world by the boundary that separates created ontic essence from uncreated ontic essence, the experientially known from the experientially unknown, sensible and measurable reality from intellectual hypothesis (*suppositio*). The field was left clear for humanity's endeavor to secure sovereignty over as much of the realm of truth as was accessible to it through its intellectual and technical abilities, to interpret and subject the reality of the world to its individual mental capacity.

§35   *The theological presuppositions of technocracy*

This subjection of the world to man's intellectual and technical capacity (what we call today our technological culture) finds its first expression as early as the Middle Ages in Gothic architecture. The builders of Gothic edifices were not interested in the *logos* of the material of the construction. They did not seek to coordinate and harmonize this *logos* to bring out its expressive possibilities. On the contrary, they subjected the material to given forms, and gave the stones a deliberate *a priori* shape with the intention of realizing the ideological objective that was envisaged by the construction.[107]

Erwin Panofsky, in his very interesting study, *Gothic Architecture and Scholasticism*,[108] has drawn attention to the attempt of both scholastic thought and Gothic architecture[109] to explore the truth intellectually and to the fact that both arose at the same time:[110] "It is a connection ... more concrete than a mere 'parallelism' and yet more general than those individual 'influences' which are inevitably exerted on painters, sculptors or architects by erudite advisors: it is a real relationship of cause and effect."[111] Gothic architecture, following soon after scholasticism, is the first technological application of scholastic thought. It sets out in visible form the scholastic attempt to subject truth to the individual intellect, drawing on the new logical structures introduced by scholastic theology. In the thirteenth century, for the first time a truth is arranged and discussed systematically, under a number of sub-divisions. A complete work is divided into books, the books into chapters, the chapters into paragraphs, and the paragraphs into articles. Each assertion is established by the systematic refutation of objections, and phrase by phrase, the reader is gradually brought to a full intellectual clarification of a given truth.[112] It is "a veritable orgy of logic," as Panofsky says of Thomas Aquinas' *Summa Theologiae*.[113]

In an analogous manner the technique of Gothic architecture is based on a structure of small cut stones of uniform shape. The stones form columns, and the columns are sub-divided into ribbed composite piers, with the same number of ribs as those in the vaulting above them.[114] The arrangement of the columns and the division of the ribs create a rigid skeleton which neutralizes the weight of the material by balancing the thrusts of the walls. Here again, thesis is reinforced by the systematic refutation of antithesis, "the supports counter the weights placed on them," and the weight of the material is neutralized by balances arranged on rational principles.

This technique conceals "a profoundly analytic spirit, relentlessly dominating the construction. This spirit considers the forces, analyzes them in terms of static diagrams and petrifies them in space,"[115] forming a unity which is not organic but mechanical, a monolithic framework. "Our sense of stability is satisfied but we are perplexed, because the parts are connected no longer organically but only mechanically: they look like a human frame stripped of flesh."[116] We see here technology, i.e., human will and logic, taming matter. The structure manifests the intellectual conception and will of the craftsman rather than the potentialities of the material – the moral obedience of matter to spirit, not the "glory" of matter, the revelation of God's energies in the *logos* of material things.

Gothic architecture is historically the first striking example of the cultural and, more specifically, the technological extensions of the anthropocentric cosmology of European theologians in the Middle Ages. On this cosmology was founded the whole structure of Western technological culture. However strange it may seem, the principle which refers the genesis of technocracy to theology is not an arbitrary one.[117] The development of technology in the West is not simply a phenomenon of steady scientific progress. At the same time it is also the specific embodiment of a particular attitude towards the world, which recapitulates all the phases of Western man's evolution: the subjection of truth to the intellect, the denial of the distinction between God's essence and energies, and consequently the sharp divide between the transcendent and the immanent, the transformation of the personal relation with the world into an attempt to dominate nature and historical reality. The development of Western technology expresses a particular ethos, that is, the principles of a specific cosmology (since, as we have seen above, humanity's relation with the world is the fundamental moral problem),[118] both as a phenomenon of the organic detachment of humanity from the whole rhythm of the world's life, and as a phenomenon of history's being caught up in a nexus of threatening impersonal powers, which make it impossible for the uniqueness of personal human existence to be presupposed – such as the appearance of the capitalist system and its socialist counterparts, which alienate human life within the context of an impersonal economy trapped in the rationalistic balancing of production and consumption.

This is not the place for an extended discussion of all the historical consequences of Western cosmology and the problems surrounding each of them. Perhaps the most important stage in the historical evolution of the new relationship of humanity with the world initiated by the scholastic theology of the Middle Ages is the problem of the pollution of the environment, which in our time has become an increasing threat. The poisoned atmosphere of industrial zones, lands turned to desert wastes, waters made toxic, and the assertions of statisticians that in twenty-five years or less large areas of the globe will be rendered uninhabitable – all these reveal in a direct way some fault in humanity's relation with the world. They demonstrate the failure of humanity in its effort to subject the reality of nature to its individual needs. This subjection has been achieved by the power of the human mind materialized in the machine, but proves today to be the tormenting of nature and its corruption, which is unavoidably also a tormenting of human kind and the threat of death. For human life and human truth cannot be separated from the life and truth of the world which surrounds us. The relationship is a given and is inescapable. Any falsification, any violation of this relationship is destructive of the existential roots of human kind.

Within the context of today's technological culture, the culture not of relation or use but of *consumption* of the world, which is imposed on the multitude with systematic techniques of persuasion and the total subjection of human life to the ideal of an impersonal and individualistic comfortable life – within the context of this culture the Orthodox theological view of the world does not represent simply a truer or better theory of nature, but embodies the converse ethos and *mode of existence*, the potentiality for a culture at the opposite pole to consumerism. Orthodox cosmology is a moral struggle which aims at bringing out, by the practice of asceticism, the personal dimensions of the cosmos and humanity's personal uniqueness. Within the context of Western culture this could become a radical program of social, political and cultural change. With the proviso that such a "program" cannot be objectivized in terms of an impersonal strategy. The possibility always remains of personal revelation, that is, of *repentance*, as also the content of the Church's preaching and the practice of Orthodox worship. In opposition to the messianic utopia of consumer "happiness," which alienates humanity, turning people into impersonal units, and which is organized in accordance with the needs of the mechanistic structures of the social system, the Church sets the personal uniqueness of the human person, as attained in the fact of an ascetic, that is, a personal, relationship with the world.

Chapter Two

The Personal Dimension of Space: Absence

§36   *Space as the accommodation of the fact of relation*

The consciousness of space is a consciousness of the *other*. Whatever is *other* defines a referential separateness. It is located as "opposite" us and consequently "within" spatial dimensions. We recognize the person fundamentally as the unique power of "being-opposite" beings, as a presupposition of the referential *disclosure* of beings and consequently as a presupposition of the cognition of space. That is to say, we recognize space as the accommodation of personal reference, as a fact of relation.

§37   *The objectifying of personal relation in local distance* (apo-stasis) *and spatial extent* (dia-stasis)

This primary experience of space within the bounds of personal relation is objectified and numbered conventionally as geometrical magnitude and measurable extent, in the degree that the personal relation itself is objectified. The transformation of the pre-conscious ec-static reference of the person in the purely intellectual sense of the *disclosure* of beings as objects (that is, the regarding of personal relation as "external" – the notion of personal relation as a fact which can be defined *outside* the experience of relation) has as a consequence the objectifying of space, the definition of space in terms of measurable dimensions: When personal relationship with the world is changed into an objective *observation of phenomena*, the "opposite" of personal reference is measured conventionally in relation to the position (*stasis*) of the observer; it is determined by the specific measurements of local distance (*apo-stasis*). The "other" as object is here or there, above or below, right or left, near or far,[1] its distance defined objectively and intellectually.

The "external" view of personal relation objectifies space as distance between the two terms of the relation, and establishes *extent* (*dia-stasis*) as the measure for the measurement of space: Space is measured between two things "which are at a distance from each other, that being here at a distance from there and being there at a distance from here are one and the same."[2] The distance "makes room" (*chôrei*) for beings; it gives them space (*chôros*). And in giving them space, it gives them boundaries (*oria*); it "defines" (*orizei*) them: the objectifying of beings means, ultimately, that they are defined in terms of distance – "now it has three dimensions, length, breadth, depth, the dimensions by which all body is bounded."[3] Thus space loses entirely the character of the personal "opposite" of dynamic ec-static reference. It becomes a boundary of beings, their measurable magnitude, the conventional notation of their dimensions. Space is identified with the *place* of objects. Place is a motionless boundary,[4] which "contains" the object. In other words, it objectifies the phenomenon in motionless magnitude: "Place is the first motionless boundary of what contains, like a vessel which is not transportable."[5]

On the basis of this definition we can arrive at an absolutely objectified understanding of the whole of physical reality, in which this movement is "the place of the place"[6] – "like a vessel on a river"[7] – a void is "a place bereft of body,"[8] and the totality of the world's space is constituted by the successive interpenetration of the local dimensions of beings as far as the furthest "limit" of the universe: "and for this reason the earth is in water, and this is in the air, and the air is in the ether, and the ether in the world, but we cannot go on and say that the world is in anything else."[9]

The objectification of physical reality, however, within the bounds of local dimensions does not in the least negate the experience of "ou-topia" (*ou topos*), which is the experience of space at the indefinite boundaries of personal relation. Within the "boundaries" of personal relation, of pre-conscious universal ecstatic reference, before any consideration of the criteria of common convention the "opposite" remains dimensionless, that is to say, metrically indeterminate. The ecstatic reference of the person is a fact that transcends the categories of measurable space, or rather, place – the *here* or *there*, the nearer or farther. The second term of a personal relation may be *here*, as a presence with dimensions, or *elsewhere*, as an absence with dimensions, defining always the same space of personal reference – a space without dimensions. In this case the space is "known" not as the noetic sense of the distance between two motionless terms, but as a dynamic non-dimensional ec-stasy with a double impetus, as a mutual personal reference, as an experienced closeness which abolishes distance, without negating the consciousness of space. And this means that whatever else, in this experienced closeness of personal reference there is always a second person or an act of personal "disclosure," a *pragma* – a "thing in itself" – never a conventionally objectified *chrêma* – a "thing to be used" – belonging to daily necessity.

Only relations between persons and the rising up of beings into the personal knowledge of their uniqueness and universality as "things" (*pragmata*) negates the measurable dimensions of *here* and *there*, of nearer and farther, and point to both presence and absence as the experience of non-dimensional nearness.

§38 *Absence as experience of non-dimensional nearness*

Yet presence with dimensions, as immediate local near-ness, is also directly linked to the noetic function of the determination of measurable distance, and is monitored by the perceptible basis of measurement, that is, by the objec-tification of space, and consequently by the difficulty, if not impossibility, of the cognition of the non-dimensional space of personal relation. The determination of the measurable distances of space with dimensions, especially when we are dealing with objects of immediate topical nearness, is an automatic function of consciousness, which can be ex-perienced as a substitute for relation, although it concerns an awareness of distance in terms of objectified space. We must therefore accept *absence* as a more important measure of the experiential cognition of the dimensionless "opposite" of personal reference.

Jean-Paul Sartre has made an exhaustive analysis of the relation between personal absence and space.[10] His inten-tion is not to demonstrate the personal dimension of space, to posit personal relationship as the presupposition for the experience of absence as a felt nearness. Nevertheless, one could maintain that from the analysis which Sartre attempts the awareness of the space of absence is confirmed as above all the possibility of cognition of the non-dimensional im-mediacy of personal relation.

Sartre uses a story from everyday life to shed light on the real relationship of absence with personal immediacy.[11]

> The story is about my friend Pierre at the café, where I usu-ally meet him. I arrive late and don't find Pierre. Pierre *is not here*. I look for him in the café and my search reveals the *reality* of Pierre's absence within the dimensions of a specific space. The café with its tables and chairs where we usually sit, with its mirrors and thick haze from the cigarette smoke, with its familiar customers, the buzz of conversa-

tion and the noise of cups and glasses, is a specific whole of certain dimensions from which Pierre *is absent*. Every element of this space makes his absence a reality.[12] The fact that Pierre *is not here* is not something I confirm simply by glancing at a familiar corner and a particular chair where I usually see him. Pierre is absent from the totality of the café's space.[13] The café "discloses" Pierre's absence to me. For me the café "is full"of Pierre's absence. And it is precisely this space that does not "contain" Pierre, the space that is empty of Pierre, that confirms Pierre's existence to me more vividly than his local dimensional presence.[14] The empirical confirmation: Pierre *is not here* is for me an experience of direct relation to him, which is evoked by the specific space of his absence.[15] Similar assertions which are also true, but only noetically (such as "Wellington is not here in this café," or "Paul Valéry is also not here") have no significance for me. They do not represent any experience relating to nearness through absence.[16]

Pierre *is not here*, and yet now for me he is has an immediacy with a specific non-dimensional nearness. The dimensional space of the café reveals Pierre's absence to me as an experiential assurance of his existence, as an experience of a non-dimensional "opposite" of my personal reference to Pierre. When Pierre is here, the space does not have the personal dimension[17] which now reveals his absence to me. When Pierre *is here*, there is a specific dimensional presence, self-evidently present to my consciousness. Now that Pierre *is not here*, what is self-evident to the automatic functioning of my consciousness is denied and the pre-conscious knowledge of the non-dimensional space of personal reference is revealed. Now Pierre is pre-eminently existent, as the second term of an immediate relation, which denies the objectified measurable distance. Pierre's absence "defines" an experiential space of existential nearness, the very cognition of existence as dynamic ec-stasy "opposite" a second personal reference.

I am, of course, exploiting Sartre's example with an inten-

tion quite different from that of Sartre himself. His reference
to Pierre's absence does not envisage the sense of a non-
dimensional personal "opposite." His intention is to define
absence as the actual reality of non-being ("non-être"),[18] the
conception of the existent with reference to nothingness. But
this same example of the experience of a personal absence
leads to conclusions which force us to transcend Sartre's abstract idea, though perhaps without denying it.

§39   *Possible ontological interpretations of the fact of absence*
      as experience of the nothingness of ontic disclosure

Without doubt, the awareness of absence confirms the existence of the other by nullifying perceptible accessibility, demonstrating the reality of the existence through the experience
of *non-being*. The sensing of the reality of *non-being*, as con-
firming existence, constitutes a tragic experience of the power
of existence to be embodied both in *being* and in *non-being* –
which Sartre calls *anguish*, that is, a consciousness of the existential identification of *being* with non-being (knowledge that
my being, that which I am now, is my future as *non-being*).[19]
   This anguish, which constitutes an immediate experiential
knowledge of *being* and *non-being* as possibilities but also
as potentialities of existence, confirms existence both as an
immediately accessible dimensional presence and as a nul-
lity of dimensional presence – always on the basis of the
experience of the existential immediacy of absence. Thus the
awareness of absence, as an experiential presupposition *also*
of anguish, is a form of existential cognition which nullifies
the measurable and perceptible accessibility, demonstrating
the actual reality of the non-dimensional nearness of *non-
being*: the objective *other* of existential cognition *is* and at
the same time *is not*. Whatever exists *is* even when it *is not* in
the dimensions of perceptible accessibility. But the question
arises, whether this annihilation of perceptible accessibility

which confirms existence refers nothingness to the *being* of beings, whether the *non-being* of dimensional absence refers to the mode by which beings *are*, whether absence, as experiential confirmation of existence, nullifies the character of being as personal disclosure and reveals the nothingness as the hidden essence of every being.

The confirmation of existence through absence as the actual reality of *non-being*, the determination of existence through the possibility even of its potential annihilation as perceptible accessibility – it is evident that this is based on a presupposition of pre-conscious experience, or intuition, as Sartre calls it.[20] Through this experience or intuition dimensional absence is revealed to us as existential immediacy. But the question is whether the experience of absence, as existential immediacy, presupposes a *relation* with the existence which is absent, a dynamic ec-static understanding and *personal* cognition of the uniqueness and dissimilarity of the other – a relation and cognition which is experienced as a fact before any conscious marking of the dimensional presence or absence of the other – or whether it simply represents the psychological confirmation of a specific void in a particular dimensional space, where the other *should have been*, that is, the cognition of the nullified but specifically dimensional onticity of existence – an experiential reversal of the dimensional-ontic concept of *being* on the cognition of the dimensional reality of *non-being*. It is obvious that the reply to this question depends on our more general position on ontological matters, on the perception that we have of *being*: whether we identify *being* with the ontic *disclosure* of objects, or whether we acknowledge it as the personal *mode of existence* – the unique and dissimilar mode by which it *is* what it is – as this mode is revealed in the context of the fact of ecstatic relation.

If we acknowledge existence as ontic-dimensional disclosure, the experience of absence – of non-disclosure – confirms the existential immediacy (in the degree in which cognition of the dimensional disclosure pre-exists) as an unavoidable and ultimately obligatory reference to nothingness, which is the presupposition of disclosure. In this case space plays the role of the specific "context" in which absence is "projected" as the dimensional *non-being* of existence. (In the above example the specific "context" of Pierre's absence is the "familiar" café.) Existence is confirmed in the specific dimensions of its nullification, absence is revealed as "another aspect" of existential disclosure, nothingness as "another aspect" of *being*: but if the truth of existence is experienced only as a fact of ecstatic *relation*, only as the non-dimensional "opposite" of our personal reference to the equally personal uniqueness and dissimilarity of the other, then the reality of absence gives *being* and *non-being* a content very different from that which is implied by Sartre's analysis.

In particular, the following question arises from the example of the experience of Pierre's personal absence: Why is the absence of Wellington or Valéry from the café I know, although also referring to the actual reality of *non-being*, not as equally confirmatory to me of their existence as the absence of Pierre? What is the presupposition (the necessary and sufficient experiential condition) which gives Pierre's absence, and not that of anybody else, the existential dimension of an immediate accessibility? Is it simply the previous experience in my consciousness of Pierre's dimensional (ontic) *disclosure* in the same space? But then the absence of any other object, whose ontic disclosure in the same space I have also experienced (e.g., a hat stand that has been moved, or an umbrella stand) should be able to confirm for me the existential immediacy of these objects in the same way that Pierre's existence is also confirmed through absence. Sartre, however, asserts that no object (no being in the state of "en-soi") can create the awareness of absence as existential confirmation of *not-being*. The object simply *no longer is*. Its absence does not disclose *not-being* ("non-être"). It only constitutes a negative affirmation, a comparison of the past with the present, which is expressed in the form of *no-longer* ("ne-plus").[21] Human existence (the unique being in the state of "pour-soi") is the only kind that can be placed "outside being" ("en dehors de l'être") by absence, that affirms existence ("pour-soi") by nullifying being as onticity ("en-soi"): "man is the only being through which nothingness comes into the world."[22]

But the question remains: What is the presupposition in human experience that affirms existence when the onticity of *being* is nullified? Why is it not any absence, but only the absence of the human existence "known to me" from previous "disclosures" that creates the certainty of existential immediacy? Is it the result of a distinct experiential clarity peculiar to the individual that on each occasion accompanies the disclosure of a person and makes him or her "known" – a clarity which is "extended" in experience as existential affirmation, when a specific space discloses to me the dimensional absence of the other? But does this distinct and peculiar – that is, unique and dissimilar – experiential clarity, which accompanies the disclosure of the person "known to me," not constitute a *personal* (pre-conscious) cognition of the uniqueness and dissimilarity of the other, a dynamic ec-static reception of the truth of the other, and ultimately a *relation* with the other – a relation which transcends any determination of existence through ontic disclosure or through the nullification of ontic disclosure in dimensional space? Is it then nothingness as an existential presupposition, or is it personal relation – the non-dimensional "opposite" of personal reference – which lies behind the "manifestations" of existence as presence or absence? Does the consciousness of absence, as affirmation of existential immediacy, refer the reality of existence to nothingness or to *being*, as the potentiality for non-dimensional personal disclosure?

A positive answer to these questions is an experiential
potentiality, not an intellectually obligatory objectivity: a
potentiality which depends on "moral" (i.e., existential-ontological, not noetic-ontic) presuppositions which refer to a
possible *mode of existence*. It depends, specifically, on the
ecstatic (ascetic) self-transcendence of individuality, which
makes the experiential approach to the *personal* existence
of the other possible.

§40   *The experience of absence as the basis for the under-
       standing of the dynamic "ou-topia" of the person*

The awareness of absence affirms existence as personal immediacy only within the limits of a dynamic-existential fact
of ecstatic relation and loving self-offering, which are non-
dimensional terms. Ecstatic relation and loving self-offering
are realized with equal "authenticity" (are experienced as
"actual reality") both in the case of the dimensional presence of the other and in the case of his or her dimensional absence. This means that the fact of ecstatic-personal relation
precedes the awareness of dimensional presence or absence.
Above all, however, the awareness of absence refutes the automatic functioning of the noetic verification of the objective
existence of the other and manifests the personal relation as
a presupposition of referential immediacy, which affirms the
existential reality of the other in a non-objective space.

In other words, the affirmation of existence through the
experience of the nothingness of ontic disclosure refers to
the personal *mode of existence* only when the *relation* has
been achieved, which is the existential experience of ecstasy
or loving self-transcendence, a dynamic movement towards
the non-dimensional "opposite" of personal immediacy.
Thus the pre-conscious ecstatic referentiality of the person,
its fundamental capacity to be "opposite" the "essence" (*ousia*) of beings, their possible presence (*par-ousia*) or ab-

sence (*ap-ousia*), is proved by the experience of absence to be not an *a priori* noetic determination of human existence but a "moral" possibility and dynamic fact – a capacity for "knowledge" both of existential essence and of the reality of *space* in the world: the essence of existence – Being – is not exhausted by the denotation of ontic disclosure and by the pre-reflective conception ("Irréflechie") of the nothingness of onticity through absence. But it is affirmed as the *mode* by which it *is* what it is, that is, as personal presence or absence, as non-dimensional immediacy within the indefinite terms of personal relation. And this experientially non-dimensional – and only conventionally dimensional and measurable – immediacy of personal relation is *space*: cosmic space is not measured (except with the conventional-quantitative measures of dimensional distance). Instead, space *measures* the ecstatic reference as consciousness of the personal "opposite." A more realistic basis for the understanding of space is experience of the dynamic "ou-topia" of the person.

With the experience and understanding of space as the "measure" of ecstatic reference as our starting-point, it becomes evident that the "definition" of the person precedes, or rather, transcends, the "hereness" of existence in the world ("in-der-Welt-sein").[23] "Being-here" ("Da-sein"), which defines the *reality* of human existence, refers not to a dimensional hereness, but to the immediacy of ecstatic *relation*. The existential reality of personal (ec-static) relation does not acknowledge any restrictions of place. From the moment a person is "opposite," it is everywhere – the "opposite" of personal reference is unbounded with regard to place. The "being-here" of human existential reality refers, unquestionably, to "hereness" in the world,[24] but the world is not exhausted of necessity in the quantitative dimensions of conventional measurement. When we hear a piece of music by Mozart, we find ourselves in the "space" of non-dimensional proximity to the person of Mozart. The same happens when we study a painting by van Gogh. It is the space of personal relation, the immediacy of personal uniqueness and dissimilarity which is experienced vividly in spite of the dimensional non-presence of the person. Van Gogh or Mozart *are* "opposite" – they exist in a non-dimensional accessibility – wherever their personal creative energy is manifested, the perceptible expression of their ecstatic reference. The personal creative energy preserves the non-dimensional immediacy of personal uniqueness and dissimilarity (more vividly in the characteristic cases of genuine artistic expression), transcending the hereness in the world of human existence as a restriction of place and time. The personal energy is the place of existential disclosure of the person, the non-dimensional place of *relation*, which reveals personal uniqueness and dissimilarity as experiential immediacy.

§41   *Personal energies as the "place" of personal relation*

The Byzantine theologians saw in personal energy the non-dimensional *place* both of the human person and of the Person of God. John Damascene specifically defines the space of God's disclosure of his personal energy as the *place* of God: "What is called the place of God is where his energy becomes manifest."[25] And God's personal energy becomes manifest primarily in the space of cosmic reality. When humanity achieves the ec-static self-transcendence of individuality which makes an experiential approach to the *personal* existence of God possible, the world is revealed "opposite" humanity as the non-dimensional *place* of divine personal energy. Cosmic space is then not measured as conventional distance (*apo-stasis*) from humanity or as the interval (*dia-stasis*) between objects. Rather, the cosmos *measures* ("*chôrei*" – "accommodates," "gives space to") the mutual ec-static reference of humanity to God and of God to humanity. In the context of the personal relation of humanity with the Maker of "things" – of the "things transacted" of cosmic reality – the world ceases to be autonomous in the conventional way as a neuter object which is measured because we lay claim to it on utilitarian grounds. The world "accommodates" – it gives space to the relation of God to humanity.

Humanity, however, discovers the accessibility of God in the fact of the reality of the world, without this accessibility annulling the *natural* distance of God from the world, the distance separating uncreated from created nature. "All things are far removed from God, not by place but by nature," says John Damascene.[26] The closeness of humanity to God within the context of the world is not *natural* but local, that is to say, it is a personal closeness – a closeness of *relation*. The world "is far removed from God" by an infinite and indeterminable *natural* distance, but at the same time the world is the "substantiation" of God's personal will, the *place* of the disclosure of his personal energy. The divine will or energy does not remain unrealized and without hypostasis, but is "immediately substantiated" "in the hypostasis and form of creation."[27] It is "substantiated" *outside* God, although at the same time it discloses the non-dimensional "topical" proximity of God.

So it is not the world that "accommodates" God or his personal energy, but the divine will and energy which "accommodates" or gives space to the world, a space "outside" God which is simultaneously God's *place*, the disclosure of the non-dimensional immediacy of his personal energy. Just as humanity's own personal creative energy (the energy of making, thinking, or loving) preserves the immediacy of personal uniqueness and dissimilarity, even in the absence of the ontic "hereness" of human existence, so too the distinction between the nature and the energies of God, without denying the reality of the *natural* distance of God from the world, preserves the world as a space of the immediate personal nearness of God and manifests God as the *place* of the universe: "For God is not contained, but is himself the place of all."[28]

The dimensional "opposite" of the world's reality, as disclosure of God's personal creative energy, reveals to humanity God's existence as a non-dimensional "topical" proximity, an immediacy of *relation*. And within the "boundaries" of God's topical proximity, which are the boundaries of the cosmos, the cosmic "hereness" of human existence transcends conventionally objectified topical restrictions, the definitions of *here* and *there*, of nearer and farther. The "being-here" of human existential reality signifies "being-in-the-world" and, consequently, in the space of a relation, a non-dimensional personal immediacy. The *here* interprets the *mode* of being, and this mode is one of personal ecstatic reference: *being-in-the-world* signifies *being-opposite* the divine, personal, creative disclosure.

§42   *Eros as transcendence of ontic topicality, a non-dimensional mode of existence*

But the experience of the non-dimensional space of personal relation indisputably finds its fulfillment in direct interpersonal communion, that is, in the fact of *eros* – the dynamic movement of loving self-offering. For the Fathers of the Greek East the fullness of non-dimensional erotic unity is the loving interpenetration of the Persons of the Holy Trinity: God is "the all of eros"[29] – "this eros is love, and it is written that God is love."[30] Eros proves the divine hypostases to be "non-dimensional": "for they are not divided by essence, nor are they separated by power, or place, or energy, nor are they apportioned by will, since their abiding in each other and their interpenetration are inseparable."[31] Athanasius the Great "describes" the non-dimensional immediacy of the personal communion of the Father and the Son, interpreting the seat of the Son "at the right hand" of the Father:

> Sitting then on the right, yet he does not place his Father
> on the left; but whatever is right and precious in the Father,
> that also the Son has, and says, "All things that the Father
> has are mine" (John 16:15). Therefore the Son, too, though
> sitting on the right, also sees the Father on the right, al-
> though as a man he says, "I saw the Lord always before my
> face, for he is on my right hand, that I might not be moved"
> (Ps 15:8). This shows, moreover, that the Son is in the Fa-
> ther, and the Father in the Son; for the Father being on the
> right, the Son is on the right; and while the Son sits on the
> right of the Father, the Father is in the Son.[32]

The disavowal of any topical delimitation in the relation
of the Persons of the Holy Trinity necessarily implies the
transcendence of any ontic attribute and any dimension
concerning a God who is "beyond every essence." But this
transcendence is not exhausted merely by an apophatic approach, on the human side, to the mystery of the divine life.
The transcendence also affirms cataphatically the revelation
of God – the voluntary and active disclosure of God "outside
himself" – as the fullness of personal-triadic communion.
The loving relation and erotic interpenetration of the divine
Persons disavows any measure of dimensional onticity and
reveals the Trinity as "beyond the 'where,'"[33] as "non-dimensional unity,"[34] and as "non-dimensional connection"
without beginning or end, measure or quantity.[35] The place
of God is the non-dimensional personal-loving relation, the
eros of triadic communion. The distinction of the hypostases,
"timeless and loving,"[36] "absolutely beyond any 'where,'"[37]
reveals the *mode* of the divine existence, which is love: love
is the *place* as *mode* of existence – "he who abides in love
abides in God, and God abides in him" (1 John 4:16).

The "theologians," says Dionysius, call God eros and love
"in accordance with divine revelation,"

> since only he is the beautiful and the good in itself, and is
> as it were a manifestation of himself through himself, and

is the good procession and simple erotic movement of the transcendent unity, which is self-moved, self-motivated, preexistent in the good, and gushing forth to beings from the good, and again returning to the good. In this the divine eros shows itself in the highest degree to be without end and without beginning, going round on an unerring intro-verted course, like an eternal circle, the good from the good and in the good and to the good, and the same and in the same way, and always proceeding and remaining and being restored.[38]

The "uncaused" and "transcendent" eros of the triadic communion is not exhausted in the apophatic "terms" of the mystery of the divine life but "proceeds by transition" and "acts ecstatically" – "moved itself to operate according to the superabundance productive of all things."[39] "It goes forth to the things that are outside it" by a "life-giving" and "natu-ral" erotic movement "outside itself," a movement and en-ergy which establishes and sustains the spiritual and material creation, so as to return through it again to God as the erot-ic-personal response of creatures to the love of the Creator: "He who is the cause of all things in the superabundance of his goodness loves all things, makes all things, perfects all things, sustains all things, returns all things. And the divine eros is good, of the good, for the good."[40]

§43   *The world's eros. The erotic unity of the world's space*

The erotic movement from God towards creatures, and from creatures back towards God recapitulates the *mode* by which what is *is*, and reveals the space of the whole universe as the unquantified and unmeasured *how* of a loving com-munion – a space which can be understood only in poetic categories ("in the good, from the good, to the good"), only as dynamic disclosure "outside God" of the mystery of the love of the Trinity.

This expression of an integrated view of the cosmos as the non-dimensional space of erotic communion is characteristic of Maximus the Confessor. He sees the whole of creation from the angels to inanimate matter as a unified and non-dimensional erotic fact, an erotic relation dynamically arranged in a hierarchy and a universal erotic movement, which constitutes creation – both personal and impersonal, animate and inanimate – in a "social" interconnection with reference back towards God.[41] Maximus says:

> The first cause of heavenly eros is God, who is transcendent and without cause. For if this eros is love, as has already been said, and it is written that "God is love," it is evident that the eros or love that unifies all things is God. From there it passes over to the angels. Hence it is also called "angelic," that being especially where one may find the divine eros of unity. For there is nothing disharmonious or factional among them. Then after the angels there is said to be also an intellectual eros, that is, among human beings full of divine wisdom, who are the members of the Church. To them Paul says: "that all of you agree," etc. (1 Cor 1:10); and the Lord: "that they may be one, even as we are one" [John 12:11]). This refers to Christians who are of the truth. But then it also concerns humanity as a whole, amongst whom there is the law of affectionate attraction. And he called rational souls "intellectual" because he named them so from the divine mind. And he called the eros of irrational creatures, the affectional attraction of the senses, "psychic," because it is evidently not of the mind. For it is from this erotic force that birds fly in flocks, such as swans, geese, cranes and crows and the like. And there are similar creatures on land such as deer, cattle and the like. And there are marine creatures such as tunny and mullet and the like. And those creatures that do not gather in herds or shoals seek the companionship of others of the same species. He calls "natural" the eros of inanimate and insensate things according to their habitual propensity, which belongs to their quality, things that are drawn erotically to the creator because

they are sustained by him. And therefore according to their
vital force, which is their natural movement, these things
too return towards God.[42]

The cosmic "hereness" of humanity is the unique power
not only of the disclosure, but also of the actualization of
the erotic unity of cosmic space, of the world's erotic re-
versionary reference to God. Humanity's role as "mediator"
between God and the world is fulfilled in the dynamic recapitulation of the erotic interdependence of creation in its
personal reference to God. Humanity is the unique potentiality of *personal* realization of cosmic eros. If eros is the
mode of created orderliness, the "cosmos" of creatures, if it
is the *place* of the relation of the created with the uncreated
(the place (*topos*) as mode (*tropos*) of existence), and if the
relation is fulfilled only in personal ec-stasy, then the human
person is the place of the world, the disclosure of the truth of
the world as erotic response to the personal energy of God.

But the personal realization of cosmic love, the rational-
izing of the erotic orderliness of creation by human kind, is
nothing other than the disclosure of the erotic archetype of
divine life, the image of the triadic prototype. In the degree
that humanity recapitulates the erotic mutual relationship of
the world in a personal reference to God, it interprets and actualizes and sanctifies life as an erotic movement of God towards creatures and of creatures towards God.[43] It becomes
the *place* of this dual loving impetus, the place of the world
and also the "place of God,"[44] the disclosure of that unique
mode of existence which is the eros of the communion of the
Trinity. And the more immediate the personal relationship
of humanity with God becomes – ever increasing without
limitation – the more God, who is trihypostatic, and humanity, which is multi-hypostatic, interpenetrate each other lo-
cally (not naturally) within the non-dimensional bounds of
the non-quantifiable place of personal relation.[45]

§44   *Absence, death and the triadic adumbration of the*
        fullness of existence

Within the context of the reality of the world, the personal
immediacy of God is affirmed through his ontic absence. If
the experience of absence affirms existence as non-dimensional immediacy of personal relation, that is to say, if relation precedes the consciousness of phenomenal onticity, if as
a cognitive potentiality it transcends the sensory confirmation of objectified individuality, then in reality "the absence
is God,"[46] because God is the fullness of personal relation,
the existential transcendence of objectified individuality.
The formulation by Christian revelation of the mystery of
God who is One and simultaneously Triadic, the relation
$3 = 1$, which abolishes all quantitative and arithmetical objectivity, preserves the truth of existence as transcendence of
ontic individuality, as a fact of erotic communion and loving relation. God is One, without this oneness constituting
an existentially lonely and intellectually ontic individuality,
because there are at the same time three Persons without the
Trinity of Hypostases dividing the unity of God, which the
ontic understanding of the number three would have imposed. The formula "Trinity in Unity" means that it is impossible for God to be defined using ontic-atomistic categories. It means that God's existence is revealed only as a fact
of personal relation, the only "definition" of God being *love*
(1 John 4:8) – "God is the whole and the partial eros."[47] The
formula "Trinity in Unity" is not only a way of preserving
the apophaticism of the mystery of divine existence. It is
also an adumbration of the truth of the *personal* existence
(of the unique *mode* of existence) which is revealed only
in the transcendence of autonomous individuality, only in
the immediacy of the loving relation and erotic self-offering.
The truth about the Triadic God therefore also reveals and
interprets the truth of humanity, the dynamic-moral "end" of

this truth, which is the *personal* existence of humanity, the
non-dimensional personal immediacy of human existence.[48]

Existence, as non-dimensional personal immediacy, as
truth which is known only within the terms of relation and
loving self-offering, interprets the fact of *death* as entry into
the space of the definitive transcendence of ontic individuality, just as it also interprets Orthodox *askesis* as the voluntary death of egotistic individuality and dynamic, and reveals
even death – the dissolution of physical individuality – as
preeminently the potentiality of entry into the space of the
fullness of personal relationship, into the space of existential
fulfillment. Death is a reality of life which is experienced
fundamentally as the dimensional absence of existence, as
a fact of the nullification of sensory accessibility. But when
absence is experienced as personal immediacy and loving
relation, death affirms the existential reality of the person
as a reality of life precisely in the fact of *relation*, not in the
dimensions of measurable space. The loving relation itself,
as a dynamic-moral realization of the existential truth of humanity, as self-transcendence of moral individuality, of individual wishes and desires, is an experience of death which is
felt as a reality of life and existential fulfillment.[49]

Outside the boundaries of personal relation, however, when
the person "declines" into the objectified individuality of
egotistic autonomy, death is only the anguished awareness
of the temporally inevitable and existentially undeniable annihilation of dimensional immanent onticity – a "phenomenon of life" once more ("Death, in the widest sense, is a
phenomenon of life," as Heidegger said),[50] but in the degree
in which it reveals the truth of life as an undeniable and inevitable annihilation of ontic existence.

But if God is Triadic, if the truth of existence reveals the
relation $3 = 1$, death is the potentiality of true life, that is to
say, the potentiality of humanity's personal-existential fulfillment.[51] If personal existence is seen as the fact and real-

ity of life, as ontic hereness, then the non-dimensional "opposite" of personal reference is not limited by death. Death is then *absence* as existential affirmation of the person. It defines the "decline" of the physical, the objective and the ontic, the "swallowing up" of the mortal,[52] the entry into the personal space of non-dimensional accessibility.

As consciousness of the eventual and undeniable annihilation of ontic hereness ("in which we have received being"),[53] that is, as consciousness of a gap between the phenomenal and dimensional ontic reality of existence and its dynamic-personal perfection, death remains necessarily the supremely testing, painful and agonizing experience of existential individuality. But at the same time it proves to be an act of "divine philanthropy,"[54] the supreme transcendence of the impersonal objectification of humanity, of the daily failure to enter into the space of non-dimensional personal immediacy, a "natural" opposition to the absolutizing of the conventional dimensions of dimensional existence.

In the language of Scripture, dimensional individuality is what is "partial" with regard to existence, and death abolishes the "partial" so as to preserve the "perfectly whole": "When the perfectly whole comes, the partial will pass away[55] ... it does not yet appear what we shall be."[56] What is "partial" with regard to existence means partial knowledge and fragmentary self-understanding dimly in a mirror. It means a relative and partial communion through our conventional "tongues" – "for our knowledge is partial ... we see dim reflections in a mirror"[57] – while the "perfectly whole" abolishes tongues, abolishes the partial, and brings us into the space of personal immediacy: "as for tongues they will cease; as for knowledge it will pass away ... then I shall know as fully as I am known ... face to face."[58] The only thing that does not pass away on entry into the space of personal immediacy is the existential foretaste, that is, *love*, the preliminary experience of personal universality: "love will never end."[59]

§45   *The non-dimensional place of ecclesial communion*

The personal dimension of space and the experience of absence as non-dimensional immediacy are encountered by the
Church above all in the fact of *worship*. Worship, rooted in
the eucharistic assembly, is the actualization and formation
of the Church as a "body," that is, as that existential reality which transcends partial individualities in order to attain
and reveal the simultaneous existential unity and multiplicity of the *communion* of persons, to adumbrate the mystery
of the Triadic "mode of existence" which is the truth of "true
existence." Within the *local* terms of worship, terms of personal immediacy, there is no distinction or distance between
present and absent, living and departed. Every local gathering for worship recapitulates the *whole* of the Church – the
catholic Church – the entire "roll of the saints," the dynamic
interpenetration of loving self-offering, the world's erotic-
eucharistic response to God. Worship recapitulates the erotic
reciprocity of creation in a personal reference to God – "in
the person of Jesus Christ."

In the person of Christ, which is the *natural* union of God
with humanity (an organic union, like that of the head with
the members of the body), the world's erotic structure and
movement and "function" (*leitourgia*) finds its personal expression and realization "opposite" the personal God: Christ
is the recapitulation of the erotic movement of God towards
creatures and of creatures towards God, the *place* of this
dual loving impetus, the non-dimensional immediacy of the
personal union of the created with the uncreated.

In the Church's Eucharist Christ is bread and wine. He is
the world in its existential fullness, as *place* of the personal
union of the created with the uncreated – body and blood of
Christ. Body and blood signify *life* (and "abundant life," life
in its fullness, in its unity with the eternal Source of life),
which is communicated in and participated by actualizing

the Church as existential unity and multiplicity, as personal disclosure of the world's erotic decorum and possibility of entry into the eros of the communion of the Trinity. This bread and this wine are not the objective creation, which is contested and divided up by individual desire and will. It is the body of him who "has died and has risen again." It is creation "beyond" the death of autonomous individuality. It is the restoration of life to its Triadic fullness, in its existential unity and multiplicity. And the life "beyond" death abolishes the distance between those present and those absent, the living and the dead. The life in the Eucharist "is love." Humanity exists in the personal immediacy of the Triadic *mode* of existence. "Understand this in a holy way," we read in the Dionysian corpus. "When the venerable symbols are placed on the divine altar, by which Christ is signified and through which he is partaken, the roll of the saints is present non-dimensionally, manifesting their indivisible solidarity in their transcendent and sacred union with him."[60]

The non-dimensional presence of the saints defines the *place* of the Church as *mode* of existence, where the living and the dead, those on earth and those in heaven, the earliest and the latest are united in the one body of Christ – "in that unity which has as its teacher the Holy Trinity."[61] The architectural and iconographic adumbration of the non-dimensional unity of the eucharistic body in Byzantine liturgical space is telling: in a Byzantine church the Pantocrator in the dome with the angelic powers that encircle him, and the prophets of the Old Testament that follow, and the life of Christ in a lower register, from which we pass to the Evangelists in the four pendentives – all this "heavenly hierarchy" is united organically with the full-figure representations of the saints at eye level, complementing the presence of the faithful filling the church, in a unified body. The Pantocrator, the angels and the saints, together with the living "remnant" below are all in a single unity of life and personal immediacy, "in one uniform

unanimity,"[62] "in a godly sameness of disposition,"[63] with
Christ as the *principle* of unity with those who have gone before." "The divine rite of the *synaxis*," says Dionysius again,
"even though it has a unified, simple and inclusive principle,
is multiplied out of love for humanity in the sacred variety of
the symbols, and goes so far as to accommodate the whole of
the thearchic representations, yet contracts again in a unified
way from these into its own oneness, and confers unity on
those raised up to it in a sacred manner."[64]

Worship is the power of disclosure, but also the measure of
the personal dimension of space, the non-dimensional and
one-like "opposite" of personal reference, the realization of
the erotic unity of the world's space, the realization of the
world's regressive reference to God.

Chapter Three

The Personal Dimension of Time: Presence

§46   *The understanding of personal ec-stasy as temporal*
        succession

The ecstatic referentiality of the person, the fore-conceptual universal *relation* with objective beings and other persons,
also becomes conscious as experience of *time*. Personal relation is the existential presupposition for the cognitive *disclosure* of beings, their rising up from oblivion into truth. This
rising up and disclosure of beings both as fore-conceptual
cognition and as automatic conscious marking, necessarily
constitutes an experience of *change* (*metabolê*). Change is
the experience of the transition from one state to another –
"every change is from something to something" as Aristotle
says.[1] The passage, then, from non-relation to relation, from
oblivion to truth, is an experience of change – an experience which is the starting-point for bringing the *disclosure*
of beings into consciousness. The ec-stasy of the person
from non-relation to relation only dynamically, that is to say,
referentially, may therefore be defined as change. But even
change cannot be conceived of without an ecstatic character, "for change in itself," as Aristotle says, "makes things
depart from their former condition."[2] And it is the experience of ec-stasy as change "from something to something"
that becomes conscious as transition from a state of "before"
to one of "after," that is to say, as time. "Every change ...

is in time"[3] and "time is not independent of movement and change."[4]

Ec-stasy is "temporalized" as change; time is the under-standing of ecstasy as change, the now conscious cognition of succession from oblivion to truth. This means that the consciousness of time is an experiential co-ordination of the disclosure of beings, the rising up of beings into personal relation. The personal relation is the existential presuppo-sition of the phenomenicity of phenomena, of the *change* from oblivion to truth, that is to say, of the experience of time. The experience of time presupposes the personal rela-tion – the ec-stasy of the person and the presence of beings with reference to the person. Presence (*parousia* from *par-eimi*) defines and presupposes a dyadic relation, one term of which is the person, and the relation "is measured" as time. "Is measured"[5] as successive and repeated *change*: it is defined "not by a term but by a ratio."[6] Time, then, "exists" only as coordination of personal relation, as experience of the "measurement" of ecstatic change from oblivion to truth, of the presence of beings that is referential to the person.

Insofar as it is "temporalized" as change, ec-stasy does not cease being a *personal* experience. It invariably presupposes the person as a "horizon" for the disclosure of change. It is al-ways experienced as dynamic reference and dyadic relation, always as presence, as *par-ousia*, or "being-beside." This means that the fact of the rising up of beings from oblivion into truth, that is, the phenomenicity of phenomena, does not define the presence of beings in respect of referentiality to the person as temporality, but is defined as temporality by reason of the ec-static character of the reference to the person. We can accept that even temporality is ecstatic,[7] but only as *disclosure* of the ecstasy of the person, the change from oblivion to truth, as experience of the presence of be-ings in respect of referentiality to the person – as the mode by which the truth of beings is experienced as change.

In other words: it is not time as an objective reality that is measured by ecstatic change (that is, by the truth of beings), but ec-stasy, as the presence of beings in respect of referentiality to the person, that is measured as time. Time is not an objectively or consciously independent operation of the disclosure of beings in the person's "horizon." Nor is time the existential presupposition of the disclosure of beings. It is the reference to the person, the dyadic relation as presence, the rising up from the oblivion of non-relation, that is measured as time. Beings *are disclosed* in the "horizon" of the person, not in the "horizon" of time. The person "defines" the *disclosure* of beings, while time "measures" this disclosure, is the measure of the personal relation, through beings.[8]

§47   *Time as the "measure" of personal relation*

By interpreting time as an experiential coordination of ec-static change, and as a *measure* of the personal disclosure of beings, that is, as "signifying" the personal *mode of existence*, we transfer the problem of time to a different level from that of phenomenology and objective definitions. We transcend the conception of both *objective* and *subjective* time, and the attempt to conflate the two ideas. (Typical examples in the history of philosophy of conceptions of objective and subjective time and their combination are the Platonic view, which identifies time with the movement of the heavenly bodies,[9] which it sees as "instruments of time,"[10] the Plotinian view, which sees time as an "energy of the soul," that is, it attributes to the soul alone the ability to "exist in time,"[11] and the Aristotelian view, which combines the other two approaches, defining time as a relation of measurement, which flows from the coupling of the objective and subjective factors, as a commingling of cosmic movement with a psychological function.[12])

The phenomenological conception of time – objective and

subjective[13] – has as its starting-point the objectification of the experience of ecstatic change as change subject to measurement, the objectification of conscious information for the *disclosure* of oblivion and truth as a measurable succession. If beings only become true in a relation referring to the person, and if this relation as ecstatic change is "signified" by time, then it is evident that time becomes the *measure* by which truth is understood, that is to say, the *being* of beings. But if the experience of ecstasy as change is objectified as conscious information of measurable succession, then the measure of ecstatic reference is identified with the very fact of reference, that is to say, time, is identified with the being of beings. Aristotle says: "It is clear that a thing whose being is measured by [time] will have its being in rest or motion."[14] This is the starting-point for the conception both of so-called *objective* time (the measurable movement of the heavenly bodies, of biological growth, of historical becoming, etc.) and of so-called *subjective* time (time as the conscious flow of temporal experiences). In both cases, time is understood not as the "significant" experience of the ecstatic reference which *measures* the ecstatic reference, but as *measurable* ecstatic reality, whether objective or in the consciousness, which "defines" the truth of beings as numbered movement of ecstatic succession. That is to say, it defines the *being* of beings. The rising up into truth, the ec-stasy from oblivion, is understood not as *relation* and reference to the "horizon" of the universality of the person before thought, but as the fact of ecstatic change which is *measured* as movement from a "before" to an "after" (where the "before" and the "after" constitute a semiotic complex of objective events of a given succession of experiences of a given flow of consciousness) and this movement constitutes the sole possibility for beings to be understood as that which they *are*. Thus the succession of "before" and "after," whether as natural-measurable time or as flow of consciousness, becomes the existential presupposition of beings.

§48   *The "now" as motionless time: the nothingness of
         successive intervals of events or the non-dimensional
         time of personal immediacy*

The distinction and differentiation of time from the presence of beings that is referential to the person – the rising
up from the oblivion of non-relation – is expressed characteristically by Sartre: that which separates what is before
from what is after is *nothingness*, he says.[15] The notion of
this *nothingness*, however, presupposes an understanding of
time as objective and measurable ecstatic change, that is, as
a numbered succession of objective events, which are understood, that is, *disclosed*, only as a semiotic complex of "variables." *Nothingness* is the mental conception of the midpoint in ecstatic change, the notional separation of events,
the non-quantitative difference between successive values
taken on by the variables of the temporal semiotic whole.
    Aristotle was the first, in consequence of his understanding
of time as numbered movement, to define the "between" of
before and after[16] as the indivisible unit of numbered time,
the "now,"[17] which being indivisible is also unmoved – the
nothingness of movement and time.[18]
    But Aristotle also interprets the *now* as a "middle-point"
which at the same time includes the beginning and the end
("the now is a kind of middle-point, uniting as it does in itself
both a beginning and an end"[19]) and this definition permitted
Byzantine thought to see in the *now* the continuous present
of personal immediacy. John Damascene defines the *now* as
time "without quantity,"[20] and Basil the Great refers the *now*
to the divine "perception" of time,[21] which knows no motion
or change. Maximus the Confessor sees in the *now* the truth
of "unmoved time," that is, of "eternity," since "eternity …
is time when it ceases from movement, and time is eternity
in motion, so that eternity … is time deprived of movement,
while time is eternity measured by movement."[22] "Eternity"

is the time of the fullness of the personal relationship between man and God, because time "is deprived of movement" only when "nature is united immediately with Providence."

At the non-dimensional boundaries of this "union," that is, of the fullness of the personal immediacy of man and God, nature "finds Providence a principle (*logos*) which by nature is simple and stable, and is not subject to any circumscription at all, and therefore is entirely without movement." Circumscription signifies a boundary, a barrier, a limitation. It signifies objective individuality and, consequently, movement "from something to something" – it signifies the limitation or the destruction of non-dimensional personal immediacy. Consequently, in the physical world of objects, the personal ec-stasy of nature is necessarily measured as time and "movement in accordance with life has become a source of change for what exists in time," because the world is a "limited *stasis*" in comparison with the unbounded and non-dimensional immediacy of personal relation with God. The movement that causes change in temporal nature refers to a breaking of relations – not to the natural condition of "him in whom the monad has come to be" – and is revealed as the "estrangement" of time and decay. Only "when it has come to be in God" does nature transcend time, transcend *stasis* and movement, "and will possess an ever-moving *stasis* and a stable ever-movement, having come to have its being eternally that which is same and one and alone."[23]

Thus the meaning which we attribute to the *now* proves to judge not only the problem of time but also the problem of existence. These two problems receive radically different responses, depending on how we understand the *now*: as *nothingness*, the void of the midpoint of ecstatic change, or as the non-dimensional time of personal immediacy. The concept of nothingness, of the void which opens up between what precedes and what follows, presupposes and defines time as a given succession of objective events, and the existence of beings and humanity as suspended in the void of the measured apartness of events. The events are phenomenal destructions of the void; beings *are* because they are not *nothing*. Existence is necessarily understood in immediate correlation with nothing (the *nothingness* of temporal apartness) and the nothing as starting-point, end and uninterrupted content of temporal existence.

But when the preceding and the subsequent are not signs of an objective succession, which defines and exhausts ecstatic truth, but are "stations" (i.e., the measures or terms) in the experience of the person's relationship with beings, in the progressive and dynamic *disclosure* in the person's "horizon" of the referential presence of beings, then the succession from preceding to subsequent *measures* the ecstatic reference, the person's motion towards universality, the universal synthesis and recapitulation of the *personal* truth of the world. And when we say that the temporal succession measures the person's motion towards universality and the "one-like unity" of relation, we mean that in the space of the world's objects time measures the fragmentary character of personal relation (the "becoming" of relation), while the measure of this measuring is the relation itself, the non-dimensional time of *now*, the erotic time of personal immediacy, the one-like (*henoeidous*) relation of the creature with the Creator.

§49   *Counted time. "Motion" and "continuity"*

We have discussed the phenomenological understanding of time – objective and subjective – which has as its starting-point the objectification of the experience of ecstatic change as measurable change, the objectification of the information provided by consciousness about the *disclosure* of beings as a numbered succession of the oblivion and truth of beings. We must return to this concept and investigate its implications in the field of ontology.

We have said that time, as objectified measurement of ec-static change, represents the confirmation, in the conscious-ness, of truth as a succession of objective events or temporal experiences, and is identified with the very event of change from oblivion to truth, that is, with the *being* of beings. Time is no longer the "signifier" of the truth of beings, the measure by which we count the *disclosure* of beings, but is itself the counted extent, the "horizon" of the disclosure of beings as beings. Aristotle says: "Time, then, is what is counted, not that with which we count."[24]

If time is "what is counted," it is counted by the ec-stasy of beings, that is, by their disclosure in the "horizon" of time and, consequently, by conscious information about truth as disclosure. Time, as "horizon" of the disclosure of beings, *contains* the beings – "it is necessary that all the things in time should be contained by time."[25] It is the existential presupposition of beings, since the mode by which they are what they are is temporality as ecstatic disclosure: beings *are* only as exposed to time, that is, only insofar as they are *disclosed*, which means they are defined by conscious infor-mation about truth as ec-stasy in time. Time is thus interpret-ed as the understanding of *being* – without time, being is not conceivable, and without *being*, time is not conceivable.[26]

Thus the temporality of time, its successive mutability, is made autonomous. It is not the experiential articulation of the dynamic motion of human kind towards its universality that *counts* the personal relation. Nor is it the articulation of the presence of beings that is referential to the person, nor the definition or "semantics" of ec-stasy as change. Temporality is made autonomous as objective extent, which is *counted* by the ecstatic disclosure of beings. Put in other terms: time exists not when change as movement from before to after *counts* the personal relation, but when movement as change from before is after is counted: "For time is just this – num-ber of motion in respect of 'before' and 'after.' Hence time is not movement, but only movement insofar as it admits of enumeration."[27] In this way truth ends up by being an objective event and, at the same time, a simple phenomenicity, which does not interpret the ontological problem of the essence of beings, since it is restricted to the affirmation in the consciousness that what is true simply emerges from oblivion, that *being* is simply not nothing. The ecstatic change is an objective item of information about truth as counted movement: "Time is not a number with which we count, but the number of things which are counted ...."[28] What is in time is so in the same sense as what is in number is so."[29]

Time is interpreted and judged finally in the context of the ontological distinction between *individual* and *person*, between individual existence and personal existence. The imprisonment of time in the phenomenological objectification of ecstatic change presupposes the sense of the human person as an autonomous ontic individuality – humanity as individual consciousness and intellection, as a psychological ego. By contrast, the experience of time as *measure* of personal ecstasy and reference, that is, as presence, as experience of rising up from the oblivion of non-relation, presupposes the "moral" achievement of the universality of the person, the dynamic self-transcendence of individuality, the erotic recapitulation of nature in the person, the person as disclosure of unisimilar human substance.

In the former case, the phenomenological objectification of time seems to have a pragmatic verification in every area of existential experience, as a fact of progressive *decay*. The movement of change is experientially tied to the confirmation of decay. "Movement changes what exists," says Aristotle.[30] Movement transposes existence to an "after" which is always less incorrupt that the "before." "Those things ... which are subject to perishing and becoming – generally, those which at one time exist, at another do not – are necessarily in time."[31] Generation and decay in living organisms, or increase and diminution in inanimate matter (where increase must be conceived as "change in quantity"[32] – size) are the immediate experiential data which bring about the consciousness of time as "local movement," that is, as temporal change within the bounds of individual existence.[33]

But "in local movement there is on the one hand motion, and on the other increase and diminution" – where *motion*, as the necessary succession of before and after, is the cause of generation and decay,[34] the cause of their succession, that is, the cause of the *continuity* (*synecheia*) of time[35] (here in the sense of cohesion (*synochê*) within specific limits). Individual existence is made to cohere by the passage of time, since generation and decay, being continuous – "coming-to-be and passing-away happen to things continuously"[36] – have their cause in motion. Thus the passage of time, as a necessary succession of generation and decay, or increase and diminution, defines consciousness of temporality as experience of "coming-to-be" and "passing-away." And *continuity*, as a permanent cohesion of time at the limits of generation and decay, defines consciousness of temporality as experience of permanent finitude.

§50   *Death as temporal "continuity" and total ecstatic "motion" of individual existence*

On the basis of these phenomenological presuppositions of conscious experience, we may understand the necessarily central fact of existential-temporal self-awareness, the fact of *death*, in immediate correlation with the consciousness of temporality as decay and continuity. Death belongs to the consciousness of temporality as continuity (*synecheia*). It contains (*synechei*) temporality as motion is itself and "temporalized" as decay. Death is not the end of temporality, the interruption of the succession of before and after at some supervening "moment." It is the permanent reality of the continuity of temporality, the consciousness of motion as permanent finitude. Thus the succession of before and after, as permanent change, is the experience of decay ("for it causes change by increase and diminution"), and as temporal continuity, that is, as permanent finitude, it is consciousness of mortality. Time is experienced as the submission of existence and of the world to decay and death. The temporality of time "is permanent" as decay and the continuity of time is permanently limited by death. This is a very pragmatic experiential conception and understanding of time, which could become the stimulus for referring even the objective cause of natural decay to time: "A thing, then, will be affected by time," says Aristotle, "just as we are accustomed to say that time wastes things away, and that all things grow old through time, and that people forget owing to the lapse of time, but we do not say the same of getting to know or of becoming young or fair. For time is by its nature the cause rather of decay, since it is the number of change, and change removes what is."[37]

The ec-stasy of existence, as change which is "temporalized" in the succession of before and after, is confirmed as decay. But ec-static existentiality ("existing in a state of ec-stasy") is also experienced as a consciousness of the total *continuity* of temporality. That is to say, it is a confirmation of death. The ec-stasy of existence is recapitulated in the fact of death: death is existence's potentiality for total ecstatic reference – reference to the *nothing* of ontic individuality, ec-stasy from *being* to *nothing*. Hence the awareness of death can constitute the recapitulatory self-awareness of individual existence, the self-cognition of existence as temporal finitude and ecstatic reference. We understand the reality in the world of individual existence as temporal *continuity* (*synecheia*) and total ecstatic reference only in the fact of death. The temporality of individual existence is *contained* (*synechetai*) by death; existence *is* as permanent finitude; the *being* of individual existence – the *mode* by which it is –

may be defined as *being-towards-death* ("Sein zum Tode"),[38] as a total ecstatic motion towards death. The consciousness of death is the potentiality of individual existence for recapitulatory self-awareness, a potentiality for self-cognition of existence, as total ecstatic reference.

But the potentiality of individual existence for total referential ecstasy is also, at the same time, a first possibility of entry into the space of personal *presence* (here with the sense of uninterrupted immediacy). Temporal existence may be recapitulated not only in the total ecstatic impetus towards death, not only in the *continuation* of death, but also in the duration of personal energy, that is, in every fact of the disclosure of the personal uniqueness and unlikeness of existence, in very fact of *presence*. Presence *endures* as personal energy, as immediacy of universal ecstatic relation, creating a chink in the cognition or awareness of the temporal finitude of existence.

§51   *The "duration" of personal energy*

This transition from the awareness of temporal continuity and the total ecstatic motion of individual existence to the experience of personal referential catholicity, the passage from the recapitulatory self-awareness of individuality to the experience of the fact of *presence*, that is, of a non-dimensional personal immediacy which is not contained by time, is of course a potentiality, not a necessity. Nevertheless, there are many specific experiential confirmations of this potentiality. There are ecstatic projections – total disclosures – of individual existence which are not recapitulated in the temporal finitude of individuality, that is, in the fact of death, but endure beyond and outside temporal continuity. To such ecstatic disclosure belongs every work of art and every true erotic communion. A painting, a piece of sculpture, a musical composition, a poem preserves the unlikeness and unrepeatable uniqueness of the person, as an experience of non-dimensional immediacy and relation, beyond the boundaries of the temporal finitude of individual existence.[39] With the understanding of the arithmetical succession of time and its correlation with the finite limits of individual existentiality, the human existence of the artist van Gogh is a *continuity* of life of thirty-seven years. Nevertheless, van Gogh certainly "exists" beyond these temporal limits. He is a personal *presence* which transcends the temporal finitude of individuality and *endures* as a universal ecstatic disclosure in each of his works of art, that is, in each disclosure of his personal energy. Each van Gogh painting *is* van Gogh. It reveals his *presence*, the non-dimensional immediacy of the unique and unrepeatable unlikeness of the person van Gogh, his personal otherness.

One could also say, comparatively speaking, that van Gogh *is*, "exists" – as a universal ecstatic disclosure of his personal otherness – much more in one of his paintings than as a historical individuality and objectively confirmed temporal existence. The properties and characteristics of individual character and life, which we bring together with a view to determining and knowing the individual existence of the painter van Gogh, the interpretations of his work and the circumstances of his life which influenced it, always remain objective-conventional determinations which can just as well describe other individuals and inevitably leave the personal otherness of van Gogh, the immediacy of his presence, inaccessible. Every painting of van Gogh, that is, every disclosure of his personal energy, every work of art he produced, is a potentiality for *knowing* van Gogh incomparably more immediate than the totality of information *about* van Gogh, a potentiality for realizing a *relation* with him which transcends every local and temporal limit.

And this relation, which preserves the universality of the ecstatic reference of existence, that is, the immediacy of personal presence, abrogating the temporal finitude of individual life, is not a potentiality necessarily bound to the genius and technical skill of the artist. Artistic genius simply discloses, in emphatic terms, personal energy as duration and immediacy of presence. But the personal energy is the real presupposition for the disclosure and the knowledge of the personal otherness of *every* human being. It refers to the very existential truth of the person, his or her ecstatic character. The problem does not lie in the differentiated margins of the potentiality for expression – in the degree to which a distinct expressive capability in each person is innate or cultivated – but in the dynamic ("moral") transition from the temporal self-awareness of individuality (as ec-stasy towards death) to the experience of the universal personal reference which abrogates temporal *succession*. The temporal ecstasy of individual existence is, inevitably, an impetus towards death (since the only possible existential metathesis of ontic individuality is *nothingness*, the opposite of disclosure, oblivion) while the ec-stasy of the person is an impetus towards *relation* and the realization of relation, an experience of the non-dimensional presence of personal immediacy. And it is possible even for this anguished experience of temporal continuity, that is, the anguish of the certainty of death, of the certainty of the inescapable ec-stasy of individuality towards the *nothingness* of phenomenal onticity, to be objectified as conscious experience without touching on the certainty of the potentialities for non-dimensional personal ecstasy. It is possible for it to be only anxiety in the face of the objective certainty that "one dies."

§52   *The erotic transcendence of temporal "continuity,"*
      "divided eros" and "true eros"

The transition from the self-awareness of the total ec-stasy of individuality to the experience of personal universal reference may serve as a preliminary definition of the *erotic* fact.

We could define eros fundamentally as the existential impetus towards transcending the boundaries of individuality, towards abrogating temporal continuity and inevitable decay. The consequently total ecstasy from individuality may not only be an impetus towards death, but also erotic ecstasy. Erotic ecstasy from physical individuality, however, is not sufficient to transcend it. It is not this which determines the erotic fact of personal universal reference. We must distinguish the erotic ecstasy of physical individuality, from the erotic-universal reference of the person – or, in the words of the Dionysian writings, we must distinguish between "real eros" and the "empty image" or the "lapse" from "real eros," which is a "partial," "physical" and "divided" eros.[40]

The erotic ecstasy of individuality is, fundamentally, a *natural* necessity, nature's obligatory reproductive *urge*, which aims at the self-preservation of nature through the perpetuation of the individual species and is realized as a movement of self-satisfaction of individuality, the satisfaction of the natural desire of the individual's feelings. This obligatory natural urge is certainly a fact of existential ec-stasy – "a faint echo" of "the desire for life,"[41] of the existential need for the transcendence of temporal continuity and natural decay. But individual existence "stands-out" (*ex-istatai*) always within the bounds of nature. It encounters the "other" not on the level of personal otherness but on the level of nature, as a similarly individual *species*, as object and insurmountable limit of individual pleasure. That is to say, it realizes and confirms the partition of nature into individualities. And the erotic ecstasy of individuality is fulfilled in having children, in this objective manifestation of the inescapable slicing up of nature, in the "condemnation" of the newly born human being to be the bearer of an individual nature. Philosophical terminology can suggest, but lacks the capacity to describe, the erotic ecstasy of individuality as the experience of existential transference to *nothingness*, as the tragic awareness of the void which is revealed by egocentric eroticism. Only some passages of poetry or literature can "signify" this experience.

The dynamic ("moral") transition from the self-awareness of the total ec-stasy of individuality to the experience of personal universal reference, is the definition of "real eros." Doubtless, the erotic ecstatic impetus of individuality is the natural presupposition of personal universal reference, since the person is not an existential reality separate from nature. Maximus the Confessor sees the natural presupposition of humanity's "power of love"[42] in the "power of desire": "Without the power of desire there is no longing, and so no love, which is the issue of longing; for the property of desire is to love something. And without the incensive power, intensifying the desire for union with what is loved, there can be no peace, for peace is truly the complete and undisturbed possession of what is desired."[43] Of course for Maximus *desire* refers not to sensual pleasure but to the pleasure of the mind[44] – and the *mind* (*nous*), in his own language, signifies the *personal* powers of humanity.[45] The reference of desire to sensual pleasure is, for the Fathers, an existential distortion, as we shall see below. But this distortion does not destroy the natural basis of "true eros."[46]

"True eros" presupposes the natural *impulse* of erotic ecstasy that belongs to individuality, the *loving-power*[47] that is "mingled" with nature and at the same time transcends and destroys the natural *continuity* of this ecstasy, the containing of eros within the bounds of nature. Eros transposes existential ecstasy to the unrestricted bounds of personal reference, to the dynamic and dimensionless immediacy of personal reference – it discloses existential ecstasy as universality and *duration* of communion. Eros is the "disclosure," that is, the unmediated experience of personal universality and of the non-dimensional present of personal immediacy.

This *present* is always a fact of *presence*. It is the truth of the person, the rising up of the "other" from the oblivion of non-relation – a rising up that abolishes temporal succession in the human experience of a universal existential *astonishment*, referring to the otherness of presence. Presence endures as immediacy of unique, incomparable and dissimilar relation, and time can only measure this duration in a conventional way – since duration is experience in connection with presence and does not depend on the objective–conventional counting of temporal succession - presence *enduring* as the non-dimensional present of erotic communion, that is, as transcending and abolishing the objective counting of temporal succession.

The confirmation of this truth is empirical and immediately accessible, both as duration of personal energy in every creative "disclosure" of the person (which is all the more "erotic" the more integrally, that is, the more universally it is expressed), and as duration of the immediate erotic communion of the sexes. The time of an erotic encounter, objectively measured, may be the same as the time spent waiting for a delayed train, or carrying out a tedious duty, but these equal tracts of time differ with regard to *duration*.

§53   *The "estrangement" of time in decay and death as connected with the use of the world*

The definition of the *duration* of time as correlative to *presence* in no way implies a kind of "subjective" or "psychological" time. Such an implication inevitably restricts research on the problem of time to the field of individual consciousness. But time, as empirically correlated with existential experience, cannot be restricted exclusively to the realm of consciousness, however much consciousness seems to include the necessary and sufficient condition of the phenomenicity of the phenomenon of temporal succession. There is without doubt a primary given conscious function which constitutes the experience of time as the cognition of temporal succession, without the intervention of objective factors of measurement,[48] a function which can be disrupted in cases of mental illness. As a definition of this given primary conscious function one may start by accepting Husserl's statements,[49] to which modern psychology does not seem to be opposed. It would, however, be arbitrary to restrict the problem of time simply to the function of consciousness which puts together temporal experience as a cognition of temporal succession. We would then be leaving unanswered essential questions referring to the empirically confirmed correlation between time and the fact of progressive *decay*, which itself necessarily transfers the problem of time from the field of consciousness to the realm of universal existentiality.

Neither the experience of decay nor the consciousness of the total continuity of temporality, that is, the certainty of death, can be interpreted only on the givens of the conscious functioning of time. Time as decay and time as cohesion of existence in the enduring finitude of death cannot be interpreted except in the context of the fact of personal relation, except in respect of the *duration* of presence.

I said above that time is interpreted and judged in relation to the ontological distinction between the *individual* and the *person*, between conscious individuality and personal universality. The imprisonment of time in the conscious operation of bringing together temporal experience as the cognition of temporal succession has as its starting-point the understanding of existence as ontic individuality, as the self-awareness and psychological ego of the individual. By contrast, when we see time in the context of the world's challenge, which for humankind is decay and death, this presupposes the experience of the universality of the person – the person as a referential-ecstatic recapitulation of nature and the reality of the world as the result and disclosure of a personal energy.

In other words, an interpretation of time which is confined

neither to the bounds of a conventional syllogistic procedure, nor to the bounds of an exclusively conscious operation, must be based on the experience of personal relation as
a dynamic-existential ascent to the worldly universality of
the person and the personal universality of the world.

As human beings we necessarily realize an immediate relationship with the world, a relationship of existential communion. We are not observers or students of the world's
reality. We engage with the world immediately both as food
and as material for our technological achievements, with a
view to the maintenance of our existence. And although this
relationship and communion between humankind and the
world, the daily and organic assumption of the world by us,
seems to preserve human existence, at the same time this
very relationship gradually consumes human individuality,
coordinating it existentially with the progressive decay of
every ontic individuality – the decay which is *measured* as
time. The relationship between humankind and the world
is not only conceptual or conscious. It is a dynamic *movement* and existential transposition towards the world, which
is realized as assumption of the world and is simultaneously
"temporalized" as decay: the movement towards the world
is an ec-stasy which changes existence, and the ec-stasy is
measured as time. The relationship of humankind with the
world, even though an existential-real communion, seems to
have its "end" – its essential goal – outside the relation itself.
It seems to tend towards an unattainable personal-erotic immediacy, towards an unrealizable *duration* of presence. That
is why it also constitutes a movement which is not completed
(which does not arrive at its natural "end"), an uninterrupted
metabolic change which destroys duration and is "temporalized" as decay.

Time as decay, but also as *continuity* of death, is then the
measure of the relationship between humanity and the world,
a relationship whose failure and disorganization and persistent

finitude is measured by time. The relationship has life, that is, the *duration* of existence, as its essential-natural "end." The failure of the relationship is a "missing of the mark" with regard to the end (that is, *hamartia* – the Greek for "sin" – in the primary sense of the word[50]) – the relationship being realized as decay and keeping life within the enduring finitude of death, never arriving at existential *duration* of personal immediacy, at the non-dimensional present of existential fulfillment.

And the relation does not attain to the duration of *personal* immediacy, because humanity's engagement with the world has in view not a personal loving relationship with the world, but an individualistic claim on it, the subjection of the world to individual desire and will. Engagement with the world, humanity's existential ec-stasy towards the world, does not serve a personal relationship with the world, but is subjected to the "natural" necessity and *urge* of the self-preservation of the individual, an urge which "becomes temporal" as decay. And it "becomes temporal" as decay because the "natural" urge of the self-preservation of the individual is an ec-stasy of the individual within the bounds of nature, not an ec-stasy of nature outside-of-nature, that is, within personal existentiality, within the personal *mode of existence*.

The individual's urge of self-preservation is "natural" because it is defined by nature and is exhausted within the bounds of nature. That is why it inevitably comes into conflict with the equally "natural" urge of the self-preservation of other individuals. But these opposing ec-stasies of individuals, within the bounds of nature, split nature into fragments.[51] They are the cause of the existential finitude of individuals and their progressive decay. And if the "end" of nature is life as *duration* of existence, then the "natural" impulse of the self-preservation of the individual proves to be an impulse "contrary to nature," which destroys the "natural" existentiality of nature, that is, life as *duration*.

§54   *The ascetic experience of life as "duration"*

If, therefore, it is personal immediacy – the non-dimensional present of erotic communion – which is the only empirical possibility for the experience of life as *duration*, and if the essential-natural "end" of humanity's relation with the world is the *duration* of existence, then this relation is "according to nature" only when it is a *personal* relation. And humanity's relation with the world is personal when our reception of the world, our existential ec-stasy towards the world, is not subjected to the necessity and urge of the self-preservation of the individual and does not subject the world to the individual's desire and will, but transcends natural individuality and objective ontic phenomenicity, in order to encounter the personal *logos* of "things," to disclose the personal dimension of the world.

This dynamic ec-stasy of nature *outside-of-nature*, the discovery and reception of the world's personal immediacy, is a specific work and attainment. It is the empirical content of the Church's *askesis*, as it has been defined in an earlier chapter. Asceticism is our dynamic and practical refusal to be subjected to the necessity and urge of self-preservation of the individual or to subject the world to the individual's will and desire. Our ascetic relationship to the world transfers the ecstatic urge of the self-preservation of the individual *outside-of-nature*, to the existential discovery and recognition of a personal *presence*, whose principle and disclosure is nature.

The personal *logos* of "things" refers to the presence of the Creator Logos, to the disclosure of the person of the Logos, to the personal God-Logos. And the presence of the Logos endures as personal energy in the character of beings as "things," in the "personal" uniqueness and dissimilarity – the beauty and wisdom – of the beings constituting the world's reality. The *logos* of the beings constituting the world's real-

ity is *outside* their self, is a *logos* referring to the Person of
the Logos (just as the *logos* of a painting by van Gogh is not
exhausted by the painting itself but refers to the person of
van Gogh, *discloses* the person of van Gogh). This reference
is not a necessity but an ecstatic potentiality, a possibility of
truth, a rising up from the "oblivion" of objectivity, a possibility of erotic *surprise* before the personal uniqueness and
dissimilarity of "things," before the personal beauty of the
world (like the surprise before the incomparable and unique
beauty of every erotic offering, which transforms the gift
into an image of the beloved).[52]

Conversely, when our relationship with the world is exhausted within the limits of individual need and desire, in the
"weakness of the senses," the *logos* of beings is restricted to
their own selves and loses any personal reference – beings
are only objective "things-to-be-used," in the service of the
individual, their truth is exhausted in their objective disclosure,[53] and their temporal change is experienced only as an
ecstasy of decay, as an enduring transition to nothingness.

§55   *Liturgical time*

The dynamic ec-stasy of nature *outside-of-nature*, the existential discovery and recognition of the *presence* of the
Logos in the world, as the experiential content and work
of ecclesiastical *askesis*, finds its "final" realization in the
Church as a fact of *eucharistic thanksgiving*. The Church,
as a fact of eucharistic thanksgiving, is the world's communion under the forms of bread and wine with the flesh of
the Logos, the reception of the world as immediacy of relation with the personal God-Logos. But this relation, as a fact
and the reality of the transformation of the world into the
flesh of the God-Logos and the transformation of humanity
into a partaker of the divine nature, presupposes a reciprocal ec-stasy, a self-transcendence not only of the human but

also of the divine nature: personal *askesis* finds its "final" realization in the Church's Eucharist, not only as nature's ec-stasy *outside-of-nature*, not only as the dynamic self-transcendence of individual nature, but also as encounter with the corresponding ec-stasy of God towards nature.[54]

In the Eucharist the *personal* assumption of nature by humanity encounters the nature that has been assumed by God, the nature that is not simply the result of the personal energy of the God-Logos, but is the flesh of the God-Logos. This assumption of nature by God, the incarnation of the God-Logos, is the one unique event which fully recapitulates the Church's truth about existence and temporality, about humanity, the world and God. In the person of Jesus Christ, the incarnate God, the personal dimension of the world and the existential ecstasy of the physical individuality of humanity find their "final" personal consummation, their "final" realization and fulfillment, as an event of hypostatic union of the created with the uncreated.

The incarnation of the Logos does not mean that God becomes the world and the world becomes God.[55] It means that the world's personal potentialities and their universal recapitulation in the human person, the unisimilar existential truth of personal universality towards which every form of existence tends dynamically, reaches its natural "end" in the theanthropic person of Christ, in the unconfused, immutable, undivided and unseparated unity of the divine and human natures – of God and the world[56] – in one person and one hypostasis.[57] This union and communion and unconfused mutual interpenetration of the two natures is a "new" existential reality, which abolishes existential ecstasy as temporal succession and decay and the finitude of death, or rather, fulfills existential ecstasy as immediacy of personal communion and grants existence its physical *duration*.

The incarnation of the Logos, as immediacy of personal communion of the created with the uncreated, is a "new" existential, and consequently temporal, reality: it is a cutting into time which destroys the *continuity* of time, or temporality as enslavement to the "before" and "after" – it inserts into time the *duration* of the "physical" communion between humanity and God. God intervenes with a chink of potentiality in phenomenal reality. The potentiality is of an immediate relationship with him – the incarnation being a chink in objective temporality, revelatory of the non-dimensional time of personal relation, the transcendence of time in the boundless present of loving communion. The Church's faith in "eternal life" refers not to an endless extension of temporal succession, but to a present of loving relation, to a non-dimensional fact of erotic communion, that is to say, to that *mode of existence* which restores humanity to the fullness of its personal truth, free from the limitations of physical individuality, limitations of time, space, decay and mortality.

The taste and experience of this incorrupt time of personal communion is approached by the believers within the Church's *liturgical* time. Each liturgical-eucharistic assembly is not a repetition, imitation or symbol of the world's communion with the flesh of the Logos, but the ever-present potentiality of participation in this communion, in the fact of the "physical" union of humanity and God. As a repeated yet nevertheless unchanged and ever-present potentiality for communion with the Logos, the Eucharist dissolves the past and the future in the immediacy of *presence*: the offering and realization of the Eucharist is an act of universal existential unity, which abolishes every moral or temporal difference: the living and the dead, the near and the far, the holy and the sinful, the first and the last, are all present *here* and *now* "before" Christ and "in Christ" – in the immediacy of the personal relation with him. The experience of eternal life within the Church, the eternity of the Church, is not interpreted (except relatively and symbolically) by the philosophers' "immortality of the soul." The incarnation of God saves not "spirits" but the whole human person, as assumed by Christ in his theandric flesh.[58] The eternity of the Church is the experience of the transfiguration of time in the immediacy of *presence* – of the incarnate presence of the Logos and the temporal presence of the Body which participates in the Logos.

The Church's liturgical time transforms temporal succession into a festal witness of the presence of salvation. Parallel to and, essentially, outside and beyond the arithmetical time of measured decay, the Church has her own cycle of time, the ever-dynamic cyclicality which unifies life "around the same one and alone" of erotic oneness (*henoeidia*) – the assurance of salvation expressed as daily celebration. The cycle of her feasts is *movable* and *immovable* – unchangeable movement and movable stability – reciprocal fissures in the horizontal time of corruptible change, fissures of the potentiality for the experience of "non-dimensional and infinite life," the experience of "eternal" time, "of participating in eternity" – "of participating in every being."[59] Liturgical time is the time of the liturgy of one Body, where the members participate in the same experience of personal immediacy. It is the time of the *Kingdom* of God, the non-dimensional present of the "Eighth Day": in contrast to the "week that measures out time,"[60] the Eighth Day "suggests the mode of that condition which is beyond nature and time"[61] – the non-dimensional present of the Eighth Day is a mode of existence; it is the fact of the relation between humanity and God as *duration* of erotic communion.

The incarnation of the Logos abolishes not only the continuity but also the impetus of time, impetus as history – that utopia of temporal potentialities of dynamic "change" and evolutionary improvement of objective "conditions," the imagined eternity of an endless "becoming" which is woven together from human suffering, violence, antagonisms, horrific hatred, bestial exploitation, and inadequate good intentions. For history is only that which can be objectified within time. That is why the immediacy of personal relationships – worship, love, art and politics as justice and self-denial – is not history. And those manifestations of personal life that are commemorated expressively and prove victorious over time are not historical fossils objectified in the memory but convey the immediacy of personal presence, uninterruptedly current possibilities of personal participation in life. The incarnation of the Logos abolishes history, because it recapitulates human "becoming" in the present of an existential confrontation with truth. It recapitulates life in truth and reveals truth as life. In the context of this confrontation, history as a succession of possibilities of dynamic change proves to be a form of slavery to objective time. The human person, imprisoned in historical "becoming" is a temporal unit either submissive or rebellious within the bounds of the objective "conditions" that limit it, a unit hopelessly tied to the gearing of the social balancing of rights and duties, to the vicious circle of time and money.

The incarnation of the Logos abolishes not only the *continuity* and *impetus* but also the *decay* of time, for it abolishes the finitude of the "moment," transforming desire into erotic fullness of *duration*. The Logos becomes incarnate "of the Virgin," and this virginal birth is the incorruption of nature, since love transcends the "natural" necessity of the ec-stasy of the individual, to be fulfilled as universal ec-stasy of nature *outside-of-nature*: In the flesh of the Virgin the whole of God and the whole of man are united unconfusedly, immutably, indivisibly and unseparably within the bounds of the fullness of the erotic ecstasy of the two natures, which is virginal because it is free from insatiable individual desire. From now on love becomes a *mystery* of the manifestation of the unity of Christ with humanity, and every love has the potentiality for a fulfilling duration as virginity of self-transcendence. Longing is free from its temporal bondage to the "moment."

Erotic time is no longer the recurring cycle of the tragedy of the Danaids.[62] Love becomes again a possibility for humanity to transcend its physical individuality, its enslavement to the temporal succession of the moments of desire, for it to realize the mystery of the communion of the natures in the non-dimensional space of erotic self-offering.

One final observation: it is evident that the "eternity" of humanity, the existential self-transcendence of individuality and entry into the space of personal immediacy, differs from the eternity of God as much as human nature differs from the divine nature: when we were discussing the *eternity* of God, we were referring to the conceptually unapproachable mystery of the fullness of the personal communion of the three divine persons within the unity of the one indivisible nature. This communion, which does not presuppose a self-transcendence of individual existences, is as unknowable to us as the divine nature itself. Our reference to the eternity of God is only relative, on the basis of the experience of the "eternity" of the liturgical time of ecclesial communion.

PART THREE

The "Semantics" of Personal Disclosure

Chapter One

The Logos as Disclosure of the Person

§56   *The logos as "declaration" and the logos as "logic"*

The primary sense of *logos* is derived from *legô*. It means collection (*syl-logê*), gathering, assembly. Homer says: "Let us gather up (*legômen*) the bones of Patroclus, son of Menoetias."[1] Originally *legô* meant I assemble, I bring together partial elements or attributes into the unity which is indispensable for that which exists to become manifest. Philo of Alexandria's later interpretation reflects this original meaning: "seeing that the *logos* of being is the bond between all things, as it is said, and holds all the parts together and constrains them, preventing them from disintegrating and falling apart."[2] *Logos* is identified with the presupposed original unity of being, with the initial potentiality for the unitary character of the universality of being to be revealed, that is, with that which being *is* when regarded as a "whole" or as "essence" (*ousia*). "The essence is one, the *logos* of the essence is one, and the name is one," Plato says.[3] And he adds that the unicity of the *logos* of the essence preserves the unisimilar character of being: "the essence of which we define the *logos* of being is the same."[4] Which means that the *logos* of being is identified with the essence of being. It refers to that which being fundamentally *is*, as a given universal unity. That is to say, it precedes the determination of properties and attributes (the *predicates* of being).

159

The relationship between the *logos* and the *ousia* of being is analyzed systematically by Aristotle. In Aristotle's
language the partial elements of the unity of being as *universal* (matter, form and "in a third sense the compound of
these"⁵ – "the compound of both taken universally"⁶) like the
properties of being as a *whole* – the synthetic totality of the
predicates of being ("a certain quality or quantity of some
such other predicate asserted of it"⁷) allow the possibility
of "speaking [of being] in many ways," ⁸ yet "all referring
to one principle"⁹ – always with reference to the original
unity of being, to the *essence* or *nature* of being. When we
say the tree *is* woody (quality), the tree *is* tall (quantity), the
tree *is* in the forest (place), the tree *is* ancient (time), the tree
is fruit-bearing (energy), etc., we define this *one* being "in
many senses," the being which is the tree. But we presuppose the single definition of its essence or substance: this *is* a
tree – the initial unity of this being, the unicity of its essence
("the essence of each thing is one"¹⁰ – "and unity is nothing
apart from being"¹¹). The *logos* of being precedes the predicates, that is, the properties of being as a *whole*. Hence it is
manifested as a presupposition for understanding the units of
being: "It is said to be one ... when the *logos* of what it is is
one and the same."¹² And this unity has a universal character.
It refers to all the partial existent units of being, to whatever
"is said to be one" – it is always a *logos* of the "universal"
("the *logos* is of the universal"¹³), it is "the *logos* in respect of
the thing."¹⁴ The *logos* of being refers *to* something; it is not
the *logos about* something. It concerns the initial question:
"What is it and what is this?"¹⁵ that is to say, in its essence.
"While 'being' has all these senses, obviously that which
is primarily is the 'what,' which indicates the substance of
the thing."¹⁶ The identification of *logos* with the power of
manifesting the essence or substance of being immediately
shows the character of *logos* as *declaration*. Not every *logos*
is declaratory.¹⁷ But the declaration – the presupposition that

being should be manifested in its essence – is always *logos*.[18] The *logos* is declaratory when it refers to essence (*pros ti*),[19] when it tells us that something is or is not, exists or does not exist, when it is disclosed (rises into truth) or is hidden.[20]

The activity of disclosing, that is, the function of the *logos* which discloses the essence of being, or allows it to appear, presupposes the gathering (*syl-logê*) and assembling of the partial elements and predicates of the universal entire unity of being. But it also presupposes the exclusion of other elements and predicates which do not belong to this unity. We are thus led to the sense of *logos* as *definition*, that is, as a boundary of the distinguishing presuppositions of the unity of every being's essence. *Logos*, which is declaratory of essence, *defines*, that is, circumscribes and distinguishes, the elements which "signify" the uniqueness and unity of the essence. It separates and differentiates these elements from other elements which "signify" other essences. The definition refers to the unitary character of essence ("it is one thing, the *logos* of which we call a definition"[21]), presupposing the differentiae which bring out the singular uniqueness of the essence: "clearly the definition is the *logos* which comprises the differentiae."[22] And this unity always has a universal character, referring either to the uniqueness of the actual unity of being ("some man or some horse" – *primary substance*, or individuals) or to all the partial actual units of being, "all that are called one" (*secondary substance*).[23]

In both cases the *logos* of the distinguishing differentiae subsists in the unisimilar *logos* of the "universal," which is declaratory of the essence. The definition *defines* the unity of the essence as *logos* "from the differentiae": "the last differentia will be the substance of the thing and its definition."[24] Thus the energy of disclosure, the declaratory *logos*, reveals not only the unity of being as "universal," but also the *mode* of this unity: it preserves both the *logos* of the distinguishing differentiae, which *define* the universal unity of substance, and the *logoi* of the incomplete "parts" or elements which make up the *order* of the unitary universality of substance: "the *logos* of the parts must be present in the *logos* of the whole"[25] – "the *logos* of what the essence is contains the parts of the thing defined."[26] Consequently, the *logos* as definition corresponds not only to the "semantics" of the unitary universality of the essence, but also to the disclosure of the *mode* of the combination of the incomplete "parts" or distinguishing differentiae which manifest the unitary universality of the essence – the *logos* corresponds to the *mode* or the *how* of the existence of essences. Therefore so long as beings are disclosed *with* the *logos*, they are also disclosed *according to* their *logos*. The mode of their disclosure is determined by the *logos* that is declaratory of their essence. It is a *logical* mode, referring to a harmonious and ordered (with an etiological harmony and order) combination of distinguishing differentiae and incomplete "parts" which manifest the unity of the universal essence – that which being *is*: "order is every *logos*,"[27] "that which for the sake of which it is is in the *logos*."[28] Thus we arrive at the meaning of *logos* as *logical*, organic and etiological series and order.

But the *mode* by which essence *is*, the unitary universality and uniqueness of the essence, constitutes its *form*, its dissimilar shape. Consequently definition, as a declaratory *logos* (a *logos* which discloses the unitary and unique character of the essence) refers to the *form* and is productive of it: "for definition is of the universal and of the form."[29] And the distinguishing differentia, which manifests the unitary uniqueness of the essence, is a "differentia productive of form" (*eidopoios diaphora*): "for the *logos* that comes from the differentiae belongs to the form"[30] – "for every differentia productive of form along with the genus makes a species."[31] But the *form* (or *species*) can only be "signified." That is to say, it can only be connected with the experience of its uniqueness, which is why *logos* as definition is a "sign" of the uniqueness of the essence: "the *logos*, of which the name is a sign, becomes a definition."[32] The same name, as an uttered expression, has no meaning when it is not a "sign," that is, a *symbol* – when it does not "symbolize" (in the etymological sense "put together," "unify") the incomplete experience, of the form which each of us possesses separately, with a view to signifying" being, that is, to defining it: "no name is a name naturally, but only when it becomes a symbol."[33] The signified form names the things: "the species gives names to the individuals that belong to it."[34] The *logos*, consequently, both as declaration and as logic, is identified with the potentiality of disclosure of essence only when it functions significantly and symbolically, that is, only when it presupposes the experience of the form and refers to this experience. Here we could add that *experience* of the form also presupposes and discloses the pre-conceptual *relation* of humanity with the "personal" uniqueness and dissimilarity of beings, and consequently the *logos*, as declaration and as logic, presupposes and discloses the personal relation of humanity with the things that are, since relation is the necessary and sufficient presupposition of the experience of the form "signified" by the *logos*.

§57   *Logos as "mode" of the person's ecstatic reference*

We saw earlier that the rising up of beings from oblivion into truth presupposes a "horizon" (a possibility of disclosure) which is the existential reality of the person. We could say now that it also presupposes a *mode* or *means* of disclosure (not only the *where* but also the *how* of disclosure) which is the *logos*. Beings become true, are disclosed in the "horizon" of the person, as *logos*. Their declaratory and logical disclosure has been discussed above, with the help of Aristotle's analysis, as a semantic and symbolic function of the *logos*, that is, as reference to the unitary uniqueness

of the universal unity of being – to the *form* (*eidos*). And we
went on to say that the semantics of the form presuppose the
experience of the form and refer to it, with the result that
they refer to the primary potentiality of the person's *relation*
with beings, which is a relation of the disclosure of beings
in the "horizon" of the person. The *logos* is identified with
the *mode* or the *how* of the disclosure, so that the distinction
of the *mode* of disclosure from the *horizon* of disclosure is
more a conceptual distinction than a real possibility: what
we call a "horizon" of disclosure, before being a specific
where, a specific "place" of either reflective or conceptual
knowledge, is a dynamic *how* of ecstatic reference, an existential fact of pre-reflective *relation*, which constitutes the
necessary and sufficient presupposition for the disclosure
and truth of beings. But if we keep the distinction between
the *mode* and the *horizon* of disclosure for the sake of systematic (if conventional) exposition, we can express it more
specifically as follows: the dynamic-ecstatic referentiality
of the person constitutes *as a potentiality* the "horizon" of
the disclosure of beings, and *as a result* or consequence the
truth of beings, the cohesive unification of the elements of
ontic individuality as declaration, as a declaratory definition
of the essence of being. In both cases – as potentiality for
disclosure – the ecstatic reference of the person is realized as
logos and constitutes *logos*. In the first case, the potentiality
for the disclosure of beings in the "horizon" of the person is
constituted as a readiness for *logos*, a potentiality for "logical" reception of the *logos* of things, a presupposition for
dialogue (*dia-logos*), that is, for *relation*. In the second case,
the result of the person's ecstatic reference, the disclosure of
beings, that is, their truth, is also *logos*, a "semantic" determination of pre-reflective experience of the form, that is, of
humanity's personal *relation* with the "personal" uniqueness
and dissimilarity of beings. Here we might add that as a invitatory operation of interpersonal relation (speech, written

and emblematic representation, facial expression, gesture, work of art, manifestation of love) the person's ecstatic reference is again *logos*. We can therefore conclude that the personal in its ecstatic reference is always *logos*.

§58   *Logos as "signifier" of personal relation*

Logos, consequently, is the *mode* of the person's universal-ecstatic reference. That is to say, it is an existential fact, the fact of *relation*, the ontological transcendence of ontic individuality, the dynamic denial of individual self-sufficiency – the supreme disclosure of the person. The conception of the *logos* of beings, the disclosure of their essence, proves to be a fact much broader than the reflective-conceptual function of connecting objects with the conventional "signs" of the common linguistic idiom. Knowledge of the *logos* of beings, as universal experience of the personal truth of beings, experience of their disclosure in the "horizon" of the person, is not exhausted in the coincidence of sense with the thing thought, or in the "acoustic image" which conventionally indicates this connection. It is not exhausted within the framework of the automatic matching of names to objects, such as is imposed by the need for daily communication.[35] The "logical" disclosure of beings in the "horizon" of the person presupposes both the personal *logos* of beings as "things" and the pre-reflective universal-ecstatic reference of the person in this *logos*, its dynamic reception – and consequently a *relation* of the person with the beings.

We can perhaps see a suggestion of this relation, which as universal experience transcends the simple intellectual marking of objects, in Aristotle's identification of sensory perception with *logos*: "The sensory perception and the *logos* are the same."[36] Aristotle refers specifically to the "concord" of an external stimulus with the experience of its sensory reception: "If voice is concord, and if the voice and the hearing of it are in one sense one and the same, and if concord is a *logos*, hearing as well as what is heard must be a *logos*."[37] The *logos*, as "concord" of the sensory experience with the external stimulus, represents in a very specific way the function of the "logical" disclosure of beings in the "horizon" of the person. Aristotle does not oppose sensory experience to the epistemic powers of the soul. On the contrary, "thinking and understanding are regarded as akin to a form of perceiving (for in the one as well as the other the soul discriminates and is cognizant of something which is) and indeed the ancients go so far as to identify thinking and perceiving."[38] We could say that both the sensory experience and the mental capacity constitute phases or manifestations of the universal-ecstatic reference of the person, which is always "logical," just as the external stimulus is also always "logical," that is, the *form* (*eidos*) of beings or language as *informative* (*eidopoios*) marking of beings. In the context of this theory "the language of the soul's epistemic activity is symbolic" – "for the *logos* is the activity and the disclosure of the mind," as Maximus the Confessor very concisely puts it.[39] The epistemic activity of the soul or mind is here simultaneously expressions of it which refer to the ecstatic reference of the person, which is always "logical."

In other words, the *logos*, as a function of *disclosing*, signifies the existentially universal (not merely the mental or conscious) fact of personal cognition, the experience of humanity's "logical" reception of the *logos* of "things," that is, the fact of humanity's *relation* with the world. Hence *logos* is also defined as the supreme *personal* power, as the power which is fundamental to the person and the source of everything else. "While there are some wild animals in which imagination is found, there is no *logos*," observes Aristotle.[40] *Logos* is the differentia that distinguishes humanity from irrational (*a-logê*) nature, the differential of the personal power of ecstatic reference and universal relation with beings. It is this relation that defines the truth of beings, their rising up from oblivion (non-relation). Before being objectified conventionally in the realm of the automatic functioning of daily necessity (before language is "devalued" and transformed from a symbol "of the soul's epistemic activity" to a conventional *sign* of daily utility for facilitating human co-existence), this definition of beings in terms of the operation of disclosure has a unique experiential character which is dissimilar and unrepeatable, since the universal *relation* of every person with beings or other persons is unique, dissimilar and unrepeatable. What we call the *logos* of being is the affirmation of the essence (*ousia*) of being as presence (*parousia*), as reference, in the "horizon" of personal uniqueness and dissimilarity.

We arrive consequently at an interpretation of *logos*, which we can "define" as a person's power to reveal and express the uniqueness and dissimilarity of its ecstatic reference and its universal relation with beings or other persons. Before being objectified as a conventional "naming" of being, *logos*[41] is a personal disclosure, the revelation of a unique, dissimilar and unrepeatable *relation*. Every partial mode or phase in the disclosure and expression of this relation, every mode of utterance (speech, written word, facial expression, gesture, work of art, manifestation of love), before being a definition declaratory of the essence of being is a *logos*-definition of the person, a disclosure of personal uniqueness and dissimilarity.

§59   *The "logic" of aesthetic experience*

It should be clear from the above that the primary meaning of *logic* is not the putting together of a hermeneutic and determinative structure in accordance with a certain objective agreed order and set of rules, but the personal power of the reception and cognition of the *logos* of "things," the encoun-

ter and coordination of the human *logos* with the world's
logos. On the basis of an objectively and conventionally
established "logicality" (*ratio, raison, Venunft*), this personal coordination can only be expressed as indeterminacy,
or disorder and asymmetry. The *logical* structure of a phenomenon implies not the objective cogency of a systematic
intellectual polishing and reflective interpretation or definitive classification, but the witness or disclosure of humanity's personal coordination with the world's *logos*. And this
witness or disclosure may be expressed either in intellectual
or in sensory categories. It may be manifested by speech,
writing, facial expression, gesture, a work of art, or a demonstration of love.

Logos's decline to the impersonal conventionality of the
"semantics" of objects (its becoming autonomous and its
subjection to the usefulness of the "naming" of objects, or
the detachment of *logos* from the existential fact of *relation*),
that is, neutralized speech (*language*[42]), and the restriction
of logic to the power of constructing objectively compelling
syllogisms,[43] has restricted the function of disclosure – the
character of *logos* as the manifestation of personal uniqueness – to a very few areas of life, perhaps chiefly to the expression of love and artistic activity. A work of art always
remains the *logos* of a person, the "logical" disclosure of a
person, the "sign" of the artist's personal coordination with
the personal *logos* of the object which he undertakes to represent. Artistic activity *defines* the facts, and reveals their
truth. That is to say, it restores their personal reference. And
this definition of the facts, in the case of a work of art, is a
personal *logos*, a unique, dissimilar and unrepeatable witness to the personal discovery and reception of the *logos* of
the facts. It is a witness to and disclosure of a person. Van
Gogh's painting of a pair of old country boots *defines* these
boots in an unrepeatable way. It reveals their unique truth,[44]
their emergence into the space of the artist's existential ex-

perience – into the "horizon" of his personal cognition – and their representation becomes a personal *logos*, a disclosure of the very person of van Gogh. When we stand in front of the painting, we say: this *is* van Gogh.

Here we might add that the evaluation of a work of art refers to the degree in which the artist's *logos* has represented the uniqueness of his or her personal *relation* with the object of the work. It refers to the degree in which the artist's interpretation transcends the impersonal and conventional versions of objects. The revelation of the artist's personal relation with the object of the work "draws up" the object from its impersonal neutrality, inviting the beholder (or reader, or listener) of the work of art to an equally personal participation in the personal uniqueness of the object. Accordingly, a work of art is always a *symbol*, for it brings together (*sym-ballei*) the partial experiences of personal participation in the personal uniqueness of the object. The artistic expression or disclosure of the artist's personal encounter with the personal *logos* of the object (which is always a *logos* of beauty, not of concepts) opens up a new path. It calls forth and brings together our partial personal participations in this *logos* – it coordinates and reunites the presence of beings with the "horizon" of their truth, which is the human person, manifesting the dynamic universality of the one personal relation. And being a *symbol*, a work of art is also an *allegory*, in the ancient meaning of the world. It manifests the *logos* of the object as a witness to the person who has received this *logos*. The object of the work of art refers to a reality which is *other* than its conventional ontic version: it "allegorizes," in the etymological sense that it says something other.[45] Thus the *logos* of art is more universally immediate the more personal it is, the more it succeeds in expressing the universal power which is personal relation, the power of the personal uniqueness and dissimilarity of the object to be disclosed in the personal "horizon" of disclosure. It is precisely because the person "contains" and recapitulates universal human nature – because the person is the ecstatic power of nature and nature is the content of the person – that the *logos* of art is more universal and more admitting of common epistemic experience when it succeeds in expressing personal ecstasy, that is, when it transcends the expression of merely individual experiences (individual emotions or inspirations).

In other words, artistic expression is a "moral"-erotic achievement that transcends individuality, or the dividing up of nature into discreet items. It is an achievement that ascends to the universality of a personal relationship with the world. The transcendence of individuality is attained by the artist's submitting to the internal "laws" which govern the "coherence" of the *logoi* of physical reality – a "coherence" of the *logoi* of physical reality – a "coherence" which constitutes the onticity of beings.[46] This submission endows art with the potentiality for an essential "asceticism," makes it a way of restoring the person to its existential authenticity, and identifies artistic creation with the experience of the world's personal dimension, with the personal discovery and manifestation of the personal *logos* of things. Hence when artists seek not simply to give a perfect *impression* in their personal rendering, but to convey the truth about life – even if they do not succeed in experiencing or expressing any more than humanity's existential failure – when they approach the frontiers of personal creative expression, they always experience something of humanity's bliss before the Fall. Revealed behind every work of art is the abyss of the mystery of the person and of the world beyond any conventional representational rendering. In the degree in which the person is the nearest and the farthest, it is at the same time also the inexpressible. Art is the *logos* of this inexpressibility.

§60   *Natural energies as the logos of personal otherness*

We are now in a position to say that the *logos* constitutes a disclosure of the person through the natural *energies*, as we have defined them in an earlier chapter, as nature's universal power to reveal the personal mode of its existence. We know nature only as the content of the person. That is, we know only the *mode* by which nature *is*, and this knowledge becomes accessible to us through nature's *energies*, which reveal to us the *logos* of personal otherness. Speech, the written word, facial expression, gesture, the production of art, the manifestation of love are energies-potentialities of universal nature of such a kind which disclose the *logos* of personal otherness. The person in its ecstatic reference is always *logos* and this *logos* is the disclosure of nature's energies which always reveal the personal otherness.

Within the context of this ontological approach to *logos* we can reappraise the reality of the world's *logos*, we can look at the world as the *logos*-disclosure of a personal creative energy. Approaching beings as "things" refers the *logoi* of beings to the energies or to the "acts of will" of a creator person. In the words of Maximus the Confessor:

> Since the *logoi* of beings, having been prepared in God before the ages, as he himself knows, are invisible, and are customarily also called good desires by the saints, they are observed by being apprehended mentally from created things. For all of God's creatures, when contemplated intellectually by us in accordance with nature and necessary knowledge, secretly reveal to us the *logoi* by which they have been brought into being. And they manifest the divine purpose which is in every creature just as the heavens tell of the glory of God and the firmament proclaims the work of his hands. There is an eternal power and divinity that is the providence that embraces beings and the energy that in accordance with it deifies what has been providentially conceived of.[47]

The entire reality of nature is "logical" in the degree in which the *logoi* of beings are not exhausted in themselves, but disclose the personal energies and "acts of will" of God, composing a symphony of *logoi*, "in which this whole and the parts of the whole naturally appear to and do contain the whole of their cause shining with a brilliant radiance."[48] The "logical" structure of the world, the cosmic symphony or operation of the *logoi* of ontic reality, adumbrates the unity of the existential principle of beings, the person of the God-Logos as he is revealed through the energies of the divine essence.[49]

Consequently the power of knowing God through the witness borne by the world does not refer the *logos* of the world to an impersonal causal principle. It refers the *logos*, as the power of personal disclosure, to God himself. And this is not a reference of the particular to the general, of the relative to the absolute, since in the realm of personal disclosure there are no quantitative categories. The reception of the *logos* of beings signifies the experience of a personal relation. It reveals the world's *logos* as the second term of this dialogue-like relation, which can be experienced only as personal communion, a communion of ecstatic-loving reciprocity. Within the context of this experience of communion, the "logical" existence of humanity and the "logical" structure and unity of the world reveal their "in the beginning" existential presupposition, the person of the God Logos: "In the beginning was the Logos, and the Logos was with God, and the Logos was God. He was in the beginning with God; all things were made through him, and without him was not anything made that was made" (John 1:1-3).

Chapter Two

The Image as "Signifier" of Non-conventional Logos

§61   *Phenomenological ontology as a presupposition of conventional semiology*

If we take as our starting-point for the problem of knowledge the etymological meaning of the Greek word for "truth," *a-lêthia*, which is truth as *disclosure*, as rising up from oblivion (*lêthê*), our definition of the "horizon" of disclosure defines the problem of knowledge, and becomes the basis for the construction of an epistemology. If the truth of beings, their rising up from oblivion, both defines and presupposes an objective "horizon" of disclosure – the horizon of time in Heidegger's ontological approach – epistemology is necessarily phenomenological. Knowledge is exhausted in the phenomenal, temporal rising up from oblivion, in the distinguishing of presence from absence, in the disclosure, that is to say, of our epistemological distance from the essence. Knowledge is not the raising up of the phenomenal to the universal "idea," or to the mental conception of its essence. It is the awareness of disclosure as the *mode* by which what is *is*, the understanding of disclosure as determinative of time, which is the only horizon in which that which *is* comes into the light, or is *disclosed*.

The disclosure of distance from the essence, which is the knowledge of beings as *phenomena*, ends up as being experience of the distance between humanity and the inaccessible essence of objective beings. Humanity understands the *mode* by which beings *are* – the truth of beings as disclosure and disclosure as temporality – but the understanding of the disclosure, or awareness of time, as an exclusively human potentiality is only the necessary and sufficient condition for the phenomenicity of phenomena. It does not annul the self-hiddeness of the essence, the distance between humanity and the veiled essence of beings.[1]

Our distance from beings, which *defines* objects, is illuminated by the *logos*. The *logos* bridges the void between the subjectivity of knowledge ("die Subjektivität des Erkennens," as Husserl puts it[2]) and the objectivity of the semantic content of knowledge ("die Objektivität des Erkenntnisinhaltes"). Knowledge is always experience or awareness of a disclosure, but a disclosure of *a particular thing*. Knowledge always has some semantic content. Thus it finds in the *logos* the schematic-objective expression of its semantic content, with the result that its pragmatic use, the delivery of practical consequences through necessarily conventional forms, then becomes possible.

Consequently, although it is dependent on the awareness of distance from essence, on truth as temporal phenomenicity, the epistemology that emerges from a phenomenological understanding of ontology inevitably objectifies the knowledge of "essences" in the space of the "semantics" of objects. The objectivity of the content of knowledge is shaped by the *logos* as concept, as what is *signified* ("signifié"), so that the *signifier* ("significant") might be expressed – through the acoustic image ("image acoustique") – linguistically.[3] Thus the boundaries of knowledge are transposed to the boundaries of language. Nothing is differentiated, no knowledge is determined, before it is expressed linguistically. The conceiving of the concept ("concept-signifié")[4] is possible only through its conjunction with the acoustic image ("significant") – we think in acoustic images even when we do not express our thoughts aloud.[5]

The acoustic image shapes, or defines and exhausts, the semantic content of knowledge. It becomes the "sign,"[6] the schematic expression of the concept, which now loses its relationship with the existential experience of the relativity of knowledge in respect of the self-hiddenness of the essence. Knowledge is necessarily relative, since not only is the *signifier* arbitrary in its conjunction with the *signified*,[7] but the *signified* itself is only phenomenal – "it stands apart from the essence." The relativity of knowledge nevertheless establishes an absolute affirmation of linguistic expression as means of cognition, that is to say, a linguistic positivism, which is to confine knowledge within the boundaries of language.[8] We know reality only in its logical form and structure, that is to say, only in respect of the possibility it offers us to signify it with the *signs* of our common linguistic idiom. The common element which binds language to reality is logical form and structure as reflected in language. Consequently, we know only what can be expressed or reflected within language, only what has *meaning*, what corresponds to logical form and structure. Thus truth cannot be expressed except by rules of "linguistic logic."[9] It must depend on the rules of linguistic logic, even if this logic is merely "semantic," or a conventional knowledge useful only for its practical consequences.

Saussure's basic thesis, that the linking of signifier to signified is absolutely arbitrary, reveals the exclusively relative and conventional character of linguistic logic. The truth of the statement "a tree is a plant" and the falsity of the statement "a tree is a mammal" depend totally on the conventional arbitrary designations of the names "plant" and "mammal." And yet this relative and conventional linguistic expression and logic is the "vague" and "imprecise" common daily language which we use to create the "precise" symbolic language of scientific positivism.[10] No knowledge can be expressed apart from the conventional linguistic idiom of a human group.[11]

§62   *The ontology of the personal "mode of existence" as a presupposition for knowledge as a universal relation*

If we now accept the human *person* as the "horizon" of the disclosure of beings (their rising up from oblivion to truth), knowledge becomes the experience of the disclosure within the context of the person's relation to objective beings. Our understanding of the existential and cognitive fact of *relation* depends on ontological presuppositions necessarily different from those relating to phenomenology. There is one common presupposition, the denial that essence can be defined in ontic categories, or the denial of the identification of essence with the idea or concept of being a "universal." Consequently, in neither case is knowledge the disclosure of essence. The essence remains inaccessible not only on the phenomenological but also on the *personal* cognitive level. Beyond this common presupposition, however, our approach to the problem of essence is radically different.

In an earlier chapter[12] I gave a brief description of the void which a phenomenological approach to the problem of essence leaves in ontology as such. This void permits both Western apophaticism's absolutized *mysticism of essence* and the conventional intentionality of a "semiological" epistemology. Against the phenomenological approach to the problem of essence I have proposed here a distinction of essence from persons, and also a distinction of essence from the essence's *energies*, which are always personal. These two distinctions respond to the question concerning the *mode* by which that which exists *is*: the essence, or Being, "conceals itself" in the *mode* by which whatever is *is*, and this mode is the *persons* (the bearers of the energies of the essence), and the "things" or "acts"[13] of the persons (the results of the essence's energies), which are always personal.

Consequently, the "self-hiddenness" of essence does not imply here an arbitrary mystification of essence, leading inevitably to a nihilistic interpretation of it. The "self-hiddenness" means that essence is never identified with ontic individuality, or with conceptual definitions, or with the phenomenological version of oblivion-truth. Essence can only be known within the context of the existential fact, the *mode of existence*, and this knowledge constitutes a possibility of potentiality, not the delineation of a given objectivity.

The ontological problem is summarized exhaustively in the reality of the person (a reality never circumscribable linguistically), which is the only possible way in which essence is disclosed, essence's *mode of existence*. The reality of beings, their mode of being, is not bound up with our understanding of ontic individuality. It is not exhausted by objective temporal phenomenicity and our intellectual conception of non-phenomenicity, of oblivion or nothingness. Objective beings are forms of *energy*, and in this assertion the ontological views of the Eastern Church Fathers on the "logical" character of the simple qualities of matter resemble the ideas of modern microphysics.[14] The ontological problem is transposed from the realm of the phenomenicity of ontic individualities, or the conventional "semantics" of meaning and the contents of consciousness, to the realm of personal existence, to that dynamic and universal fact of *relation* which is the person as ecstatic existence, or the result of personal energy as invitation to personal communion. It is the personal relation that constitutes the dynamic realization of an authentic *mode of existence*. And it can be known only as a fact of living experience. No intellectual definition can exhaust the *mode* by which that which is *is*, that is, essence (Being) as personal existence and personal energy. The fact of *relation* alone constitutes a universal existential and cognitive potentiality, the fullness of existence and knowledge. Being (the *mode* of existence) "is hidden" not because it is indeterminate or difficult of intellectual access, but because it is the existential and cognitive content of a dynamic-*moral* attainment of freedom, an ascent to an authentic (or *natural*) mode of existence. The dynamic self-transcendence of ontic individuality (the transcendence of the splitting up of nature into separate individuals and of existence into partial functions or potentialities), the ascent to the ecstatic unity of nature, or to the dynamic universality of the person, which is realized within the context of loving self-offering and relation, is a *moral* achievement. It is a dynamic-personal expression of existence, not an ontic one. It is an experiential expression, which means one that is morally accessible. The *personal* unity of existence and knowledge is realized dynamically as a unity of mind and heart, of *logos* and *praxis*, of morality and being, a unity which transforms the whole of existence into a cognitive instrument, ensuring the universal immediacy and experiential certitude of "true knowledge."

§63   *The unity of knowledge as a fact of universal relation*

This ontological theory remains within the bounds of experiential reality – without recourse to *a priori* principles – even though it represents an experiential potentiality rather than an objective certainty. The space of Being is covered by the personal presence of God and the personal presence of humankind. It is identified with the dynamic fact of this personal relation. In phenomenological terms we could say that the "horizon" of disclosure (the true person) and the beings that are disclosed (the things accomplished by the divine energy) are the two terms of the relation within which the ontological problem is summarized. Whatever *is* – the reality of beings and the whole of what happens within the bounds of reality – is situated within the single fact of the personal relationship between God and humankind. Beings are "things" or products (*pragmata-pepragmena*) of the divine energy, which reveal the divine personal presence, and constitute forms and structures of beauty, that is, a world or *cosmos*, a complete adornment (*cosmêma*), of God's erotic invitation to a personal relationship with humankind. And the entire process of cosmic and historical becoming is the positive impetus of acceptance, or the converse movement of rejection, of this personal invitation to communion between the created and the uncreated – the existential fact of personal freedom in its pragmatic and cosmic dimensions.

Mode of being is thus not an escape from the problem of essence. It leaves no room for a mysticism of essence, which interprets the self-hiddenness of essence both as ontic-temporal disclosure and as the purely notional conception of non-disclosure, that is, of oblivion or nothingness. The mode of being summarizes the ontological problem exhaustively in the existential fact of personal relation, which is a universal experiential possibility, not a conventionally signified phenomenicity.

The possibility of personal relation refers to the primary "definition" of a human being, to that which a human being fundamentally *is*: a possibility of erotic self-transcendence and loving communion. And *possibility* also implies the admissibility of non-self-transcendence, an individualistic imprisonment in the subjective contemplation of the phenomenicity of the phenomena of an irrational world. In the latter case, the truth of beings is an intellectual conception and conventional description of their rising up from oblivion or nothingness, and knowledge is a "semiological" set of conventions. In the first case, truth is an erotic wonder, a revelation of the world's personal dimensions, and knowledge is a dynamic-moral fact, a bodily and spiritual attainment of ascetic self-denial and loving self-offering. *Knowledge of the world* is possible only within the context of human-

ity's dynamic-personal relation with God. We *know* beings
not through a conventional description which identifies the
object with the concept or uses the concept to define temporal phenomenicity, so as to make it available for practical
use through its acoustic image. We *know* beings as dynamic
disclosures of God's personal energy, as the *logos* of this energy or as an invitation to a personal-erotic relationship with
him. And the knowledge of the invitation itself is already
an erotic participation in the relation. It is *eros* as a unique
mode of existence. It is the unity of the fullness of existence
and knowledge.

§64   *Logos and language – language and morality*

Knowledge, as a personal relation, is necessarily expressed
by the *logos*, but the *logos* is not restricted to the combining
of the semantic content of subjective understanding with the
linguistic expression that has been established by the common conventional idiom. The *logos* possesses wider margins
of possibility for the disclosure of personal relationship and
the realization of personal knowledge that are ignored by
both phenomenology and linguistic neopositivism. In the
context of the reduction of the person to an objectified individuality, to its alienation as a social or psychological unit,
these two schools of thought complement each other very
well. But they do not arrive at the conclusions imposed by
the erotic *logos*, the *logos* of art, the *logos* within the words
and beyond the words,[15] the immediacy of the *logos* of humanity's bodily expression.[16]

The common linguistic idiom of a human group is a means
or instrument which serves the expression or disclosure of
the personal *logos* of every specific person. It can therefore
be the bearer of cognitive "surprise" beyond any pre-existing
subjective knowledge. We can isolate words as the "acoustic
images" and conventional "signs" of common communica-

tion, but this isolation of words and study of their conventional character, the technique or "mechanism" of language[17]
and its presentation as "phonetic matter" which organizes
thought,[18] is inadequate for interpreting the working of language, which always discloses the personal *logos* within
and beyond the words. The separation of language from the
personal uniqueness and dissimilarity of the personal *logos*
is an arbitrary intellectual act. Language, separated from its
personal bearer, is not the complete fact of humanity's linguistic expression, the fact of life, which is the relation and
communion of human beings through language – just as the
cadaver on the dissecting table is not the complete fact of human existence. Even an utterly conventional and artificially
constructed linguistic register that functions purely as a code
for practical communication does not cease to be life, that
is, the *logos*-disclosure of an ethos of non-communication, a
denial of personal relation.

"The language of the soul's cognitive energy is symbolic,"
says Maximus the Confessor.[19] The soul's "cognitive energy" is a *personal* power to receive the *logos* of "things" and
of other persons, and an ecstatic-*logical* power to disclose
the person to the external world within the context of the
relationship with "things" and other persons. This personal
"power" is a personal *energy*, the disclosure of the unique,
dissimilar and unrepeatable *mode* by which every human being *is*. And language is the result of this personal energy (of
cognitive-logical energy, of the soul), a result inseparably
interwoven with its organic cause – language is *symbolic*:
it conjoins (*sym-ballei*) the soul's cognitive energy with the
disclosure or result of such energy.

Under no circumstances can language be separated from
the person who speaks it. It cannot cease being the *logos* of
a specific human being, a disclosure of his or her uniqueness
and dissimilarity. And if we describe as human morality the
measure of the differences or dynamic grades between a per-

sonal-loving relation and an egocentric self-sufficiency (or between a personal mode of existence "according to nature" and an individualistic mode "contrary to nature"), language is then one of the supreme disclosures of human morality. When it is made subject to an egocentric individuality, language becomes a conventional means or an instrument for the satisfaction of individual needs, desires or demands. It is restricted to the arbitrary intentionality of an interaction serving individuals. The words do not refer to common experience. They are no longer bridges to communion but material which people use to express themselves and buttress themselves as individuals. That is why they often support the sense which each person wants to give them. We speak the same words and each of us understands what we want to understand, not what will bring us into communion with things and other people. Words like justice, love, freedom, reverence, democracy, beauty and truth lose their symbolic character. They cease to "signify" and coordinate personal experience. They become variables veiling the most diverse individual meanings.[20] Linguistic neopositivism has sought to restrict the arbitrariness, imprecision and polysemy of everyday language, proposing the putting together of strictly logical systems for constructing or clarifying linguistic proportions. That is to say it has proposed a rational reconstruction and refurbishment of everyday language.[21] Naturally, a linguistic approach of this kind aims simply at a more objective reinforcing of the conventional character of language. It wants to construct a stricter convention which still ignores the moral character of language – the identification of language with life, with the mode of existence of the human person. It aims at the subjection of life to language, not language to the dynamics of life.

The opposite linguistic morality to that expressed by a linguistic "semantics" which has been made autonomous (or by the subjection of language to the arbitrariness of individualistic egocentricity) is manifested in that use of language which maintains and serves personal relationship. When we speak of a *use* of language which serves personal relationship, we should understand this as a dynamic-moral fact of freedom: the ascetic subjection of the egocentricity of individual existence to the *common logos*, to the "semantics" of personal experience.[22]

This subjection of an arbitrary individualism allows the *logos* of personal disclosure to be possible. It makes language a personal potentiality and energy, a fact of cognitive relation and communion. The common linguistic idiom then functions as the disclosure (or consequence) of personal energy. Language serves the dialogue of personal relation. It expresses, provokes and coordinates personal experience. It is a dynamic *invitation* to communion and relation. Language functions as an invitation to personal relation in the degree to which it embodies personal energy, since the energy is always invitatory to communion and relation and accessible only within the context of the fact of relation. Language as invitation represents a semantic expression of the fact of personal energy. It "signifies" – that is, it calls forth, ensures and preserves – the existential power of relation. Of course, language does not cease primarily to "signify" objects and the reality of life. Nevertheless, its "semantic" character may perhaps not be exhausted in the conventional meaning of objects, in the linking of a commonly agreed acoustic image with a specific *phenomenon*, whether object or fact. Language has the power to "signify" phenomena as facts of personal energy, to disclose the personal *logos* of "things" and events, to encounter this *logos*, since it is itself a personal *logos* or energy, within the bounds of the existential fact of relation[23] – and this power represents the authentic function of language. The "semantics" of language become complete when language refers to, or rather, *passes over* to, the person – and we should understand this reference or passage as a dual dynamic thrust: language shows the bearer of the *logos* and what is signified by the *logos* as the two terms of a personal relation.

§65   *The image as analogous knowledge*

Within this context the Greek East understood the *image* as a means for expressing the truth of persons and things, and spoke an iconic language that signified the disclosure of the person of God and the person of humankind. Image is the signifier of personal relation, the "logical" disclosure of personal energy as invitation to communion and relation. This means that as a cognitive category the image is not exhausted within its own terms. It does not represent a static signified thing," or substitute a reality or fact simply by an "example," but discloses a personal energy invitatory to communion and relation, and preserves the character of knowledge as a fact of dynamic relation.

The understanding of the image as a category of cognition which was developed by the Christian Greek world differs both from the ancient concept of the image and from the modern use of the term in analytical philosophy.

The ancient Greek concept of the image relies on analogy (etymologically deriving from the verb *eikô*, "I give way to") and means a likeness, a representation, an analogous expression of the form. The image may be a material representation of real or imaginary objects, that is to say, a painted or sculpted impression,[24] or it may be a reflection – the phantom of an object in any mirror[25] – or it may even be the representation of facts and realities in the human mind.[26] Finally, the image may be an *allegory* (*allêgoria*), a sensible form that speaks (*agoreuei*) of something other than itself, referring symbolically to another reality or idea.[27]

The concept of the image is also analogical in modern analytic philosophy – at least in Wittgenstein's early work.[28]

Only here the analogical relation of the image to the reality depicted is based on the analytical correspondence of logical relations which link together simple objects both in reality and in the image. For every fact we form a corresponding image[29] – the image is analogous to a fact, that is, it is analogous to a certain combination of objects[30] and to the mode in which objects are combined, or to the structure and form of the fact.[31] The image has the logical form of depiction in common with the thing depicted:[32] the combination of objects in the context of the depicted fact and the combination of the elements of the image[33] by which the fact is depicted have a common form and structure which is *logical*. The image is a model of reality,[34] which means that the logical form and structure of the image is also the form by which we can know reality, the mode by which we can reach out to it.[35] Every image is at the same a logical image[36] and only as a logical image can it depict the world[37] (i.e., the totality of the facts[38]). And since we know the facts (i.e., the world) only by forming images, it follows that the only possibility we have of cognitive access to the world is the logicality which is identical to the possibility of depiction. The identification of logic with depictable form implies the identification of image and meaning: what an image represents is its sense.[39] " 'A state of affairs is thinkable': what this means is that we can picture it to ourselves."[40] The image is the mode of knowledge-understanding. Thought constitutes the possibility of knowledge, because it is image: every thought is a logical image of the facts.[41]

The Byzantine understanding of the image, or the possibility of depiction, also presupposes an analogical relation between depictable form and depicted reality. Only here the *analogy* cannot be fully investigated in the correspondence of the analytical-conceptual correlation of both the simple objects of reality and the elements of the image. The *logos* of reality is not a *measurable* correlation of objects that constitutes a state of affairs, and the *logos* of the image is not purely and simply a *form* of depiction, or *rule of measurement*, that corresponds to the structure or correlation of objects in a particular state of affairs. The depiction lies not in a correspondence of correlations (which leaves the question of what the correlated things *are* unanswered) but in a relation between *logoi*: in the relation between the *logos* of things and the *logos* of human beings, in the capacity of the human *logos* to encounter and disclose *logically* the *logos* of reality. The *logos* of reality is the *logos* of the things themselves as "things accomplished" (*pepragmena*). It is a *personal logos*, the *logos* of an *event*, that is to say, the *logos* of the personal energy of God, the "accomplished" *logos* (*pepragmenos logos*), the *logos*-thing (*logos-pragma*). And the *logos* of the image has to do with energy, not measurement. It is the personal-logical reception of the *logos* of reality by humankind. It is the logical mode by which the *logos* of humankind encounters and discloses the *logos* of "things."[42]

Consequently the possibility of depiction is exhausted not in logicality as the bond and structure of the partial, but in logicality as existential fact, as the possibility humanity has of encountering and disclosing, by its own *logos*, the personal *logos* of objective "things." "Through mental imaging (*logismos*) the *logos* arrives at spiritual reality (*ta logika*)," says Maximus the Confessor.[43] If we accept mental imaging as a "logical" expression of the "personal" particularity of things, of their "personal" *logos* or beauty,[44] this is then the *mode* by which the human *logos* encounters the logical nature of things. "When anything is depicted, it is not the nature but the hypostasis that is depicted," declares Theodore the Studite.[45] Apart from its importance as a fundamental theological reference, this statement clearly indicates that the image does not depict the very essence or nature of things. It depicts their hypostasis, the mode by which the nature or essence *is*. And this mode is always logical – the hypostasis is known only as the bearer and disclosure of the *logoi* of nature, of its energies, which are always personal.

In this way the boundaries of knowledge are transposed to the boundaries of personal-logical relation, to the mode of "existence in accordance with *logos*." Such existence cannot be grasped in the measurable or formal structure or correlation of what is partial. It is grasped only in their referentiality – by reference to the hypostasis itself of the partial, which is a *logos*, a disclosure of the *logoi*-energies of the essence. And the knowledge of partial *logoi* is always *logical*. It is the fact of the "encounter" between two personal *logoi*, the fact of personal *relation*. The problem of the knowledge of simple objects, or even of essences, is transposed from the domain of conceptual-conventional marking to the experience of the energies of the essence, which are always personal, because they are personal *logoi*. And since the energies of the essence are personal-logical, they are always invitatory to relation. They invite us to knowledge of the hypostasis, which only becomes known through the energies of the essence. The semantics of this knowledge is the image. The *logos* of the image "signifies" an energy, an invitation, "whence it is called 'beauty.'"[46] Consequently, the image is a language of beauty, not of objectified concepts or correlations. In contrast to the concept, which corresponds to an intellectual grasping of the essence, and also in contrast to logical correlation as an objectified structure which is also exhausted in the act of grasping intellectually, the *logical* beauty of the Image presupposes experiential participation, a universal existential response to the invitation to personal communion.

In other words, the Image, in the patristic view, represents the semantics of a language of which the instrument is not our partial and fragmentary capacity for intellection, but the whole person in its existential integrity, in the unity of mind and heart, *logos* and action, morality and being, in short, in its whole human hypostasis.

§66   *The Greeks and "contemplation"* (theôria)

We might perhaps suppose that this understanding of the image and its cognitive function as logical beauty has its historical and experiential roots in ancient Greek art. There is, of course, an analogy between the Byzantine icon and the function of the image in Greek art, particularly the art of the fifth century B.C. In both Byzantium and classical Greece the image manifests a dynamic-personal approach, a *conscious view* of things.[47] The Greek artist of the fifth century B.C. did not aim at the faithful representation of a physical original or its artificial reproduction. He aimed at the form of representation which permitted an immediate vision of the *logos* or essence of the thing. Accordingly, he effected a kind of *subtraction* of the individual and incidental features of the object represented so as to ascend from the particular to the universal aspects of logical harmony and coherence. Thus "a work of art, an *agalma*, served as a *measure of the beauty of the physical original*, not the reverse."[48] The work of art is an *agalma* [an image rendering honor, from the verb *agallô*, I "glorify" or "exalt"] because it offers us the joy and exultation of a true contemplation of the world. It expresses a vision of the object *along with its logos*, referring its sensory aspects to their *logical* reality, which is more real than their circumstantial impression: art offers us a mode of vision which *interprets* the world.

More generally, sight for the classical Greek was the highest power of a relation which permitted participation in the visible. It is the mode by which the *logos* of things is "recorded" in our rational consciousness – in our mind (*phronêma*).[49] Democritus in particular transfers this cognitive function of sight to language, and sees words in terms of mental vision – he calls the names of the gods "sound-statues."[50] Language is made to function "through names as it does through images."

The Platonic identification of knowledge (*gnôsis*) with contemplation (*theôria*), the vision of truth, does not differ very much from this epistemological understanding of Democritus. We come to know sensory reality through our bodily eyes and intellectual reality, which is real truth, through the eyes of the soul. Our cognitive instrument is sight, that is to say, the complete recapitulation of all our cognitive and experiential powers in one immediate vision, which is simultaneously participation in what is known – sight does not objectify knowledge and what is known in reflective syllogisms.[51] Plato calls true philosophers "those who are fond of contemplating the truth."[52] They do not seek the truth by relying on their own private opinion, which only generates ignorance.[53] They try to *see* the truth by "the eye of the soul"[54] – "for only by this eye is the truth seen."[55] The unit of knowledge is the idea in its primordial etymological sense (from *idein*, "to see"), as a consequence of the dynamic-energetic vision of things.[56] The ascent to the Idea, that is, to the dynamic vision of things, presupposes something much more than simple observation. It presupposes the complete experience of and participation in the beauty of what is beheld. The knowledge of beauty is not a detached experience of only an intellectual or emotional character. On the contrary, it presupposes the coordination of all our cognitive and experiential powers, and this coordination is a dynamic-existential movement towards the beauty of what is beheld, an experiential-internal relationship with it, an *eros* towards the beauty that is beheld. Sight is consequently a cognitive instrument as the experiential starting-point of love, which constitutes supreme knowledge. The "ascending steps" of progress in knowledge are steps of erotic love. They depend on the successive contemplation-vision of the beauty of bodies, and occupations, and laws, and sciences, which leads to erotic *astonishment*, to the unexpected vision of beauty in itself, which is one and eternal, and in which the philosopher remains, "turned towards the open sea of beauty and con-templating it."[57]

The scope of this study precludes a systematic attempt to demonstrate the priority of the universal-experiential *vision* of truth in Aristotelian cognition theory – to demonstrate the wrongness of the opposition which Western interpreters have seen (from the period of the Scholastics to the present day) between Platonic contemplation and Aristotelian logic. I shall simply confine myself to a statement of the view, without trying to prove it, that Platonic contemplation as an epistemological approach finds in Aristotle its natural continuity and development. Aristotelian logic presupposes the right *logos* as the right definition and right structure of concepts and syllogisms, but does not exhaust knowledge in the definition and structure. Knowledge refers to "con-templating logically."[58] It is the soul that encounters the knowable concept – "when the soul becomes absorbed in some concept"[59] – and the soul is the whole human being,[60] which moves towards knowledge by "contemplating and reflecting."[61] Learning by intellection structures, organizes and combines pre-existing items of knowledge – "all teach-ing and all intellectual learning come about from already ex-isting knowledge."[62] And the immediacy of cognitive expe-rience always remains non-demonstrable – "understanding in the case of immediates is always non-demonstrable"[63] – just as there are aspects of knowledge which cannot be put in words – "for there will often be *logoi* for which there is no name."[64] Finally, contemplation is "the most pleasant and best" aspect of knowledge,[65] but it is also its metaphysical goal. The meaning of human life lies in "the contemplation of God," in "contemplating and serving God."[66]

§67   *The language of images. A code for readers*

With the comparative standard or help of the classical

Greek understanding of contemplating (*theôrein*) and imaging (*eikonizein*) (which does not survive into the age of
Neoplatonism) we can now return to the Byzantine understanding of the image. As an initial definition of the difference between the two approaches we could say that again it
centers on the truth of the *person*, that fundamental presupposition of patristic ontology. The Greek Fathers saw in the
language of images a language expressing the beauty of *personal* disclosure. They saw the beauty of the created world
as an image and *logos* of God,[67] as a consequence of the personal energies of the divine essence,[68] as a personal disclosure of the God Logos.[69] And they identified knowledge of
God with the experience of the contemplation of the "noetic
beauty" of the Lord's person.[70]

But how does language function as a cognitive instrument
when it borrows the mystagogic depths of the image in order
to facilitate the possibility of personal disclosure?

We could begin by saying that language functions icono-
logically when it attempts to preserve an interior *logos* by
transcending the autonomy of concepts, that is, when it does
not exhaust the signified in the established use of the signifier. This transcendence of the conventional character of
words is achieved mainly through an oppositional use of established concepts, that is, through a scheme of linguistic-
conceptual contradictions which are nevertheless not *logical* contradictions as well. In the writings of the Byzantine
Church Fathers concepts often conflict with each other and
refute each other to make their transcendence possible, so
that through these conceptual contradictions the transcendence of the conventional objectification of meanings and
the experiential participation of the whole of ourselves (not
just our thought) may be attained in the truth that is expressed. Thus the Church's God is "supraessential essence"
and "mind beyond mind" and "ineffable *logos*." He is the
"nameless name," the "Godhead transcending Godhead,"

the "principle of origin beyond origin," and his name is "incomprehensibly comprehensible." The knowledge of God is "knowledge through ignorance," and "imparticipable participation." Theology is "shapeless shape," "non-symbolical symbol," "formless form," "perfection beyond perfection." It expresses "dissimilar similarities," "grasping all things in a relationless combination." Truth is identified with mystical experience, theology with seeing God, which is perfectionless perfection itself. Theologians who are visionaries of the divine "see invisibly the ineffable beauty of God himself. They hold intangibly, they comprehend uncomprehendingly his formless form, his shapeless shape, and his unconfigured configuration, unvariagatedly variegated in an uncompounded beauty, through a visionless vision."[71]

The simultaneous reference of two contrary concepts to the same signified indicate a concept which cannot be confined to the objective-conventional understanding of one of the two concepts. The common and unified sense to which the pair of contrary concepts refers presupposes the entire noematic content of each concept and simultaneously their mutual noematic negations. Each concept is valid as a complete meaning. That is to say, we must understand the signified as both a noematic thesis and the negation of that noematic thesis. Each term of the conceptual antithesis expresses a likeness with the signified, which in the context of the unified antithetical expression can only be conceived of as *otherness*. And this is precisely the cognitive content of the image. In every image the representation is like the object represented but at the same time in its essence is unlike it. Conversely, in an iconic linguistic expression which uses contrary pairs of concepts both the noematic thesis and its noematic negation have a likeness to the thing signified, a likeness which must be understood not as noematic identity but as *iconic* likeness, which presupposes the essential unlikeness.

In other words, the simultaneous and unified reference of

both the noematic thesis and the noematic negation to the same signified permits a dynamic imaging of the signified truth, that is, the transcendence of the exhaustion of knowledge in the coincidence of the concept with the thing thought, a dynamic transition or "passage" (*diabasis*) to another kind of knowledge, the organ or instrument of which is not the conventional-common linguistic idiom and our conceptual encounter with it, but a much more general experiential-cognitive human capacity. This very much more general human capacity for knowledge is the capacity for a personal relationship with the signified, and it is the image that calls us to the realization of this dynamic relationship.

Let us apply the above analysis to a specific example: the knowledge of God through ignorance or "unknowing." The knowledge of God cannot be restricted to the understandable-conventional concept of knowledge, which is valid for the space of the knowable. In comparison with knowledge of the knowable (*gnosis*), the knowledge of God is inevitable "unknowing" (*agnôsia*) – since it transcends the limits of the knowable – without ceasing to be a kind of knowledge of *dissimilarity* to the knowledge of the knowable. But neither can "unknowing," with respect to God, be identified with the noematic content given to it by the common linguistic idiom, only because cognition of our ignorance of God, in relation to our knowledge of the knowable, is a kind of knowledge without ceasing to be ignorance similar to ignorance of the knowable. Both the concept of knowledge and the concept of ignorance or "unknowing" have a noematic (iconic) similarity to the signified truth of "knowledge through 'unknowing,'" which nevertheless must be understood as essential dissimilarity. Thus the expression "knowledge through 'unknowing'" functions only iconically. It becomes a "sign" or image that "signifies" the possibility of a personal cognition beyond any conventional noematic objectivity established by the common linguistic idiom.

In an analogous way the (imagistic) iconography of the
Byzantines transcends not only a naturalistic (or rather, "pho-
tographic") representation of objective individuality but also
its allegorical-analogical interpretation, and refers ("passes
over") to the prototype,[72] the personal uniqueness of which
can only be represented as unlike likeness and can only be
known as a fact of personal relation. The amazing technical
skill of Byzantine iconography succeeds in transcending the
sensory onticity of physical individuality without resorting
to a schematic-aesthetic impression or idea or to a commem-
orative allegory. When the Byzantine icon depicts specific
persons, it succeeds in representing, or rather, "describing,"
a mode of existence: the transcendence of ontic individuality, the restoration of the person to its existential wholeness,
the unconfused union in the sensory person of created and
uncreated nature, or of created and uncreated energy. The
depiction of the "archetype" (of the person of Christ, or of
the Theotokos, or of the saints) functions as a call to participation in a personal mode of existence, and only as a fact
of dynamic response to this call (that is, with the limits of a
"moral" achievement) is a cognitive "passage" to the archetype possible.

Consequently, in both cases not only in the iconology but
also the iconography of the Byzantines, the truth is "signified" without being exhausted in its "semantic" expression.
The semantics of the image "presents otherness, but otherness as likeness." And it is precisely this dynamic way of expressing an unlike similarity[73] (ever calling us to a personal
and objectively undetermined relation) that encounters the
cognitive category of the image.

§68   *Truth's iconic disclosure and essential hiddenness*

I have suggested that the language of the Christian philosophers of the Byzantine period functions iconologically,

with the intention of preserving an interior *logos* beyond the words, by transcending the objectification of concepts within the framework of the common linguistic idiom. This preserving of the *logos* from the objectification of concepts presupposes the iconic similarity between signifier and signified and at the same time their essential dissimilarity. Consequently we could say that language functions icono-logically when it aims at both the disclosure and the con-cealment of the truths signified (in their iconic disclosure and essential concealment).[74] The following passage from Dionysius the Areopagite is very illuminating on this point:

> Now there are two reasons for proposing types for the type-less, for giving shape to what is without shape. First we lack the ability to raise ourselves up directly to conceptual contemplations. We need our own ascents that come natu-rally to us and can offer us those forms of formless and mar-velous visions that are attainable by us. Second, it is most fitting to the mystical passages of Scripture that the sacred and hidden truth about the celestial intelligences should be concealed through the inexpressible and the sacred and be inaccessible to the many.[75]

According to this passage the iconic function of language *proposes* (offers the possibility of) a dynamic ascent to the vision of "formless" and "shapeless" truths, through the "forms" and "shapes" that are accessible to our cognitive powers. But precisely because the "forms" and "shapes," which are accessible to human language and a conceptual approach to it, refer to truths which transcend the level of language's given semantics, the iconic proposal operates in two ways, or represents two possibilities. It is a "sign" or invitation to engage in a dynamic ascent towards a universal (not merely intellectual) knowledge (vision) of truth. But at the same time it is also an unutterable enigma hiding the truth and making it inaccessible to those who approach it simply through the instrument of language's given semantics.[76]

In other words, the enigmatic aspect of images functions objectively as concealment and personally as revelation of truth. It thus represents not only a very deep respect for truth, which must be preserved from the alienation of objectification, but also a supreme attitude of love for humanity,[77] a desire to protect humanity from the danger of transforming truths into "intellectual idols." The sacred enigmatic aspect of images refuses to present truth as an object of the intellect,[78] since this would have implied a denial of truth, the truth of the personal God, of the human person, and of the personal dimension of the world. The language of images conceals the truth like a dynamic leaven in the mystagogic space of personal relation and ecclesiastical communion. Access to the truth through the language of images presupposes a "moral" achievement – an ascetic transcendence of the ego, a denial of the individual's intellectual or emotional self-sufficiency, an entry into the space of loving self-offering, that is, of personal relation and communion.

§69   *The image as a category of sensory, logical and intellectual beauty*

The cognitive function of the image may also be approached through Maximus the Confessor's distinction between three levels of knowledge. These three levels are the senses, *logos* and mind. Each represents a human cognitive power together with a corresponding domain of knowledge or mode of regarding reality.

The sense refers knowledge to the immediacy of objective beings, to their material hypostasis, their form or shape, which differentiates every ontic individuality. They also refer to the experience of the natural relations which bind together the objects constituting the reality of the word and form the world's facts. Consequently, sense perception is the human cognitive power to "perceive objects in their form as a whole."[79] This simultaneous perception of the formal differentiation of beings arises from the cognitive power made available to us by the senses, the power to distinguish "the difference of the subject."[80] The formal differentiation of every ontic individuality is a differentiation made through the senses which constitutes the starting-point of knowledge. The knowledge of beings "impressed formally in the senses by the shapes of sensory things"[81] goes on to find the measure or standard of distinguishing difference in the *logos*.[82] But the fundamental cognitive function of the senses, the pre-*logos* cognitive approach to sensory forms and shapes which makes possible our initial access "to the practical" (reality as a whole), is realized through the *phantasia*, or imagination,[83] (here meaning the sensory experience of phenomena).[84]

The *logos* is the mode or means and potentiality for personal knowledge, the link between sensory experience and the generalization of knowledge which is represented by the "mind." The forms and types of sensory things are conveyed to the mind as *logoi*,[85] thanks to our "rational faculty," our ability to order the information of the senses "logically," to transform sensory experience into "scientific" knowledge.[86] Thus the competency of the *logos* is identified both with "human intelligence,"[87] or the operation of thoughts (*logismoi*),[88] and with "the natural faculty of the rational appetite which is also called the will of the intellectual soul."[89] The rational will reveals the wholeness of the operation of the *logos*, which is not exhausted simply in the capacity for syllogistic reasoning. Our rational power weaves together our faculties of cognition and will, and therefore becomes the starting-point of erotic ecstasy, which constitutes supreme knowledge.[90] Before being made whole in the "movement" of the "power of love,"[91] rational knowledge is restricted to "natural" or "Gnostic contemplation," "since it lies between types and truth."[92] It represents the power of transcending conventional "types," but cannot approach truth itself. The knowledge "which lies only in the *logos* and in conceptions"[93] is necessarily "relative." It emerges "from the analogy of beings,"[94] "from that which is relative to something" (*pros ti*), and is inseparable from "the things that are understood in connection with each other."[95] It corresponds to the natural necessity for a practical cognitive intentionality, "by which our present life is governed."[96]

Finally, the mind (*nous*) is "the soul's contemplative organ,"[97] its power of contemplation or vision of truth. The vision of truth is an experiential knowledge: knowledge "in the true and proper sense is found only in experience through an operation apart from *logos* and concepts."[98] This no longer concerns sensory experience, the experience of sensible types and forms. It concerns the "sensing" of the mind, which transcends not only the experience of the bodily senses but also the cognitive experience of the *logos* – "the experience of the reality itself puts an end to the *logos* about it."[99] It is a cognitive power incomparably more general even than thoughts and concepts. It is the knowledge that is brought by the general existential fact of relation, that is, by participation – "participation in what is known, which is manifested after every act of intellection."[100] We must refer the cognitive immediacy of participation, which transcends every conceptual objectivity, exclusively to the space of personal disclosure and communion, to personal truth which is unique, dissimilar and unrepeatable, because "it does not belong to anything relative, for it does not possess anything at all which is to be understood in connection with something else."[101] Personal relation or participation is a knowledge that is attained dynamically – "by subtracting actively (*kat' energeian*) the knowledge that lies in the *logos* and in concepts"[102] – and therefore is never possessed definitively, so that it can be transformed into an objective cognitive category, but is "ceaselessly active ... furnishing the whole sense perception of what is known by participation."[103]

Consequently the mind or *nous*, as the bearer of the personal possibilities of participation in truth, is "a power that unifies us with God,"[104] "through which in an unknowable and indemonstrable way we are united with God in a union that transcends intellection."[105]

We may say now that the cognitive function of the image is realized dynamically on all three levels of knowledge (sensation, *logos* and mind) defined by Maximus. The "semantics" of the image, through types and forms, "ascend to the mind from the senses, communicating to it the things that pertain to the senses, and descend to them from the mind, submitting to the senses what pertains to the mind." In the space of the Orthodox Greek East, the cognitive category of the image, which is a category of sensible, rational and intellectual beauty, refers to "active" knowledge, to that personal, dynamic relation and participation that is "in ceaseless operation." "In everything depicted," says Theodore the Studite, "it is not the nature but the hypostasis that is depicted." Natures or essences are not depicted. They are defined in intellectual categories which necessarily exhaust their cognitive content within their boundaries. They presuppose the ontology of ontic categories or the phenomenicity of ontic individualities. The image, however, as a category of sensible, rational and intellectual beauty, or of universal-experiential knowledge "putting a stop through experience to the *logos* about things," refers to persons or hypostases which are objectively dissimilar and unrepeatable ("are not towards anything") and are known only by a dynamic, active and ceaseless knowledge.

Chapter Three

On Analogy and Hierarchy

§70   *The way of knowledge by analogy*

By seeing knowledge as an existential problem and by linking the possibility of knowledge with the dynamics of relation
as a "mode of existence," we are led to the notion of hierarchy, which is the way and mode of articulating relation (the
transmission and appropriation of knowledge), the reference
of the power of cognition to the successive stages or levels of
humanity's existential authenticity or spiritual perfection.

(a)   *Analogy in Plato*
The notion of hierarchy interprets the mode by which the
Christian East understood the analogical way of knowledge
or analogical participation in knowledge. The analogical possibility of knowledge has, of course, its starting-point in its
intellectual formulation by Plato.[1] In Plato's view every being participates "proportionately" (*ana ton logon*) in its Idea,
and every Idea is "the offspring of the good, which the good
begot to stand in proportion (*analogon*) with itself."[2] The *logos* represents the possibility of cognitive participation in the
truth of being through the analogy of beings and Ideas (the
being possesses "the same *logos*" as its Idea). Consequently,
it also represents the possibility of participation in the good
through the analogy of Ideas and the good. Access to the
analogy of beings and ideas becomes easier with every cre-

ative act. Every creative act discloses (brings to light) the common *logos* of Idea and thing made. It presupposes the "vision" of the Idea of the thing that is made, while the Idea itself remains "beyond" any creative possibility:

> And are we not also in the habit of saying that the craftsman who produces either of them fixes his eyes on the idea or the form, and so makes in the one case the couches and in other the tables that we use, and similarly of other things? For surely no craftsman makes the idea itself. How could he?[3]

By recognizing the *logos* of beings we "contemplate" the truth of the Ideas and participate analogically in the space of incorruptible and eternal truths. This contemplation is participation in the good, because the good is "the reality that gives the truth to the objects of knowledge and the power of knowing to the knower."[4] The good is participated "analogically" through the contemplation of the Ideas or essences, because it is the cause both of the essences and their contemplation, since it is "beyond essence"[5] – "an inconceivable beauty." The truth and its proportionate (*ana ton logon*) knowledge and "essential" manifestations are "products" of the good and means of analogical participation in the good.

The instrument or mode by which knowledge-contemplation and participation are attained is the mind (*nous*), and it is evident that here the mind is not confined simply to its intellectual capability but represents the soul's general power of cognition.[6] The mind participates in the good in a manner analogous to that in which the faculty of sight participates in the vision of the sun. The vision of the sun is not the same thing as the sun itself, but is a "most sunlike" perception. "And the sun is not vision but the cause of vision."[7] Thus the mind is not the good but "goodlike," being the supreme power of "vision of the good, and the good is not mind but the cause of mind."

The analogy that links the "most sunlike" faculty of sight

with the sun and the "goodlike" mind with the good is the power of cognitive "participation," a power which is given and yet is also a dynamic possibility. Analogy represents the *logos* of the fitness of the eyes to receive light or the fitness of the mind to recognize the good.

> You are aware, I said, that when the eyes are no longer turned upon objects upon whose colors the light of day falls but that of the dim luminaries of night, their edge is blunted and they appear almost blind, as if pure vision did not dwell in them. – Yes, indeed, he said. – But when, I take it, they are directed upon objects illumined by the sun, they see clearly, and vision appears to reside in these same eyes. – Certainly. – Apply this comparison to the soul also in this way. When it is firmly fixed on the domain where truth and reality shine resplendent it apprehends and knows them and appears to possess mind, but when it inclines to that region which is mingled with darkness, the world of becoming and passing away, it opines only and is blunted, and it shifts its opinions hither and thither and now seems as if it lacked mind.[8]

Plato's understanding of analogy, then, is not a comparison of quantities or dimensions. Nor is it the proportionality of arithmetical relations or measurable aspects of similarity. Analogy is an iconic relation, a relation between image and that which is depicted, and the knowledge of this relation is a dynamic fact which presupposes the mind's aptitude for cognition and the mind's participation in that which is depicted through its image.

In other words, analogy, as an iconic relation, presupposes the *logos* more generally as a cognitive power of participation, not as an apodictic proof of measurable-quantifiable relations. The classic example of analogy in the *Gorgias* ("sophistic is to legislation what beautification is to gymnastics, and rhetoric to justice what cookery is to medicine"[9]) presupposes precisely the experience of the identity of the *logoi*, the experiential knowledge of these analogous human activities. Plato seems to have had a clear understanding of the dangers of self-deception when analogical relations are absolutized and used as apodictic proofs. That is why he notes in the *Sophist*: "A cautious man should above all be on his guard against resemblances; they are a very slippery sort of thing."[10]

(b)   *Analogy in Aristotle*

The formal statement, however, of an analogical relation (to have an analogy to something = to have the same *logos*) also applies to purely measurable-quantifiable relations. Perhaps the actual origin of analogy is fundamentally mathematical rather than a comparison of qualitative similarities. At any rate, in Plato's time the Greeks were aware of the mathematical concept of analogy – the relation $a : b = c : d$ (e.g., $2 : 3 = 4 : 6$) and the derivatives of this relation.[11] The critical problem for philosophy is the transfer of mathematical analogy, as an epistemological and apodictic principle, to the field of the investigation of truth. First Aristotle transferred the mathematical concept of analogy to the space of ethics, to prove that "the just is proportional" and "the unjust is what violates proportion."[12] He defines analogy not as (qualitative) identity of *logoi* as principles, but as (quantitative) *equality* of *logoi* as ratios,[13] because only by quantitative-measurable analogy can the distribution of the just be maintained within the context of human society.

This need for analogical balance leads Aristotle to introduce into the space of ethics the concept of the *tertium comparationis*, an objective measure for the qualitative balancing and objective measuring of the work produced by every member of the community and the proportional (or "analogical") distribution of the just. The specific measure of comparison in the space of social exchange is the *nomisma* (money). The *nomisma* balances and measures the product of work, whether the shoes made by the shoemaker or the house built by the builder.[14] Money is a conventional measure of comparison: "money has become by convention a sort of representative of demand; and this is why it has the name 'money' (*nomisma*) – because it exists not by nature but by law (*nomos*)."[15] It nevertheless represents the objective power of the practical application of proportional equality. The work that the builder offers to the shoemaker must be proportional to the work which the shoemaker offers to the builder:

> Now proportionate return is secured by cross-conjunction. Let *a* be a builder, *b* a shoemaker, *c* a house, *d* a shoe. The builder, then, must get from the shoemaker the latter's work, and must himself give him in return his own.[16]

This proportionate return is effected by the common reference of the work of both of them to the objective measure of money, which is the "third of the comparison" of shoes to houses – the possibility of balancing shoes and houses proportionately. In the relation $a : b = c : d$, the farmer's recompense in money (a) and the work produced by the farmer (c) must be proportionate to the recompense received by the shoemaker (b) and the work he has produced (d) – whereby "a farmer is a, food c, a shoemaker b, his product equated to d ... so that as farmer is to shoemaker, the amount of the shoemaker's work is to that of the farmer's work."[17]

Besides his transfer of mathematical analogy to the field of ethics, however, Aristotle does not ignore the analogy of the image. His best discussion of this is in the *Poetics*, where he offers an interpretation of poetic metaphor:

> Metaphor consists in giving the thing a name that belongs to something else .... That from analogy is possible whenever there are four terms so related that the second is to the first, as the fourth to the third; for one may then put the fourth in place of the second, and the second in place of the fourth. Now and then, too, they qualify the metaphor by

adding on to it that to which the word it supplants is relative. Thus a cup is in relation to Dionysus what a shield is to
Ares. The cup accordingly will be described as the "shield
of Dionysus" and the shield as the "cup of Ares." Or to take
another instance: as old age is to life, so is evening to day.
One will accordingly describe evening as the "old age of
the day" – or by the Empedoclean equivalent; and old age
as the "evening or "sunset of life."[18]

So in poetic metaphor the relation $a : b : = c : d$ is applicable,
or in the specific example, life : old age = day : evening. The
relationship of old age to life is analogous to the relationship
of evening to day. The analogy permits the poetic metaphor,
that is to say, it permits the relationship $b : c = a : d$. We can
thus speak proportionately or analogously (*kata logon*) of
the old age of the day or the evening of life.

The analogy of poetic metaphor was used later by the scholastic theologians of the Middle Ages, but in their case to
demonstrate iconic analogy (the "externa analogia proportionalitatis impropriae") as the transfer ("translatio") of iconic
relation to a reciprocal correspondence of literal meanings.[19]
A characteristic example of this kind of metaphor is Paul's
speaking of the Church as the body of Christ (1 Cor 12:12).
As the body is one, but with many members, so the members
of the ecclesial community constitute a unified whole, and
this whole is Christ. The analogous relationship of body and
members, ecclesial community and members, permits the
transference ("translatio"-*metaphora*) of the image ("imago"-
sôma) to the concept ("notio"-*Ekklêsia*), the reciprocal literal
correspondence of image and concept, by a common reference to the members, which are the "third of the comparison"
("tertium comparationis") between body and Church.

(c)   *Analogia entis*
The most important application of the relationship of analogy, with regard to historical consequences, was that which

was undertaken in the field of ontology. This was the analogical relation between beings and Being, or beings and essence, known in the Middle Ages as "analogia entis."

The origins of this lie again in Aristotle. He began with the statement: "There are many ways in which a thing may be said to 'be,' but they are related to one central point, one definite kind of thing, and are not homonymous."[20] To define being we use the verb "is" (*esti*), which affirms onticity, or participation in Being – and we use it to define being "in many ways": as quality, quantity, place, time, relation.[21] We say the horse *is* white, the horse *is* two meters tall, the horse *is* here, etc. It is evident that in defining the horse "in many ways" we always use the verb "is" *analogically* in relation to a principle: the horse *is* white in analogous relation to whiteness as such; the tree is tall in analogous relation to tallness as such. Consequently, the knowledge we have of the onticity of a specific horse or of a specific tree is analogous.[22] It relies on the analogy of its attributes – the analogy of quality, quantity, place, time and relation ("analogia attributionis," as the Scholastics were to call it).

But even if we use the verb "is" to define "in many ways," the onticity of the subject on the basis of the analogy of its attributes, the primary determination of the onticity of being is still always made with reference "to one thing," that is, with reference to what the specific subject "is." We say primarily that this *is* a horse and this *is* a tree. We define the specific subject by reference to the *one* horse and the *one* tree, that is, to the *essence* of horse and the *essence* of tree: "While 'being' has all these senses, obviously that which is primarily is the 'what,' which indicates the essence of the thing"[23] – "the essence of each thing is one."[24] And the reference of the specific subject to the "first one," that is, to the essence, is also analogous. Every specific subject participates "according to the same *logos*" in the common essence. It has the same *logos* as the essence – "for it is in virtue of the *logos* of the essence that the others are said to be … for all will be found to contain the *logos* of the essence."[25]

It is evident that determining the subject not only on the basis of the analogy of attributes but also with reference to the *logos* of its essence exhausts analogous relation as a possibility of defining or knowing being. Aristotle uses the concept of analogy to safeguard the unity of the subject. He does not extend analogy to mean a relation of ontological identity, the participation of beings in Being as such. The relation of beings to Being is for Aristotle a relation of cause and effect – a relation of transition from potential being (*dynamei on*) to actual being (*energeiai on*), a relation of moved and mover ("whence comes movement")[26] – not a relation of analogical participation in Being. The regressive sequence of effect and cause, moved and mover, refers the Being-as-such of nature to a principle which transcends nature, to the "first unmoved mover,"[27] "which moves without being moved, being eternal, essence and actuality."[28]

The Scholastics were the first to use the analogical relation of beings and Being to define Being in itself, or God, the "first mover," the transcendent First Cause of Being. Every being participates in Being. It is an "ens per participationem," whereas God, the "first and ultimate" being, the "eternal and best," does not participate in Being but constitutes Being in itself, "ens per essentiam," self-existence, in analogy to which whatever is, *is*.

The relation of beings to the Being-as-such of nature, and the relation of the Being-as-such of nature to God, the Cause of Being, can, in the scholastic view, lead to the analogical knowledge of God, since relation itself is analogous, with only one unknown term, namely, God. The Being-as-such of nature occupies the position of the "third of the comparison" between beings and God. The Scholastics used as their model the mathematical analogy $a : b = c : d$ ($2 : 3 = 4 : 6$), in which when one term is unknown it can be defined by the productive combination of the remaining three. If the unknown term is d, we have the relation $a : b = c : x$ ($2 : 3 = 4 : x$, $2.x = 3.4$, $x = 3.4/2 = 6$).[29]

Thus the relation between beings and Being, and between Being and God, may be expressed according to the Scholastics with the precision of mathematical analogy: beings: Being $=$ Being $: x$, where x represents the Cause of Being, namely, God. In this case, the analogical participation of beings in Being is the key for understanding the analogical participation of the Being of beings in its divine Cause, and God, the Cause of Being, is defined *analogously* in relation to *Being*, the cause of beings.

We have seen that the participation of beings in Being was defined by Aristotle as the subject's analogical reference to its essence, and as the analogy of the attributes of the subject to the attributes of Being-as-such.

In the former case, the subject "is spoken of" (is known) according to the *logos* of its essence. The participation of the subject in Being is defined as an *analogical* participation in its essence. On the basis of this definition of the relation between subject and essence, we can say by analogy that in God this relation is a relation of identity: the subject that participates in the essence is the essence itself. The Being of God is God himself, and the essence of God is his very existence.[30]

In the latter case, the subject "is spoken of" (is known) "in many ways," on the basis of the analogy of its attributes to the attributes of Being-as-such (quality, quantity, place, time and relation). The analogical participation of the subject in the attributes of Being-as-such necessarily exhausts the knowledge of Being within the limits of experience in the world – since the experience of quality and quantity, of place, time and measurable relation always refers to the sensory reality of the world. It is nevertheless possible for us to recognize in beings that are partial and incomplete certain

attributes which transcend the Aristotelian categories of being. These attributes can, through an intellectual ascent to the
absolute ("regressus in infinitum"), disclose the perfections
of Being. That is to say, they can make known to us by analogy the transcendent attributes of God.[31] Thomas Aquinas
and Albert the Great summarized these attributes, which can
be the foundation of a transcendent analogy, in the predicates: "unum, verum, bonum, res, aliquid" (one, true, good,
thing, something).[32] Being in itself is real, a reality ("res").
By transcending the partial and incomplete, it is always one
("unum"). In contrast with the other beings, it is something
("aliquid"). With regard to the knowledge we have of it, it is
true ("verum"). And with regard to its willed intentionality,
it is good ("bonum"). The Scholastics called these five predicates of being "transcendentals" ("transcendentalia"). Their
reference to God constitutes not an experiential analogy, but
a *transcendent* analogy, an intellectual extension ("extensio")
of these predicates beyond the limits of experience in the
world, in the space of the transcendent absolute.[33] Thus we
can come to know the attributes of God's essence, namely,
unity, goodness, truth, supreme onticity and supreme otherness, with the aid of the intellect ("per lumen intellectus"),[34]
through the analogical elevation of the perfections of beings
to the absolute and transcendent perfection of God, which is
the Cause of every perfection.[35]

§71   *Scholastic analogy as theological epistemology*

We can draw two basic conclusions from this brief account
of scholastic teaching on analogy as an epistemological path
and method.

1. The knowledge of God by analogy, as established by the
Scholastics, is confined to an intellectual approach to the essence of God, which is a transcendent but nevertheless ontic
essence – a transcendent object ("objectum") of the intel-

lect.[36] Scholastic analogy ignores the *personal* existence of God, the Triad of the divine persons, the mode of existence of the divine essence, which is personal. They thus introduce into the field of Christian theology not only the "poverty" of Judaic monotheism, but a conception of God which is incomparably inferior. For the personal God of biblical revelation and ecclesiastical experience they substitute the impersonal conception of a transcendent "object," a logically necessary absolute cause and origin of beings.[37]

This transcendent "object" is accessible only through the subject's ability to rationalize. It is understood solely in the context of the antithesis between the absolute and the relative, the infinite and the finite. God is separated from the world by the sharpest possible contrast between the transcendent and the immanent, the empirically existent and the empirically non-existent, sensible reality and intellectual conception.

Consequently, the analogy of the Scholastics established an ontology of exclusively ontic categories. It left the existential problem untouched, the problem of the mode of existence of God, humanity and the world. It accepted existence *a priori* as logically determined. Matter remained ontologically unexplained, and the origin or principle of what exists was transferred to the necessity of the things that determined essence, not to the freedom of the person, not to triadic love as the self-determination of the mode of existence.

2. Scholastic analogy ignored the personal mode of existence, not only as an ontological reality but also as a means of cognition. It ignored the cognitive power of personal relation, the disclosure – the unmediated knowledge – of the person through the energies of the essence, which are always personal. It ignored the immediacy and universality of the knowledge, beyond any conceptual signification that accompanies erotic "astonishment," the unexpected revelatory cognition of personal uniqueness and dissimilarity that arises in the relationship of love.

Thus for the Scholastics even the knowledge of God was not a universal (rather than just intellectual) cognitive experience of the revelatory disclosure of the *person* of God within the limits of a dynamic interpersonal relationship between God and humanity. For them it was not the *eros* of God for humanity and humanity for God that reveals unutterably and discloses indefinably the uniqueness and dissimilarity of the mystery of personal existence. But it was the human intellect ("la raison seule"[38]) which objectifies God's existence as the logical necessity of an impersonal principle and cause of the world.

Consequently, the Scholastics established an epistemology that exhausted the possibility of cognition in the conventional categories of objective syllogisms and restricted the truth to the coincidence of the concept with the object of thought, or opened up the way to a mysticism of essence, a *contemplation* of an impersonal absolute, which precisely because it is impersonal permits no solution other than pantheism or agnosticism.[39]

§72   *The analogy of dissimilar similarities*

If Western theology preferred the Aristotelian concept of analogy as a guiding principle, Byzantine theologians were more inclined towards Plato when seeking to express the Church's experience of knowledge. They saw analogy as a cognitive method for manifesting experiential participation in truth, as the *logos* of the fitness of the soul's "eyes" for receiving the "light" of truth.

In contrast, then, with the scholastic understanding of analogy, which is no more than the intellectual ascent from relative predicates to absolute ones, and from partial predicates to universal ones, analogy for the Byzantines refers, as a cognitive method, to the possibility that existence can be led by the call to personal relation to the actual realization of the relation. That is to say, it refers to the analogical grades of the power of existence to participate wholly (not only intellectually) in truth.

A revealing example of the difference between the two approaches is the distinction between analogy, in the sense of a comparison of similarities, and the idea of analogical similarities as dissimilarities. Analogy as an intellectual ascent from partial to universal and from relative to absolute predicates is necessarily an analogy of similarities. It presupposes "the same *logos*" (or "ratio") of relative and absolute, partial and universal. By contrast, analogy as a possibility of ascent from the partial call-to-personal-relation to the universality of knowledge promised by the actualization of that relation is based on the transcendence of objective similarities, on a cognitive approach to similarities as dissimilarities – "taking the similarities as dissimilarities," as Dionysius says.[40]

In the latter approach, analogy functions qualitatively-iconically, not quantitatively-measurably. The quantitative-measurable version of analogy can be used to compare essences, that is, common objective attributes, while iconic analogy, which presupposes the understanding of similarities as dissimilarities, aims at a dynamic cognitive transition from the objective attributes of the essence to personal otherness, to the mode of existence, to the uniqueness and dissimilarity of personal existence. Personal existence cannot be known definitively through analogical similarities, since its "definition" is its otherness, its unique, dissimilar and unrepeatable character. Personal otherness can be marked (that is, "depicted" iconically) by analogical similarities, but only by similarities which must be understood as dissimilarities. If we try to define personal existence, together with personal energies and the effects of personal energies (the *pragmata-pepragmena*, or "things" and deeds of the person), simply by analogical similarities, it shows that we are unaware of personal otherness, that we are taking ignorance for knowledge.

As a cognitive method, the analogy of dissimilar similarities represents an epistemology at the opposite pole to objective demonstrative proof. It represents the refusal of the Greek Fathers to objectify knowledge, to subject it wholly to utilitarian ends. It implies the strongest possible defense of the truth of the person, of the limitless limits of knowledge which personal otherness reveals.[41]

Analogical similarities have a cognitive value only because they mark and depict the dissimilarity and uniqueness of persons and "things" as this is revealed in the dynamic fact of personal relation. Analogical similarities therefore have a cognitive value only when they mark the possibility of personal relation, when they express the relation and lead to the relation. But they are empty intellectual predicates when they are without the cognitive experience of personal relation.

The analogy of dissimilar similarities also helps to clarify the radical difference between the apophaticism of the Greek theologians and the negative theology of the Western Scholastics. Negative theology (*theologia negativa*) compares objective dissimilarities, just as cataphatic theology (*theologia affirmativa*) compares objective similarities. In both cases the purpose is the comparison of essences and ontic attributes. Of course, the similarities do not constitute identity. They therefore presuppose a percentage of given dissimilarities, which permits cognition of the relative character of knowledge. Nor do the dissimilarities constitute absolute otherness. They therefore presuppose a percentage of given similarities, which does not permit a complete agnosticism. The Fourth Lateran Council (1215) adopted the view that no significant likeness could be posited between the Creator and creature without presupposing an even greater unlikeness ("quia inter creatorem et creaturam non potest similitudo notari, quin inter eos maior sit dissimilitudo notanda"[42]). It is evident that even in this statement dissimilarity does not refer to the otherness of the personal mode of existence. Dissimilarity coexists with similarity in a quantifiable-measurable relation. The analogy of similarities, which presupposes at the same time even greater dissimilarities, does not cease to represent objective predicates, or to constitute a quantitative comparison of objectified magnitudes.

By contrast the analogy of dissimilar similarities, by which I mean the apophaticism of the Byzantine theologians, is based not on the quantitative comparison of objective dissimilarities, permitting also a percentage of similarities, but on taking the objective similarities themselves as real dissimilarities. That is to say, it refers the dissimilarity to the otherness of the personal mode of existence, to the priority which existence has in relation to the understanding of objective essences. This means that for the analogy of dissimilar similarities to function as a cognitive method, a dynamic transformation is presupposed of objective predicates into experiences of personal cognition, a transition from the cognitive level of intellectual categories to the space of the universal knowledge provided by the experience of personal knowledge.[43] This dynamic transition is a possible fact which when accomplished becomes a "moral" achievement. It is a self-transcendence of the natural individuality and objective demands of the individual intellect, an entry into the space of personal relation,[44] an ascent to a personal mode of existence and the completeness of knowledge which this mode reveals.[45]

This means that the epistemology of the Byzantine theologians is not just another method of cognition, better or worse, more appropriate or less appropriate than the way of affirmation and the way of negation. It is a dynamically possible "moral" fact, a cognitive potentiality that accompanies the dynamic restoration of humanity to its existential authenticity, its progressive acquisition of the personal completeness of existence.[46] The epistemology of the Eastern theologians presupposes "the transformation of the understanding,"[47] the unification of the fragmented cognitive human faculties (the unit of mind and heart, of *logos* and action, of morality and being), the single cognitive "contemplation" which is attained within the dynamic limits of ascetic self-transcendence and loving-erotic ecstasy and self-offering.[48]

Thus treating similarities as dissimilarities presupposes, as a cognitive method, the moral-dynamic character of knowledge, the linking of knowledge with the stages of humanity's existential perfection[49] (the non-alienation of the relations which form the existential fact of subjectivity and make it known). Ultimately, it presupposes a hierarchical ordering of the personal powers of knowledge, which are always analogous to the hierarchical ordering of the stages of existential perfection. It signifies analogy as a *hierarchy* of cognitive-existential powers and perfections.

§73 *Hierarchy as teletarchy, as the ordered perfection of the transmission of knowledge*

The notion of analogy as hierarchy was interpreted definitively in the Areopagitical writings of the fifth century. Much work has been done by scholars to identify the Platonic and Neoplatonic sources used by the author.[50] But from a systematic point of view the idea of hierarchy, as analyzed in the Areopagitical writings, finds its proper place in Byzantine theology, where it has been integrated into the whole structure of the Church's teaching.

Analogy as hierarchy – knowledge as a power analogous to the stages of existential perfection, or the transcendence of alienation – does not represent in the Areopagitical writings an intellectual-methodological scheme for grading the quantitative differentiations of knowledge, but articulates an existential reality with knowledge as an experiential-universal participation in this reality. The moment we recognize that knowledge transcends a static-intellectual understanding of objectively signified essences and refers to a dynamic-universal cognition of the otherness of persons and "things" (the personal mode of existence and the effects of the personal energy), we are bound to accept a hierarchical ordering of knowledge, a hierarchical order of the powers, not the quantitative differences, of knowledge.

But this hierarchical ordering is not simply a graded arrangement of the subjective powers of knowledge on analogy with the stages of existential perfection. It is at the same time also the reality of a universal mode of transmitting knowledge, a comprehensive "sacred order" within whose bounds the transmission and every personal existence is "raised up in proportion" (*analogôs*) "to the imitation of God"[51] (the imitation of the truly existent). The "imitation of God" is the way and the goal of all knowledge, the practical mode and unperfectable perfection of knowledge. For if knowledge is not exhausted in the intellectual marking of objective essences, but refers to the dynamic-universal cognition of the otherness of persons and "things," and if this cognition is only achieved in the fact of a personal-loving relation, then the imitation of the triadic mode of divine existence – the fullness of personal-loving communion, the existential model of non-estranged relations – is pre-eminently the *praxis* that conveys knowledge.

So the entire existential and cognitive hierarchy is an order and energy which ascends dynamically "to the imitation of God." It is a "sacred arrangement, an image of the divine beauty,"[52] a disclosure of the beauty of the triadic communion. The "beauty befitting God" is "simple," "good" and moreover "teletarchic," which means "transmitting to each, according to their merit, a share of his own light."[53] This teletarchic transmission of knowledge is accomplished by means of the mode of existence of its bearers, who are "clear and spotless mirrors, receptive of the divine ray of primordial light. On the one hand they are filled in a sacred manner with the radiance that is granted to them, on the other, they generously illuminate others in succession in accordance with the divine laws."[54]

Therefore hierarchy, as mode by which knowledge is transmitted, constitutes a universal and unifying communion and relation, a united teletarchy of the reciprocal transmission of knowledge, the beauty of an entire "mode of existence," reflecting the deiformity of the loving communion of the Trinity: "Therefore when one speaks of hierarchy, one means in general a certain sacred arrangement, an image of the divine beauty, which performs the mysteries of its own illumination in an ordered way and with hierarchical knowledge, and is assimilated, so far as permitted, to its own source."[55]

The beginning and end of this hierarchical order, in accordance with which knowledge is dynamically activated, is God. He activates the dynamic realization of knowledge as "assimilation to" and "union with" "his own most divine beauty."[56] And those who participate in this teletarchic unity are "co-workers with God," who cooperate with the hierarchically accomplished divine energy and disclose "the divine energy manifested in them so far as possible."[57]

The cooperation of "those who have been allotted a share of hierarchy" follows the divine order of loving-kenotic communion and beauty. That is to say, it is actualized as a dual dynamic impulse. The transmission of knowledge is effected as love and the reception of knowledge as humility, "because it belongs to the order of hierarchy for some to be purified and others to purify, for some to be illuminated and others to illuminate, for some to be perfected and others to bring about perfection."[58] The transmission of knowledge constitutes purification and illumination and perfection, that is, "mystagogy,"[59] an energy of love that perfects those who are loved. And the reception of knowledge is also a dynamic readiness to respond to this work of "mystagogic" love. It is a self-emptying of any individualistic self-sufficiency, an act of humility. The cognitive path of hierarchy is summarized in these two basic Christian "virtues," which are not conventional moral predicates, but existential categories, dynamic disclosures of a mode of existence which is "according to nature."

§74   *The hierarchic unity of truth*

Finally, the author of the Areopagitical writings sees the whole of creation as participating in the "sacred order" and "universal arrangement" of deisimilar hierarchy. He sees all beings as participating in the hierarchic unity of communion with the Godhead, in proportion, or analogously, to the mode of existence which each one embodies.[60] The analogical gradation of modes of existence is also triadic. Inanimate beings participate in the dynamically accomplished divine energy, which constitutes creation, because they participate in the Being which God provides. Living beings participate in life, which is accomplished dynamically as a gift of the divine life-giving power and energy. And rational and intellectual beings participate in the personally-energetically manifested divine wisdom, dynamically summarizing the whole hierarchic arrangement of the world in the immediacy and unity of personal relation between created and uncreated.[61]

This theory of the whole world as a uniform hierarchy and thearchic arrangement represents a unified approach to the problem of knowledge, the problem of Being, and the problem of the end or goal of existence – what today we call epistemology, ontology and ethics. It would require a separate study to show how this unified epistemological-ethical approach is implemented in practice in the organization and structure of ecclesiastical life – in the symbolism of worship, the structure of the administrative hierarchy, the "canonical" presuppositions of the regulation of Church life, and the cosmological synthesis expressed by Church architecture and the iconographic schemes within them.

It would also require a separate study to show how the idea of hierarchy is founded on the presuppositions of a comprehensive mode of life, that is to say, a culture at the opposite pole to the culture of analogical-quantitative relations. The difference between Byzantium and the West is a difference between two comprehensive epistemological-ethical views of the world, humanity and God, views which find their specific cultural expression in the organization and structures of public life, and in art, politics, economics and technology. Finally, this difference could be summarized in the contrast between the objective-quantitative understanding of analogy and the understanding of analogy as hierarchy – a difference between two cultures, whose consequences for human life we are only just beginning to evaluate.

Also worth a separate study is how the same idea of hierarchy interprets the Greek East's understanding of the Church's Tradition. In the Orthodox view Tradition functions as a dynamic, hierarchic teletarchy and progression. It follows the divine order of a loving-kenotic communion and beauty. That is to say, it is expressed as a dual dynamic impulse: the transmission of experience, knowledge and virtue, which is handed on as a dynamic expression of love, and comes to be accepted as a humble readiness to participate in and cooperate with the hierarchically accomplished teletarchic unity of truth.

PART FOUR

The Fall and Nothingness

Chapter One

Nothingness as "Outside" Personal Relation

§75   *Nothingness as the distantiality of ontic individuality*

In the course of the preceding chapters, we have examined the main lines of an ontology summarizing the truth of Being, or the truth of every existent and existential reality, in the light of the relation between a personal God and the human person. This relation presupposes the ecstatic character of personal existence. That is to say, it presupposes the recapitulation and self-transcendence of essence or nature in the fact of personal otherness, the disclosure of the essence only through the essence's *energies*, which are always personal. The person is the bearer of the essence's energies, which means that the essence's mode of existence is personal otherness. It is persons and the "things-deeds" of persons, the effects of the essence's energies, which are always personal. The knowledge of persons and "things" represents a personal potentiality. It is possible only through the fact of relation, of an empirical-universal participation in the personal energies or in the effects of the personal energies, which is participation in the *logos* of the personal otherness of "things." The energies make participation-relation possible as existential self-transcendence, loving self-offering, and erotic communion, which is why eros is the fullness of a non-alienated relation, the fulfillment of the potentialities of

223

the knowledge of persons and things. The erotic knowledge of things reveals the world as personal energy: the sum total of the things-deeds of the divine personal energy constitutes the world. And the world is a dynamically activated erotic summons of God to communion and relation.

Relation, however, as ecstatic self-transcendence, constitutes an existential potentiality, not a given existential necessity. The potentiality also implies the possibility of failing to transcend nature through personal relation. It points to a fact of limitation, an estrangement or "falling away" of the person to the existential limits of natural atomic individuality. The failure to attain a personal relation does not mean the absence of any relation at all with the objective world. It means the loss of the ecstatic character of this relation, a character that underlines personal otherness and makes erotic participation and communion possible. The loss of the ecstatic character limits the relation to an intellectual noting of objective essences. It identifies existence with thought, being with thinking. The intellectual potentiality or energy of nature does not distinguish and is not distinguished as personal otherness in the fact of relation. It is objectified as a common and impersonal natural power, and is subjected to the objective utilitarianism which serves the self-sufficiency of atomic individuals. Human existence ceases to recapitulate the universal mode of existence, the personal oneness of Being. It falls away to the existential limits of natural atomic individuality. It is an ontic unit simply endowed with individual self-consciousness and a capacity for rational thought. The capacity for rational thought, and often individual self-consciousness as well, are objectified within the context of the conventional relations imposed by ordinary social life and common linguistic usage.

We are thus speaking of the falling away of the person with a view to defining its alienation or estrangement physically in terms of a more or less undifferentiated individuality, intellectually in terms of mental capacity and psychologically in terms of a self-conscious ego. This falling away corresponds to the ontic definition of existence according to "classic" metaphysics – the metaphysics of Aristotle, as interpreted by the Scholastics and the postscholastic Western philosophical tradition. That is to say, the ontic definition of existence reflects the presuppositions of an ontology founded on a mental-abstract concept of Being, Being as a notional universal, on the causal connection between Being and beings, and on ignoring any question about the difference between Being and beings, essence and energies. The notional sense of Being always refers to the Being of being, that is to say, to the nature of being, to the concept of being as a universal, and to the identification of existence with onticity in general. Consequently, within the context of "classic" metaphysics both Being and existence remain categories of *physics*, that is to say, they remain conventional objective definitions. "Physics," says Heidegger, "determines from the beginning the substance and history of metaphysics. Even in the theory of Being as *actus purus* (Thomas Aquinas), as absolute concept (Hegel), as eternal return of ever the same will to power (Nietzsche), metaphysics steadfastly remains physics."[1]

We saw earlier that Heidegger, on the basis of the givens of the phenomenological method, denied the intellectual conception of Being as nature as a whole, but without transcending the ontic sense of existence. We "know" Being through intellection and the use of reason as the mode by which whatever is *is*, that is to say, as *lêthe* and *a-lêtheia,* oblivion and truth, or as disclosure and hiddenness. The disclosure of beings nevertheless only becomes accessible to us in the distance of ontic individuality. In the end Heidegger's ontological discussions show clearly that the ontic sense of phenomena, even with the transcendence of the physical sense of Being, leads inevitably to a nihilistic ontology, to an identification of the potentiality of being with the potentiality of not-being, or nothingness (*Nichts*).[2] The phenomenal object, as an entity enclosed within its simple identity ("a being as a being") is that which it is and nothing else.[3] The phenomenicity of phenomena is significatory of objective ontic individuality. It presupposes the assertion: *this* and *nothing* else, referring existence to the possibilities both of the phenomenon and of nothingness. A being becomes apparent because it is not nothing, and consequently the mode by which the being *is* presupposes both disclosure and nothingness.

It is evident that here "nothing" does not refer to a mental conception of the opposite to essence, to the notion of non-existence derived syllogistically from the notion of existence. Nothing represents the presupposition of individuality, the disclosure of objects as ontic individualities. Nothing is revealed as the presupposition of the phenomenicity of phenomena, that is to say, as the distantiality of objects. It is revealed as the presupposition of the disclosure of beings "in themselves" as "a synthesis of themselves with themselves." Distantiality (*apo-stasis*) defines their static individuality. It is the opposite of ecstasy (*ek-stasis*), the dynamic referential self-transcendence of individuality, which reveals the unity of persons and "things," the universality of the *logos* of personal otherness. Nothing is the void of the distantiality of objects, which is disclosed when *relation* is destroyed and the personal-energetic unity of existential reality is cut up into objects. It is the absence of relation which leaves ontic individuality existentially suspended – it is that which is outside personal reference.

The existential potentiality of personal relation, or the falling away from this potentiality (the alienation of relation as dependence, subjection, egocentric defensiveness, and delusive self-sufficiency) proves to be the key problem of ontology, a dynamic-moral possibility which underpins two radically different answers to the question of existence, two radically different ontological theories. The failure or denial of personal relation, the falling away of the person to the existential level of physical individuality, is consequent upon the exhaustion of the truth of beings in the intellectual and conscious marking of phenomenal ontic individuality, revealing nothing as the "other face" of ontic disclosure, as the hidden essence of every being. And this identification of essence, that is, of Being, with nothing is the most shocking revelation we owe to Heidegger's ontology: nothing proves to be the only metaphysical reality.[4]

The person's falling away, its inability to transcend the self, that is to say, the person as an individual, is unable to conceive of beings as "things," as the *logos* of personal otherness. It embodies the non-rationality (*a-logon*) of things, the non-essential (*an-ousia*) existence of beings, the disclosure of beings as the silent response of nothingness to the question about existence. The inability to attain a personal relation nullifies beings in the apartness of individuality. Individual presences are transient and unexplained breaches in the universal ontological reality of nothingness. The absence of personal relation also nullifies the bearer of the consciousness of nothingness in his or her perfect non-rational aloneness, in the lethargy of the self-completeness of the atomic individual. Thus nothing proves to be the basic ontological category and the only existential reality, which is experienced directly as absence of relation, as outside reference to the person.

§76   *The Fall as existential alienation or estrangement*

The elevation of the fallenness of humanity into an ontological reality, rather than simply a conventional category of moral evaluation, is something we also find in Heidegger,[5] even though he defines it somewhat differently. For Heidegger the Fall ("Verfall, Verfallen, Verfallenheit") is an uninterrupted falling away of human existence from

its authentic self-motivated existential potentiality to a neutralized "world" of "everydayness" – a falling away from
being (*Sein*) to being-with-another ("Miteinandersein") in
the space of coexistence.[6] This coexistence constantly neutralizes humanity's being, creating a "middle term" of our
presence-in-the-world ("Durchschnittlichkeit des Daseins,"
or "averageness of *Dasein*"). In the context of "everydayness" the mode is disclosed by which individual existence
("Alltäglichkeit des Daseins," or "everydayness of *Dasein*,"
also usually *is* by a middle term, and this mode is the neutralized unit of coexistence, the neutral "Man," or "somebody."[7]
The "somebody" is not anybody specifically, and although it
is all of us, it is all of us not as a whole, but as disclosures of
the mode by which anybody-is in everydayness.[8]

Heidegger declares that the present technocratic age most
emphatically magnifies the neutralization of human existence within the context of mass coexistence. Modern public information systems, mass means of communication,
political and ideological propaganda, and consumer adver-
tising, all impose habits, and the same mode of thought. In
different forms, the "dictatorship of publicness" ("Diktatur
der Öffentlichkeit") and "enslavement to publicness"
("Verknechtung an die Öffentlichkeit")[9] inevitably alienate human existence and transform it into an anonymous
arithmetical unit.[10] The alienation of humanity, however,
in today's consumer society is not just the subject of philosophical investigation, nor is it dealt with exhaustively in
Heidegger's discussions. It is one of the central problems
of our globalized Western culture. On a popular level, the
term "One-Dimensional Man" has gained currency through
the work of Herbert Marcuse as a definition of the type of
person created by modern technocratic societies.[11] A uniform
technological and economic system, the product of relent-
less organizational necessity, creates a directed consciousness serving inevitably, if unwittingly, to enslave the mind.

But such observations are now commonplace. Here we must advance beyond the point where Heidegger leaves us and go on to investigate the ontological content of humanity's falling away, the alienation of our personal uniqueness and dissimilarity. I have said above that the absence or denial of personal relation, the inability to attain ecstatic self-transcendence, leaves ontic individuality existentially in suspension, revealing the void of the distantiality not only of objects but also of individual existences, the bearers of the consciousness of the void. Distantiality is experienced principally as absence of the *logos* which makes relation possible as existential participation in the personal-energetic unity of reality as a whole. The irrationality (*a-logon*) of existence restricts its truth to a transitory rising up from the abyss of *nothing-else*, from the void of the absence of any other existential reference whatsoever apart from ontic individuality. This void of the distantiality of ontic individualities is bridged conventionally by the substitutes for existential relation, which make our obligatory coexistence within the framework of the world's reality productive in a utilitarian sense. Our capacity for reasoning, and often our self-consciousness as individuals, are objectified in the conventional relations which are imposed by the common life we share and by our common linguistic usage. These conventional relations serve objective usefulness, subject the existence of the individual to objective usefulness, and alienate the existence of the individual as a neutralized interdependency of objective usefulness.

This means that while the many social manifestations of humanity's alienation within the framework of the conventional relations of everydayness refer principally to the existential distantiality of individualities, such distantiality is expressed and manifested within the framework of coexistence and being-with. The distantiality of individuality is the *fact* of existential neutrality, while coexistence, or being-with, is simply the potentiality and the context for the manifestation of this fact. In other words, coexistence in society is not the cause of humanity's alienation. Alienation is the effect of the deterioration, or falling away, of the ontological reality of the person. The person is the only ontological reality which counters the falling away of atomic individualities and bridges the gulf between the part and the whole, between otherness and universality, between a specific dissimilar, unique and unrepeatable existence and human nature in general. The person is the only ontological reality which counters the antithetical correspondence of being and nothingness, [12] since the absence of the person does not negate its existential immediacy, and the "opposite" of the person is not its ontic negation but the existential fact of non-relation, or neutralize ontic individuality.

The shape of this neutralization of human existence within our Western consumer culture is a matter for historical rather than ontological analysis. The ideological and theoretical presuppositions of this culture are based on a view of the person as an atomic individual. They identify existence with the capacity of the individual for rational thought and individual psychological self-consciousness.[13]

By denying the ontic definition of Being in Western metaphysics – the exhaustion of the truth of being in the coincidence of concept with object conceived ("adaequatio rei et intellectus") – Heidegger laid the foundations of a new (to the West) ontology springing from the question of the difference ("Differenz") between beings and Being.[14] By insisting, however, on the phenomenal individuality of being and on the individuality of immanent existence ("Dasein"), and by finding the only solution in a general reference, to the horizon of *time*, Heidegger was led unavoidably to pose the question of Being as a dilemma between temporal disclosure and self-concealment, between being and nothingness: "Warum ist überhaupt Seiendes und nicht vielmehr Nichts?"

(In §10 above it should have become evident that time, taken as the general horizon of ecstatic reference, or as the potentiality for understanding Being, is a pseudo-solution to the fundamental problem of the ontological difference between beings and Being, or otherness and universality, since time [*chronos*] is a product and measure of relation and only "becomes temporal" [*chronoutai*] as a dimension of personal relation. And this fundamentally *personal* dimension of time is revealed indirectly by Heidegger himself when he refers temporality to existential consciousness in terms of "care" [*Sorge*] or when he distinguishes "Historie" from the "Geschichtlichkeit des Daseins."[15])

The individuality of temporal immanence defines the falling away of beings, the possibility of their disclosure or nullification, that is to say, the mode by which beings are and which the Being of beings is. The Being of beings is identified with the possibility of their transitory emergence from the abyss of "nothing else" or their sojourn in this abyss: Being is the falling away of individuality, the potentiality of beings to become truth or nothing.

Of course the ontological nihilism into which Heidegger's thought leads us, and which is the unavoidable result of reliance on individuality as mode of existence, does not destroy his contribution to ontology. The question of the difference between beings and Being has now been posed within the terms of the Western approach to philosophical problems. It has overturned the ontic-intellectual definitions of nature-essence and existence, and can therefore lead Western thought much further than any imprisonment within the confines of the distantiality of individualities. In Heidegger's case, his fundamental question has as a more positive result (in comparison with the denial represented by the popular nihilism of the consumer society or the disappointing self-sufficiency of metaphysical intellectualism) the disclosure of the "transcendent" character of Being[16] as truth or as nothingness, that is to say, the identification of the limits of thought as an instrument of cognition and respect for them.[17] Here I shall try to show that the same question may express the ontological difference between the person and nature, which is the basis for the ontological theory of the problem of existence as understood in the theological thought of the Christian East, the basis for an apprehension of the existential content of truth and nothingness.

§77   *The existential fact of freedom: the ontological difference between person and nature*

In earlier sections I described nature as the content of the person, and person as nature's mode of existence, or the existential recapitulation of our nature as a whole. The ecstatic otherness of the person is not defined by its nature, since it transcends (as otherness) the fixed boundaries of the common attributes that constitute the nature. But the person fixes the boundaries of its nature or essence, since it constitutes nature's mode of existence. This means not that every human person is a part of humanity's being, a part of human nature, but that it "contains" the universal nature, or is the existential instantiation of that nature. Human nature exists only "in persons," only in a personal mode, only as disclosure of personal otherness. Personal otherness is instantiated and disclosed with respect to the common attributes of nature. It presupposes the common nature, although it transcends it as an ecstatic fact in the case of every specific human existence.

This relationship between nature and person in our Being and specific existence cannot be exhausted in ontic-intellectual definitions. It is not a relation of the whole to the part, but a primary ontological reality, an existential fact, the mode by which a human being fundamentally *is*. We know the Being of humanity (the mode by which a human being *is*) as personal otherness, but the personal otherness is instantiated in respect of the identity of the common characteristics of our nature in the fact of a single human existence. The existential relation between person and nature presupposes their ontological difference. The person recapitulates the nature, as existential reality, without exhausting it and simultaneously transcends the nature, as ecstatic otherness – it determines the nature without being determined by it. The ontological difference between person and nature, the simultaneous existential identity and otherness, constitutes the single human existence as a specific existential fact of *freedom*: freedom of the person with regard to the nature, freedom of the determination of the nature by personal otherness.

It is obvious that within the context of this theory freedom does not represent an abstract idea – a predicate of an idealistic axiology or a social demand for a rational arrangement of the individual's rights and obligations. Freedom is the constitutive precondition of personal existence, the immediate empirical existential fact of the relation between person and nature, which is experienced by the single human existence as ontological difference between existence and essence, as natural identity and existential otherness.

As the ontological difference between person and nature, freedom is an immediate experiential reality which is so specific as an existential potentiality that it can destroy itself. What we call freedom is not simply our power to make rational choices among the possibilities presented to us, but the immense potential we have for the self-realization of the person, a potential that destroys itself. The self-destruction of freedom, which is the most tragic way it has of affirming itself, signifies the voluntary subjection of the person to the impersonality of the nature. It is what we call the "Fall," a deterioration or reversal of the primordial relation between person and nature, an existential alienation of their ontological difference.

Thus the Fall is defined as an existential potentiality of the person, as the fact of the self-annihilation of freedom in terms of the relation between person and nature. The person is subjected to the nature and is defined by the nature. It becomes an atomic individual – an impersonal unit of the nature.[18] The determination of the person by the nature signifies the deterioration of the ecstatic reference of existence, which ceases to transcend nature and is exhausted within the bounds of its natural identity. It signifies the existential alienation of personal otherness, the dominance of the common attributes of the nature over the uniqueness and dissimilarity of the person. Ecstatic transcendence of the nature in the fact of personal otherness degenerates into an ecstasy of the individual within the bounds of the nature – and the antithetical ecstasies of the individual entities within the bounds of the common nature divide up the nature, fragmenting it into small pieces. The nature is fragmented into atomic individuals who are distinguished from each other only by the quantitative differences belonging to the impersonal attributes of the common nature. Existential otherness gives way to a static individual self-consciousness, which sets the nature of the atomic individual, as the ego, against other natures of atomic individuals.

§78   *The exercise of freedom: opposition to the passions*

The existential experience of the fact of freedom, as the ontological difference between persona and nature, is the foundation both of the anthropology of the Greek Fathers and the Orthodox practice of asceticism. The ascetic struggle against the natural desires, the natural will, and the natural demand for pleasure refers neither to a Platonic evaluation of spirit over matter, nor to a Stoic view of the negative character of the passions, those natural movements of the soul and the body which war against the rational element. Christian asceticism is not the struggle of the spirit against matter, nor is it the opposition of the rationality of the mind to the irrational elements of human nature. It is a dynamic transcendence of the autonomy of nature – an autonomy which is irrational (*a-logos*) because it does not arise out of the dialogue (*dia-logos*) of personal relation and communion. Asceticism fights not against nature but against the autonomy and self-sufficiency of individuality which is the irrationality of non-relation. Asceticism "forces" the autonomous natural will in order to subject it to the personal will of communion and relation. It "forces" nature to achieve the freedom of the person from nature, the ecstasy of nature, the realization of the truth of the person which is "in accordance with nature," which is the personal otherness of nature, the transcendence of the alienation of the person as an impersonal unit of the common nature.

Maximus the Confessor defines freedom as the "voluntary movement of intelligent life"[19] and Gregory of Nyssa as "assimilation to that which is uncompelled and self-determining."[20] Voluntariness, self-determination and non-compulsion are the opposite to subjection to natural necessity, to the impersonal laws of survival which mould nature, subjecting it to the common necessity for the sake of self-preservation and perpetuation of the species. Nature in itself, in its biological identity, is governed by necessity, while personal otherness presupposes the ecstasy of nature from subjection to necessity, because it is realized only as *relation*, only as uniqueness and dissimilarity of communion, free and undetermined by any *a priori* necessity. "The precise meaning of freedom is to lack nothing whatsoever," says John Chrysostom:[21] perfect deliverance from every necessity, from every impersonal natural need for survival, is the fullness of the powers of life as personal relation, the fullness of freedom.

We have seen in an earlier chapter[22] that personal otherness is not defined simply in a comparative sense with regard to objective beings and other persons. It is realized principally with regard to the natural individuality of personal existence.

Natural individuality recapitulates, as an existential fact, the common-objective properties of nature. Nature is "enhypostatized" in individual existence. It subsists as a real existential fact only within the bounds of individual existence.[23] This means that personal otherness is actualized principally with regard to natural individuality, differing not essentially but only existentially from natural individuality. Personal otherness is differentiated from natural individuality as a mode of existence which presupposes the self-transcendence of natural individuality. It is differentiated with regard to another mode of existence which is the non-self-transcendence of natural individuality, that is to say, its existential self-completeness, autonomy and self-sufficiency.

The existential fact of freedom therefore presupposes the ontological reality of the simultaneous natural identity and existential otherness of the person – of the personal otherness and common-natural properties of each single individual existence. The common properties of nature, "enhypostatized" in individual existence, disclose the personal otherness when the individual nature "stands out" (*ex-istatai*) as a fact of personal communion and relation. They are natural *energies* capable of revealing personal otherness. In which case the common properties of nature do not determine the mode of existence but are the natural preconditions for the disclosure of the personal mode of existence. But when natural individuality does not actualize its ecstatic self-transcendence in the fact of personal relation, the objective properties of nature themselves determine the mode of existence. They destroy the personal otherness of natural individuality and existence "suffers" the existential deterioration of falling away into the impersonal neutrality of the individual "form." The objective properties of nature are proved then to be "passions" of existential individuality, "unnatural" energies of individual nature.[24]

The ascetic literature of the Christian East sets forth the struggle against the passions as the only way to attain freedom,[25] and identifies freedom with the "restoration" of nature to its personal otherness – with the restoration of the person to its existential integrity. The existential integrity of the person signifies the fullness of a personal erotic relation with creation and God. It signifies the discovery of the world's personal dimension, and entry into the "darkness of theology,"[26] which is immediate communion with God, or "empirical" knowledge of the mystery of divine existence,[27] that is to say, of true life. Thus freedom in the end signifies the *salvation* of human kind. And to "save" (*sôzein*) means to "make whole" (*sôon*), to restore humankind to its existential integrity, to the fullness of life.

§79   *The moral paradox of freedom: justice and love*

The struggle against the passions, as the only way to realize freedom experientially, implies a moral "paradox" – one corresponding to the ontological "paradox" of the simultaneous existential identity and otherness of person and nature that is the presupposition of freedom. The struggle against the passions implies subjection to the commandments and laws of the ascetic life if the transcendence of every law and the realization of the freedom of the person is to be achieved. Our nature's identity also supplies the identity of the "rules" for transcending our nature's autonomy. Yet the otherness of personal freedom is realized as subjection to common presuppositions for transcending our nature's autonomy. The commandments and laws of asceticism are general and objective precisely because they represent the identity of the common presuppositions for transcending our nature's general objective need for autonomy and self-sufficiency. Our nature must be subjected personally (that is, dynamically and freely) to the "rules" of freedom, which are the commandments laid down for the works of *askesis*,[28] and this subjection is the starting-point for the realization of personal works of *askesis* (the works which militate against the impersonal wills and desires of our nature that have become autonomous) arising from universal experience and also from the revelation of the divine will for the salvation and freedom of humankind.[29]

In Orthodox ascetic practice, subjection to the commandments is intended to achieve freedom and is realized as *justice* towards nature[30] and as *love* towards God. Our nature's autonomous self-sufficiency, as expressed in the impersonal demands of the passions, is an *injustice* towards the nature itself,[31] since the passions are natural energies which are "contrary to nature." It is an injustice towards the existential authenticity of our nature, which is the personal mode of its existence. That is why Orthodox writings describe the works of asceticism as "works of justice" and a "path of justice."[32] They are also *bodily works*, specific acts of resistance against the autonomous natural will.[33] Christian ascetics reject subjection to the need for food, the need for bodily pleasure, the need for sleep and bodily relaxation, not because they despise the body and matter through some spiritual idealism,[34] but in order to impose on the body and on matter the *justice* of a mode of existence that is "according to nature": so that the ascetic may rediscover the body, and matter, and the beauty of the world in their true, personal dimensions, that is to say, within the bounds of the fullness of a personal-loving relation[35] that is free from the autonomous imperatives of the nature of the atomic individual. And it is only through the freedom of the person from subjection to the necessitude of its nature that nature as a whole, the totality of creation, is freed from the corruption of an aimless independence from the Creator, and is revealed as the "glory" and disclosure of God, the personal *logos* of its Creator. The freedom of the human person also frees creation from its self-containedness and subjection to decay. It gives it back its personal otherness, the beauty of the erotic fact, of the loving summons of God which it embodies. In Paul's words to the Romans

(Rom 8:19-23) we have the primordial Christian expression of the cosmological dimensions of the fact of freedom.[36]

But the dynamic *askesis* of freedom through obedience to the commandments which counter the autonomy of natural atomic individuality is not exhausted in the keeping of the commandments, in the imposition of *justice* on nature. It aims at the ecstatic self-transcendence of nature, at the realization of the primary relation that is free from the bonds of the autonomy of the creature – at man's love for God. If the subjection of nature, the suppression of its desires, becomes an end in itself, freedom from nature remains unattainable, since the self-annihilation of nature is exhausted within the bounds of the nature of the atomic individual, with nature being transcended as the indeterminacy and otherness of personal relation.

Furthermore, the self-annihilation of nature within the bounds of atomic individuality remains merely conceptual. Ascetic experience confirms that "it is not possible for nature to overcome itself."[37] It is impossible for the natural self-sufficiency and self-completeness of atomic individuality to be transcended when the subjection of the autonomous desires of our nature is not set in the context of an erotic fact. The subjection of our nature is not simply a rational arrangement and moderation of natural selves, the purpose-less self-sufficiency and self-completeness of our atomic individuality – and this can only be achieved as an ecstatic loving relation and self-offering. Personal freedom is a fact of love, and love is the existential ground of freedom.

The moral "paradox" of freedom reaches its completion in love, for love is free from any law, from any subjection to commandments and natural or conventional fetters,[38] while at the same time it voluntarily subjects itself to any kind of privation, fetter or limitation in order to be realized as a fact of self-offering. Love is "the life which is not subject to the law and therefore is above all natural necessity and change;

and he who has attained it is as if liberated from the outer flesh ... for what is partial within him has been abolished."[39] But the transcendence of natural need and the departure from the flesh (the ecstasy of nature) which lead to the fullness and universality of existence (to the abolition of "what is partial") presuppose a simultaneous subjection to precisely those laws which militate against the natural need of "the flesh" for autonomy. These laws and the commandments of *askesis*, as presuppositions for the freedom of love, cannot be impersonal. They are not simply objective legal ordinances but disclose and define a fact of relation and communion, the fact of *ekklêsia*. The commandments of *askesis* aim at incorporation into the ecclesial body, which knows no other law than the life "which is not subject to the law,"[40] the life which is realized as the transcending of justice and as erotic self-offering and freedom "in all things."[41]

§80   *The limit to the self-annihilation of freedom: the dissimilarity of distantiality*

The dimension of person and nature, the evolution of their ontological difference into an existential antithesis, as directly experienced in the life of everydayness, is not a finished actuality but a dynamically constituted existential fact. It is a ceaseless antithetical bipolar force, a tragic duality in us as human beings, the first and last test of our freedom, or of our power to actualize ourselves as persons. In everyday experience the "falling away" of the person into natural individuality, the neutralization and alienation of existence, is not always the result of a consciously willed process or decision. It is often a more or less involuntary subjection to the nature's dynamic urge to be liberated in terms of atomic self-completeness, to prove itself (as natural individuality) to be self-determining.

Before defining more precisely what I mean by "the nature's dynamic urge to be liberated in terms of atomic self-completeness," I should note, as a given of immediate experience, that the evolution of the ontological difference between person and nature into an existential antithesis, the falling away of the person into atomic individuality, does not signify the total and definitive destruction of the elements of personal otherness, of the personal mode of existence. If earlier I defined the falling away of the person into atomic individuality in starkly schematic terms and with reference to clear-cut states, that was in order to analyze as accurately as possible the semantic content of the notion of a "fall." The experience, however, of everyday reality confirms that the falling away of the human person into atomic individuality is not a definite transition from one state to another (as would have suited a schematic concept), but a progressive dynamic urge to downgrade personal otherness and freedom of will without leading to its final extinction. Even when objectified and neutralized in the greatest possible degree, human nature does not cease to differ ontologically (as a mode of existence) from irrational ontic units. There is a limit to the self-destruction of freedom, and this is constituted by its ontological ground and constitutive starting-point, namely, the given ontological difference between person and nature, the specific difference of humanity and marking it off definitively from the rest of ontic reality. A human being can fall away experiencing a serious deterioration of his or her existential reality, but cannot destroy this reality utterly. ("Humanity is condemned to be free," says Sartre,[42] noting from another perspective the impossibility of freedom to destroy itself totally as an ontological reality. But if the limit which exists to the self-annihilation of freedom is an absolute prerogative or an absolute condemnation, this is a judgment which, as we shall see, is defined by the hermeneutic presuppositions of the existential fact.)

The "preservation" of the person, in spite of its progressive falling away into atomic individuality, is not confined only to the maintenance of the givens of the individual uniqueness and dissimilarity of a human existence (uniqueness and dissimilarity of *logos*, facial characteristics, psychological peculiarities, powers of expression, physical and spiritual capacities, erotic uniqueness, etc.) All of these presuppose the ecstatic transcendence of the common properties of the nature within the limits of individual existence – a self-transcendence which, however greatly limited, always remains the point of departure for the personal mode of existence. The consequence of the "fall" is not the complete loss of the power of an ecstatic self-transcendence of the nature, but the confining of this self-transcendence within the limits of the existential self-completeness of atomic individuality, the inability of the self-transcendence of the nature to be accomplished as a mode of existence which is not defined by the needs of the nature, but defines the nature as a personal otherness of communion and relation.

We must therefore say (defining more precisely the expressions used at the beginning of this chapter) that the falling away to atomic individuality does not destroy but downgrades the personal ecstasy of the nature out-of-the-nature to an ecstasy of atomic individuality within the boundaries of the nature. It downgrades the ecstasy (*ek-stasis*) of the person to the distantiality (*apo-stasis*) of an individual self-completeness, to a domineering individual self-consciousness and psychological ego. The downgrading of ecstasy to the distantiality of individual self-completeness breaks up the nature into dissimilar and objective atomic individualities. The dissimilarity of the individual existences is not the otherness of beloved persons that summons to a unifying communion and relation, but becomes a distantiality of objective individualities within the limits of the common nature. The otherness of the persons is the otherness of a mode of existence which transcends the limitation of existence by the

nature. It is revealed only in the fact of loving communion
and relation – unifying the nature as a mode of the nature's
existence free from natural necessity – while the dissimilarity of atomic individualities is revealed only as a distantiality which separates atomic individualities as existential units
within the limits of the common nature, breaking the nature
up into fragments.

Dissimilarity as distantiality is the existential reverse of
otherness as relation and reveals the falling away of the person into an objectified individual. Awareness of dissimilarity
is experience of the distantiality which objectifies the existence of the "other" and opposes me as an object to every
"other." Sartre has analyzed at some length how atomic existence becomes aware of its objectification through the gaze
of the other ("le regard d'autrui").[43] The gaze, the faculty of
sight, which is the initial potentiality of the immediacy of
relation, the primary potentiality of experience of personal
otherness, proves to be, with the falling away into atomic
individuality, the supreme experience of objectification. The
gaze of the "other" turns me into an object, sets me opposite
the atomic autonomy of his existence, against the autonomy
which works against the self-completeness and self-determination of my own individuality.

§81   *Distantiality as nakedness and shame*

Of particular relevance to our understanding of what the
Fall means is Sartre's observation that the objectification of
my existence is revealed primarily in the sense of shame that
I feel under the gaze of the "other":

> Shame is a sense of the original Fall, not because I have com-
> mitted this or that transgression, but simply because I have
> fallen into a world, among things, and need the mediation of
> the "other" in order to be that which I am. The conscious-
> ness and, especially, the fear that I will be caught in a state

of nakedness is nothing other than a symbolic representation of ancestral shame: in this event the body symbolizes our defenseless objectification. To dress yourself means to cover your objectivity, to claim the right to see without being seen, that is, to be only a subject. That is why the biblical symbol of the Fall, after the original sin was committed, is the fact that Adam and Eve knew that they were naked.[44]

The reference to the biblical account of original shame sheds light on the falling away of humanity from *person* to *individual*. In the personal mode of existence before the Fall there was no shame, because such a mode of existence did not have the defense of atomic individuality with which to protect itself from transformation into an object useful to the individual pleasure and self-sufficiency of the other. In the personal mode of existence before the Fall the body is a complete expression and disclosure of personal otherness, a potentiality for universal loving relation and self-offering, a dynamic summons to the realization of mutual ecstatic self-transcendence and communion. The sense of nakedness and the shame of nakedness begins the moment the loving relation and the mutual ecstatic self-offering are destroyed and the distantiality of objective individualities is created. Love has no knowledge of the sense of nakedness, because it has no knowledge of the distantiality of objectification. And it has no knowledge of the defense of an individuality that has become autonomous: "Love knows no shame .... It is a natural property of love not to feel shame and to be oblivious to its appearance."[45] In true eros the body as a whole reveals the personal otherness, the beauty of the prelapsarian integrity of the person. True eros is the fullness of mutual ecstatic self-offering, and therefore is unaware of the distantiality imposed by defense and imposition, while the "partial and divided" eros of atomic existence "is not truly eros, but an idol or rather a falling away from authentic eros."[46] It parts and divides because it aims at the satisfaction of atomic individuality and, consequently, sets the other apart in the distantiality of nakedness and defends itself against the demands of the other with shame.

Shame is the defense of atomic individuality against its objectification, the claim of its freedom to remain subjective within the limits of an objectified nature. The freedom of the atomic individual is not a self-transcendence of nature for the sake of loving communion and relation. It is the denial of the objectivity of nature so that the subjectivity of atomic individuality can be facilitated and made autonomous. Atomic freedom is the knowledge and the defense of subjective self-completeness, which is why the distantiality of atomic individuality is defined by the freedom of the "other" that undermines the autonomy and sovereignty of my own subjectivity. Thus every other atomic individuality is revealed as a threat to my own atomic freedom. The atomic freedom of the "other" inevitably turns me into an object. It subjects me as an object to the defense of his own subjective autonomy – between the "other" and me there opens up the void or distantiality of freedom, the existential chasm or experience of nothingness that sets apart the autonomous subjectivism of atomic individualities.[47] This is the annihilation of relation, the void that surrounds ontic individuality, the condemnation of existence to an irrational loneliness.

§82   *Nothingness as erotic experience of the absence of relation*

In the space of our fragmented postlapsarian nature, shame and nakedness and atomic freedom and individual dissimilarity are experiences and disclosures of the existential distantiality that separates atomic individuals, occasioning the sense of nothingness, which is the absence of relation. But the sense of the distantiality of nothingness, which divides atomic existences, necessarily presupposes an initial potenti-

ality for ecstatic reference and the experience of the impossibility of realizing this reference as relation. The impossibility of a personal universal relation refers the potentiality for
ecstasy to the void of atomic distantiality, to nothingness as
outside personal relation.

This last statement calls for amplification. It is not possible
for the ecstatic reference of natural individuality to be fully
explained by the sense of atomic distantiality. It ceases to be
ecstasy when it is confined within the limits of nature, fragmenting nature into dissimilar individualities. Ecstasy necessarily defines a transcendence of nature, and is therefore
realized as the existential dissimilarity of atomic individuals, that is to say, as an existential fact which transcends the
objective properties of nature. And this existential fact of the
ecstatic self-transcendence of natural individuality can only
be a relation outside-of-nature, or else the failure of this relation, a failure which leads to the experience of nothingness
as outside personal relation.

And of course the basis for preserving the ecstatic reference
through the failure of a relation outside-of-nature is not the
"other" of our normal social life. The "other" is the disclosure of atomic distantiality, that which occasions the sense
of existential loneliness. But it is only that which occasions
it. The fact itself of existential loneliness, which preserves
the potentiality for ecstasy, although as the impossibility of
universal personal relation, presupposes a second person to
whom the ecstatic reference is directed as failure of relation–
a person and not an atomic individual at a distance. Only a
person who has not fallen into the distantiality of atomic individuality, but continues to send out to me an ecstatic summons to personal universal relation, only such a person can
preserve my own ecstatic reference as a failure of relation
and experience of existential loneliness.

An empirical confirmation of the presupposition of a second person who preserves the ecstatic reference as a failure

of relation is our sense of erotic absence. Erotic absence is the sense of a universal ecstatic reference which is not realized as relation, yet neither does it recognize the distantiality of individuality. The beloved person has then been revealed as an ecstatic summons to a personal universal relation, beyond and outside the self-completeness of atomic individuality. That is why he is absent from everywhere. The absence of the beloved person is not an experience of distantiality, but a confirmation of his existential reality. It is an experience of inaccessible immediacy – an experience of that which is outside personal relation. Within the context of the ontology defined by the truths of eros and the person, the definition of nothingness refers directly to erotic absence: the definition of nothingness is not an intellectual abstraction. Nothingness is not the void of ontic absence, or absolute non-existence, or the opposite of being, or non-being. Nothingness is an erotic experience of the absence of relation. Nothingness as *outside* personal relation presupposes the universal ecstatic reference of the person as failure of relation. Consequently, the experience of nothingness confirms the existential reality of a second person; it is the experience of an erotic absence.

This ontological (because it refers to the mode of existence) presupposition of a person who has not fallen away into the distantiality of atomic individuality and who preserves, as an ecstatic summons to a personal universal relation, the reality of the human person (i.e., preserves the ecstatic reference of human existence as relation or as failure of relation) leads us to the theological truth of a personal God whose summons to personal-erotic communion constitutes the fundamental presupposition of the human person and the limit to the self-annihilation of humanity's personal otherness.

If God is not personal, but is the absolute subject which can never become an object, since he "only sees without being seen," Sartre's view is justified that the existence of God precludes human freedom because it turns human beings de-

finitively into objects, without their being able to preserve
their subjectivity by objectifying the invisible and absolute
subject on equal terms.[48] Sartre's view could be justified in
this way because the concept of the subject presupposes the
existential autonomy of atomic individuality and, consequently, the existential distantiality which only the truth of
the person can remove.

One might venture to make the somewhat schematic and
general, yet not arbitrary, observation that behind the rejection of God as absolute subject, and indeed behind most
forms of Western atheism, there lies the same theological
void which is also characteristic of the Western metaphysical
tradition as a whole, namely, ignorance of, or disregard for,
the truth of the person. Western atheism does not reject the
personal God of Christian revelation because, very simply, it
does not know him. It rejects the theologically and morally
necessary being of Western theological rationalism.[49] When
denouncing the contradictoriness of the concept of God as
absolute subject, Sartre does so within the context of an existential conflict between the individual freedom of human
beings and the absolute threat to that freedom posed by God
in the distantiality of the absolutized subject. But this conflict occurs principally in the context of Western theological
rationalism: theology was subjected to an anthropocentric
attempt to objectify God, to change him into an intellectual
object with the aim of safeguarding the individual autonomy
of human beings, the individual freedom of subjectivity confronted with transcendent absoluteness. The West changed
God into an absolute transcendent subject, which human individuality could nevertheless confront on equal terms, subjecting God as an object to the individual human understanding, to the rules and presuppositions of human logic. But this
subjection is logically and ontologically contradictory, and it
is this contradictoriness in the concept of God that Western
atheism denounces.

Chapter Two

The Personal Dimension of Nothingness

§83   *The existential grounds of personal otherness*

We know the human person as ecstatic reference "pre-served" within the context of the realization or failure of a relation – a relation transcending the distantiality of atomic individualities. We have defined this "preservation" as the last barrier to the self-annihilation of human freedom, the freedom of the person with regard to nature, and we have seen it as a hypostatic "response" to an equally ecstatic summons to personal universal communion presupposing a second person to whom the ecstatic reference is directed as relation or as failure of relation.

Before this summons becomes a certainty of erotic ab-sence, it can (as we have discussed in an earlier chapter) be the experience of our participation in a fundamentally dialogical relation with the reality of the world. The real-ity of the world as a whole in its logical structure, that is, as a fact of disclosure of the world's *logos*, presupposes the human person as the second term of the dialogical relation, which reveals the truth of beings as "things – deeds," as the effect of a personal creative act, as the *logos* of a personal existence. The disclosure of the world's *logos* presupposes humanity's personal mode of existence, and this presuppo-sition is not an intellectual necessity but a real potentiality for humanity's immediate experiential relationship with the beings that constitute the world's reality. When this relation transcends the conventionality of the *use* of things (the sense of beings as "things-to-be-used" or "currency" [*chrêmata*]), it becomes inevitably a dialogical relation, the experience of a summons to participation in and communion with the *logos* of the world's personal otherness. Consequently, beings as "things," as the *logos*-disclosure of a personal otherness, summon the human person, that is to say, "preserve" it in the ecstatic reference which is the ground of its dialogical relation.

This means that we "know" the human person, or preserve the existential potentiality for personal otherness, only in the measure in which we actively experience the reality of the objective summons of the world's *logos* – only as a hypostatic response to this summons which transcends individual distantiality. In other words, the mode by which we know the reality of the human person is not by studying humanity's specific temporal being-there ("Da-sein"), because this can be exhausted within the limits of individual distantiality. We know the person only in the fact of relation, and consequently only as response to the primary summons which "preserves" the person as the realization or failure of relation. And since the person is the response to the summons to an ecstatic relation, it is the summons that defines its existential grounds. Consequently, the truth of the person lies beyond the given being-there in the world of individual existence. It lies in the fact of the summons which defines the person as an ecstatic potentiality. And this summons – a fundamental potentiality of the person which is disclosed as the *logos* of the world's personal otherness beyond the limits of the distantiality of ontic individualities – is a personal presence which transcends the being-there in the world of individual existence. This is why in the theology of the Christian East we approach the reality of the human person from the starting-point of the revealed truth of a personal God – in contrast with Western theology, which seeks to discover the truth about God by anagogical and analogical means, focusing primarily on the reality of the human being.[1]

§84   *The triadic summons: the fundamental starting-point of personal otherness*

We know the person of God not in the distantiality of atomic individuality, but as experiential immediacy of personal relation and communion through the divine energies – the potentialities by which the unknown and inaccessible divine nature reveals its mode of existence, which is personal. Thus the first cognitive given with regard to the knowledge of the personal God is the creative effect of the personal divine energies, that is to say, the objective beings constituting the reality of the world that rise up in the "space" of personal relation as "things," as acts-deeds of a creative person.

Beings as "things" disclose the *logos* of personal otherness which is distinctive of the divine creative energy, the universal referential ecstasy of the Godhead, the ability of the divine essence to offer itself as a relation of personal communion. But the ecstatic reference and "logical" disclosure and self-offering is the personal mode of existence. This means that God does not *become* personal only in the ecstasy that manifests him, but *is* personal as divine existence. Revealed ecstatically, the personal character of the Godhead refers ontologically to the mode by which the Godhead *is* in itself, that is to say, in a given relation and communion of persons. We approach the mode by which the Godhead *is* in itself as a communion of persons, in the measure in which it is revealed to us through the divine energies, as referential ecstasy calling us to communion and relation. The mode by which we recognize the summons to personal communion and relation which God addresses to humanity reveals the Godhead in its manifestatory ecstasy as a communion of hypostatic characteristics which "distinguishes" the divine nature or essence as a triad of persons without impairing the unity of the nature or essence. Without impairing the unknown and inaccessible character of the uncreated divine nature, we "distinguish" the triad of persons because it is the mode by which we recognize God's summons to humanity, which reveals a triadic energy of the one undivided divine nature.[2]

(a)   *Essential monad and existential triad*

The mode by which we recognize the summons to personal communion and relation which God addresses to humanity reveals a triadic energy in the measure in which it is disclosed as the power of participation in the fullness of a personal mode of existence – in a fullness of personal life. By "fullness of personal life" I exclude both individual distantiality (*apo-stasis*) and a dyadic (and therefore mutliple[3]) division (*dia-stasis*) in the divine nature. God is revealed as one God, a monad of divine essence, but not in the monad's arithmetical sense, which constitutes an existential individuality in a state of distantiality (*apo-stasis*). And the transcendence of the arithmetical monad is not accomplished as an internal division (*dia-stasis*) within the unitary essence: the monad is not divided into an existential dyad. The mode of existence of the Godhead transcends both the existential atomicity of the arithmetical monad and the existential division (and dynamic multiplicity) of the dyad in a unique ("monadic") unity of fullness which the triad reveals as the transcendence of both atomic individuality and dyadic division. The monad or oneness of the Godhead "subsists triadically." It is a monad which exists as an undivided triad of persons, without the *existential* triad impairing the *essential* monad.[4] The truth of the divine life transcends the onticity of numbers.[5] It is "at the same time wholly a monad and wholly a triad." It is the one *essential* unity of the fullness of the triadic communion of the persons.

(b)   *Triadic "perichoresis"*

In the theological language of the Greek East "perichoresis," or mutual indwelling, is the mode of existence that transcends the ontic atomicity of numbers without impairing the hypostatic otherness of the persons, and discloses the oneness of the nature as an essential unity of the existential communion of the persons.[6] The hypostatic otherness is revealed in the "dynamic" reference and total communion of each divine person with the other persons of the Trinity, by a kind of self-concealment of each of the persons in the relation of communion with the other divine persons, or by the perfect absence of any element of existential self-completeness – and this mode of existential communion is called "perichoresis." It is the transcendence both of atomic distantiality (*apo-stasis*) and of dyadic (and therefore multiple) division (*dia-stasis*) in the divine essence. None of the Persons stands apart (*aph-istatai*) as individual self-completeness, nor is the nature divided (*di-istatai*) as an existential multiplicity.

This mode of existence, which indicates the fullness of personal otherness without impairing the unity of the nature, is revealed in the referential ecstasy of God outside his nature, in the summons to communion and relation which the personal God addresses to the personal human being. Only in the context of the historical experience of this summons do we gain access to the mode of divine existence which refers primarily to the inner relations of the divine persons, to the "space" of the unknowable and inaccessible divine essence. On the basis, and only on the basis, of the historical experience of the summons to personal communion and relation which is revealed as triadic energy,[7] do we define the otherness of each person of the Trinity in categories reflecting the intellectual capacity of the human mind – do we use the relative, but nevertheless experiential and existential human categories of "fatherhood," "sonship" and "procession" to refer to the fundamentally inaccessible mode of divine existence as a communion of persons in the "space" of the individual and unitary divine nature.[8]

This last phrase calls for further comment. When we speak of the mode of divine existence as a communion of persons in the "space" of the undivided and unitary divine nature, we are not attempting to "define" the divine nature as a unitary, simple and undivided whole, supposing the persons to be parts of the whole or internal relations of the essence, so as to confirm the logical necessity of the simplicity of the essence. We are not subjecting the persons to the abstract ontological conception of one divine essence, one creative and motive Cause of all that is. The only "definition" of the essence is its mode of existence, that is to say, the persons who are described or named from their mutual relations[9] without these relations being identified with the persons so that the persons are regarded as the internal relations of the essence.[10]

We distinguish the persons of the Father, Son and Holy Spirit in the disclosive energy of humanity's call to personal communion with God, and this distinguishing defines the mode of divine existence. The disclosive energy of the call to personal communion is triadic, revealing a universal mutual coinherence or perichoresis of the persons, whose internal relations and order, while inaccessible and ineffable in themselves, that is to say, objectively indefinable, may be expressed in our intellectual categories by the numerical formula $3 = 1$, which signifies that they are beyond and above any arithmetical and ontic definition. The relation $3 = 1$, which abrogates any quantitative and arithmetical objectivity, expresses the experience of the summons which the human person receives to participation in the fullness of the personal mode of existence and this mode is the perichoresis of life and energy of the divine persons.

Thus we refer the disclosure of the energies of the Godhead to the person of the Spirit.[11] The divine energies, however, which are communicated through the Spirit reveal the per-

son of the Logos: the Spirit actualizes the personal revelation of the Logos in the infinite "actual" disclosure of the
divine energies.[12] We "know" the personal presence of the
Spirit as a dynamic self-concealment, as an energy revelatory of the person of the Logos. But the Logos, too, who is
revealed by the Spirit, is the Logos of the Father. He witnesses not to himself but to the person of the Father, the unique
source and existential principle of the Godhead.[13] The Logos
is manifested in order to make the Father known, just as the
Spirit operates in order to manifest the Logos. Finally, even
the person of the Father hides itself in this universal mutual
coinherence of personal communion, eternally "begetting"
the Logos and causing to Spirit to "proceed."[14]

(c)   *Hypostasis – kenosis*

By destroying any possibility of atomic distantiality the
Godhead's mode of existence demonstrates the reality of
hypostasis, the mode of the fullness of personal existence
that is *hypostatic*. "Hypostasis" signifies the dynamic reality
and wholeness of personal existence in its ecstatic mutual
perichoresis and total communion, the antithesis of the distantiality of atomic self-containedness.

The knowledge of the Godhead's hypostatic mode of existence, or the truth of the hypostases, is accessible to humanity within the context of historical experience, experience
of the specific fact which embodies the Godhead's mode of
existence historically – that is to say, only in the person of
Jesus Christ. The two specific paths or possibilities for approaching the truth of God, as we have frequently noted in
the preceding pages – that is to say, giving priority to the
conception of God's essence, or giving priority to the knowledge of the hypostases which are the essence's mode of existence – do not simply constitute two different theoretical
methodologies; they constitute two radically different attitudes to the truth of God.

Giving priority to the conception of the essence implies an intellectualist approach to truth, an etiological and anagogical definition of the concept of God (as an abstract divine essence or supreme being which is logically the necessary principle and cause of existence) and leads unavoidably to the theory of the hypostases as internal relations within the essence.

Consequently, giving priority to the hypostases focuses on the primary and specific experience of relation through the historical disclosure "in the flesh" of the person of the Logos, a disclosure which alone reveals the mode of divine existence, the reality of the triadic communion. We are speaking here of the mutual indwelling of the divine persons which "distinguishes" the divine essence as a trinity of hypostases without destroying the unity of the divine essence and energy, because we know the mode of existence which the incarnation of the Logos revealed, namely, the kenosis of Christ.

We call "kenosis" the dynamic "self-concealment" of the deity of the Logos in a relation of communion with human nature, a relation which reveals to us the "emptying" of every element of existential self-containedness. This is a new mode of existence in terms of human experience and human categories of thought. It is the hypostatic mode of existence of the Logos who is enfleshed by the energy of the Holy Spirit in order to disclose the Father, the mode of existence of the triadic perichoresis which reveals to us the mystery of the One Triadic God in the kenotic mode of the Logos's assumption of human nature.

Thus the truth of kenosis is revealed as humanity's unique possibility of knowing the truth of God in the specific context of historical experience. And the truth of kenosis is not simply a new category of thought. It offers us the possibility of experiential coordination with the truth and authenticity of existence, that is to say, with the hypostatic mode of personal existence. The idea of Christian asceticism and Christian virtue summarized in the practice of humility means nothing other than the effort to achieve this kenosis, this "emptying" of the elements of individual self-containedness. It is an attempt to achieve the personal fulfillment which is the realization of hypostasis – in the etymological sense of hypostasis, which is "standing-under," hiding oneself as an atomic individuality in a comprehensive ecstasy ("standing-out") of erotic communion.

§85   *The energies of the divine nature as the ontological presupposition of a relation "outside of" that nature*

We approach the Godhead's mode of existence as a communion of persons, the truth of the mutual coinherence of the hypostases in the fact of the ecstatic reference of the divine essence "outside itself," through the divine energies, that is to say, as a realization of our own relation and communion with the Godhead "outside" the divine essence. The personal mode of existence of the divine essence is revealed "opposite," that is to say, in relation to a second possibility of personal existence, a possibility for the realization or denial of ecstatic relation, the acceptance or rejection of communion with the Godhead. The ecstatic reference of the divine nature through the divine energies constitutes a summons which substantiates or establishes the personal potentiality of "being opposite" the divine personal existence. The summons of God is substantiated in the human person. The potentiality for the realization of a personal relation "outside" the divine nature is the fundamental ground of the human person.

The human person represents a potentiality of total communion with God, but this total communion of life constitutes a relation "outside" the divine essence: humanity communes totally with the Godhead without participating in God's uncreated essence, because as in the case of every created be-

ing it "stands apart from God not spatially but by nature."[15]
The ecstasy of God, his power of "standing out of" his nature, of offering himself as the potentiality for total personal
communion,[16] refers to the distinction of the divine nature
from the divine energies – to that distinction which is the
"specific difference" in Aristotelian terms between Orthodox
theology and every other theological or philosophical ontology. The ecstatic power of God belongs to his will: in the
Fathers the divine energies are identified with divine acts of
will.[17] The personal mode of existence of the divine essence
does not necessitate the actualization of an ecstatic relation.
It is simply revealed in the ecstatic relation, and it is revealed
as erotic goodness and consequently as freedom from any
natural predetermination. The triadic energy of God, as a
summons to the actualization of a relation "outside of" the
divine nature, is a free act of will revelatory of the personal
mode of existence of the divine essence, not a natural necessity.[18]

The nature's will or energy is distinguished from the nature
itself. It refers to the nature's personal mode of existence, to
the personal potentiality for the realization of relation outside of the nature. There is no necessity which determines
the divine nature and can be regarded as the obligatory cause
of the ecstatic summons that is the ground of ontic individuality and of humanity's personal existence. The Platonic and
subsequently Augustinian and Thomist approach that refers
the eternal causes of created beings to the essence rather than
the volitional energies of God[19] attributes to God's creativity
a character of natural necessity. At the same time it denies
the ontological priority of the persons in relation to the nature, the fact that the nature's will or energy is expressed
and realized only as personal disclosure, as a free act which
is not determined by the nature but reveals the nature's personal mode of existence.[20]

If the ideas of beings are their eternal causes that are in-

cluded in the essence of God, in the intellectual content of
the divine essence ("in mente divina"), if they are determinations of the essence to which created beings refer as to
their exemplary cause, the divine essence not only takes
precedence but also becomes existentially autonomous with
regard to the persons, and we are led inevitably to maintain
that the principle of that which exists is predetermined by necessity, not by freedom. God in that event cannot not be that
which he is required to be by his essence, and consequently
the personal existence and freedom of God is dissolved by
the necessity of the existential predeterminations imposed
by the essence. On the epistemological level, we arrive at
an ontic interpretation of the essence or at the identification
of the essence with the intellectual conception of the whole.
Any conception of the essence or nature in itself, as distinct
from the mode of existence of the essence which is the persons, is a conception which is entirely schematic, divorced
from the givens of existential experience, the experience of
relation. The conception of the essence in itself, the rendering of the essence autonomous with regard to the persons,
is the basis of an intellectualist ontology which restricts the
question of being to an intellectual-etiological tracing back
of beings to a causal universal (in the double sense of a common principle or a supreme divine cause) and restricts the
fact of existence to the limits of ontic individuality, with no
inkling of any question concerning mode of existence or the
mode by which whatever is *is*. It thus becomes impossible
for the uncreated divine essence or nature to share a common
mode of existence with created human nature. It becomes
impossible for God to be able to exist in the flesh as a person
who unites two natures existentially, and it becomes impossible for man to be able to exist as a partaker of the fullness
of the life of God.

The whole of Western metaphysics, both theological and
philosophical, having denied the primary ontological distinc-

tion between essence and energies (the difference between
the essence and its mode of disclosure through the energies,
which are always personal), is inescapably imprisoned in an
intellectual conception of essence[21] and in an etiological interpretation of existence.[22] It thus sets essence and existence
in antithesis to each other, polarizing the abstract and the
concrete.[23] This leads inevitably to the deterministic idealism of the principle "essence precedes existence," which
traces back the ideas or causes of beings to the intellectual
content of the divine essence, and presents ontic existence as
the only existential reality.[24] At the same time this antithesis
polarizes the divine and human natures not only ontologically but also existentially, and consequently interprets the
"salvation" of humanity by the legal model of the justifi-
cation of the individual or by positing the intervention of
an ontologically inexplicable (and therefore rather magical)
"grace."

By contrast, the ontological concepts of Eastern theologians were grounded primarily on the experience of personal
relation that is attainable through the energies of the essence:
The energies differentiate and reveal the personal, otherness
while simultaneously disclosing the *homoousion* of the persons, since they are the common energies of a common nature
or essence. The ontological concepts of the Eastern theologians are consequently based on the priority of the mode of
existence in relation to the essence.[25] We know the essence or
nature only as personal mode of existence, the nature existing only as the content of the person. That is why the acts of
will or energies of the nature, as the potentiality for revealing the mode by which the nature *is*, are not identified with
the nature but are distinguished from it, for they refer to the
nature's mode of existence.

Thus in the theological understanding of the Orthodox East
created beings are the result of the divine acts of will – the
natural acts of will – which are expressed as a personal tri-

adic energy revelatory of the personal mode of the divine existence and also of the one common undivided divine nature. Since they have their cause in the will or energy of the divine nature and not in the divine nature itself, created beings differ in essence and nature from the Godhead. They constitute an entirely different natural and essential reality with regard to the divine nature or essence, an essential potentiality of otherness *opposite* the divine essence, that is to say, a personal potentiality to *be-opposite* the divine personal existence.

The triadic energy of God as a summons to the realization of a relation *outside of* the divine nature is actualized in every created being. Every created being embodies the divine summons, because every created being is a "combination" and "union" of *logoi*[26] revelatory of the divine energy. But at the same time the "logical" constitution of created beings points to their power of also embodying the "logical" response to the dynamically actualized summons of God to communion and relation, of manifesting the essential otherness of the world *opposite* the divine essence as a personal potentiality of communion with the divine personal existence.

Even though all created beings embody the divine summons to the realization of a relation with God outside of the divine essence, nevertheless only human personal existence has the existential potentiality to *realize* this relation by actualizing and recapitulating the "logical" potentiality of created beings to embody the "logical" response to God's dynamically active summons to communion and relation. Human personal existence is the only existential potentiality for the *logos* of created beings to become a *logos* of response to the active summons of God – that is to say, a fact of relation with him. In this respect the human person wholly recapitulates nature as the consequence of the divine will for personal communion – it recapitulates not only human nature as a whole but also the whole of what in essence is outside of God.

Created beings, then, exist as a disclosure of the potential-

ity for personal relation with God of the entire world, of the
created with the uncreated, a relation which can only be realized through the human person. We can thus see here more
clearly that the *truth* of the beings that constitute the world's
reality is their rising up to the "horizon" of personal relation,
before any other intellectual or conscious determination. It is
the disclosure of their "logical" constitution which embodies
both the divine summons to communion and relation, and
the power of responding to this summons. In other words,
the personal relation between humanity and God is the existential presupposition for the disclosure of their truth. Beings
become true as a disclosure of this universal relation, as a rising up from that which is "outside of" the personal relation.

When humanity "discovers" in the "logicality" of created
beings the otherness of the personal *logos* of their Creator,
when it enters into a relationship with beings as "things-acts"
of the Logos, it transforms their created "logicality" into an
erotic-logical relation with the uncreated Logos – into a relation of existential freedom from the createdness of creatures.
Conversely, when this does not happen, humanity abandons
objective beings to the non-related "logicality" of the merely intellectual determinations of created self-containedness,
that is to say, to a *logos* which refers only to itself, to the
uninterpreted dialectic of the phenomenon and nothingness.

§86   *Ecstatic otherness with regard to nature, and the an-
       tithetical dimension of person and nature*

Humanity's personal existence constitutes the only existential potentiality for the realization of the world's response
to the divine summons, in the measure in which it embodies nature's ecstatic potentiality, the potentiality for nature to
"stand outside" itself, as personal otherness and freedom, in
the fact of *relation*. This "ecstasy" of nature also constitutes
the unique potentiality of *existentially* bridging the gulf of

the *natural* distance between the world and God – and this unique potentiality is embodied in the human person. It is the potentiality of the person's freedom with regard to nature, the possibility that nature will transcend itself in the dynamics of personal relation by bridging the natural distantiality between the world and God, or the possibility that nature will make itself autonomous outside of God.

In other words, humanity's freedom is defined as the specific potentiality of the human person experientially to realize or to abolish the natural distantiality of the world from God, the possibility that humanity can reveal this distantiality as the irrationality or "non-logicality" of that which is outside of the divine essence, by rejecting personal communion with the divine personal existence, or else that it can abolish this distantiality through the realization of an all-encompassing ecstatic relation with God. The first possibility (that of personal reliance on distantiality, on the autonomy and self-containedness of nature) results in the Fall of humanity, which also drags the world with it into the irrationality (*a-logon*) or absurdity (*para-logon*) of ontic self-containedness, referring nothingness to the truth of beings: the truth of beings is identified with temporal phenomenicity, the phenomenal "rising up" of beings from *nothing*.

The Fall fragments human nature itself into as many individual self-contained units as there are personal rejections of the transcendence of natural distantiality from God. In the same way, the Fall also shatters the harmonious polyphony of the *logoi* of created beings. The *logoi* of created beings cease to refer to the one unified Logos of the world. They cease to be *logoi* summoning to the one unified relation of the created and the uncreated. The *logoi* of created beings refer to the multiplicity of individual understanding or to the conventional semantics of a common utilitarian necessity. Turned into partial concepts of a semantics which remains as a whole irrational and conventional, they serve to support human individual self-containedness.

The biblical narrative of a Fall affecting the whole of human nature refers to the initial choice that the first human beings made of individual self-containedness. It refers to the fundamental fragmentation of nature into atomic individuals – a fragmentation which was subsequently extended in the generations that followed. The unity of human nature before the Fall is manifested as an existential fact. Nature existed as a communion and relation of persons. The personal mode of existence distinguished nature as personal otherness without dividing up and destroying nature as atomic individualities in opposition to each other. The oneness of human nature, of course, presupposes the referential ecstasy of every natural atomic individuality to the unity of the mode of existence which constitutes the personal relation. It presupposes the recapitulation of nature in the personal mode of existence and consequently in every fact of personal otherness, that is to say, in every personal existence. The oneness of nature is identified with personal otherness with regard to the nature, or with the personal self-transcendence of the nature, which has its initial presupposition and its dynamic fulfillment in the realization of a relation "outside-of-nature"; in the acceptance of the divine summons to personal communion and relation.

The moment humanity denies communion with God and relation to him, its personal existence ceases to be ecstatic with regard to nature as a whole, ceases to recapitulate nature by a referential movement outside-of-nature. Personal ecstasy (*ek-stasis*) becomes no more than atomic distantiality (*apo-stasis*) within the bounds of nature, and nature is fragmented into self-contained individual units.[27] That is also why the first fragmentation of nature is definitive. The first free choosing of individual self-containedness shattered nature once and for all and condemned the will of all the remaining persons to be simply an individual will, not the

common will of a unified nature coordinated with the freedom of a relation outside-of-nature. Personal freedom with
regard to nature becomes a mutually hostile separation of
person and nature, a ceaseless antithetical bipolar impulse, a
tragic bisection of the unity of the person.

What I called in the previous chapter "nature's dynamic
urge to be liberated in terms of atomic self-completeness"[28]
is this subsequently inescapable fragmentation of nature in
every generation, the "condemnation" of the human person
to be the bearer of an individual natural will. Every new human being is born subject to nature. Its very birth marks a
further fragmentation of nature. Its initial orientation (that is,
its freedom) is not ecstatic otherness towards nature but its
antithetical separation from nature.

There is therefore much truth in Sartre's aphorism: "My
original fall is the existence of the other."[29] The existence
of the "other" in the objective distantiality of individuality
is the disclosure of my fragmented nature. The "other" is
the confirmation of the inescapable fragmentation of nature.
Every "other" is an immediate empirical proof of the impossibility of the person to annul the dynamic impulse towards
the fragmentation of nature into individually self-complete
units. The "other" is my condemnation to be the bearer of an
individual natural will.

Thus it is the "other in his individual distantiality who de-
prives me of an existential potentiality, the potentiality for my
nature to be transcended in the personal mode of existence.
The *freedom* of the other" separates me from possibility of
transcending the atomic individuality that belongs to nature
and realizing that mode of existence (the *personal* mode)
which might substitute for it the existential unity (rather than
the existential fragmentation) of our common human nature.
For freedom after the Fall no longer constitutes the ecstatic
otherness with regard to nature which would have permitted the unity of the personal mode of existence. Freedom is

identified with the denial of the objectivity of nature, so that the subjectivity of atomic individuality can be supported and made autonomous. Atomic freedom is the knowledge and defense of subjective self-completeness. Freedom is identified with the will that differentiates atomic individuality in its biological and psychological self-defensiveness.

The identification of freedom with the natural will, that is to say, with instinctive individual self-defensiveness, fragments nature into existentially self-complete units and consequently annuls the existential unity of our common nature, abandoning individual existence to an abyss of existential loneliness. The necessarily personal ecstatic impulse of atomic existence towards the realization of relation collides against the hard shell of the "freedom" of the "other," that is, against his atomic self-defensiveness. Movement towards relation is experienced as a tragic sense of the impossibility of relation, the tormenting experience of the nothingness of relation imposed by the "freedom" of the "other." The freedom of the "other," the objective existential self-completeness of his atomic nature, *annuls* my own possibility of transcending nature.[30]

That is why "hell is other people," as Sartre says.[31] For him this expression clearly means that hell is not some external objective punishment. The hellish element in the human hell is "other people." The failure of the restoration of personal existence in its existential fullness, its falling away into a state of natural atomic individuality, sets it against the individual natures of the "other people." The "other" is the confirmation of my existential failure, my inability to smash the shell of the "freedom" which has been identified with the natural will, with the self-defensiveness of the biological and psychological ego. The "other" is hell because he torments me by revealing the condemnation that is my "freedom," that is to say, the tragic loneliness of my existential self-containedness, my inability to relate to the "other," and consequently the irrationality of my existence, the impossibility of dialogue, my incapacity to express love. That which is outside of personal ecstasy is shown to be an abyss of atomic distantiality, a hell of tragic and insurmountable loneliness.

Before Sartre, Dostoyevsky had already defined hell in a similar way but more fully, summarizing the theological teaching on hell in the Orthodox tradition: "Hell is the torment of not loving."[32] It becomes evident from this definition that "other people" are the occasion of my own hell, although the cause lies in my own inability to relate to them, in my imprisonment in the egocentric autonomy of atomic individuality, in my own "freedom." Hell is therefore all the more tormenting when the "other" is not an atomic individual at a distance from me who nullifies the possibility of relation, but is a person who presents himself to me as a loving ecstasy of self-offering and calls me to a fulfilling communion and relation which for me remains unattainable. This inability to relate, the punishment of someone not loving, is the ultimate failure of existence which summarizes the Church's teaching on eternal punishment. It is not God who is the punisher and creator of hell. What we know of God is a ceaseless outpouring of love, a "passion of erotic goodness." Hell is freely chosen by humankind. It is the tormenting loneliness of an atomic nature made existentially absolute. It is the willed refusal of communion with the divine erotic goodness.

§87   *The ontological content of "salvation"*

The original choice of the first human beings in favor of individual self-containedness was the first and definitive fragmentation of human nature, a universal condemnation to the hell of existential separation from the fullness of life, which is communion with God. This hell is destroyed in the person of Christ, in the event of the incarnation of God, in the union of the divine nature with human nature.

The meaning of the *salvation* of humanity "through Christ" and "in Christ" refers to the reality of a "new" united and indivisible nature, a "new creation" which is recapitulated primarily and initially in the personal existence of Christ. In the person of Christ the ecstatic reference of human nature to its existential *telos* was restored (the *telos* being a living communion with the uncreated cause and fullness of life, with the unlimited duration of life) so that what was restored was humanity's immediate universal relation to God and communion with him. This communion is the *logos* of existence, its meaning, its cause and, at the same time, the goal and fullness of its truth. Every ontological and existential theory is made whole in Christ because he is the Logos of every existing and existential reality. He is the Logos-hypostatic revelation of God, but also the *logos* of created beings, the disclosure of God's personal creative energy. He is also the *logos* of human existence, its existential *telos* and meaning – the recapitulation of the "logical" harmony of the world and of the *logos* of history in God's relation with humanity.[33]

This vital communion of Godhead and humanity in the person of Christ was not only volitional but first and foremost *natural*. In the person of Christ the divine and the human natures were united without division or confusion and without change. This union of the two natures, the now *natural* relation and communion of Godhead and humankind, has resulted in a definitive change in humanity's existential capabilities. The possibility of the ecstatic mode of existence, the personal possibility of ecstatic otherness with regard to nature, which after the Fall had been condemned to be exhausted within the limits of nature itself as individual distantiality – this personal ecstasy of nature outside-of-nature now becomes a natural possibility within the bounds of the theanthropic nature of Christ. It is now the nature which goes out of itself and is in total communion with the Godhead, and it is left to the freedom of the person to coordinate itself with this natural ecstasy, that is to say, to deny the existential autonomy of individuality, to abrogate the distantiality of individual self-containedness, to raise itself up to the totality of the ecstasy of nature, which is realized existentially in the person of Christ.

Of course, the union of the divine and human natures in the person of Christ is defined by the Church as a mystery inaccessible to objective categories of thought, that is to say, as a fact accessible only to the knowledge provided by living experience as a whole.[34] Hence the change that takes place in humanity's existential powers cannot be described exhaustively in philosophical language. The self-transcendence of natural individuality, the "kenosis" or self-emptying of atomic self-containedness and the restoration of the person to the fullness of hypostasis, that is to say, to the total perichoresis of loving communion, is an existential potentiality with which humanity is "graced" by God (the cause of every existence) – it is a "grace" or charisma given by God as a response to humanity's free and dynamic will to commune with the Godhead. And the charismatic restoration of *personal* communion with the Godhead is experienced as a "mystical participation" in the existential fact of the *natural* union of divinity and humanity.

This existential fact of the natural union of divinity and humanity is a new nature, that is to say, a new mode of existence – since we know the nature only as an existential fact. It is the "new" theanthropic nature which has as its "head," or its fundamental personal recapitulation, Christ himself,[35] and as its "members" all those who participate in the mode of existence which he inaugurated, all those who participate *personally* in the total *natural* union of divinity and humanity. The "head" and the "members" form a *body*, the body of the Church, the concrete realization of the "new" nature of the incarnate Logos, the ontological reality of a new mode of existence – new compared to the mode of existence of a nature fragmented into atomic individuals. The Church is a "gathering together of those previously scattered" atomic individuals of fragmented nature into the unity of personal loving perichoresis and existential communion with God.[36]

The Church, then, does not simply represent a sociological or moral fact or a "religious" manifestation of fallen humanity. The Church is an ontological reality, the existential fact of a "new" human nature, which communes wholly with the Godhead, or which realizes an existential "impulse" opposite to that of the Fall. It realizes existence as love and eros, not as survival as an atomic individual. Human freedom does not cease, even within the "limits" of the Church's life, to be an antithetical dimension of the person and of "fallen" nature. To be grafted onto the "common" nature of the Church is a personal achievement, an attainment of personal freedom, which becomes possible "by the power of the Incarnation."[37] Overcoming the Fall, the "kenosis" of natural atomic individuality, represents not an automatic alteration, but a dynamic fact of progressive *metanoia*,[38] a change of outlook, and consequently a change of mode of life – in the end a fact of existential rebirth. It is the "death" of the "old man" of atomic self-containedness and the "resurrection" of the "new man" of total personal self-offering and relation.

The whole meaning of the Christian ascetic practice and mystical life is summed up in the dynamics of this existential change.[39] And this change is possible because the inability of nature to realize an ecstatic relation of communion with the Godhead has been definitively lifted. The human person is no longer condemned to remain within the existential limits of natural individuality. It can now realize dynamically the presupposition of its existential fullness, the movement and reference outside-of-nature within the dynamic context of the natural union of God with humanity.

This brief review of Christology brings the Church's teaching on hell into focus. Hell is a mode of existence. It is the existential distantiality of atomic individuality, the impossibility of natural ecstasy, the unattainability of communion and relation. This mode of existence is obligatory and universal after the Fall, but the obligatory and universal character of the Fall is expunged in the existential fact of the Incarnation of God, in the union of the divine nature with the human. The distantiality of atomic individuality, which is the denial of the existential fullness of the person, that is to say, of communion with God, is now a matter of free personal choice, a voluntary refusal to ascend to the totality of natural ecstasy which was realized existentially in the person of Christ.

God's union with humanity is an existential fact that is definitive and total. Our free personal response to this *natural* union with the Godhead restores humanity to the fullness of its existential potentiality, to the fullness of life. The free refusal of personal participation in this natural union with the Godhead perpetuates the "unnatural" mode of existence of the Fall, which is humanity's hell.

The "eternal life" the Church speaks about is the abrogation of time within the ceaseless present created by the immediacy of God's relation to humanity or within the ceaseless bounds of the tormenting experience of the annihilation of relation. "At the end of the ages," says St. Maximus the Confessor, that is to say, when "time ceases from motion," the union of God with humanity will be revealed in its universality: it will have included every human being. For the "worthy," those who will be able to respond to the fullness of God's loving self-offering, this union will be "by grace" and a source "of divine and inconceivable pleasure." For the "unworthy," those who remain existentially unable to enter into relation, union with God will be "contrary to grace" and a source of "indescribable pain."[40] The eternal salvation or eternal damnation the Church speaks about are existential possibilities beyond the conventional categories of punishment and reward which are verified by direct experience.

§88   *Nothingness as personal power and choice*

The power of the human person to accept or refuse the natural distantiality separating the human from the divine nature, the possibility that we might reveal this distantiality to be the irrationality [*a-logon*] or absurdity [*para-logon*] of existential self-containedness, that is to say, to be the void or the abyss of being outside-of-Being, leads us to an ontological rather than ontic-intellectual understanding of nothingness.

In philosophical thought, nothingness is defined by the logical necessity of that which is the dialectic opposite to being. "Of opposites one of each pair is a privation," says Aristotle, "and all things are traced back to being and non-being."[41] Thus nothingness belongs to an ontic category, is defined by being, is the opposite of being, is the denial of being, is non-being. In short, it is purely conceptual. But in the ontology of existential categories – the ontology which starts with the question, "what is the difference between being and Being?" or "what is the difference between nature and nature's mode of existence?" – nothingness has an existential meaning which confirms a fundamental ontological difference.

We know Being only as existential fact, only as the mode by which whatever is, *is*. We know nature in its totality only as ecstatic otherness with regard to its common attributes, only as personal immediacy or as the effect of personal energy: we know it in the fact of the relation which recapitulates nature outside-of-nature. The personal ecstasy of nature is the mode of existence of the whole, the only mode by which Being becomes accessible to us in its ontological totality and not in the quantitative narrowing of fragmented ontic individualities. Yet every personal refusal to refer nature to the fact of the relation which recapitulates nature in personal otherness (a refusal based on the existential potentiality defined by the ontological difference between person and nature) exhausts the meaning of the existential ecstasy of nature in the distantiality of atomic individuality, or in the "unnatural" self-containedness of atomic nature. Personal insistence on the distantiality of atomic individuality, the free choice of atomic self-containedness, does not refer the ecstasy of nature to the fact of a total personal relation, which recapitulates the mode of existence as a whole (the only mode by which Being becomes accessible to us in its ontological totality); it refers the ecstasy of nature to the fact of the absence of relation, of the nothingness of the existential totality, that is to say, to *nothingness* as an existential reality.

In other words, nothingness is a mode of existence which is defined by insistence on natural individuality. A possibility of free personal choice, it is the distantiality (*apo-stasis*) of atomic individuality as against the ecstasy (*ek-stasis*) which recapitulates the total unity of existence in personal otherness. Nothingness is the existential reality of *being outside-of-Being* as the fullness of personal existence, that is to say, outside the relation and communion of humanity with God, the only relation which recapitulates nature in its totality in a personal ecstatic reference outside-of-nature. As experience of the absence of ecstatic reference, nothingness is not purely and simply the existential (atomic) experiencing of the nothing on which atomic existence depends. It is the existential consciousness or anxiety of falling away from Being, of the essential non-existence of existence, of imprisonment in the irrationality of atomic existence.[42]

Nothingness constitutes a *personal* potentiality of existence because it is the denial of the hypostatic mode of existence which the person alone can attain (or refuse to attain). It is the opposite of "kenosis," the hypostatic mode of existence which was revealed by the incarnation of God. As free personal choice, or as personal existential potentiality, nothingness refers to the ground of personal existence, which is the summons of God, the fundamental possibility to-be-opposite the divine personal existence. Thus we could say that nothingness, as existential experience of ecstatic referentiality outside-of-Being, confirms the existence of a personal God. It is the consciousness of the existential possibility of the ecstasy of existence *outside-of-nature* either towards the existential fullness of personal relation, or towards the nothingness of existence that is the absence of relation.

The personal dimension of nothingness, nothingness as a personal existential possibility, is revealed not only in the fact of human freedom, which preserves the truth of the person even within the limits of the existential self-containedness of atomic individuality, but also as the experiential assurance of the personal existence of God, in the dynamic of the existential ecstasy which reveals him as either immediacy of relation or failure of relation.

Chapter Three

The Moral Dimension of Nothingness

Morality and Being: identity and difference

The meaning of morality (*êthos*) refers to the mode of existence: "character (*êthê*) is what makes us ascribe certain qualities to the agents."[1] The reference to the "quantity" of being presupposes the truth of existential authenticity and, at the same time, its distortion or alienation, that which we call the Fall of man, the falling away from the mode of existence "according to truth." The falling away from existential authenticity is defined anagogically by reference to the prelapsarian integrity of existence, and the *measure* of this reference we call *ethos* or morality. As a measure of existential authenticity, morality finds its fulfillment or wholeness in the mode of existence "according to truth." Morality which has been made whole or integral is existence "according to truth."

This definition attributes to the concept of morality an ontological and existential meaning, not a conventional or legalistic one. It identifies the ontological content of morality with the "quality" of the mode of existence, that is to say, with the truth of being or with the distortion of this truth. What I call the prelapsarian integrity of existence is the unity of morality and being, the refusal to make an ontological distinction between the two, or to differentiate at all between morality and being.

If the truth of being is defined by the freedom and other-

275

ness of the *personal* mode of existence, then morality, as the measure of the reference to existential authenticity, defines the nearness or distance from the fullness of the truth of the person, of personal communion and relation, of freedom from the self-containedness of atomic individuality. With regard to the divine existence, where there is no occurrence of a fall from existential authenticity, the morality or ethos of God is identified with Being (the mode of divine existence), with the triadic communion and mutual interpenetration of the divine persons. When Christian revelation lays down that "God is love" (1 John 4:8), it refers not to a partial property of God's conduct but to that which God *is* as the fullness of the triadic communion of persons within the "framework" of an undivided nature. The communion and mutual interpenetration of the divine persons, that is, the mode by which the Godhead *is*, reveals the morality of the divine life, the love and the Being of God. But with regard to human existence, which introduces a fact of *fall* from existential authenticity, morality is differentiated from being by the concept of the difference between the measure and the measured: As a measure of reference to the truth of Being (to the freedom and otherness of the personal mode of existence), morality defines and "measures" the fact of the "preservation" of the person within the bounds of the realization, or failure to realize, a *relation* beyond and outside of the distantiality of atomic individuality.

§90   *Morality as convention and an axiological ontology*

But this ontological-existential interpretation of morality presupposes, of course, a more general approach to the ontological problem wich identifies Being with the personal mode of existence, or alternatively, recapitulates in the person and in the personal energies-deeds of the person the truth of every existent and existential reality.

By contrast, an ontological approach which identifies Being with an intellectual conception of onticity "as a whole," that is to say, with the concept of an ontic totality, or an ontological approach which identifies Being with temporality as the mode by which whatever is *appears*, that is to say, with not-being-nothing, in both cases result either in a definition of morality determined in objective, individualized categories, or in a sense of morality simply as convention. When the truth of Being is separated from the mode of existence "according to truth," that is to say, from the experience of personal relation and personal energies, the concept of morality inevitably acquires a conventional content. It is exhausted in the axiological measuring of objective advantages, which are founded on the demands or goals of social survival, that is to say, which have their beginning and end in individual and social usefulness (the latter idealistic to a greater or lesser degree).

The objectivization of morality within a framework of an axiological gradation of social demands enshrines an individualized morality as the basis of all moral values. And this individualized morality is absolutized and projected anagogically in order to define the idea of an "absolute good" – just as being, or ontic atomicity, is absolutized intellectually in order to provide an anagogical definition of Being. These two corresponding abstractions can then converge to form a single fundamental theory of ontic reality as an axiological synthesis, that is to say, to define the framework of an axiological ontology. Such an axiological ontology is necessarily dualistic. It confronts the problem of existence within the framework of a bipolar ontological antithesis between good and evil, spirit and matter, soul and body. The purest form of existence is spirit, outside any necessity or suffering, that is to say, outside any limitation imposed by ontic individuality. The spirit is existence "as a whole," existence at its most integral and unlimited. It is both the absolute good and the definition of Being. A falling away from the universality of the good and the integrity of Being creates inferior, coarser forms of existence. These are the material forms that are divided up into ontic individualities. The experience of the senses is experience of falling away from the good and from the universality of Being. But the mind can ascend progressively as far as the absolute ontological antithesis of good and evil, spirit and matter, that is to say, as far as a cosmological and theological dualism attributing two principles or causes to the world. The objective standard by which this ontological gradation, or antithesis, is measured is morality as determinative of the individual, and the good as the fundamental summary of the properties which serve atomic individuality or justify its absolutized existential demands.

(a) *Scholastic axiology*

The approaches and systematic theories which provided the framework of an axiological ontology and ethics underwent an often contradictory development (from Plato's axiological idealism, the identification of Being with the "Idea of the Good,"[2] to the dualism of Plotinus,[3] the Hermetic Corpus[4] and the Gnostics[5]) before finally arriving at the rationalistic synthesis of Roman Catholic scholasticism which either positively or negatively has influenced almost the whole of Western thought. The Scholastics[6] defined the concept of the good or of virtue on the basis of the rules of logic: "Virtus moralis bonitatem habet ex regula rationis."[7] Every act or habit that conforms to the demands of reason is good or virtuous, while any disobedience against reason, whether actual or implied, is evil or a sin.[8] And this is because human reason is an anagogic faculty, or an existential microcosm of the divine reason, in which all the eternal laws of ethics and existence are summarized.[9] Hence disobedience against reason is contrary to nature and its eternal laws. It is disobedience against God himself and the divine will.[10]

Thus Roman Catholic scholastic axiology summarizes Being and the good in an intellectual approach to the absolute. It introduced an individualized ethics as the measure of the good, as the measure of the submission of individual nature to the intellect and of the intellect to the eternal laws of divine reason. In this manner Roman Catholicism has established the rationalism and subjectivist ethics of modern European culture. The personal God of historical revelation and of the Church's experience is transformed into an abstract "source" and "cause" of all natural, ethical and social legislation.[11] Human individuality is subordinated to the authority of absolute reason, or else it rebels violently against it, with the result that European history takes the shape of a tragic polarization between totalitarianism and revolution.

(b)   *The Kantian imperative*

Kant marks an important stage in the history of the problem. He sought to soften the stark contrast between transcendent reason and human reason by abolishing the metaphysical dimension of scholastic axiology[12] and raising moral subjectivism to a rational rule of absolute validity: "Handle so, dass die Maxime deines Willens jederzeit zugleich als Prinzip einer allgemeinen Gesetzgebung gelten könne."[13] This stark contrast was consciously substituted by the dialectical opposition between the moral imperative and an absolutized abstract conception of nature or Being.[14] But the moral imperative, for all the support it finds in individual experience, does not cease itself to be a mental absolute, a tracing back of an individualized morality to the absolute. And an individualized morality inevitably represents a standard of conventional values, a utilitarian estimate of objective human relations, without the slightest reference to the problem of existence, to the question regarding a mode of existence "according to truth" – a non-alienated existence.

Even modern value-theorists who wish to define the good

as beyond the conventional and relative limits of a utilitarian standard have not succeeded in combining ethics with the problem of existence, the essential transcendence of abstract mental forms. The following statement of Nicolai Hartmann might be taken as an example: "The good is not the ideal being of value or its inner meaning, nor is it the simple actual existence of the thing valued. It is simply the teleology of value – with evil as the teleology of non-value – in the space of reality."[15] The attempt to define the good not comparatively (*hôs pros*) or referentially (*pros ti*), but in itself, apart from any comparison and relation, in a teleological combination with *a priori* recognized "values," inevitably ends up as a bare concept of the good, or a schematic idea without existential content.

§91   *Heidegger's combination of morality and Being*

The most serious attempt in modern Western philosophy to combine morality and ethics with the ontological problem was made by Heidegger. The transition from a metaphysics of ontic categories (the causal linking of beings to Being) to an ontology of the difference between beings and Being was accompanied by an attempt to establish an ontological (not "ontic" and categorical) definition of morality, to identify ethics with fundamental ontology ("Fundamentalontologie") as Heidegger calls the interpretation of humanity's *being*, which is the knowledge of Being as the power of ecstasy, or as the consciousness of temporal phenomenicity.[16]

Heidegger himself did not go on to formulate his ontological ethics systematically, but he did define its boundaries. With Heraclitus' fragment, "man's *ethos* is his daimon,"[17] as his starting-point, Heidegger discusses the etymology of the Greek word *ethos* and its ontological content. The first use of the word in the plural means "haunts" or "abodes." "The haunts and pasture of horses," we read in Homer's *Iliad*,[18] and in the *Odyssey* we find the expression: "to sleep in their abodes."[19] The word has the same meaning in Hesiod,[20] and also in Herodotus,[21] Plato,[22] and Arrian.[23] Gradually the word begins to mean (even as early as Hesiod[24]) "the traditional ordinances prevailing in a place where people dwell together, which are shaped by the life led in that place, are established by a shared existence as fitting customs and are regarded in that place as habits which are legal and right."[25]

Heidegger notes that Heraclitus' fragment 119 must be interpreted in accordance with the first sense of *ethos*: our *ethos* is the disclosure of the place where we dwell permanently, the definition of our abiding, the specific space of our life. Consequently, when Heraclitus declares that "man's *ethos* is his daimon," that is, God, he refers *ethos* to our space or mode of life, and this mode is the existential nearness of God and our abiding in him. Thus the word *ethos* defines that which man is, man's essence.[26]

Heidegger limits himself to observing that such an understanding of *ethos* refers principally to ontology, not to ethics.[27] Nevertheless, this interpretation of *ethos* does not lead to the ethics of Western Christianity and European philosophy, the axiological ethics of an individualized morality. But Heidegger does not go on to determine the consequences that flow from the identification of ontology with ethics, the identification of morality with being, which is indicated by Heraclitus' definition. Humanity's *ethos*, as the mode by which we *are*, and, specifically, as "nearness" to and "abiding" in God (where nearness and abiding signify, of course, an existential reference and relation), necessitates an understanding of Being as a personal mode of existence. And this understanding is very different from the phenomenological sense of Being, on which Heidegger insists, the power of "disclosure" and "self-concealment," where "disclosure" is understood as temporality and time as the mode by which beings are-not-nothing.

§92   *The "ethics of freedom" in French existentialism*

The existential-ontological theory and interpretation of morality and ethics was developed most consistently in the French existentialist movement, which of course has its roots in Heidegger's "new ontology." Existentialism takes the dominance of the *absurd* in the life of the world and in historical "becoming" as an ontological reality.[28] From the moment we affirm this ontological reality existentially, from the moment we are persuaded that the absurd and "evil" are not creations of chance circumstances but are the "natural" realization of historical life, or givens which refer to the mode of our historical existence, from that moment we consciously transfer to the space of conventionality and unrealistic idealism both our attempt to achieve an individual morality and our organized action aiming at historical "change."

Existentialism affirms the absolute and definitive dominance of the absurd in the life of the world, seeking the ultimate preservation and valuing of human existence precisely through the absurd and in full knowledge of the inescapable engagement of history with the "gears"[29] of evil. It is significant that it was during the Second World War, with its horrific loss of life and the madness of the Nazi camps and crematoria, that the existentialist movement appeared in France as a desperate attempt to give some value to human existence in the face of the given absurdity of history.[30]

The preservation and valuing of humanity is realized in existentialism by the affirmation of our freedom in historical action. Historical action, a conscious and responsible resistance to the absurdity of the world, affirms human freedom as an existential differentia distinguishing it from the force of determinism and the absurd, and endows humanity with value in the face of any kind of totalitarianism.[31] Humanity *exists* not simply as the potentiality for thought, as Descartes claimed, since thought cannot interpret the absurdity of historical existence. Humanity exists as a potentiality for the dynamic realization of its freedom. It is "thrown down" into an absurd world. The circumstances in which human beings are born and grow up deny the freedom of the subject. Nevertheless these "situations"[32] are precisely the presuppositions for the dynamic realization of freedom, that is to say, for the self-realization of existence, in dynamic contrast to every "external" determination.

The basic ontological distinction which Sartre introduces between human existence as a dynamic self-realization ("pour-soi"), and every other kind of existence as always given and "in-itself" ("en-soi"), reveals the ontological content of human freedom.[33] Human freedom precedes the *essence* of man. It is its presupposition,[34] that which distinguishes the human being from all other beings which do not have the power to change the given situations by which they are determined absolutely. Even in the hands of his executioner a human being is free, not in the sense of an "interior" freedom as proclaimed by Luther and German idealism but as the power of immediate energetic action which can be realized even at the last moment.[35] This action, even if it fails, even if it is only the possibility of action, gives humanity the power to be itself and not the passive result of the situation in which it finds itself.

Thus humanity's *being* is identified with freedom: "That which we call freedom cannot be distinguished from the *being* of the 'human reality.' Man is not there *first* so as to be free *in consequence*; there is no difference between the being of man and his 'being-free.'"[36] This identification gives humanity's *being* an absolutely dynamic character: "Man is that which he does."[37] Our historical activity is the mode by which we are what we are. It is our responsibility for our own existence. The human person is responsible for that which it is, chooses that which it is, even if this choice ends ultimately in failure. To live the absurd to the extreme, *cre-*

ating (historically or artistically), filling the senseless void with images or hopes – that is a kind of "heroic despair,"[38] an absolute and tragic faith in humanity and in the ontological prize of its freedom, a noble and despairing ethics.

The identification of humanity's *being* with freedom, with responsibility for the realization of existence in the face of the given *situations* which fetter it, that is to say, historical activity as humanity's existential self-realization, is a thesis which brought French existentialism into a kind of complementary relation with the Marxist theory of historical materialism – in spite of the gulf separating Marxism from any kind of philosophical thought that presupposes cognitive categories drawn from a subjective approach to life. Marxism relied on a comprehensive theory of individual consciousness and the action which it expresses. It saw the human person only as a member of a "wider whole" with individual consciousness as a product of the historical evolution of this whole and, at the same time, as an instrument or "tool" of adaptation to historical evolution in general.

French existentialism appeared to want to fill the enormous anthropological void left in Marxism by the total dependence of the individual on the social environment and on an impersonal historical evolution, the void of the alienation of the human subject within the context of a Hegelian-Marxist "fetishistic worship of facts." It appears that it was the encounter between the two "ideologies" of existentialism and Marxism that prompted modern attempts to express an "anthropology" of historical materialism, a neo-Marxist humanism, based on the "principle" of humanity's *hope* or *denial of alienation* within the mechanistic structures of a consumerist (socialist or capitalist) society, and on the absolute priority of the human subject in relation to these structures.[39]

I shall not attempt a broader analysis of these ideas here. I will simply note that in all these cases the ontological problem of the Fall, at least as defined by Heidegger,[40] remains essentially unexamined. The absurdity of the word and of history are a given and invariable reality,[41] and nothingness is revealed to be an existential realization of humanity's being through the continual destruction of ontic identity (the "en-soi").[42] Human freedom, as a conscious and active reaction to the absurdity of the world and of history, is a tragic potentiality for existential self-annihilation without any redemptive character, and ultimately a reality of condemnation, as Sartre defined it of his own accord.[43]

§93   *Good and evil, two anhypostatic concepts*

If we accept the otherness and freedom of the person, or a personal mode of existence, as a fundamental ontological reality, it follows that on the level of morality and ethics we should go beyond not only the duality of good and evil and an *a priori* axiology but also an existential "ethics" that aims at the dynamic self-realization of existence in terms of its own freedom, that is to say, in terms of its own self-annihilation.

The truth of the person as a fundamental ontological reality necessarily denies any ontological content to the concepts of good and evil. Good and evil are two anhypostatic concepts, two intellectual categories which are created by raising an individualized morality to the level of an absolute. Conversely, the concept of an individualized morality necessarily presupposes a conventional definition of good and evil on the basis of empirical usefulness, that is to say, on the basis of an *a priori* axiological gradation of social relations.[44]

If morality has on ontological content, it cannot be exhausted in the conventional axiological categories of good and evil. The ontological content of morality refers to an existential reality, and an existential reality is always hypostatic. Morality is not an anhypostatic concept but a personal predicate. It is the "measure" of reference to a mode of existence "according to truth," that is to say, to a personal mode of existence.

In Christian theology, however, (both biblical and patristic) we often find absolute good, or good in itself, with an onto- logical content, defined as a hypostatic reality referring to the person of God ("no man is good but God alone"[45]). But it is evident that in this case the good refers to the *ethos* of the divine life, which is identified with the Being of God, with the triadic mode of divine existence, which is the fullness of personal communion and relation.[46] That is to say, it is not about the intellectual ascent to an absolute derived from a morality individualized within the context of empirical use- fulness. It is about the ontological interpretation of the good of that mode of life which is not alienated, or which is "ac- cording to truth," as revealed in the triadic communion of the divine persons.

It is striking that although the good refers to the hypostatic reality of the triadic Godhead, the Church's theologians ab- solutely refuse to allow an ontological content to the concept of evil as well.[47] And this refusal necessarily entails the re- jection of any kind of dualistic interpretation of existential reality. The Church Fathers do not recognize any mode of existence other than the personal, the fullness of which is revealed in the truth of the triadic God. Evil is not a different ontological reality. It is not a different mode of existence, but the distortion and corruption of the one unique – that is, per- sonal – mode of existence,[48] the result of a wrong use of the freedom of persons.[49] For this freedom cannot be destroyed utterly. The wrong use of it cannot eliminate its ontological ground, which is the personal mode of existence.[50]

It was precisely the danger of interpreting evil as an onto- logical reality, corresponding to the existential realization of the good in the *ethos* of the divine triadic communion, that sometimes led certain of the Fathers to reject the ontological content even of the good, the reference of the good to the Godhead, and regard the good (now with a conventional axi- ological meaning) as a simple accident.[51] Of course a conventional axiology cannot define the existential fact. Hence an axiological evaluation can only express partial passions, relations or accidents. The distortion and corruption of the mode of existence which is "according to nature" is not distinguished in an ontological or conventionally axiological manner, but only *morally*. In this moral differentiation the *ethos* signifies precisely the *measure* of the reference to the fullness of the personal mode of existence. The differentiation of the mode of existence is moral in the measure in which it manifests the difference between personal ecstasy and atomic distantiality, between Being and nothingness.

To speak of the moral differentiation of a mode of existence as disclosure of the difference between personal ecstasy and atomic distantiality implies reference to a moral dimension of both Being and nothingness. Like Being, nothingness defines the moral differentiation of the one unique existential fact, the differentiation of the personal mode of existence, as either affirmation or denial of the fullness of personal communion. Atomic distantiality is not distinguished ontologically, but only morally, from personal ecstasy. The consciousness of atomic distantiality is, of course, a personal ecstatic experience, but an experience of the moral distortion of the personal ecstatic mode of existence.

Consequently, from the ontology of the truth of the person there emerges a morality which neither recognizes nor justifies a schematic intellectual opposition between ontological (dualistic) or conventional and axiological ideas of good and evil. It recognizes only the general moral dilemma of choosing between Being and nothingness, that is to say, between "life" and "death"[52] – since Being is identified with the fullness of life, with the pleroma of a mode of existence "according to truth," while nothingness is death, or distantiality from true life, the negation of the *logos* of life, the irrationality of non-communicating individuality.

§94   *"Virtue comes through truth"*

Within the framework of this ontological morality there exists a deontology and a legal expression of its terms which aims at the restoration of humanity to its existential authenticity. Such restoration is not confined to the prescribed objective improvements of conduct, as usually happens in every system of codified ethics, where the objective consequence of the moral code is ultimately the self-sufficiency of atomic individuality.[53] The restoration refers to a total change, or *metanoia*, on the part of humanity. And *metanoia* means a change of *mind*, that is to say, a change of humanity's entire outlook, a dynamic transition from the distantiality of atomic self-containedness to the ecstasy of personal communion, a return from the individual to the person, from humanity's existential distortion to its existential truth.[54]

In other words, the goal of this ontological morality is truth, not virtue. Virtue is the ascetic practice which serves the realization of the truth of humanity – truth is not some "knowledge" subordinated to a utilitarian understanding of virtue. Maximus the Confessor clearly defines this presupposition of the ontological character of Orthodox moral teaching: "Virtue exists for the sake of truth, not truth for the sake of virtue."[55] And he distinguishes the "natural forms or expressions of virtue" from those "which are spiritual, that is, are supernatural and characteristic of God"[56] – distinguishing between the virtue which serves the self-containedness of human nature and the virtue which reveals the truth of the mode of divine existence. Putting the virtues into practice does not constitute for Maximus a quantifiable moral perfection. It creates a *unit of wisdom* which is "contemplated indivisibly" and is "perceived in a single form" through the practice of the individual virtues.[57]

Truth as the goal of virtue defines the cognitive character of ascetic practice for the attainment of the virtues and the

ascetic character of "the path of knowledge." Ascetic practice leads to knowledge, because knowledge of truth is an
existential realization, not something appropriated mentally.
Truth is approached only by "a person who knows along
with acting and who acts along with knowing." Christian
ascetic practice and Christian virtue as a moral endeavor are
summed up in the deliberate and dynamic rejection of the
egocentricity of atomic individuality, in the emptying of the
ego of atomic selfcontainedness, which is the rebellious impulse of fragmented nature to preserve itself in its ontic self-
sufficiency. Ascetic practice aims at the rejection of what is
willed by atomic nature, so that the freedom of the person
can be attained, the existential self-transcendence of atomicity in personal communion and relation, the ecstasy of nature
outside-of-nature in the existential fulfillment which is communion with the Godhead.

And precisely because the aim of Christian asceticism is
humanity's personal communion with God, and this communion is a human existential capability only because God
freely gives himself to humanity in an ecstatic self-offering
of "erotic goodness," the aim of ascetic practice is attained
only in the fact of divine grace. The grace of God is not
some indeterminate kind of divine "blessing," which is added quantitatively to humanity's natural capabilities. It is the
life-giving summons and ground of the summons ceaselessly issued by God for humanity to participate in the existential fulfillment of personal communion with the Godhead. It
is the dynamically "attractive" power of divine love, which
seeks to restore humanity to the sublime gifts which its nature received in the person of Christ, in the fact of the natural union of God with humanity. This means that even the
achievements of ascetic discipline, the human virtues, have
only a relative significance with regard to the goal of existential fulfillment, and are appropriated only through divine
grace, only by the fact that God gives himself to humanity

in a ceaselessly actualized self-offering. If human virtue becomes an end in itself, it imprisons humanity in an objective
self-sufficiency which perpetuates its atomic self-containedness, its condemnation to be distanced from life and "true
existence." Virtue finds its existential goal, the goal of truth,
only as a dynamic assent to divine grace, which is the dynamically activated summons of God's erotic goodness.

§95   *Sin, the moral content of nothingness as an existen-
       tial fact*

Abiding in the distantiality of atomic individuality signifies
the failure of humanity to be that which it is "in accordance
with truth." It signifies a falling away from Being, a kind
of "para-existence," a mode by which humanity is outside
of Being, "contrary to (para) nature." This falling away is
sin. That is to say, it is missing the mark with regard to authentic existence "in accordance with truth." It is again the
Eastern Church Fathers who insist on this interpretation of
sin as missing the mark and failure – a failure of humanity to
remain in "that which is human in accordance with nature."
Maximus the Confessor writes, for example: "Failure and
weakness open the door to evil, bringing about what is contrary to nature by the privation of what is in accordance with
nature."[58] And elsewhere he says, commenting on Dionysius
the Areopagite: "He calls sin, that is, a failure or a falling
away by someone, a privation and a missing of the mark, a
shooting wide of the target rather than hitting it, to use a metaphor from archery. When we fail to attain movement which
belongs to the good and is in accordance with nature, or order, we are borne towards that which is contrary to nature
and irrational and entirely without essence or existence."[59]
As I have already emphasized, the Greek Fathers refused
to give sin hypostatic substance as a natural reality, just as
they refused to see it in juristic terms simply as transgression

and psychological guilt. Sin is not a nature, an evil nature, which exists hypostatically as an opposite pole to the goodness of God. There is nothing in God's creation which is hypostatically and naturally evil. Sin is failure, the failure of persons to become complete as persons in an all-embracing relation and communion amongst themselves and with God. It is the product of free will, of a mistaken choice. This mistaken choice has inevitable implications for human nature, since it makes the individual will and nature autonomous and consequently fragments and distorts the personal unity and wholeness of nature.[60]

But this "remodeling" of nature does not imply its *essential* change into something evil. To exclude any such interpretation Maximus goes so far as to describe the fall of nature as blameless, in contrast to the blameworthy sin freely chosen by Adam. He writes:

> Once the faculty of free will of Adam's natural *logos* had first been corrupted, it also of itself corrupted nature, rejecting the grace of dispassion, and so sin came into being. The first and thoroughly blameworthy sin was the falling away of the faculty of free will from the good towards evil. The second sin came on account of the first. This was the blameless remodeling of nature from incorruption towards corruption. For two sins came into being in our first ancestor through his transgressing the divine commandment, the one blameworthy, the other blameless, since it had the blameworthy sin as its cause. The former arose when the faculty of free will voluntarily rejected the good, the latter when because of the faculty of free will nature involuntarily rejected immortality.[61]

The "remodeling" of nature, the falling away from Being (from the totality of personal communion) in the distantiality and fragmentation of atomic individuality, is a kind of "nonexistence," a form of existence "contrary" to existence, "contrary to nature," outside of Being. On the basis of such an understanding of sin, Eastern Orthodox theologians have refused to see humanity's relation to God in juristic or legalistic terms as an individual transgression of objective ordinances resulting in a purely psychological guilt. In Eastern theological literature, God was never understood as a vindictive inflictor of punishment. The juristic Roman Catholic tradition is quite alien to it. God "judges" human beings not in the sense of a judge in a court of law ascertaining guilt and imposing the appropriate penalty. He judges because he is what he is: the potentiality of humanity's "true life" and existence "in accordance with truth." When the human person cuts himself off voluntarily from this existential potentiality, he is "judged" with regard to this potentiality.[62] It is not God's verdict but his existence that judges it. God is only an outpouring of love, a "wealth of benignity," a "torrent of erotic goodness." But since God is love and the fullness of the truth of Being, he is a judging presence for humanity, "since (the holy and consubstantial Trinity) is one God who is by nature Creator, and exerciser of a providential and judicious care over all that he has made."[63]

Sin is a self-punishment which the human person chooses freely, rejecting communion with God, rejecting that which it has been called to be, rejecting Being, which is existence "according to nature" and "according to truth, and preferring "to miss the mark" with regard to the "natural" end of its existence and fall away from Being.

As something without hypostasis yet nevertheless a real *moral* potentiality for existential missing the mark and falling away from Being, sin refers to nothingness, whose moral dimension it "measures." Sin is the moral content of nothingness as an existential fact, the measure of the annihilation of existential fulfillment, which is a ceaseless fall into nonexistence which is never wholly accomplished, since the person is still preserved even in his ultimate self-destruction. Hence even as moral experience sin is not restricted to the cognition of a legal transgression, but is the experience of nothingness, the irrationality (*a-logia*) or absurdity (*para-logon*) of existence, the experience of the abyss of being "outside" personal communion, the pain of a nullified existential fulfillment, the "second death" of Revelation.[64]

Nothingness, then, may be defined in the end not as a concept but as a moral reality, a confirmation of the existential truth of the person, the ability of a human being to say no to God – "nullifying" but not annihilating the truth of his or her personal existence. The *ethos* of humanity is this adventure of its freedom, its never-ending choice between Being and nothingness, a choice which is ever confirmatory of its personal truth.

Thus the truth of the human person recapitulates both the ontology and the ethics of Christian philosophy. The *ethos* of the Church is its Truth, the truth for humanity and the truth for the world and for God. And this truth, which is faith and a rule of life, is the reality of the person. For the person to be restored to his or her integrity and wholeness, for the human being to become "all *prosôpon*" – "all person" – defines our existential end. It is the conclusion of our moral journey, the attainment of theosis or deification, the goal towards which the Church strives – as defined by Macarius of Egypt when he wrote: "For the soul that has been deemed worthy to participate in the spirit of his (God's) light and has been made radiant by the beauty of his ineffable glory, since he has prepared it for himself as a throne and dwelling-place, becomes all light, all face, all eye."[65]

Notes

PART ONE

Chapter One

[1] See H. G. Liddell, R. Scott and H. S. Jones, *A Greek-English Lexicon*, s.v. *ôps*; cf. D. Demetrakos, *Mega Lexikon tês Ellênikês Glôssês*, 9:8056.

[2] [*Antikeimena* in modern Greek are simply "objects" or "objective things." Here the etymological sense of "opposites" or "antitheses" is included, which is the sense in which the word was used in antiquity. Trans.]

[3] *L'Être et le Néant* (Paris: Gallimard, 1943), 33. "Being-for-itself" translates *pour-soi*, and "being-in-itself" *en-soi*.

[4] His precise wording is "unsere besondere Aufmerksamkeit auf den fundamentalen Unterschied zwischen der subjektiv-anthropologischen Einheit der Erkenntnis und der objektiv-idealen Einheit des Erkenntnisinhaltes richten" (Edmund Husserl, *Logische Untersuchungen*, 4th ed., vol. 1 [Halle: Niemeyer, 1928], 173–74).

[5] Here in the sense of a common subjective understanding.

[6] See Ferdinand de Saussure, *Cours de linguistique générale* (Paris: Payot, 1969), 144: "Des concepts tel que 'maison', 'blanc', 'voir', ecs., considérés en eux mêmes, appartiennent à la psychologie; ils ne deviennent entités linguistiques que par association avec des images acoustiques."

[7] See Martin Heidegger, *Über den Humanismus* (Frankfurt: Klostermann, 1991), 12; idem, *Einführung in die Metaphysik* (Tübingen: Niemeyer, 1958), 108; idem, *Sein und Zeit* (Tübingen: Niemeyer, 1963), 165.

[8] See Thomas Aquinas, *Quaest. dips. de veritate*, ques. 1, art. 1.

[9] "Das Ding an sich ist ein Abstraktionsprodukt aus der Reflexion auf die Dingheit" (G. W. F. Hegel, *Wissenschaft der Logik*, 1:.2.2:.1.Aa).

[10] "Das dem Wesen gegenüberstehende Sein ist der Schein ... die Erscheinung ist die Wahrheit des Seins ..."

[11] Martin Heidegger, *Nietzsche*, vol. 2 (Pfullingen: Neske, 1961), 200.

[12] Heraclitus, frag. 123 (Diels 1:178): *physis kryptesthai philei.* Cf. Heidegger, *Einführung in die Metaphysik*, 87.

[13] See *Sein und Zeit*, 189: "Das beruhig-vertraute In-der-Welt-sein ist ein Modus der Unheimlichkeit des Daseins, nicht umgekert. Das Unzuhause muss existenzialontologisch als das ursprünglichere Phänomen begriffen werden." ["That kind of Being-in-the-world which is tranquillized and familiar is a mode of Dasein's uncanniness, not the reverse. From an existential-ontological point of view, the 'not-at-home' must be conceived as the more primordial phenomenon" (trans. Macquarrie-Robinson).]

[14] See *Sein und Zeit*, 187: "Wenn sich demnach als Wovor der Angst das Nichts, das heisst die Welt also solche herausstellt, dann besagt das: wovor die Angst sich ängstet, ist das In-der-Welt-sein selbst." ["So if the 'nothing' – that is, the world as such – exhibits itself as that in the face of which one has anxiety, this means that Being-in-the-world itself is that in the face of which anxiety is anxious" (Macquarrie-Robinson).]

[15] [*Energeia* can mean either "activity" or "actuality." On the history of the term in the Greek tradition, see now David Bradshaw, *Aristotle East and West* (Cambridge: Cambridge Univ. Press, 2004). Trans.]

[16] See Klaus Oehler, *Antike Philosophie und byzantinisches Mittelalter* (Munich: C. H. Beck, 1969), 25–26: "Bei ihm (Gregor von Nyssa) wird ausdrücklich, was bei Basileios nur unausdrücklich gemeint ist: die nähere Eingrenzung des Hypostasebegriffs durch die Gleichsetzung mit dem Begriff Prosopon (*prosôpon*, Person)."

[17] See Oehler, *Antike Philosophie*, 23: "Die altkirchliche Theologie hat der neuplatonischen Philosophie viele Begriffe entlehnt. Von diesen Begriffen ist der Usia (*ousia*) der wichtigste .... In enger Verbindung mit dem Begriff der Usia erscheint in der altkirchlichen Theologie der Begriff der Hypostase (*hypostasis*), den sie ebenfalls der neuplatonischen Terminologie entnimmt." The term *ousia* was used by earlier philosophers (the Presocratics, Plato and Aristotle) in senses similar to that which Christian theology gave it. Although, according to Oehler (*Antike Philosophie*, 23), the term *hypostasis* acquired a philosophical sense with Plotinus, Helmut Köster (*Hypostasis*, in G. Kittel, *Theol. Wörterbuch zum Neuen Testament*, 8:574) attributes this to the Stoics. Before the Neoplatonists or Stoics the word *hypostasis* was used exclusively in expressions relating to physics or medicine ("the hypostasis in the bladder," "the hypostasis originating in the kidneys," "the hypostasis of weight," "the hypostasis of a cloud," etc.; see Köster, *Hypostasis*, 572–73, and Demetrakos, *Mega Lexikon*, 9:7504–5). See also Leontius of Byzantium, *Against the Nestorians* 2.1 (PG 86:1528d–29a): "What we call 'hypostasis' is said by some of the older Greek writers of the sediment and lees

of wine and similar liquids, to indicate its settling below the liquid float-
ing above it, as we call substantive signs. The movement or departure of
what was once present is also called 'hypostasis' .... The word is also
used of the acquisition of some money or income .... 'Hypostasis' is also
that which endures and does not easily collapse ... and also the proposition of some narrative or simply some speech which is particular to it and
not general; as in the expression 'in this hypostasis of boasting'. Faith
is also called a 'hypostasis' as if it were some kind of knowledge that is
apprehended ...." Köster cites three characteristic expressions using the
term in Plotinus: "truly not-being, an insubstantial image and phantasm
of bulk, a desire for hypostasis" (*Enn.* 3:5.7.13); "from the perfection
in it and its concomitant activity (*energeias*), the activity generated acquires hypostasis" (*Enn.* 5:4.2.36); "it is not appropriate to disbelieve
that it is a hypostasis and essence from an essence inferior to that which
made it" (*Enn.* 3:5.3.1). In the New Testament *hypostasis* is used five
times with different meanings, only once in the sense later given to it by
Christian theology: "as being the reflection of his glory and stamp of his
hypostasis" – i.e., of God the Father (Heb 1:3).

[18] See B. Stephanidis, *Ekklêsiastikê Istoria*, 3rd ed. (Athens: Astir, 1970),
193.

[19] See Aristotle, *Categories* 5:2ᵃ11–16: "A substance – that which is
called a substance most strictly, primarily, and most of all – is that which
is neither said of a subject nor in a subject, e.g., the individual man or
the individual horse. The species in which the things primarily called
substances are, are called secondary substances, as are also the genera
of these species" (Oxford trans.). See also *Metaphysics* 7.13:1038ᵇ9–16:
"For primary substance is that kind of substance which is peculiar to an
individual, which does not belong to anything else; but the universal is
common ..." (Oxford trans.).

In patristic literature, however, the terms *ousia* and *hypostasis* or *prosopon* acquired very early on a meaning which went beyond Aristotle's distinction of primary and secondary substance. Vladimir Lossky writes: "Il
est clair qu'une telle définition de l'hypostase [on the basis of Aristotle's
distinction] ne pouvait servir que de préambule à la théologie trinitaire,
de point de départ conceptuel vers une notion déconceptualisée, qui n'est
plus celle de l'individu d'une espèce. Si quelques critiques ont voulu
voir dans la doctrine trinitaire de saint Basil une distinction d'hypostasis-
ousia qui répondrait à la distinction aristotélicienne entre *prôtê* et *deutera ousia*, c'est qu'ils n'ont pas su démêler le point d'arrivée d'avec le
point de départ, l'édifice théologique, au delà des concepts, d'avec son
échafaudage conceptuel" (*À l'image et la ressemblance de Dieu* [Paris:
Aubier, 1967], 112).

Even though Lossky's observation is correct, it betrays a Western understanding of the Aristotelian distinction. The scholastic interpretation of Aristotle established in the West for centuries had imposed an intellectualist understanding of Aristotelian terms (substituting intellectual terms for the reality); it had stripped them of the "semantic" content which the Greeks had always seen in them. I would repeat here, too, how urgent the need is today for a Greek reading of Aristotle as well as Plato. (On this point E. Gilson makes a telling observation. With regard to the misinterpretation of Aristotle's views by Westerners throughout the Middle Ages, he says: "Réalistes et nominalistes du moyen âge, pour leurs donner leur noms traditionnels, n'avaient pas tort de se réclamer pareillement d'Aristote, bien qu'ils l'interprétassent, comme l'on sait, en deux sens diamétralement opposés" (*L'Être et l'Essence* [Paris, 1948], 57). And M.-D. Chenu completes the observation with regard to Plato: "On a vu, à propos du platonisme au XIIe siècle, que les mythes existentiels de Platon furent alors tournés en simples allégories, et, par cette désexistentialisation intellectualiste ramenés à une expression figurée de la loi metaphysique des essences" (*La théologie au XIIe siècle* [Paris: Vrin, 1966], 313.)

[20] Gregory of Nyssa, *On the difference between ousia and hypostasis* 5 (PG 32:336c).

[21] Ibid., 3 (PG 32:328b).

[22] Gregory of Nyssa, *Ep.* 24 (PG 46:1089c; ed. G. Pasquali, 76.16–17).

[23] Gregory of Nyssa, *Against Eunomius* 1 (PG 45:337b; ed. W. Jaeger, 1:109.22–26).

[24] This is the sense which Heidegger gave to the ecstatic character of human existence, creating the terms "ek-sistieren" and "Ek-sistenz" to emphasize a contrast with the term "existentia" of Western metaphysics. See *Über den Humanismus*, 15–16: "Das ekstatische Wesen des Menschen beruht in der Ek-sistenz, die von der metaphysisch gedachten existentia verschieden bleibt …. Ek-sistenz bedeutet inhaltlich Hinausstehen in die Wahrheit des Seins." And in an earlier book, before introducing the words "Ek-sistenz" and "ek-sistieren," he wrote: "Der Satz: 'der Mensch existiert' bedeutet: der Mensch ist dasjenige Seiende, dessen Sein durch das offenstehende Innestehen in der Unverborgenheit des Seins, vom Sein her, im Sein ausgezeichnet ist …. Sein ist nicht etwas anderes als 'Zeit,' insofern die 'Zeit' als der Vorname für die Wahrheit des Seins gennant wird …" (*Was ist Metaphysik?* 9th ed. [Frankfurt: Klostermann, 1965], 16–17).

[25] Dionysius the Areopagite, *On the Divine Names* 4.13 (PG 3:712a).

[26] "Latin philosophy," says Th. de Régnon, "first considers the nature in itself and then proceeds to the person; Greek philosophy first consid-

ers the person and afterwards passes through it to find the nature. The
Latins think of personhood as a mode of nature; the Greeks think of
nature as the content of the person" (*Études de théologie positive sur
la Sainte Trinité* 1:433, quoted in Vladimir Lossky, *Théologie mystique
de l'Église d'Orient* [Paris: Aubier, 1944], 57; ET, *The Mystical Theology of the Eastern Church* [London: James Clarke, 1957], 57–58). See
also H.-M. Legrand, "Bulletin d'Ecclésiologie: Introduction aux Églises
d'Orient," *Revue des Sciences Philosophiques et Théologiques* 56: 709,
where, commenting on the Western scholastic structure of P. N. Tremble-
las's *Dogmatics*, he notes: "puis vient le traité de Dieu (livre I), où le De
Deo uno précède le De Deo Trino, comme dans la Somme de S. Thomas
d'Aquin (cognossibilité de Dieu, vrai notion de Dieu, attributs divins et
après seulement le dogme trinitaire 'en général' puis 'en particulier')."
[27] See M. Schmauss, *Katholische Dogmatik*, vol. 1 (Munich, 1960),
306ff.; Karl Barth, *Die kirchliche Dogmatik*, 2:390; Ch. Androutsos,
Dogmatikê (Athens, 1907), 47ff.; P. N. Trembelas, *Dogmatikê*, vol. 1
(Athens, 1959), 186ff.
[28] See Étienne Gilson, *La Philosophie au Moyen Age*, 2nd ed. (Paris:
Payot, 1962), 241ff., and Johannes Hirschberger, *Geschichte der Philosophie*, 8th ed., vol. 1 (Freiburg: Herder, 1965), 504–5. See also M.-D.
Chenu, *La Théologie comme science au XIIIe siècle*, 3rd ed. (Paris: Vrin,
1969), 97ff., where the author affirms in the works of Thomas Aquinas a "grandiose" synthesis of theology's mystical-theoretical character
with the demands of scientific rationality: "Verbe éternel ou Verbe fait
chair, spéculation contemplative ou règles de vie morale, symbolisme
sacramentaire et communauté des saints, relèvent tout uniment du même
principe de connaissance. Les catégories si fermement tranchées du phi-
losophe entre le spéculatif et le pratique ne divisent plus ce savoir ... ces
savoirs sont campés dans un même champ d'intelligibilité, que constitue
la lumière de foi en oeuvre de science: *intellectus fidei*."
[29] This is an expression well established in the theological literature of
the Greek East, and the starting-point of its approach to the ontological problem. Cf., for example, Maximus the Confessor, *Ambigua* (PG
90:285a) and *Mystagogia* (PG 91:701a); Gregory of Nyssa, *Against
Enomius* 1 (PG 45:316c); Justin Martyr, 1 *Apology* 3 (PG 6:1209b); John
Damascene, *Against the Jacobites* 52 (PG 94:1461b).
[30] See Gilson, *La Philosophie au Moyen Age*, 589–90: "Il y a, dans le
thomisme, un acte de la forme elle-même, et c'est l'exister .... L'acte
de l'essence n'est plus la forme, *quo est* du *quod est* qu'elle est, mais
l'existence."
[31] Lossky, *La théologie mystique*, 63–64 (ET, 64–65).

[32] I have tried in an earlier study, again on the level of theoretical differences, to demonstrate on the basis of Heidegger's writings how the
scholastic theological tradition of the West leads inexorably to the modern phenomenon of "European Nihilism." See Christos Yannaras, *On the
Absence and Unknowability of God*, ed. Andrew Louth, trans. Haralam-
bos Ventis (London and New York: T & T Clark, 2005), with reference
to the Dionysian corpus and Martin Heidegger.

[33] Cf. his characteristic aphorisms: "*Sein* erweist sich also einhöch-
stbestimmtes völig Unbestimmtes" (*Einführung in die Metaphysik*,
59); "Das Sein ist das Nächste. Doch die Nähe bleibt dem Menschen
am weitesten" (*Über den Humanismus*, 20); "Die Unbestimmtheit de-
sen jedoch, wovor und worum wir uns ängstigen, ist blosses Fehlen
der Bestimmtheit, sondern die wesenhafte Unmöglichkeit der Bestim-
mbarkeit" (*Was ist Metaphysik?* 32); "Das Sein als das Geschick, das
Wahrheit schickt, bleibt, verborgen. Aber das Weltgeschicht kündigt sich
in der Dichtung an" (*Über den Humanismus*, 26). Cf. also J. Hirschberger's revealing comment on Heidegger's philosophy: "Was bleibt, ist
eine Art Mystik und Romantik des Seins, bei der alles auf die Hinnahme
ankommt" (*Geschichte der Philosophie*, 2:648).

[34] Heidegger, *Einführung in die Metaphysik*, 1.

Chapter Two

[1] "Universal" (*katholou*) means "general." See Aristotle, *De interpeta-
tione* 7:17ª38–39: "Now of actual things some are universal [*katholou*],
others particular [*kath'ekaston*] (I call universal that which is by its nature predicated of a number of things, and particular that which is not;
man, for instance, is a universal, Callias a particular)" (Oxford trans.).
See also Leontius of Byzantium, *Against the Nestorians and Eutychians*
(PG 86:1289d–92a): "Those who investigate logical problems teach that
particulars participate in universals, while universals are predicated of
particulars. And among indivisibles there is a natural participation in the
form, but among universals there is a participation in particulars according to their name. We therefore do not reject calling the particular by the
appellation of the universal."

[2] *Nature* (*physis*) and *essence* (*ousia*) originally had the same meaning, as also did *person* (*prosôpon*) and *hypostasis*. See Maximus the
Confessor, *Ep.* 15 (PG 91:549b): "Essence and nature are identical; person and hypostasis are also identical." Also: "The words *essence* and
nature are identified and given the philosophical sense of *eidos* ['form'
or 'kind']: Essence or nature are called by them [*sc.* the Fathers] that

which the philosophers call *eidos*" (Leontius of Byzantium, *Scholia* 1 [PG 86:1193a]).

[3] "For essence only signifies being itself. Hypostasis signifies not only being, but also presents how it is and of what sort" (Theodore of Rhaithu, *Proparaskeue, Analecta Patristica*, Orientalia Christiana Analecta [Rome, 1938], 204.10.16). See also Gregory of Nyssa, *Against Eunomius* 1 (PG 45:337b): "With regard to essence, it has been shown by those competent in dealing with such matters philosophically that no difference can be conceived of if one strips it bare of the qualities and properties that are considered as being in it and examines it as it is in itself according to the principle of being."

[4] "Hypostasis, that is, the indivisible subject of nature, is nature but not nature alone because it is with characteristic property. But nature is not hypostasis which is indivisible" (John Damascene, *Against the Jacobites* 52 [PG 84:1461a]).

[5] "Hypostasis ... is something which exists as a hypostasis in its own right and is the division of the indivisible essences into the number of each thing according to person; hence the Fathers understand it as being the same as person and call it such" (Leontius of Byzantium, *Against the Nestorians* 2.1 [PG 86:1529d]).

[6] "Hypostasis is a subsistent and substantial thing, in which the bundle of accidents subsists as if in one underlying thing and energy" (Theodore of Rhaithu, *Proparaskeue* 206.5). See also John Damascene, *Dialectica* 16 (PG 94:581b; ed. B. Kotter [Berlin, 1969], 86): "The accident is said to be in the underlying essence." Also *Dialectica* 43 (PG 94:613b; ed. Kotter, 109): "The holy Fathers called the same thing hypostasis and person; that which subsists individually in itself from essence and accidents, and differs in number, and indicates someone such as Peter or Paul." Also *Dialectica* 1 (PG 94:593a–96a; ed. Kotter, 94–95): "Hypostasis is naturally disposed to have essence with accidents and subsist in itself and be contemplated by sense-perception or energy."

[7] For the identification of "accidents" (*symbebēkota*) with "passions" (*pathê*), see Aristotle, *Metaphysics* 14.1:1088a17 and 1.8:989b3; *De Anima* 1.1:402a7–9. Also Maximus the Confessor, *Scholia on the Divine Names* (PG 4:412bc).

[8] "... not dividing up the unity of the essence into persons" (Gregory of Nyssa, *Against Eunomius* 1 [PG 45:405b]). See also Leontius of Byzantium, *Scholia* 8 (PG 86:1252bc): "... according to hypostasis, that is, according to existence." Also John Damascene, *Dialectica* 42 (PG 94:613a; ed. Kotter, 109): "For the essence subsists actively in the hypostasis."

[9] "Essence does not subsist in itself, but is contemplated in the hypostases" (John Damascene, *On the Orthodox Faith* 3.6 [PG 94:1001d]).

See also Leontius of Byzantium, *Against the Nestorians and Eutychians* (PG 86:1280a): "An hypostatic nature, that is, essence, can therefore never exist. Nature is not hypostasis, because they are not conversely predicable. For hypostasis is also nature, but nature is not yet also hypostasis. For nature admits of the principle of being, but hypostasis admits also of being in itself. For the one points to the principle of the form, while the other reveals the being of something. And the one indicates the character of the universal thing, while the other demarcates the property of what is common."

[10] "... nature ascends towards that which subsists" (Maximus the Confessor, *Theological Chapters* [PG 91:200d]).

[11] *Metaphysics* 5.26:1023b29–31 (Oxford trans., modified). See also Heidegger, *Was ist Metaphysik?* 11: "Allein die Metaphysik antwortet nirgends auf die Frage nach der Wahrheit des Seins, weil sie diese Frage nicht fragt. Sie fragt nicht, weil sie das Sein nur denkt, indem sie das Seiende als das Seiende vorstellt. Sie meint das Seiende im Ganzen und spricht vom Sein. Sie nennt das Sein und meint das Seiende als das Seiende."

[12] We encounter the existential-ontological interpretation of the term *nature*, as a rule, in the ascetical writings of the Orthodox East. Orthodox ascetical teaching is based on the assumption of a dynamic self-transcendence of nature within the bounds of personal existence and the belief that this is possible. Cf. the expressions "to triumph over nature," "defeat of nature," "the flesh, the hostile friend that is mine and not mine" (John Climacus); "to go out of the bounds of nature," "to sanctify nature," "when he attains love, he transcends nature," "to renew nature" (Isaac the Syrian); "to alter and change nature," "to be altered and changed into another state and nature" (Macarius of Egypt).

[13] See Chenu, *La théologie au XIIe siècle*, 302: "Les concepts de *nature* et de *personne* impliquent le rapport de l'abstrait (quo est) et du concret (quod est) dans les êtres existants .... Jeu philosophique de l'abstrait et du concret."

[14] See *Summa Theologiae* 1:29.2 and *De Potentia* 9:1–2. See also in relation to this Johannes Hirschberger, *Geschichte der Philosophie*, 1:490–91, and Chenu, *La théologie au XIIe siècle*, 303: "Le mot *res* sortira de son neutralisme (chose) pour désigner, grâce à l'alliteration de la formule technique *res naturae – natura rei*, la densité réelle d'une chose concrète existante, en equivalence *d'hypostasis*."

This loss of the existential content of the concept of hypostasis, its acquisition of the sense of ontic atomicity, led rapidly in the West, as early as the twelfth century, to the objectification of all existential categories in the field of theology. M.-D. Chenu observes perceptively: "Even if from Anselm and Abelard to the great Masters of the thirteenth century, metaphysics continues to exhibit insight [I believe that Chenu means metaphysical insight into the transcendent as opposed to the limitation of metaphysics to rational analysis], it is nevertheless interesting to distinguish in this insight two fields that are significantly different in spite of being contiguous. One field, in which the most prominent figure was Abelard, is marked by the use, within the bounds of theological synthesis, of dialectical methods which in themselves were purely secular ("profanes") instruments (of knowledge) but which were nevertheless used because their value in the realm of the sacred was acknowledged.... Gradually, another field took shape in which it was not only syllogistic *modes* that were introduced into the study of God's word, but new *objects*, which had recently been confirmed in the context of the world and the nature of things. What was important now was no longer the reference to God, through the symbolic or dialectical path, of created realities, which by reference to their final cause lose their specific meaning and earthly significance. It was an independent knowledge of humanity and of the world, with an absolute validity within the context of secular knowledge, actually effective in theory and practice, now transformed into theological science. Thus while they had long been accustomed to using the distinction between form and matter to analyse the structure of sacramental symbols, now ... they discovered the metaphysical truth of hylomorphism, they understood humanity as a form bound to a matter, they constructed a corresponding view of the universe, they defined matter as the substance of things .... The theologian appropriated, within the context of the organic structure of his wisdom, the objects *supplied* to him by the rationalistic branches of science, the sciences of the universe and its laws, the sciences of humankind and its capacities" (*La théologie au XIIe siècle*, 314).

[15] Presocratic writers "On Nature" discuss what today we would call ontology. See also John Damascene, *Dialectica* 31, ed. B. Kotter, 94.27: *to de einai kai pephykenai tauton esti.*

[16] See Heraclitus, frag. 1 (*Die Fragmente der Vorsokratiker*, ed. H. Diels and W. Kranz [Zurich/Berlin: Weidmann, 1964] 1:150), where the expressions *kata logon* and *kata physin* are treated as identical. See also Heidegger, *Einführung in die Metaphysik*, 100: "*Logos* ist die ständige Sammlung, die in sich stehende Gesammeltheit des Seienden, d.h. das Sein. Deshalb bedeutet in Frg. 1 *kata ton logon* dasselbe wie *kata physin*. *Physis* und *logos* sind dasselbe."

[17] "L'existence précède l'essence" (Jean-Paul Sartre, *L'existentialisme est un humanisme* [Paris: Nagel, 1962], 17–18).

¹⁸ In Sartre, *L'existentialisme*, 21: "Il y a au moins un être chez qui l'existence précède l'essence, un être qui existe avant de pouvoir être défini par aucun concept et cet être c'est l'homme." There is a fuller analysis in my *Schediasma Eisagôgês stê Philosophia* [FT, *Philosophie sans rupture* (Geneva: Labor et Fides, 1986)], §29.

¹⁹ See *Über den Humanismus*, 17.

²⁰ See ibid., 12, 17; *Einführung in die Metaphysik*, 108.

²¹ "Die in ihrer Wesensherkunft verborgene Unterscheidung von essentia (Wesenheit) und existentia (Wirklichkeit) durchherrscht das Geschik der abendländischen und der gesamten europäisch bestimmten Geschichte" (*Über den Humanismus*, 18).

²² "Das 'Wesen' weder aus dem esse essentiae, noch aus dem esse existentiae, sondern aus dem Ek-statischen des Daseins bestimmt" (ibid., 16).

²³ "Ek-sistenz bedeutet inhaltlich Hinausstehen in die Wahrheit des Seins" (ibid.).

²⁴ "... insofern die 'Zeit' als der Vorname für die Wahrheit des Seins gennant wird ..." (*Was ist Metaphysik?* 17).

²⁵ "Als der Ek-sistierende steht der Mensch das Da-sein aus, indem er das Da als die Lichtung des Seins in 'die Sorge' nimmt" (*Über den Humanismus*, 16).

²⁶ "Ek-sistenz ist nich identisch mit dem überlieferten Begriff der existentia, was Wirklichkeit bedeutet im Unterscheid zu essentia als der Möglichkeit" (ibid., 15).

²⁷ "Existence, meint dagegen actualitas, Wirklichkeit im Unterscheid zur blossen Möglichkeit als Idee" (ibid., 16).

²⁸ "Das 'Wesen' des Menschen beruht in seiner Ek-sistenz ... 'der Mensch eksistiert' antwortet auf die Frage nach dem 'Wesen' des Menschen" (ibid., 15–16). See also *Sein und Zeit*, 42: "Das 'Wesen' des Daseins liegt in seiner Existenz."

²⁹ "Making in themselves idols, an intellectual idolatry" (Basil the Great, *On Isaiah* 96 [PG 30:276c]).

³⁰ "Das Nichts gehört, auch wenn wir es nur im Sinne des völlingen Nicht von Anwesendem meinem, ab-wesend zum Anwesen als eine von dessen Möglichkeiten. Wenn somit im Nihilismus das Nichts waltet und das Wesen des Nichts zum Sein gehört, das Sein jedoch das Geschick des Überstiegs ist, dann zeigt sich als Wesensort des Nihilismus das Wesen der Metaphysik" (Heidegger, *Zur Seinsfrage* [Frankfurt: Klostermann, 1956], 33; cf. 38). See also *Einführung in die Metaphysik*, 62, 64.

³¹ "Wenn sich demnach als das Wovor der Angst das Nichts, das heisst die Welt als solche herausstellt, dann besagt das: *wovor die Angst sich ängstet, ist das In-der-Welt-sein selbst*" (*Sein und Zeit*, 187 ["So if the

'nothing' – that is, the world as such – exhibits itself as that in the face of which one has anxiety, this means that *Being-in-the-world itself is that in the face of which anxiety is anxious*" (Macquarrie-Robinson).]

[32] "Da-sein heisst: Hineingehaltenheit in das Nichts .... In der hellen Nacht des Nichts der Angst ersteht erst die ursprüngliche Offenheit des Seienden als eines solchen: das es Seiendes ist – und nicht Nichts. Dieses von uns in der Rede dazugesagte 'und nicht Nichts' ist aber keine nachgetragene Erklärung, sondern die vorgängige Ermöglichung der Offenbarkeit von Seiendem überhaupt, das Wesen des ursprünglich nichtenden Nichts liegt in dem: es bringt das Da-sein allererst vor das Seiende als ein solches" (*Was ist Metaphysik?* 34–35).

[33] "Das Nichts gibt nich erst den Gegenbegriff zum Seienden her, sondern gehört ursprünglich zum Wesen selbst. Im Sein des Seienden geschieht das Nichten des Nichts" (*Was ist Metaphysik?* 35). And on p. 39: "Das Nichts bleibt nich das unbestimmte Gegenüber für das Seiende, sondern es enthüllt sich als zugehörig zum Sein des Seienden."

[34] "... beide gehören in Eins zusammen" (*Einführung in die Metaphysik*, 62).

[35] In the patristic literature of the Greek East, *relation* is always revelatory of hypostasis. Cf. Athanasius the Great, *Dialogues on the Trinity* 1.25 (PG 28:1153d): "the term 'god' indicates the nature, the term 'father' the relation with the son." Also Gregory of Nazianzus, *Oration* 29.16 (PG 36:96a): "The Father is neither the name of an essence ... nor of an energy, but of a relation." Also Gregory of Nyssa, *Against Eunomius* 2 (PG 45:473b): "The name 'father' does not represent an essence, but indicates the relation with the son" (ed. Jaeger, 2:319.1–3).

[36] This is based on Heidegger, *Sein und Zeit*, 68: "Die Griechen, hatten einen angemessenen Terminus für die 'Dinge': *pragmata*, d.i. das womit man es im besorgenden Umgang (*praxis*) zu tun hat." ["The Greeks had an appropriate term for 'Things': *pragmata* – that is to say, that which one has to do with in one's concernful dealings (*praxis*)" (Macquarrie-Robinson).]

[37] This again is based on Heidegger, *Sein und Zeit*, 38: "Höher als die Wirklichkeit steht die Möglichkeit. Das Verständnis der Phänomenologie liegt einzig im Ergreifen ihrer als Möglichkeit." ["Higher than actuality stands *possibility*. We can understand phenomenology only by seizing upon it as a possibility" (Macquarrie-Robinson).]

[38] This is based on Heidegger: "Das Seiende, das wir je selbst sind, ist ontologisch das Fernste" (*Sein und Zeit*, 311). ["The entity which in every case we ourselves are, is ontologically that which is farthest" (Macquarrie-Robinson).]

[39] "Das Sein ist weiter denn alles Seiende und ist gleichwohl dem Menschen näher als jedes Seiende .... Das Sein ist das Nächste. Doch die Nähe bleibt dem Menschen am weitesten" (Heidegger, *Über den Humanismus*, 19–20).

[40] It may be noted that when modern physics refers every form of matter in the end to forms of energy, it confirms the character of beings as "things" (*pragmata*). It reveals the totality of Creation as an accomplished act (*praxē*). See my *Schediasma Eisagôgês stê Philosophia* [FT, *Philosophie sans rupture*], §31.

[41] "For every house is built by some one, but the builder of all things is God" (Heb 3:4).

[42] *On the Divine Names* 4 (PG 3:712ab).

[43] *Scholia on the Divine Names* (PG 4:261b).

[44] *Ambigua* (PG 91:1260).

Chapter Three

[1] This expression is used by Leontius of Byzantium with reference to the union of the divine and human natures in the Person of Christ. See *Against the Aphthartodocetans* (PG 86:1380b).

[2] See Ioannes Karmires, *Ta dogmatika kai symbolika mnêmeia tês Orthodoxou Katholikês Ekklêsias*, 2nd ed., vol. 1 (Athens, 1960), 175.

[3] There is a vast bibliography on the bicomposite character of human nature in the Bible and the meaning of the terms body-soul-flesh-spirit. See, e.g., Ernest de Witt Burton, *Spirit, Soul and Flesh* (Chicago: Univ. of Chicago Press, 1918); Daniel Lys, *Nephesh, Histoire de l'âme dans la révélation d'Israel* (Paris: PUF, 1959); K. Galling, *Das Bild vom Menschen in bibl. Sicht*, Mainzer Universitäts-Reden 3 (1947); A. Gelin, *L'homme selon la Bible* (Paris: Cerf, 1968); Gerhard von Rad, *Theologie des Alten Testaments*, vol. 1 (Munich: Kaiser, 1962), 166–67; Rudolf Bultmann, *Theologie des neuen Testaments*, 4th ed. (Tübingen: Mohr, 1961), 204ff.

[4] "Holy Scripture says many things, and often assigns names loosely [*katachrêstikôs*]. Some belong to the body but are used of the soul. And again, those of the soul are used of the body, and Holy Scripture does not distinguish them" (Isaac the Syrian, *Extant Ascetic Works* 83, ed. Spanos, 317).

[5] John Chrysostom, *Homily on Genesis* 14.5 (PG 53:117).

[6] Clement of Alexandria, *Stromateis* 8.4 (PG 9:573b) and *Fragments* 38 (PG 9:769c).

[7] Gregory of Nyssa, *On the Creation of Man* 14 (PG 44:176).

[8] Didymus the Blind, *On the Holy Spirit* 54–55, 59 (PG 39:1079–82).

[9] Hesychius of Sinai, *To Theodulus* 2.24 (PG 93:1520a): "The tripartite nature of the soul ... anger ... the appetitive ... and the rational." And Clement of Alexandria, *Paedogogus* 3.1 (PG 8:556a): "Since the soul consists of three parts, the intellectual, which is called the rational, is the inner man ... but the irascible part, being brutal, dwells near to insanity; and the appetitive, which is the third part, is multiform."

[10] Basil the Great, *On Isaiah* 1.13 (PG 30:140).

[11] Gregory of Nyssa, *On the Creation of Man* 27 (PG 44:228).

[12] Basil the Great, *Homily* 31 (PG 31:1340d).

[13] Basil the Great, *Homily* 3.7 (PG 31:213c).

[14] Cyril of Jerusalem, *Catechetical Lectures* 4.21 (PG 33:481b).

[15] Macarius of Egypt, *Spiritual Homilies* 1.5 (*Die 50 geistlichen Homilien des Makarios*, ed. Dörries, Klostermann and Kroeger [Berlin: Walter de Gruyter, 1964], 6).

[16] Maximus the Confessor, *Chapters on Theology* 1.12 (PG 90:1088b).

[17] Macarius of Egypt, *Spiritual Homilies* 1.5.

[18] Cf. John Climacus, *Ladder of Divine Ascent* 15.83: "What is the mystery concerning me? What is the principle of my constitution?" (ed. Sophronios [Constantinople, 1883], 97).

[19] Gregory of Nyssa, *On the Creation of Man* 29 (PG 44:233).

[20] See Gen 2:7: "And God formed man of dust from the ground and breathed into his face the breath of life, and man became a living soul."

[21] "He breathed even at the beginning into the face of the first created human being" (Gregory Palamas, *On the Procession of the Holy Spirit* 2.8, ed. P. Chrestou, vol. 1 [Thessalonica, 1962], 85).

[22] "... that which is in the divine image and likeness the soul has in its entirety, since the soul is unitary in the mind and reason and spirit" (ibid., 2.9.85). See also Macarius of Egypt, *Spiritual Homilies* 1.7 (ed. Dörries, Klostermann and Kroeger, 9): "[the soul] is a created thing which is intellectual, beautiful, great, wonderful and good, a likeness and image of God." See also Gregory of Nyssa, *On the Making of Man* 6 (PG 44:140): "for there is one faculty, the implanted mind itself, which passes through each of the organs of sense and grasps the things beyond. This it is that, by means of the eyes, beholds what is seen; this it is that, by means of hearing, understands what is said, that is content with what is to our taste, and turns from what is unpleasant, and uses the hand for whatever it wills" (trans. Wilson, *NPNF*).

[23] "As the members of the body are many parts, yet they designate one man, so also the members of the soul are many: the mind, the conscience, the will, 'thoughts accusing and excusing' (Rom 2:15), yet all these are bound together in one soul even though there are many members. The

soul, however, is one, the interior man" (Macarius of Egypt, *Spiritual Homilies* 7.8 [ed. Dörries, Klostermann and Kroeger, 76; trans. Maloney, CWS]). See also Gregory Palamas, *On the Holy Hesychasts* 3.2–22 (ed. P. Chrestou, 1:673): "The soul is one, simple and non-composite."

[24] "Moses says that the body was fashioned from earth ... but the rational soul was breathed in by God into the face [*prosôpon*]" (Clement of Alexandria, *Stromata* 5.14 [PG 9:140a]).

[25] "For the form of the soul is given its image in accordance with the divine beauty. Therefore when the soul looks at its archetype, then it perceives itself accurately" (Gregory of Nyssa, *To Mourners for the Departed* [PG 46:509cd]). See also Gregory of Nyssa, *Dialogue on the Soul and Resurrection* (PG 46:52a): "The soul is a likeness of God ... whatever is alien to God is outside the boundaries of the soul." See also Gregory of Nazianzus, *Oration* 38.11 (PG 36:321d): "taking the body from matter already existing and putting in it breath from himself (which the Logos knew to be an intelligent soul and image of God)."

[26] "Now, by a provision of the supreme Mind there is a blending of the intellectual with the sensible world, in order that nothing in creation may be rejected as worthless, as the Apostle says (1 Tim 4:4), or be left without its portion of the divine fellowship. On this account it is that the commixture of the intellectual and sensible in man is effected by the divine nature, as the description of the cosmogony teaches us. It tells us that God, taking dust from the ground, formed man, and by his own inbreathing he planted life in the work of his hand, that thus the earthly might be raised up to the divine, and so one certain grace of equal value might pervade the whole creation, the lower nature being mingled with the supramundane" (Gregory of Nyssa, *Great Catechetical Oration* 6 [PG 45:27d–28a; trans. Moore, *NPNF*, modified]). See also Gregory of Nyssa, *On the Making of Man* 27 (PG 44:228): "the blending is nothing else than the mixture of the elements – by elements we mean those which furnish the substratum for the making of the universe, of which the human body also is composed, while the form necessarily remains in the soul, as in the impression of a seal ..." (trans. Wilson, *NPNF*, slightly modified).

[27] "What is the principle of this blending ... therefore never by reason of the yoking, which only he who has bound them knows" (John Climacus, *Ladder* 15.83, 26.54 [ed. Sophronios, 97, 143]). See also Christos Yannaras, *Ê Metaphysikê tou Sômatos* (Athens: Dodoni, 1971), 65ff.

[28] Gregory of Nyssa, *On the Making of Man* 12 (PG 44:160): "the mind should be thought to permeate each part equally by the ineffable principle of blending." See also ch. 15 (PG 44:177): "The communion of the mind with the corporeal presents a union which is inexpressible and

inconceivable; it is neither within it (for the incorporeal is not contained within the corporeal), nor does it surround it from outside (for what is incorporeal does not contain anything); but the mind approaching our nature in some inexplicable and incomprehensible way, and coming into contact with it, is to be regarded as both in it and around it, neither implanted in it nor enfolded with it" (trans. Wilson, *NPNF*, modified).

[29] "The highest union possesses both identity and difference; or identity of essences and difference of persons and vice versa. In the case of the holy Trinity identity is of essence, difference is of persons .... In the case of humankind identity is of person, difference of essences. For although a human being is a single entity, the soul is of one essence, and the flesh is of another" (Maximus the Confessor, *Theological and Polemical Chapters* [PG 91:145b]).

[30] "That which is enhypostatic sometimes means the essence, as when it is contemplated in hypostases. But sometimes it means each of the things that come together to form a single hypostasis, as in the case of soul and body" (John Damascene, *On the Composite Nature, against the Acephali* 6 [PG 95:120c]). See also Maximus the Confessor, *Theological and Polemical Chapters* (PG 91:149b): "That which is enhypostatic is what is common according to the essence, that is, the species, which exists in a real way in the individuals under it, and is not regarded in a merely conceptual fashion. Alternatively, that which is enhypostatic is what is composed and subsists in a different way according to the essence for the formation of a person and for the genesis of a hypostasis, and in no way is known as it is in itself."

[31] "cette désexistentialisation intellectualiste" (Chenu, *La théologie au XIIe siècle*, 313). See also Chenu, *La théologie comme science*, 42: "Saint Thomas, lui faisant prévaloir la consideration de l'objet, s'engage ainsi dans une recherche qui d'une part ménagera le concept authentique de science, et qui surtout *l'amènera à accepter l'objectivation de la connaissance de foi dans la théologie*" (my emphasis). And on p. 83: "La foi a pour objet la révélation (revelatum), tandis que la théologie a pour objet les conclusions que nous en pouvons tirer, le révélé 'virtuel' (revelabile)."

[32] "Maintenant ... on découvre la vérité métaphysique de l'hylémorphisme, on considère l'homme comme une forme liée à une matière" (Chenu, *La théologie au XIIe siècle*, 314).

[33] See above, pp. 9–11.

[34] The distinction between nature and persons is entirely ignored on the anthropological level even by the modern Greek dogmatic theologians Christos Androutsos (*Dogmatikê* [Athens, 1907], 129–64) and Panayiotis

Trembelas (*Dogmatikê*, vol. 1 [Athens, 1959], 456–568), typical representatives of a radically Westernized and estranged Orthodox theology.

[35] See, for example, Thomas Aquinas, *Summa Theologiae* 1:76.1.

[36] *De Anima ut forma corporis*; see H. Denzinger, *Enchiridion Symbolorum*, 31st ed. (Freiburg: Herder, 1950), 222–23, §481. See also Aristotle,
On the Soul 2:1.412^{a}27, 412^{b}5–9: "the soul is an actuality [*entelecheia*]
of the first kind of a natural body having life potentially in it .... If, then,
we have to give a general formula applicable to all kinds of soul, we
must describe it as an actuality of the first kind of a natural organized
body. That is why we can dismiss as unnecessary the question on whether the soul and the body are one: it is as though we were to ask whether
the wax and its shape are one, or generally the matter of a thing and that
of which it is the matter. Unity has many senses (as many as 'is' has), but
the proper one is that of actuality" (Oxford trans.). See also Gilson, *La
Philosophie au Moyen Age*, 627: "Le concile de Vienne venait de décré-
ter (1311–1312) que la substance de l'âme raisonnable, ou intellective,
est vraiment et par soi forme du corps humain."
The Council of Vienne is for the Roman Catholics the Fifteenth Ecumenical Council (see *La Foi Catholique, Textes doctrinaux du Magistère
de l'Église*, trans. Gervais Dumeige [Paris: Ed. de l'Orante, 1961], 161–
62).

[37] See the references to Aquinas relating to this theme in Hirschberger,
Geschichte der Philosophie, 1:517–18.

[38] See the *Theological and Polemical Chapters* (PG 91:48d, 192c, 193a).
See also 45cd, where Maximus says: The Fathers "wisely called the will
[*thelêma*] the natural appetite of intelligently ensouled flesh, but not the
gnomic appetite of a particular human being, meaning the appetite that
arises through the movements of the mind, since the former has a natural
power of a desire for being, naturally moved and moulded by the Logos
for the fulfilment of the economy .... The power of speech is an innate
property of nature; but how one speaks belongs to the hypostasis. It is
the same with naturally willing and willing. If naturally willing and willing are not identical (for the one, as I have said, belongs to the essence,
the other to the deliberate intention [*boulê*] of the person who wills) ..."
etc.

[39] For an interesting example, I strongly recommend Igor A. Caruso,
Psychoanalyse und Synthese der Existenz (Vienna: Herder, 1952). The
importance of this book lies in its attempt to approach the basic problems
of psychoanalysis using the criteria of Orthodox theology. With regard
to the unified character of psychosomatic manifestations, Caruso writes:
"It is in the recognition of the close and inseparable union of spirit with
matter that the solution should be sought of anthropology's central prob-

lem … The absolutizing of the 'Nestorian' view has led to what is chiefly and specifically human being distinguished in a merely quantitative way from the psycho-physical element of animal life. By contrast, the 'mono-physite' view of humanity saw the distinguishing aspect only in the spirit and in freedom. Both views among the integrists were one-sided. Neither the psycho-physical nor the spirit are what distinguishes humanity. What distinguishes humanity is the incarnation of the spiritual: the fact that flesh became spirit and spirit flesh" (279). "The concept of human neuro-sis cannot easily be understood either in terms of pure metaphysics, since the humanity is not just spirit, or in terms of pure biology. Human neuro-sis has a meaning which transcends the biological, the psycho-physical and the spiritual levels, and this should be taken into account on all its levels" (p. 110; page references are to the – unsatisfactory – Greek trans-lation by Athanasios Karantonis [Athens, 1953]).

[40] *Über den Humanismus*, 14: "Der Leib des Menschen ist etwas wesen-lich anderes als ein tierischer Organismus."

[41] *L'Être et le Néant* (Paris: Gallimard, 1943), 368.

[42] See Thomas Aquinas, *Summa Theologiae* 1:93.4-8. See also J.-H. Nicolas, *Dieu connu comme inconnu*, Bibliothèque Française de Phi-losophie (Paris: Desclée de Brouwer, 1966), 332ff.: "C'est par son intel-lectualité que l'être spirituel est à l'image de Dieu Trinité …. Si l'être intelligent créé est à l'image de Dieu, c'est donc très précisément à ce point d'actualisation suprême de sa vie intellectuelle où il est donné de communier ineffablement à l'intellection divine …" (339). "Une infinité de degrés est possible entre la dernière des intelligences, l'âme humaine, et l'Intelligence infinie, identique à l'Être premier, et qui est simultané-ment *Esse et Intellegere*" (334). See also Christos Androutsos, *Dogma-tikê*, 137: "Obviously the image of God does not refer to the corporeal *part* of humanity …. The divine image in humanity belongs to its spiri-tual *part*" (my emphasis). Also P. N. Trembelas, *Dogmatikê*, 1:487: "The 'in the image' … refers to the immaterial and spiritual make-up of hu-manity, that is, to the soul …. In other words, the 'in the image' consists in the rationality with which the Creator endowed humanity's spiritual nature, and in the indispensable *completion of this*, free will, through which humanity is led to moral personality …" (my emphasis).

[43] "How many ways do we use the phrase 'in the image'? According to rationality, intellectuality and free will, according to the principle that begets the mind and puts forth spirit; according to sovereignty" (John Damascene, *On the Two Wills in Christ* 30 [PG 95:168b]).

[44] Here with the Aristotelian sense: "I call universal that which is by its nature predicated of a number of things" (*De Interpretatione* 7.17ª39 [Oxford trans.]).

[45] "Si toutes les créatures ressemblent à Dieu, c'est-à-dire à la Trinité, seules les créatures intellectuelles lui ressemblent en propre, car elles procèdent de Lui selon une similitude qui se prend selon la perfection spécifique (*similitudo speciei*), bien qu'elle soit, évidemment, analogique: mais la *ratio analogata*, en cette analogie, est l'être sous la forme où il est caractéristique de l'Être divin. C'est ce caractère analogique, impliquant la multiplicité et la hierarchie à l'interieur de cette ressemblance, qu'exprime la formule: à l'image de Dieu" (J.-H. Nicolas, *Dieu connu comme inconnu*, 335).

[46] On this point Vladimir Lossky writes: "St. Augustine takes as his starting point the image of God in man, and attempts to work out an idea of God, by trying to discover in Him that which we find in the soul created in His image. The method he employs is one of psychological analogies applied to the knowledge of God, to theology" (*Mystical Theology of the Eastern Church*, 114–15).

[47] See Origen, *Against Celsus* 6.63 (PG 11:1896a): "If the nature that is in the image of God is in the body alone, the superior part, the soul, is deprived of being in the image, and this exists in the corruptible body. Not one of us holds this view. But if the words 'in the image of God' apply to both together, God must be composite .... The remaining possibility is that that which is made in the image of God is to be understood of the inward man" (trans. Chadwick). See also Cyril of Alexandria, *Against the Anthropomorphites* (PG 76:1068a): "Everyone agrees that man is in the image of God, but the likeness is not corporeal; for God is incorporeal." Also Gregory of Nyssa, *On the Making of Man* (ed. Hörner [Leiden: Brill, 1972], 9): "How are the words 'in the image of God' to be understood? One should conceive of nothing corporeal and earthly."

[48] See Gregory Palamas, *Prosopopoiia* (PG 150:1316c): "Man should not be said to be only a soul, nor only a body, but the two together, which God is said to have made in his image." Also his *One Hundred and Fifty Chapters* 63 (ed. Sinkewicz [Toronto: Pont. Inst. of Med. Studies, 1988], 156): "In company with many others you might say that also the threefold character of our knowledge shows us to be more in the image of God than the angels, not only because it is threefold but also because it encompasses every form of knowledge. For we alone of all creatures possess also a faculty of sense perception in addition to those of intellection and reason" (trans. Sinkiewicz). See also Cyril of Alexandria, *Commentary on St. John's Gospel* 9 (PG 74:277d): "To achieve the property of a perfect nature through both, I mean through soul and body, the Creator implanted the Holy Spirit, that is, the breath of life, like a seal of his own nature, through which he formed a beauty after the archetype, and completed the 'in the image' of the Maker, directed towards every idea

of virtue by the power of the spirit dwelling within him." Also Irenaeus, *Against Heresies* 5.6.1 (PL 7:1137a): "Now the soul and the spirit are certainly a part of the man but certainly not the man, for the perfect man consists in the commingling and union of the soul receiving the Spirit of the Father, and the admixture of that fleshly nature which was moulded after the image of God" (trans. and ed. Cleveland Coxe, *ANF*).

[49] See Theodoret of Cyrus, *On Genesis*, ques. 20 (PG 80:108ab): "The mind begets the word, and the spirit goes forth together with the word, not begotten like the word but always witnessing to the word and going forth with the begotten. These are present in man as if in an image. For the word is not for pleasure or without substance, nor is the spirit." See also Anastasius of Sinai, *From the sermon 'in the image'* (PG 89:1148bc): "Let us come to the most important thing about the words 'in the image' that we might demonstrate ... the unity of the Deity in Trinity .... It is clear that our own soul, and its intelligent word, and the mind [are also three in one] .... The soul is unbegotten and without cause as a type of the unbegotten and uncaused God and Father. But its intelligent word is not unbegotten; it is begotten from it ... without passion as a type of the begotten Son. The mind is neither without cause nor begotten, but is made to proceed ... in the image and likeness of the all-holy and proceeding Spirit."

[50] See Gregory of Nyssa, *On the Making of Man* (ed. Hörner, 16): "where the power of ruling is, there is the image of God." Also, John Chrysostom, *Homily on Genesis* 9.2 (PG 53:78): "Learn what the words 'in the image' mean, because they do not refer to essence but are a likeness of sovereignty. God did not mean 'in the image of the form,' but 'according to the principle of sovereignty.' Therefore he urged them to have dominion over the fish" etc. Also, Diodore of Tarsus, *Commentary on Genesis* 1.26 (PG 33:1564cd): "Some have taken the creation of man 'in the image of God' to mean according to the invisibility of the soul. They have not considered that if an angel is invisible, so is a demon .... How then is man an image of God? In his sovereignty."

[51] See Gregory of Nyssa, *On the Making of Man* 16.10.11 (PG 44:184b): "But since the list of individual good gifts is a long one ... the language of Scripture expresses it concisely by a comprehensive phrase, in saying that man was made 'in the image of God' ... but preeminent among all is the fact that we are free from necessity and not in bondage to any natural power, but have the free will to do as we please." See also Cyril of Alexandria, *Commentary on John* 9 (PG 74:277d): "[Man] being possessed of free will, and entrusted with the reins of his own will; for this too is a share of the image, for God exercises dominion over the products of his own will."

[52] Aristotle, *Metaphysics* 10.2:1053^{b}25.

[53] Ibid., 3.2:1003^{a}33.

[54] Ibid., 3.2:1003^{b}5.

[55] Cf. Heidegger, *Über den Humanismus*, 12: "Die Metaphysik stellt zwar das Seiende in seinem Sein vor und denkt so das Sein des Seienden. Aber sie denkt nicht den Unterschied beider."

[56] Aristotle, *Metaphysics* 7.3:1029^{a}2–5 (Oxford trans., modified).

[57] Ibid., 7.13:1038^{b}16 (Oxford trans.).

[58] "Our theory [*logos*] seems to confirm the phenomena and to be confirmed by them" (Aristotle, *On the Heavens* 1.3:270^{b}4 [Oxford trans.]).

[59] Aristotle, *Metaphysics* 7.11:1036^{a}28 (Oxford trans.).

[60] Aristotle, *Metaphysics* 7.3:1028^{a}6.

[61] "Therefore if the form is prior to the matter and more real, it will be prior to the compound also for the same reason" (Aristotle, *Metaphysics* 7.3:1029^{a}5–7 [Oxford trans.]).

[62] Aristotle, *Metaphysics* 7.10:1035^{a}20–21.

[63] Ibid., 7.12:1037^{b}11–12.

[64] Aristotle, *Physics* 1.5:189^{a}5–8. See also *Metaphysics* 4.11:1018^{b}32–33: "For according to the principle, universals are prior; according to the sense-perception, particulars."

[65] Aristotle, *Metaphysics* 7.11:1037^{a}5–7 (Oxford trans.).

[66] Ibid., 7.3:1028^{b}36–37 (Oxford trans., modified).

[67] Aristotle, *Metaphysics* 7.10:1035^{a}6–7.

[68] See above, pp. 47–48.

[69] See N. Augeles, "Ê hyperbasê tês physikês ston Aristotelê," *Philosophia* (K. E. E. Ph. Yearbook of the Academy of Athens) 2 (1972), 293.

[70] *Against Eunomius* 2 (PG 45:564b; ed. Jaeger, 2:402.16–26).

[71] *On the Divine Names* (PG 3:645cd; trans. Luibheid-Rorem, CWS).

[72] "Without energy, nature neither is nor is cognizable" (Gregory of Nyssa, *Fragments*, in F. Diekamp, ed., *Analecta Patristica*, Orientalia Christiana Analecta 117 [Rome, 1938], 144). See also Basil the Great in F. Diekamp, ed., *Doctrina Patrum de Incarnatione Verbi* 14.9 (Münster, 1907), 88.19ff.: "For neither is essence without energy in accordance with nature, nor is energy ever without essence, or rather, we are cognizant of the essence through the energy, since we have the energy itself as evidence to assure us of the essence." See also Maximus the Confessor, *Theological and Polemical Chapters* (PG 91:200c): "the lack of this [natural energy] either makes the nature not be a nature, or makes them all identical with each other and one instead of many, confusing them all together through the abrogation of what constitutes them." See also his *Ambigua* (PG 91:1037c): "The principle of the natural energy is the term of the essence, naturally characterizing all in which it has been implanted

according to the essence. For what is predicated in common and in general is the term of their essence." See also Gregory Palamas, *Defense of the Holy Hesychasts* 3:1.24 (ed. P. Christou, 1:637.6): "You would not be able to see any essence whatsoever without a natural energy;" and 3:3.6 (Christou, 1:685.9): "The holy fathers clearly state ... that no nature whatsoever can either exist or be known without the energy that belongs to it essentially."

73 See Cyril of Alexandria, *Thesaurus* 18 (PG 75:312c): "nature and energy are not identical." See also Basil the Great, *Against Eunomius* 1.8 (PG 29:528b): "How would it not be absurd to say that the power of creation is an essence, and the power of providence also an essence, and the power of foreknowledge an essence too, and in general that every energy is an essence?" Cf. 2.32 (PG 29:648a): "The things he has made are indicative of power and wisdom and skill but not of the essence itself, and neither do they present of necessity the whole power of the Creator." See also Gregory Palamas, *One Hundred and Fifty Chapters* 142 (Sinkiewicz, 246): "energy affects something else, not identical with the operator" (trans. Sinkiewicz). Cf. Gregory Palamas, *On Deifying Participation* 29 (P. Christou, 2nd ed., 2:162.5): "So when you hear us saying that the essence is one thing and the energy another, you should understand us to be saying that each of these has its own meaning."

74 See *Metaphysics* 7.2:1069^{b}15–20.

75 Aristotle, *Physics* 8.5:256^{a}14 (Oxford trans.).

76 *Metaphysics* 7.6:1071^{b}12–14. Cf. N. Augeles, "Ê hyperbasê tês physikês," 300.

77 *Summa Theologiae* 1.2:3 (trans. and ed. Pegis).

78 Ibid.: "If that by which it is moved be itself moved, then this also must needs be moved by another, and that by another again. But this cannot go on to infinity, because then there would be no first mover, and, consequently, no other mover, seeing that subsequent movers move only inasmuch as they are moved by the first mover; as the staff moves only because it is moved by the hand. Therefore it is necessary to arrive at a first mover, moved by no other; and this everyone understands to be God."

79 Aristotle, *Metaphysics* 7.6:1071^{b}14–16 (Oxford trans.).

80 Aristotle, *Metaphysics* 7.6:1071^{b}19–20.

81 "and the first mover must itself be unmoved" (Aristotle, *Metaphysics* 4.8:1012^{b}31 [Oxford trans.]).

82 "But it is impossible that movement should either come into being or cease to be; for it must always have existed. Nor can time come into being, or cease to be; for there could not be a before and an after if time did not exist. Movement also is continuous, then, in the sense in

which time is …. There is therefore a mover which moves without being moved, being eternal substance [*ousia*] and actuality [*energeia*]" (ibid., 7.6:1071^{b}6–10 and 7.7:1072^{a}24–26).

[83] This transference took place within the context of the subordination of theology to Aristotelian epistemology: "Par l'introduction de l'epistemologie aristotélicienne, s'était constituée au XIIIe siècle, dans une réflexion explicite, la théologie comme science. Saint Thomas d'Aquin était le maître de cette opération" (Chenu, *La Théologie comme science*, 9). And on p. 11: "Saint Thomas le premier a su – et osé – poser nettement le principe d'une intégrale application du mécanisme et des procédés de la science au donné révélé, constituant par là une discipline organique où l'Écriture, l'article de foi est non plus la matière même, le sujet de l'exposé et de la recherche, comme dans la *sacra doctrina* du XIIe siècle, mais le *principe*, préalablement connu, à partir duquel on travaille, et on travaille selon toutes les exigences et les lois de la *demonstratio* aristotélicienne."

[84] Cf. *Summa Theologiae* 1.1:7: "The object of our science is God …. In sacred science the ruling idea, to which everything is subjected, is God …." See also Chenu, *La théologie comme science*, 55: "La foi qui a pour object la Vérité première …."

[85] Dionysius the Areopagite, *On the Divine Names* 3 (PG 3:869c).

[86] Maximus the Confessor, *Theological and Polemical Chapters* (PG 91:32bc).

[87] "For energy is the essential movement of the nature, and what is operative is the nature, from which the energy issues" (John Damascene, *On the Orthodox Faith* 59 [ed. Kotter, 144]).

[88] A reference to Basil the Great by Gregory Palamas, *One Hundred and Fifty Chapters* 143 (PG 150:1220d; ed. Sinkiewicz, 248).

[89] "Willing and the 'how' of willing are not identical, any more than seeing and the 'how' of seeing. For willing, like seeing, belongs to nature, and is an attribute of all beings of the same nature and race. But the 'how' of willing, like the 'how' of seeing … is the way in which willing and seeing are used. It is an attribute only of the one who exercises it and separates him from the others with what is commonly called a difference" (Maximus the Confessor, *Disputation with Pyrrhus* [PG 91:292d]).

[90] "By the principle of nature the will is shown to be one for all; but by the way it is moved it is different" (Maximus the Confessor, *Theological and Polemical Chapters* [PG 91:25a]).

[91] Basil the Great, *Letter* 189.8 (PG 32:696b). See also Maximus the Confessor, *Theological and Polemical Chapters* (PG 91:200d): "For the energy is referred back to the one who operates, and the nature in turn to the substratum."

[92] Gregory Palamas, *In Defense of the Holy Hesychasts* 3:1.31 (ed. P. Christou, 1:643.15–17).

[93] Dionysius the Areopagite, *On the Divine Names* 5 (PG 3:593ab).

[94] Ibid., 7 (PG 3:645a).

[95] Gregory Palamas, *In Defense of the Holy Hesychasts* 3:2.10 (ed. Christou, 1:664–65.9, trans. Gendle, CWS). There is an echo here probably of Plato's *Cratylus*: "My notion would be something of this sort. I suspect that the sun, moon, earth, stars, and heaven, which are still the gods of many barbarians, were the only gods known to the aboriginal Hellenes. Seeing that they were always moving and running, from their running nature they were called gods or runners (*theous, theontas*) and when men became acquainted with the other gods, they proceeded to apply the same name to them all" (397c8–d9 [trans. and ed. Hamilton-Cairns]). See also Gregory of Nyssa, *Against Eunomius* 2 (PG 45:960; ed. Jaeger, GNO 1:268): "On the one hand God is in himself what he is believed always to have been; on the other, he is called by those who invoke him not that which he is (for the nature of beings is inexpressible), but is believed to have the divine names from the effect he has on our lives."

[96] *On the Divine Names* 9 (PG 3:825a). See also Maximus the Confessor, *Scholia on the Divine Names* (PG 4:332cd).

[97] Maximus, *Ambigua* (PG 91:1265d–68b). The whole passage is as follows: "There are said to be two universal energies among beings, one of which is the one that naturally brings forth from beings that which is homogeneous, of the same essence and identical to themselves in every way .... The other energy they say is the one that is productive of external things, according to which one constructs something different from some preexisting matter alien to one's own essence, to do with energies that are external and heterogeneous. The latter energy they say is constituted with knowledge and skill."

[98] "Therefore Basil the Great says: 'God poured out the Holy Spirit abundantly on us through Jesus Christ. He poured it out; he did not produce it. He bestowed it, he did not create it. He gave it; he did not make it.' What then did God pour out and bestow and give us through Jesus Christ? Was it the essence or the grace of the Holy Spirit? Surely it was the deifying grace, in accordance with which John, the Golden-mouthed theologian, said: 'it is not God but grace which is poured forth.' For through this grace the nature of the Spirit, being uncreated, is both made known and shown, since it has no manifestation in itself. Clearly, then, this grace is uncreated, and so clearly, that its result is that each of those who have been divinely graced and deified I say to be unoriginate, eternal and unending ... not through created nature, through which being began and came to an end, but through the grace that is divine and uncreated and

is for ever beyond all nature and time, since it is from God who is for ever" (Gregory Palamas, *To Akindynos* 3.17 [ed. Christou, 1:308.2–14, 23–26]).

[99] "the whole [of God] having interpenetrated (*perichorêsantos*) the whole of those who are worthy, as becomes his goodness" (Maximus the Confessor, *Ambigua* [PG 91:1076c]). See also Gregory Palamas, *On the Divine Energies* 28 (ed. Christou, 2:116.24–28: "Even if deifying grace is not the nature of God – for the latter is imparticiple – it is nevertheless a natural energy of God, naturally consequent on God and always contemplated inseparably around him. Therefore he who is an heir to this is said to be an heir of God."

[100] Dionysius the Areopagite, *On the Divine Names* 9 (PG 3:825a).

[101] "Everything that God is, the person who has been deified by grace will also be, except identity according to essence" (Maximus the Confessor, *To Thalassius* 22 [PG 90:320a]). See also *Ambigua* (PG 91:1308b, 1237ab).

[102] "Creatures are indicative of its power and wisdom and skill, but not of its essence" (Basil the Great, *Against Eunomius* 2.32 [PG 29:648a]).

[103] "Every divine energy by itself, according to the true principle, indicates God as indivisibly whole in each thing in which it is individually in accordance with some principle ... and God without being divided or apportioned is wholly in all things in common and in each being individually. He is neither expanded in various ways by the differences of the beings in which he is, nor contracted by the individual existence of the one, nor does he contract the differences of beings in accordance with the one single wholeness of all things, but is truly all things in all things, though he never goes out of his own undivided simplicity" (Maximus the Confessor, *Ambigua* [PG 91:1257ab]).

[104] Maximus the Confessor, *Chapters on Theology* 5 (PG 90:1377ab). See also Nicolas Cabasilas, *On the Life in Christ* (PG 150:644d–45a): "The love-potion utterly changes the lovers of humanity."

[105] "For there is one faculty, the implanted mind itself, which passes through each of the organs of sense and grasps the things beyond: this it is that, by means of the eyes, beholds what is seen; this it is that by means of hearing, understands what is said; that is content with what is to our taste, and turns from what is unpleasant; that uses the hand for whatever it wills" (Gregory of Nyssa, *On the Making of Man* 6 [PG 44:140; trans. Wilson, *NPNF*]). On the mind as humanity's energy, see Gregory Palamas, *In Defense of the Holy Hesychasts* 2:2.26 (ed. Christou, 1:5.33.25–27), and Basil the Great, *Letter* 233.1 (PG 32:864d).

[106] "It tells us that God, taking dust of the ground, formed the man, and by an inspiration from himself he planted life in the work of his hand, that

thus the earthly might be raised up to the divine, and so one certain grace of equal value might pervade the whole creation, the lower nature being mingled with the supramundane" (Gregory of Nyssa, *Great Catechical Oration* 6 [PG 45:27d–28a]).

[107] "An energy of man is a house or a ship" (Gregory of Nyssa, *Against Eunomius* 1 [PG 45:381b; ed. Jaeger, 1:149.12–13).

[108] "Any essence of which the essential energies are created must itself necessarily be created" (Gregory Palamas, *In Defense of the Holy Hesychasts* 3:1.31 [ed. Christou, 1:643.4–5; trans. Gendle, CWS).

[109] See Thomas Aquinas, *Summa Theologiae* 1a:12.2: "Hence as other intelligible forms, which are not identical with their existence, are united to the mind according to a sort of mental existence by which they inform and actualize the mind, so the divine essence is united to a created mind so as to be what is actually understood and through its very self making the mind actually understanding" (Blackfriars trans., 3:11). Also 1a:12.5: "When however a created intellect sees the essence of God, that very divine essence becomes the form through which the intellect understands" (Blackfriars trans., 3:19.). Cf. P. N. Trembelas, *Dogmatikê*, 1:139: "Man, being intelligent and possessing the capacity to know God, is led up by automatic reasoning from visible things to those which are beyond the senses and proceeds through the mind to the investigation of God."

[110] See Thomas Aquinas, *Summa Theologiae* 1a:12.1: "If therefore the created mind were never able to see the essence of God, either it would never attain happiness or its happiness would consist in something other than God .... The view is also philosophically untenable, for it belongs to human nature to look for the causes of things – that is how intellectual problems arise. If therefore the mind of the rational creature were incapable of arriving at the first cause of things, this natural tendency could not be fulfilled. So we must grant that the blessed do see the essence of God" (Blackfriars trans., 3:5). The same conclusion is found in the *Summa contra Gentiles* 3:51: "Possibile sit substantiam Dei videri per intellectum."

[111] "A person can neither pray nor even sacrifice to such a God ('causa sui'). Before the First Cause a person can neither fall on his knees in awe, nor can he praise or worship him. That is why atheistic thought which denies the God of philosophy, God as First Cause, is perhaps closer to God as he really is ('ist dem göttlichen Gott vielleicht näher')" (Heidegger, *Identität und Differenz* [Pfullingen: Neske, 1957], 70–71). "The final blow against God and against the suprasensible world ... did not come from those outside, those who do not believe in God, but from the believers and their theologians" (Heidegger, *Holzwege* [Frankfurt: Klosterman, 1963], 239–40).

[112] [The Greek expression: *klêsê prosôpikê ... heterousiôs ousiômenê* conveys more elegantly than the English the hypostatic reality of God's reaching out to us in the third Person of the Trinity. Trans.]

[113] My setting down here the difference between the acceptance or rejection of the essence-energies distinction highlights what is perhaps a genuine weakness, or even *non sequitur*, in this book as a whole: I speak of the priority of personal relation and experience and the transcendence of conceptual definitions, using, however, conceptual definitions which I set out systematically. It is therefore possible for the reader to conclude that what this discussion is about is merely two different systems of ideas – not two radically opposed *modes* of life or *attitudes* towards it. Of course, the use of intellectual ideas and their systematic discussion can have a "semantic reference" to life, provided that the objectification of truth in concepts is constantly resisted. This resistance is not purely and simply a literary form. It articulates a social dynamic of the word. In the works of the Greek Fathers, readers may find and confirm for themselves this expression of personal experience, which gives language the iconological depth of the experiential dimension. Such an achievement is beyond my powers in the present work. Here an attempt is made to go beyond the objectification of truth in concepts, but again only through ideas expressed in concepts.

[114] See Thomas Aquinas, *Summa contra Gentiles* 2:9: "God's actuality [=*energeia*] is his essences." And 2:8: "This divine power is the essence of God." See also Barlaam of Calabria, *Against the Messalians*, in *The Works of Gregory Palamas* [ed. P. Christou, 1:300.24–301.3]): "For if even the light [of God's energies] is uncreated, what is caused and participable and visible ... is necessarily called a divinity (*theotês*), and the nature of God, which is beyond any cause and participation, vision and apprehension, naming and exposition, how will it be one and not uncreated divinities, one superior and the other inferior?" And St. Gregory Palamas replies: "Not knowing that with regard to the uncreated energies and the essence such a distinction and the superimposition (*hyperthesis*) that goes with it does not impair the fact that there is one divinity. Indeed, rather, it strengthens it, as without it the things that are distinguished could not be brought together into one divinity in an orthodox manner" (*Exposition of Impieties* [ed. Christou, 2:579.18–22]).

[115] "God's activity (*actio*), however, is not distinct from his power (*potentia*); each is the divine essence, identical with the divine existence .... we justify the meaning of power in God, not as being the principle of divine acting, which is identical with his being, but as the principle of an effect" (Thomas Aquinas, *Summa Theologiae* 1a:25.1 [Blackfriars trans., 5:155]).

[116] See the expression of this in the encyclical *Mystici Corporis* of Pope Pius XII: (in *La foi catholique – Textes doctrinaux du Magistère de l'Église* [Paris: Ed. de l'Orante, 1961], 364): "Ce qu'il faut rejeter: tout mode d'union mystique par lequel les fidèles, de quelque façon que ce soit, dépasseraient l'ordre du créé et s'arrogeraient le divin au point que même un seul des attributs du Dieu éternel puisse leurs être attribué en propre." And cf. the Eastern viewpoint expressed by Gregory of Nyssa: "Man transcends his own nature, becomes immortal from having been mortal, and imperishable from having been perishable, and eternal from having been transient, and wholly god from having been man .... For if what he [God] is by nature he grants as a property to human beings, what else is this other than that he promises an equality of honour through kinship? (*On the Beatitudes* 7 [PG 44:1280cd]).

[117] See Chenu, *La théologie au XIIe siècle*, 294n. See also *La foi catholique*, 321: "La grace est gratuite et surnaturelle," with references to Roman Catholic dogmatic sources. See also Nicolas, *Dieu connu comme inconnu*, 218ff. On created grace there is a characteristic fragment of Gregory Akindynos cited by Gregory Palamas: "The hypostasis of the All-holy Spirit creates deifying grace in the saints, but in spite of that this created grace is said to be a hypostasis of the All-holy Spirit. And those who receive this created grace are said to receive the Holy Spirit, the very essence and hypostasis of the Spirit" (*To Athanasius of Cyzicus* 33 [ed. Chrestou, 2:443.20–25]).

[118] See the study of Stylianos Papadopoulos, *Ellênikai metaphraseis thomistikôn ergôn: Philothomistai kai antithomistai en Byzantiô* (Athens, 1967), 20, 137.

[119] See above, pp. 37–38.

[120] Dionysius the Areopagite, *On the Divine Names* 4 (PG 3:712ab).

[121] "Do you see this void above our heads? It is God. Do you see this crack in the door? It is God. Do you see this hole in the ground? Again, it is God. The silence is God. The absence is God" (*Le Diable et le Bon Dieu* 10:4).

[122] "I am walking in your darkness: give me your hand. Tell me, the darkness is you, isn't it? The darkness, the heart-rending absence of the universe! Because you are the one who is present in the universal absence, the one who is heard when there is absolute silence, the one we see when nothing more is visible" (ibid., 8–9:2).

[123] "Is it then so painfully impossible for anyone to apprehend God with the senses? Why does he hide behind a fog of half-spoken promises and invisible wonders ... ? I want knowledge, not faith, not conjectures. Knowledge, I want God to put his hand out, to reveal himself

to me ...." (Ingmar Bergman, from the scenario of *The Seventh Seal* [Greek trans.]).

[124] *Le Diable et le Bon Dieu* 10:4. See also Christos Yannaras, "The Theology of Hell," in *Ê krisê tês propheteias* (Athens: Domos, 1981), 153ff.

[125] *Homily 5 on Romans* 6 (PG 60:430).

[126] *Ladder of Divine Ascent* 7.1 (trans. Luibheid-Russell, CWS).

[127] *Mystical Prayer of Symeon our father among the saints*, cited by Lossky, *Mystical Theology*, 160–61.

[128] John Climacus, *Ladder* 30.1.

PART TWO

Chapter One

[1] Diels 1:105.24–25.

[2] Diels 1:71.11.

[3] Frag. 8 (Diels 2:36.14).

[4] Frag. 1 (Diels 1:406.25; trans. Kirk-Raven-Schofield, 325).

[5] Frag. 7 (Diels 1:270.16ff; trans. Kirk-Raven-Schofield, 396).

[6] The expression (*koinon tês poleôs kosmon*) is Plato's, illustrative of the use of the word *kosmos*. See *Laws* 8:846d5–6 (Hamilton-Cairns).

[7] Frag. 1 (Diels 1:89.11ff.; trans. Kirk-Raven-Schofield, 108, modified). See Konst. Michaelides, "Kosmos und Ethos bei Anaximander und Heraklit," *Philosophia* 1 (1971), 141–54.

[8] "In this way, using the language of probability, we may say that the world came into being – a living creature truly endowed with soul and intelligence" (*Timaeus* 30b6–8 [Hamilton-Cairns, modified]).

[9] Plato, *Gorgias* 507e6–508a4 (Hamilton-Cairns).

[10] Plato, *Timaeus* 92c5–9 (Hamilton-Cairns, modified).

[11] Plato, *Timaeus* 32cl.

[12] Ibid., 32d1–2.

[13] "That the world is correctly said to be most beautiful ... is easy to comprehend. For first the visible beauty of the heavens, the order of the cycles, the divisions of time, the harmony of the elements, and the proportions extending through all things show those who are not completely benighted that the universe is most beautiful" (Proclus, *Scholia on Plato's Timaeus* 11:101d [ed. E. Diehl 1:1903.332.18ff]).

[14] "Of the things which are by nature visible, no unintelligent creature taken as a whole could ever be fairer than the intelligent taken as a

whole, and again intelligence could not be present in anything which was devoid of soul. For which reason, when he was framing the universe, he put intelligence in soul, and soul in body, that he might be the creator of a work which was by nature fairest and best" (Plato, *Timaeus* 30b1–6 [Hamilton-Cairns, modified]).

[15] "Thus, using the language of probability, we may that the world came into being – a living creature truly endowed with soul and intelligence" (Plato, *Timaeus* 30b6–8).

[16] "Then if we cannot hunt down the good under a single form, let us secure it by the conjunction of three, beauty, proportion, and truth, and then, regarding these three as one, let us assert that *that* may most properly be held to determine the qualities of the mixture, and because *that* is good the mixture itself has become so" (Plato, *Philebus* 65a1–5 [Hamilton-Cairns]).

[17] "But there are two different kinds of good things, the merely human and the divine; the former are consequential on the latter" (*Laws* 1:631b6–8 [Hamilton-Cairns]). "God is good in reality" (*Republic* 2:379b1).

[18] "Everything that is good is beautiful" (*Timaeus* 87c4–5). "For we shall not say that God is deficient in beauty or virtue" (*Republic* 2:381c1–2).

[19] "This world is good and so the creator is good" (*Timaeus* 29a2–3). "We must say that the world came into being as a living creature truly endowed with soul and intelligence by the providence of God" (*Timaeus* 30b7–31c1 [Hamilton-Cairns, modified]).

[20] "When the world began to be ordered ..." (*Timaeus* 53b1). "God who set it in order" (*Statesman* 273d4). "But others, among whom is ... Plato, claim that God made the world from pre-existent and uncreated matter: God would not have been able to make anything unless matter already existed" (Athanasius the Great, *On the Incarnation* 2 [trans. Thomson, OECT]).

[21] "God desired that all things should be good and nothing bad, so far as this was attainable. Wherefore also finding the whole visible sphere not at rest, but moving in an irregular and disorderly fashion, out of disorder he brought order, considering that this was in every way better than the other" (*Timaeus* 30a2–6 [Hamilton-Cairns]).

[22] Frag. 30 (Diels 1:157–58; trans. Wheelwright, no. 29).

[23] *Laws* 10:886a2–5 (Hamilton-Cairns).

[24] *Fragmenta Selecta, Peri Philosophias* 12a, ed. W. D. Ross (Oxford, 1964), 80 (Oxford trans.).

[25] "Die Auffassung des Weltbegriffes ist abhänging vom Verständnis des Wesens," observes Heidegger (*Vom Wesen des Grundes*, 5th ed. [Frankfurt: Klostermann, 1965], 27). See also *Was ist Metaphysik?* 11: "Inzwischen bleibt der Metaphysik während ihrer Geschichte von Anaxi-

mander bis zu Nietzsche die Wahrheit des Seins verborgen .... Allein die Metaphysik antwortet nirgends auf die Frage nach der Wahrheit des Seins, weil sie diese Frage nie fragt .... Sie meint das Seiende im Ganzen und spricht vom Sein. Sie nennt das Sein und meint das Seiende als das Seiende."

[26] "… der Weltbegriff als ein Grundbegriff der Metaphysik …" (Heidegger, *Vom Wesen des Grundes*, 27).

[27] See the very interesting study of S. Kyriazopoulos, *Ê parousia tês physikês epistêmês* (Athens, 1963), where there is a relevant bibliography. See also Marios Begzos's doctoral dissertation, *Dialektikê physikê kai eschatologikê theologia* (Athens, 1985); and Christos Yannaras, *Protaseis kritikês ontologias* (Athens: Domos, 1985). [And, most recently, Christos Yannaras, *Postmodern Metaphysics* (Brookline, MA: Holy Cross Orthodox Press, 2004), esp. "Thesis 1, The postmodern challenge: a metaphysical extension of physics." Trans.]

[28] "The mathematical study of nature could be represented from the point of view of the observer as a kind of theater. The observer holds a chronometer in his hands and marks precisely when the actors participating in the play enter and exit the stage. If one reflects that this natural knowledge has from time to time enthralled modern man, one can understand the vanity and impertinence of such a person who, relying on the precision of his chronometer, intervenes in the production to teach the participants precisely what the play is about" (Kyriazopoulos, *Ê parousia tês physikês epistêmês*, 259–60).

[29] See Sartre, *L'Être et le Néant*, 369–70, where he concludes: "La relativité de la science moderne vise l'*être*. L'homme et le monde *sont* des êtres relatifs et le principe de leur être *est* la relation."

[30] W. Heisenberg, *Das Naturbild der heutigen Physik* (Hamburg, 1955), 21.

[31] Without this meaning that the same conclusions of modern physics cannot lead towards a radically different attitude towards the world and, in particular, towards a getting round the quest for knowledge for the sake of human domination over the world, the subjection of the world to human needs and desires. "In the practical approach it is not *knowledge* which is important but *use*. A mechanical work does not have truth as its aim, but *benefit*. It is concerned not with what nature is but with what is *constructed* through nature. The practical approach is characteristic not only of those who do not participate in scientific research, but even of the natural sciences, for research only advances through technical skill. So instead of technology being presented as applied science, physics appears as a systematic development of the technical disposition. This disposition is orientated not towards theory, but *power* through theory"

(S. Kyriazopoulos, *I katagôgê tou technikou pneumatos* [Athens, 1965], 275–76). See also Panayiotis Kondylis, *Ê kritikê tês metaphysikês stê neoterê skepsê* (Athens: Gnosê, 1983).

[32] An echo of Heidegger: " 'Welt' bedeutet ... die Offenheit des Seins. 'Welt' ist die Lichtung des Seins" (*Über den Humanismus*, 35).

[33] ["products and principles" may also be translated as "poems and words." In Greek a "poem" (*poêma*) is literally a "thing made," and a "word" (*logos*) is a thought or principle until it is uttered or expressed. Trans.]

[34] "... other senses, which are receptors of impressions coming from outside, and are not accessible to rational investigation" (Gregory of Nazianus, *Oration* 28.22 [PG 36:57a]).

[35] Note the Platonic expression of this in the *Symposium*: "Whoever has been initiated so far in the mysteries of Love and has viewed all these aspects of the beautiful in due succession, is at last drawing near the final revelation. And now ... there bursts upon him that wondrous vision which is the very soul of the beauty he has toiled so long for" (210e1–6 [Hamilton-Cairns]).

[36] Clement of Alexandria, *Paedagogus* 3.1 (PG 8:557c).

[37] *The Extant Ascetical Works*, *Letter* 4 (ed. Spanos, 389).

[38] *Chapters on Theology* 1.57 (PG 90:1108b).

[39] See Hans-Georg Beck, *Kirche und theologische Literatur im byzantinischen Reich* (Munich: Beck, 1959), 347ff.

[40] *Ambigua* (PG 90:752a). On "natural contemplation" in the Fathers of the Byzantine period, see H.-G. Beck, *Kirche und theologische Literatur*, 348, 356, 357, 360, 363, 585. See also Hans Urs von Balthasar, *Kosmische Liturgie* (Einsiedeln: Johannes, 1961), 53, 114, 176, 296, 581, 639, etc. Also Lars Thunberg, *Microcosm and Mediator*, 2nd ed. (Chicago and La Salle: Open Court, 1995), 343ff.

[41] See Isaac the Syrian, *Extant Ascetical Works*, 383.

[42] "It is necessary to believe that in every being there lies some wise and skilful *logos*, even if it is beyond our powers of vision" (Gregory of Nyssa, *On the Hexaemeron* [PG 44:73a]). See also 73c: "The wisdom contemplated in creation is a *logos*, even if it cannot be expressed."

[43] Maximus the Confessor, *Chapters on Theology* 3 (PG 90:1261cd).

[44] *Homily on 1 Corinthians* 15.28 (PG 14:1312a). See also Eusebius of Caesarea, *Evangelical Demonstration* 4.1 (PG 22:252d): "He put forth his own will and power as if it were some matter and essence of the genesis and constitution of all things."

[45] For the identification of form and *logos*, see Aristotle, *Metaphysics* 2:996^{b}8, 8:1044^{b}12; *Physics* 4:209^{a}21–22, 1:190^{a}16.

[46] *Hexaemeron* 2.2 (PG 29:33a).

[47] John Damascene, *On the Orthodox Faith* (PG 94:865a; ed. Kotter, 45). See also Gregory of Nazianus, *Oration* 45.5 (PG 36:629a): "... he conceives of the angelic and heavenly powers, and the mental concept was a work, fulfilled by the Logos and perfected by the Spirit."

[48] Gregory of Nyssa, *Hexaemeron* (PG 44:73a).

[49] Basil the Great, *Against Eunomius* (PG 29:736c).

[50] Gregory of Nyssa, *On the Soul and Resurrection* (PG 46:125b; trans. Moore, *NPNF*, modified).

[51] Cf. Gregory of Nyssa, *Hexaemeron* (PG 44:73c): "By some *logos* the causative power of each thing that comes into being is brought to actualization."

[52] *Hexaemeron* 7 (PG 44:69c). See also *On the Soul and the Resurrection* (PG 46:124c): "None of these things is in itself a body – neither shape, nor color, nor weight, nor dimensions, nor size, nor anything else of what is contemplated in the qualities. On the contrary, each of these is a *logos*, and when they come together and unite with each other, a body comes into being."

[53] "If the electron, being neither a 'particle' nor a 'wave,' exceeds all the geometrical possibilities of representing it, and consequently, as regards its existence independently of ourselves, does not refer to physics, even when it can be represented by mathematical equations, it would appear in the end that it is possible for it, naturally or artificially, to become whatever object is observed. 'Particle' or 'wave,' 'force' or 'field,' are thus for modern physics symbols for position or velocity. Both this position and this velocity are nevertheless not position and velocity as such, but are constituted by observation. Therefore, if the concept of the particle symbolizes position and the concept of the wave a related succession of positions, both the one and the other are consequences of (or better: are connected with) the presence of the human observer" (Kyriazopoulos, *Ē parousia tēs physikēs epistēmēs*, 151).

[54] Gregory of Nyssa, *On the Inscriptions of the Psalms* (PG 44:441b; ed. J. McDonough and P. Alexander, 32.4–6).

[55] For the refutation of this view, which was first expressed by Augustine and subsequently became established as the common teaching of the Western Christian tradition, see Lossky, *Mystical Theology*, 91ff. See also Olivier Clément, "Le sens de la terre – Notes de Cosmologie Orthodoxe," *Contacts* 59–60 (1967): 257ff.

[56] See Lossky, *Mystical Theology*, 94–95. See also John Damascene, *On the Divine Images* 2.14 (PG 94:1300b; ed. Kotter, 105): "I venerate matter ... not as God, but as filled with divine energy and grace." Also Basil the Great, *Against Eunomius* 2.32 (PG 29:648a): "The things made are

indicative of its power and wisdom and skill, but not of its essence; nor do they necessarily represent all the power of the creator."

57 Gregory Palamas, *The One Hundred and Fifty Chapters* 142 (PG 150:1220c; ed. Sinkewicz, 246): "Hence it should be clear to those who think rightly that the divine energy is distinct from the divine substance for the energy effects something else, not identical with the operator. God effects and makes creatures but is himself uncreated" (trans. Sinkewicz).

58 *On the Holy Spirit* (PG 32:180c).

59 Procopius of Gaza, *Commentary on Genesis* 2.17 (PG 87:324c).

60 Basil the Great, *Homily on Psalm* 29 (PG 29:317ab).

61 "Not even one of the things that are is at all bereft of participation in the beautiful, if 'all things,' as the truth of the Scriptures says, "are very good" (Dionysius the Areopagite, *On the Celestial Hierarchy* [PG 3:141c; SC 58.80.32–34]). [The biblical reference is to Genesis 1:31. The Greek word for "good" used here in the Septuagint (*kalon*) also means "beautiful." Hence in the passage that follows Dionysius' play on *kalos* ("beautiful/good"), *kallos* ("beauty"), and *kaleô* ("call," "summon," or "invite"). Trans.]

62 Dionysius the Areopagite, *On the Divine Names* 4 (PG 3:701c; trans. Luibheid-Rorem, CWS, modified).

63 Isaac the Syrian, *Ascetical Works, Letter* 4 (ed. Spanos, 384).

64 Didymus the Blind, *On the Trinity* 2.1 (PG 39:452a).

65 *To Thalassius* 13 (PG 90:296bc).

66 "The divine … remains mentally ungraspable and verbally inexpressible" (Maximus the Confessor, *Letter* 6 [PG 91:432c]).

67 See Basil the Great, *On the Holy Spirit* 16.38 (PG 32:136ab), and Gregory of Nazianzus, *Oration* 45.5 (PG 36:629a).

68 See Lossky, *Mystical Theology*, 100–101.

69 "From the natural movement of beings, we learn of a being's subsistent life, the life-giving power of beings, the Holy Spirit" (Maximus the Confessor, *To Thalassius* 13 [PG 90:296d]). See also *Chapters on Theology* (PG 90:1209a): "The Holy Spirit is in all things in a simple fashion, seeing that it constitutes and exercises providence over all things, and is able to set the seeds of nature in motion."

70 Athanasius the Great, *Letter 3 to Serapion* 45 (PG 26:632bc).

71 Cf. John Damascene, *On the Two Wills in Christ* 15 (PG 95:144b): "Man indeed is a microcosm; for he has soul and body, and stands in between mind and matter. He is a combination of visible and invisible, that is, of sensible and intellectual creation." Also Leontius of Byzantium, *Against Nestorians and Eutychians* 1 (PG 86:1284c): "Neither before when [the Logos] produced the world … nor afterwards when he fash-

ioned man for himself as the great world in miniature, was he circum-scribed." Also Gregory of Nazianzus, *Oration* 28.22 (PG 36:57a): "this small world, man." And *Oration* 38.11 (PG 36:324a): "he stands on earth like a second great world in miniature." Also Gregory of Nyssa, *On the Inscriptions of the Psalms* 1.3 (PG 44:441d; ed. MacDonough-Alexander, 32.18–27): "man is a microcosm ... that which the Logos saw with regard to the great world, in all likelihood he sees in the small world ... thus in the small world too, by which I mean human nature, is perceived the music which is contemplated in the whole, in proportion to the total-ity through the part, as the whole is contained by the part."

[72] Cf. Maximus the Confessor, *Mystagogia* 7 (PG 91:684d–685a): "The whole world constituted of what is visible and what is invisible ... is man. And man consisting of soul and body is another world." On man as a *microcosm* and the world as a *macranthropos*, see Lars Thunberg, *Microcosm and Mediator*, esp. 132–43. Also W. Völker, *Gregor von Nyssa als Mystiker* (Wiesbaden, 1955), 51ff. Also Hans Urs von Balthasar, *Kosmische Liturgie*, 169–75.

[73] See H. Diels and W. Kranz, *Die Fragmente der Vorsokratiker*, 2:b34.153.4–11: "And just as in the universe we see some things only ruling, like the divine, and others ruling and being ruled, like the human (for these are both ruled by the divine and themselves rule the irrational animals), and others are only ruled, like the irrational animals, so in the same way the same is contemplated ... in man the microcosm. Some things only rule, like reason (*logos*), others both rule and are ruled, like anger (*thymos*), ... and others are only ruled, like desire (*epithymia*)."

[74] See *Timaeus* 81a–b2 and *Philebus* 29b–30a.

[75] *Physics* 8:2.252^{b}24–27: "Now if this can occur in an animal, why should not the same be true also of the universe as a whole? If it can oc-cur in a small world it could also occur in a great one" (Oxford trans.).

[76] See *Ambigua* 41 (PG 91:1304dff). See also Thunberg, *Microcosm and Mediator*, 143.

[77] *Ambigua* 41 (PG 91:1305bc; trans. Louth). See also 1305ab: "Like a laboratory in which everything is very concentrated and in itself natu-rally mediates between the extremities of each division, having been drawn into everything in a good and fitting way ... having the power of naturally uniting at the mean point of each division since it is related to the extremities of each division in its own parts" (trans. Louth, lightly modified).

[78] *Ambigua* 10 (PG 91:1193d; trans. Louth).

[79] Ibid., 41 (PG 91:1308ab; trans. Louth).

[80] Ibid., (PG 91:1308d–12b).

[81] Maximus the Confessor, *To Thalassius* 55 (PG 90:541bc; ed. Laga and Steel, CC 10.489).

[82] Ibid., 65 (PG 90:760a; ed. Laga and Steel, CC 22.285).

[83] Ibid., (PG 90:756b; ed. Laga and Steel, CC 22.279).

[84] N. Jorga, *Byzance après Byzance: Continuation de l'histoire et de la vie byzantine* (1935; 2nd ed. Bucharest, 1971).

[85] A basic bibliography would include Dimitry Obolensky, "The Principles and Methods of Byzantine Diplomacy," *Actes du XIIe Congrès International d'Études Byzantines I* (Belgrade, 1963); Arnold Toynbee, *Constantine Porphyrogenitus and His World* (London: Oxford Univ. Press, 1973); K. Lechner, *Hellenen und Barbaren im Weltbild der Byzantiner* (Munich, 1954); L. Bréhier, *Les institutions de l'Empire byzantin* (Paris: Albin Michel, 1948); P. Charanis, "On the Social Structure of the Later Roman Empire," *Byzantion* 17 (1944–45): 38–57; E. Bach, "Les lois agraires byzantines du Xe siècle," *Classica et Mediaevalia* 5 (1942): 70–91; J. B. Bury, *The Imperial Administrative System in the Ninth Century*, 2nd ed. (New York: Burt Franklin, 1963); Gervase Mathew, *Byzantine Aesthetics* (London: John Murray, 1963); J. M. Hussey, *Church and Learning in the Byzantine Empire* (London: Oxford Univ. Press, 1937); Hélène Ahrweiler, *L'idéologie politique de l'empire byzantin* (Paris: PUF, 1975); F. Dvornik, *Early Christian and Byzantine Political Philosophy* (Washington: Dumbarton Oaks, 1966); Steven Runciman, *Byzantine Style and Civilization* (Harmondsworth: Penguin, 1975).

[86] See Chenu, *La théologie au XIIe siècle*, 34ff.

[87] See M. A. Schmidt, "Johannes Scotus Eriugena," in *Die Religion in Geschichte und Gegenwart*, vol. 3, cols. 820–21; Chenu, *La théologie au XIIe siècle*, 40, 50; also Gilson, *La Philosophie au Moyen Age*, 202.

[88] "It is in this context of renaissance – where inspiration takes precedence over imitation, where also the resources of antiquity nourished new spiritual initiatives – that there developed the literary, aesthetic and doctrinal theme of the relations of humanity with nature: the human being is a 'microcosm'" (Chenu, *La théologie au XIIe siècle*, 37). See also Gilson, *La Philosophie au Moyen Age*, 327–28; Chenu, *La théologie comme science au XIIIe siècle*, 101: "Between the two great crossroads of the Carolingian renaissance and that of the Quattrocento, the twelfth and thirteenth centuries mark a stage characterized by the recovery of the capital of Antiquity."

[89] "the first attempts at a microcosm-macrocosm parallelism were of a rational, we might even say of an early scientific, type" (Chenu, *La théologie au XIIe siècle*, 41). See also Gilson, *La Philosophie au Moyen Age*, 327: "… reasoning by analogy, which consisted of explaining a being or fact by its correspondence with other beings or other facts. A

method this time legitimate and which all science makes use of .... The description of the human person as a universe in miniature, that is to say, as a microcosm analogous to a macrocosm, is a classic example of this kind of reasoning."

[90] "Confronted by the universe, the human person not only accepts the exterior world, but changes it, and seeks with its tools to compose a human world .... The thinking of the men of the twelfth century ... perceived all that art, in *forcing nature*, could reveal about humanity" (Chenu, *La théologie comme science au XIIIe siècle*, 49 [my emphasis]).

[91] See ibid., 40.

[92] "The 'interior life' calls in the microcosm, in the very name of its nature, for the intellectual and mechanical domination over the macrocosm" (ibid., 42).

[93] See ibid., 314: "There is an autonomous knowledge of this world and of the human person, valuable in its own order, actually helpful for speculation and action, which is transferable to theological science." And on p. 48: "The order is no longer simply the schema of an aesthetic imagination or a religious conviction; it is proved, sustained by a method."

[94] See ibid., 16: "In its earliest state, theology is normally a commentary, and throughout the course of its development it evolves in constant reference to structures related to the teaching of law. In the Middle Ages above all, canonists and theologians work in constant collaboration in analogous and interchangeable forms." Further research would be useful on the historical development of the legal-juridical spirit of the Roman Church even from the time of Tertullian and Augustine (who were both very well versed in legal matters). The same legal-mindedness calls for the objectivizing of particular cases, and the monarchical understanding of objective authority.

[95] See ibid., 315: "In the organic construction of its wisdom, theology takes account of *objects* which furnish it with rational disciplines, sciences of the universe and its laws, sciences of humanity and its faculties." And on p. 51: "It is the same Alan of Lille (d. 1203), this master of nature, who is also the theoretician of the 'rules of theology,' that is to say, of the method by which, as in every mental discipline, the knowledge of faith is organized and built up, thanks to internal principles which give it the appearance and value of science."

[96] The Roman Church is the only Western Medieval institution which preserves an unbroken cultural tradition and can meet the need for unity of the various nations living together in Western Europe. The exploitation of the need for such an institution had already arrived at a complete religious organization of the Western communities by the tenth and eleventh centuries. For the religious structures of the Western Medieval com-

munities and their expression in the religious art of the eleventh century, see the extremely interesting study of Georges Duby, *Adolescence de la chrétienté occidentale* (Geneva: Skira, 1967). See also Robert Fossier, *Histoire sociale de l'Occident médiéval* (Paris: Colin, 1970), esp. 43–44, 54–56; Jean Chélini, *Histoire religieuse de l'Occident médiéval* (Paris: Colin, 1968; and J. Le Goff, *La civilisation de l'Occident médiéval* (Paris: coll. "Les grandes civilisations," 1964).

[97] "The West made the unity of God (one God) a clear and firm basis (for the dogma of the Trinity) and tried to conceive of the mystery of his threeness. A fundamental formula was 'one substance, one hypostasis.' From such a formula there was a danger of arriving at one person (Monarchians, the monarchianizing bishops of Rome Victor, Zephyrinus and Callixtus). The formula favored monarchianism and assisted in the battle against Arianism" (Basil Stephanidis, *Ekklêsiastikê Istoria*, 169). The monarchian spirit of the West was revealed very clearly by the rejection of the distinction between Essence and Energies and by the relevant works which tried to support this rejection, mainly in the fourteenth century. The pro-Latin opponents of St. Gregory Palamas defined the *hypostasis* as a *referential essence* which "differs from the simple essence because the one is referential, the other detached …. The detached differs from the referential only conceptually" (John Kyparissiotes, *How the Hypostatics in the Trinity Differ from the Essence*, ed. E. Candal, *Orientalia Christiana Periodica* 25 [1959]: 132, 140, 142). St. Gregory Palamas judged from the beginning that the denial of the uncreated Energies of the Trinity conceals a hidden denial of the hypostases and their identification with the essence (see *On the Divine Energies* 27 [ed. P. Chrestou, 2:115]). And Matthew Blastares accuses the antipalamites of wanting "to contract the divine nature into one hypostasis," introducing into Christianity the Jewish "poverty," that is, Jewish monotheism (see *On the Divine Grace or On the Divine Light*, Cod. Monac. 508, fol. 150[r], cited by Amphilochios Rantovits, *To mystêrion tês Agias Triados kata ton agion Grêgorion Palaman* [Thessalonica, 1973], 25, 27).

[98] See Stephanidis, *Ekklêsiastikê Istoria*, 198–99n: "In the West the (monarchianizing) phraseology of Western Theology has through the influence of Augustine endured to the present day." See also F. Loofs, *Dogmengeschichte* (1906), 363ff. Also Chenu's conclusion (*La théologie comme science au XIIIe siècle*, 95): "Augustine's theology … is a fine piece of intellectualism" in conjunction with Stephanidis' observation (*Ekklêsiastikê Istoria*, 166): "The solution the Monarchians gave was based on rational argumentation, such that given the premises those were the ideas they would arrive at." See also N. Nissiotis, *Prolegomena eis tên theologikên Gnosiologian* (Athens, 1965), 178–79.

[99] "Theology is decidedly distinct from faith (and Scripture) in the leading scholarly circles" (Chenu, *La théologie comme science au XIIIe siècle*, 26; see also 55, 79, 83).

[100] See ibid., 26–27: "The 'scientific' regime which now established itself ... was the right of reason to install itself at the heart of the deposit and light of faith, and work there according to its own laws." See also 85–86: "Faith admits of ... a capacity for rational elaboration, exposition and proof, according to the philosophical sense of the word *argumentum* .... Even the definition of faith opens itself from now on, as if on a smooth horizon, to a rational expansion of a scientific nature."

[101] See ibid., 42: "... to accept the objectivizing of the knowledge of faith in theology ..."; and 20: "Gilbert de la Porrée (1076–1154) vigorously enunciated the principle of the transfer to theology of the formal procedures (*regulae, axiomata, principia*) customary in every rational discipline." See also 51: "Like every intellectual discipline, the knowledge of faith was organized and built up thanks to internal principles which gave it the appearance and value of science."

[102] The first part comprised the *Categories*, the *De interpretatione* and the *Prior analytics*, the second part the *Posterior analytics*, the *Topics*, and the *Sophistical refutations*. In some editions of the *Organon* the treatises *On generation and corruption* and *On the universe* were added.

[103] See Chenu, *La théologie comme science au XIIIe siècle*, 20.

[104] Ibid.

[105] "Man's encounter with nature was only accomplished in such a way that man seized this nature and put it to work for him .... To set up Nature in fact put paid to a certain Christian conception of the universe" (ibid., 44, 50).

[106] "In this mechanical universe, man ... depersonalized his action, became sensitive to the objective density and the articulation of things under the domination of natural laws ... Human science embraced the knowledge of this mastery of nature" (ibid., 48).

[107] Byzantine and post-Byzantine architecture expresses a radically opposite attitude to the material of construction. A comparison of Gothic to Byzantine buildings gives us perhaps the clearest illustration of two diametrically opposed cosmological views which lead to two diametrically opposed technical approaches. See Christos Yannaras, *Ê eleutheria tou êthous* (Athens: Ekdoseis Athena, 1970), ch. 13, "To êthos tês leitourgikês technês," 183ff.: "Every piece of Byzantine architecture is a personal exploration of the potentialities of the physical material .... In Byzantine architecture we not only find a personal use of the material of construction, but also a personal dialogue with the material, the personal encounter of humanity with the *logos* of God's love and wisdom, which

is revealed in the material creation. This dialogue, which is embodied in Byzantine architecture, conveys the measure of the truth of the entire natural world as communion and Ecclesia …. The material creation is 'shaped' as person, the Person of the Logos …." [Cf. the ET of this work by Elizabeth Brière, *The Freedom of Morality* (Crestwood, N.Y.: St. Vladimir's Seminary Press, 1984; based on the Greek of the 2nd ed., 1979), ch. 12, "The Ethos of Liturgical Art."] See also Olivier Clément, *Dialogues avec le Patriarche Athenagoras* (Paris: Fayard, 1969), 278–83; P. A. Michaelis, *Aisthêtikê theôrêsê tês byzantinês technês*, 2nd ed. (Athens, 1972; ET of 1946 ed., *An Aesthetic Approach to Byzantine Art* [London, 1955]), esp. 85–98; Christos Yannaras, "Teologia apofatica e architettura bizantina," in *Simposio Cristiano* (Milan: Ediz. dell' Istituto di Studi teologici Ortodossi, 1971), 104–12; and Marinos Kalligas, *Ê aisthêtikê tou chôrou tês Ellênikês Ekklêsias sto Mesaiôna* (Athens, 1946).

[108] Erwin Panofsky, *Gothic Architecture and Scholasticism* (Latrobe: Archabbey Press, 1951).

[109] Ibid., 27ff.

[110] "… this astonishingly synchronous development …" (ibid., 20). See also the diagrams later in the book.

[111] Ibid.

[112] "… the construction of a knowledge within faith. From this, theology is established as a science" (Chenu, *La théologie comme science au XIIIe siècle*, 70).

[113] *Gothic Architecture and Scholasticism*, 34.

[114] See Michaelis, *Aisthêtikê theôrêsê*, 89–90.

[115] Ibid., 90.

[116] Ibid. See also Worringer, *Formprobleme der Gotik* (Munich, 1910), 73 (cited by Michaelis).

[117] "Theology is the first great technical science (*technique*) of the Christian world …. The men who built the cathedrals [also] constructed the *summae*" (Chenu, *Introduction à l'étude de Saint Thomas d'Aquin* [Paris: Vrin, 1974], 53, 58).

[118] "For according to whether we use things rightly or wrongly we become either good or bad" (Maximus the Confessor, *First Century on Love* 92 [Palmer-Sherrard-Ware]).

Chapter Two

[1] "Now these are regions or kinds of place – up and down and the rest of the six directions" (Aristotle, *Physics* 4.1:208^{b}12–14 [Oxford trans.]).

[2] Ibid., 3.3:202ᵇ17–19.

[3] Ibid., 4.1:209ᵃ4–6 (Oxford trans.).

[4] "... place is motionless ... a motionless boundary ... it moves neither others nor itself" (ibid., 4.4:212ᵃ18–21, 5.1:224ᵇ5).

[5] Ibid., 4.4:212ᵃ20–1, 212ᵃ15–15; 4.2:209ᵇ1–2; *On the Heavens* 4.3:310ᵇ7–8.

[6] Ibid., 4.2:210ᵃ9.

[7] Ibid., 4.4:212ᵃ17.

[8] Ibid., 4.1:208ᵇ26–27.

[9] Ibid., 4.5:212ᵇ20–22 (Oxford trans.).

[10] See his *L'Être et le Néant* (Paris: Gallimard, 1943), 40ff. (ET, *Being and Nothingness*, trans. Hazel E. Barnes [London: Routledge, 1993], 6ff.).

[11] See *L'Être et le Néant*, 44–46 (ET, 9–11). I give the story largely in his own words.

[12] "When I enter this café to look for Pierre, there happens to be a synthetic arrangement of all the objects in the café against the background of which Pierre is given as if about to appear" (ibid., 44).

[13] "That Pierre is not there does not mean that I discover his absence in some precise spot in the establishment. In fact Pierre is absent from the *whole* café" (ibid., 45).

[14] "I was expecting to see Pierre and my expectation made Pierre's absence *happen* like a real event concerning this café. This absence is a present objective fact. I have *discovered* it and it presents itself as a synthetic relation between Pierre in the room in which I am looking for him" (ibid., 45).

[15] "And, certainly, Pierre's absence implies an original relation between me and this café" (ibid.).

[16] "... they have a purely abstract meaning ... they do not succeed in establishing a real relation between the café and Wellington or Valéry: the relation 'is not' is here merely *thought*" (ibid.).

[17] Here not as *dia-stasis* but with the metaphorical sense of a perspective of depth, of *dimension*.

[18] See *L'Être et le Néant*, 40.

[19] See ibid., part 1, ch. 1, par. 5: "L'origine du néant" (58ff.; ET, 21ff.), and especially 69: "It is precisely the awareness of my being my own future in the mode of non-being that is called 'anguish'."

[20] *L'Être et le Néant*, 45.

[21] "A witness is needed who can retain the past in some way and compare it to the present in the form of 'no-longer'" (ibid., 43).

[22] Ibid., 60: "L'homme est l'être par qui le néant vient au monde."

[23] See Heidegger, *Sein und Zeit* 1:1.2: "Das In-der-Welt-sein überhaupt als Grundverfassung des Daseins" [Being-in-the-world in general as the basic state of Dasein] (52ff.).

[24] "Zum Dasein gehört aber wesenhaft: Sein in einer Welt" [But to Dasein, Being in a world is something that belongs essentially] (*Sein und Zeit*, 13).

[25] *On the Orthodox Faith* 1.13 (PG 94:852a; ed. Kotter, 38).

[26] Ibid. (PG 94:853c; ed. Kotter, 39).

[27] Basil the Great, *Against Eunomius* (PG 29:736c).

[28] Theophilus of Antioch, *Against Autolycus* 2.3 (PG 6:1049d).

[29] Maximus the Confessor, *Scholia on the Divine Names* 4.17 (PG 4:269d).

[30] Ibid. (PG 4:268c); cf. 1 John 4:16.

[31] John Damascene, *Against the Jacobites* 87 (PG 94:1476b). See also Clement of Alexandria, *Stromata* 5 (PG 9:109ab): "Form and movement or station or throne or place or right or left is not to be conceived of in any way with regard to the Father of the universe, even if these expressions are used in Scripture …. Therefore the first cause is in a place, but beyond all place and time and name and intellection."

[32] *Against the Arians* 1:61 (PG 26:140b).

[33] *Hyper to pou* (Maximus, *To Thalassius* 61 [PG 90:640b; ed. Laga and Steel, 2:103, line 319]).

[34] *Adiastaton henotêta* (Cyril of Alexandria, *Thesaurus* 12 [PG 75:192c]).

[35] *Synapheian adiastaton* (Gregory of Nyssa, *Against the Macedonians* 16 [PG 45:1321a]). See also *Against Eunomius* 9 (PG 45:813b): "How can one measure or divide that which is non-quantitative and non-dimensional? What measure is applicable to the non-quantitative or interval to the non-dimensional? How can one conceive of infinity with an end and a beginning? For the beginning and end of dimensional finite beings is their names. Where there is no dimension there is no limit either. The divine nature is certainly non-dimensional; and since it is non-dimensional, it has no limit."

[36] Maximus the Confessor, *Scholia on the Divine Names* (PG 4:221a).

[37] Maximus the Confessor, *To Thalassius* 61 (PG 90:640b; ed. Laga and Steel, 2:103, line 321).

[38] *On the Divine Names* 4.14 (PG 3:712c–713a).

[39] Ibid., 4.10 (PG 3:708b). Cf. Maximus the Confessor, *Scholia on the Divine Names* (PG 4:261ab): "Since good eros preexisted in the good, it did not remain sterile … for the divine is operative and productive, according to the text: 'My Father is working still, and I am working' (John

5:17) .... For beneficent eros moved the divine to exercise providence, for our coming into existence."

[40] Ibid. (PG 3:708ab). Cf. Maximus the Confessor, *Various Texts* 5.87 (PG 90:1385b): "They call the subject of love and eros, that is, God, producer and begetter. For since these are within him, he brought them forth into the outside world, that is, among the creatures. That is why it is said that God is love. Moreover, he is Sweetness and desire, which is eros. That which is beloved and truly the object of erotic love is God. By the fact that the loving eros is poured forth from him, the begetter of this is said himself to move. By the fact that he is that which is truly the object of eros and love and desire and choice, he moves those things which look towards this. And the power of desiring is proportionately in them."

[41] The quotation from Maximus is a *scholion* on the following passage from the Dionysian corpus: "When we talk of eros, whether divine, or angelic, or intellective, or in the soul, we should conceive of a unifying and sustentive power which moves what is superior to exercise care for what is inferior, things of the same rank to enjoy reciprocal communion, and what is lowest to return to what is higher and superior to it" (*On the Divine Names* 4.15 [PG 3.713ab]).

[42] Maximus the Confessor, *Scholia on the Divine Names* (PG 4:268c–269a).

[43] "As active eros and love the divine itself moves, and as the object of eros and love it moves all things receptive of eros and love towards itself. To put it more clearly, it moves itself as implanting an immanent relation of eros and love in those things receptive of it, and it moves others as naturally attracting the desire of those things move towards it" (Maximus the Confessor, *Ambigua* [PG 91:1260]).

[44] See Evagrius Ponticus, *Gnostic Chapters* (PG 40:1244a).

[45] "In speaking of 'place' he does not limit the place indicated by anything quantitative (for to something unquantitative there is no measure). On the contrary, by the use of the analogy of a measurable surface he leads the hearer to the unlimited and infinite ... the place with me is so great that the one running in it is never able to cease from his progress" (Gregory of Nyssa, *On the Life of Moses* 2.242 (PG 44:405ab; ed. Musurillo, 117.15–24, trans. Malherbe-Ferguson, CWS).

[46] "L'absence c'est Dieu" (Sartre, *Le Diable et le Bon Dieu* 10.4).

[47] Maximus the Confessor, *Scholia on the Divine Names* (PG 4:269cd).

[48] For the Byzantine Fathers, the knowledge of God is the beginning and end of every kind of knowledge – knowledge of humanity as personal existence and knowledge of the world as the disclosure of the personal Energies of God – and that is why the knowledge of God, which is realized only as a fact of love, is the "true philosophy": "therefore love for

God is itself the true philosophy" (John Damascene, *Dialectica* [ed. Kotter, 56, 137, 160]).

[49] "… rational death that releases and separates the soul from the passions …" (Clement of Alexandria, *Stromata* 7.12 [PG 9:500a]). See also Basil the Great, *Homily on the Psalms* 33 (PG 29:385a): "Those who die to sin have died the death that is good and brings salvation." And Symeon the New Theologian, *Ethical Treatises* 11 (SC 129.332.46–48): "For God arranged providentially that through death we should lay hold of eternal life. Die and you will live. You don't want to? Then you are already dead."

[50] *Sein und Zeit*, 246.

[51] "… we hope to receive the whole after death …" (Symeon the New Theologian, *Ethical Treatises* 5 [SC 129.104.341–42]). See also Gregory of Nyssa, *To Pulcheria* (PG 46:877a): "If death is benign, it has become the principle and the path of our change for the better." And Basil the Great, *Homily on Psalm 115* (PG 30:109d): "Have no fear of death, for it is not corruption but the beginning of life."

[52] 2 Cor 5:4: "so that what is mortal may be swallowed up by life."

[53] See John Climacus, *The Ladder of Divine Ascent*, 26: "Only one of God's creations has its being in something else and not in itself. Yet it is amazing how it can come to exist outside that in which it has received being" (ed. Constantinople, 1883, 136; trans. Luibheid-Russell, CWS).

[54] See Gregory Palamas, *On Deifying Participation* (ed. Chrestou, 2:144.13–16): "For this is the death of the soul, estrangement from the life in God. And this death is truly terrible. The one after it, that is, the death of the body, is after it most to be prayed for, for it is an act of divine philanthropy."

[55] 1 Cor 13:10.

[56] 1 John 3:2.

[57] 1 Cor 13:9, 12.

[58] 1 Cor 13:8, 12.

[59] 1 Cor 13:8.

[60] *On the Ecclesiastical Hierarchy* 3.3.9 (PG 3:437c).

[61] Isaac the Syrian, *Ascetical Works* 84.323.

[62] "In these [the holy *synaxes*] a person who beholds in a sacred manner will see the one uniform unanimity, moved as one by the thearchic Spirit" (Dionysius the Areopagite, *On the Ecclesiastical Hierarchy* 3.3.5.432b).

[63] "The most divine, common and irenic distribution of the one and the same bread and cup lays down for those who partake of it together a godly sameness of disposition" (ibid., 3.3.1.428b).

[64] Ibid., 3.3.3.429a.

Chapter Three

[1] *Physics* 5.4:234^{b}11.

[2] Ibid., 4.13:222^{b}21. Cf. 222^{b}16: *metabolê pasa physei ekstatikon* – "it is the nature of *all* change to alter things from their former condition" (Oxford trans.).

[3] Ibid., 4.14:222^{b}30–31.

[4] Ibid., 4.11:218^{b}33–34.

[5] *Metaphysics* 1.1:1052^{b}20: "measure is that by which quantity is known" (Oxford trans.).

[6] *Eudemian Ethics* 8.10:1243^{b}29: "the measurement must be by one measure, only here not by a term but by a ratio."

[7] "Temporality is essentially ecstatical" ["Die Zeitlichkeit ist wesenhaft ekstatisch"] (Heidegger, *Sein und Zeit*, 331).

[8] "The succession of intervals as portions and hours and nights and days is not what time is. This and time are homonyms. For just as we are accustomed to calling both that which measures and that which is measured by the same name, so it is in the present case. For example, if something is measured by a cubit-rule, whether a floor, or a wall, or something else, we call it a cubit" (Maximus the Confessor, *Scholia on the Divine Names* [PG 4:316ab]).

[9] According to Plato, time is a moving image of eternity, an image in eternal orbit "according to number": "Wherefore he resolved to have a moving image of eternity, and when he set in order the heaven, he made this image eternal but moving according to number, while eternity itself rests in unity, and this image we call time" (*Timaeus* 37d5–7). See also *Definitions* 411b3: "Time is the movement of the sun, the measure of motion."

[10] *Timaeus* 41e5, 42d5.

[11] *Enneads* 3.7:7–13. See esp. 11.59–62 and 12.22–28, 40–43: "But one must not conceive time as outside soul, any more than eternity there as outside real being. It is not an accompaniment of soul nor something that comes after (any more than eternity there) but something which is seen along with it and exists in it and with it, as eternity does there [with real being] .... This is why it is said that time came into existence simultaneously with this universe, because soul generated it along with this universe. For it is in activity (*energeia*) of this kind that this universe has come into being; and the activity is time and the universe is in time. But if someone wants to say that Plato also calls the courses of the stars 'times' he should remember that he says that they have come into existence for the declaring and 'division of time,' and his 'that there might

be an obvious measure.' ... 'So, then, it will be the movement of the universe which will be measured by time, and time will not be a measure of movement essentially, but it will incidentally, being something else first, afford a clear indication of how long the movement is" (trans. Armstrong, LCL).

[12] See, for example, *Physics* 4.11:219^{a}23–30: "But we apprehend time only when we have marked motion, marking it by before and after; and it is only when we have perceived before and after in motion that we say that time has elapsed. Now we mark them by judging that one thing is different from another, and that some third thing is intermediate to them. When we think of the extremes as different from the middle and the mind pronounces that the 'nows' are two, one before and one after, it is then that we say that there is time, and this that we say is time. For what is bounded by the 'now' is thought to be time – we may assume this" (Oxford trans.).

[13] See Heidegger, *Sein und Zeit*, 326, 420. Also Husserl, *Ideen zu einer reinen Phänomenologie und phänomenologischen Philosophie* 1, Husserliana, vol. 3 (The Hague: Martinus Nijhoff, 1950), 196.29–32.

[14] *Physics* 4.12:221^{b}27–28.

[15] "Ce qui sépare l'antérieur du postérieur c'est précisément *rien*. Et ce rien est absolument infranchissable, justement parce qu'il n'est rien" (*L'Être et le Néant*, 64).

[16] *Physics* 4.11:219^{a}26, 6.1:231^{b}9.

[17] "Time contains something indivisible, and this is what we call the now" (ibid., 4.3:234^{a}22–23). "For the number of the locomotion is time, while the 'now' corresponds to the moving body, and is like the unit of number" (ibid., 4.11:220^{a}3–4) (Oxford trans.).

[18] "The same reasoning applies equally to magnitude, to time, and to motion: either all of these are composed of indivisibles and are divisible into indivisibles, or none" (*Physics* 6.1:231^{b}19–20). "Motion is always in time and never in a now" (ibid., 6.10:241^{a}15). "When, therefore, we perceive the 'now' as one, and neither as before and after in a motion nor as the same element but in relation to a 'before' and an 'after,' no time is thought to have elapsed, because there has been no motion either. On the other hand, when we do perceive a 'before' and an 'after,' then we say that there is time. For time is just this – number of motion in respect of 'before' and 'after'" (*Physics* 4.11:219^{a}30–219^{b}1) (Oxford trans.).

[19] Ibid., 8.1:251^{b}20–21 (Oxford trans.).

[20] *Dialectica* 40.52 (ed. Kotter, 116): "Time is measured in the past and in the future, and its divisions have a common boundary which unites them, the now. The now is without quantity."

[21] *On Isaiah* 119 (PG 30:312a): "The now for us signifies the integral and indivisible aspect of time. But for God all things are perceived as now."

[22] *Ambigua* (PG 91:1164bc). Plotinus had already distinguished eternity from time, referring the former to everlasting nature and the latter to material – limited nature. See *Enneads* 3.7:1.1–3: "Eternity and time, we say, are two different things, the one belonging to the sphere of the nature which lasts for ever, the other to that of becoming and of this universe" (trans. Armstrong, LCL).

[23] *To Thalassius* 65 (PG 90:760a).

[24] *Physics* 4.11:219^{b}7–8. See also 4.12:220^{b}8–9: "Time is not number with which we count, but the number of things which are counted."

[25] Aristotle, *Physics* 4.12:221^{a}28.

[26] See Heidegger, *Sein und Zeit*, 235: "Der Entwurf eines Sinnes von Sein überhaupt kann sich im Horizont der Zeit vollziehen" [Within the horizon of time the projection of a meaning of Being in general can be accomplished]; 404–5: "Alles Verhalten des Daseins soll aus dessen Sein, dass heist aus der Zeitlichkeit interpretiert werden" [All Dasein's behaviour is to be interpreted in terms of its Being – that is, in terms of temporality] (trans. Macquarrie-Robinson). See also *Was ist Metaphysik?* 17–18: " 'Sein' ist … nicht etwas anderes als 'Zeit,' insofern die 'Zeit' als der Vorname für die Wahrheit des Seins genannt wird, welche Wahrheit das Wesende des Seins und so das Sein selbst ist … Gesetzt, die Zeit gehöre in einer noch verborgenen Weise zur Wahrheit des Seins, dann muss jades entwerfende Offenhalten der Wahrheit des Seins als Verstehen von Sein in die Zeit als den möglichen Horizont des Seinsverständnisses hinaussehen."

[27] *Physics* 4.11:219^{b}1–3 (Oxford trans.).

[28] Ibid., 4.12:220^{b}8–9 (Oxford trans.).

[29] Ibid., 4.12:221^{a}26. See also 221^{b}14–16: "To be in number means that there is a number of the things, and that its being is measured by the number in which it is. Hence if a thing is in time it will be measured by time" (Oxford trans.).

[30] *Physics* 4.12:221^{b}3.

[31] Ibid., 4.12:221^{b}27–28. See also *On Generation and Corruption* 2.10:336^{b}18–24: "Thus we see that coming-to-be occurs as the sun approaches and decay as it retreats; and we see that the two processes occupy equal times. For the durations of the natural processes of passing-away and coming-to-be are equal. Nevertheless it often happens that things pass-away in too short a time, because of their mutual commingling. For their matter is irregular, i.e., is not everywhere the same; hence the processes by which they come-to-be must be irregular too, i.e., some too quick and others too slow. Consequently the phenomenon in question

occurs, because the coming-to-be of these things is the passing-away of other things" (Oxford trans.).

32 *Metaphysics* 12.2:1069ᵇ11–12, 14.1:1088ᵃ31.

33 See *Physics* 3.1:201a12–15: "of what is increasable and its opposite, decreasable: (entelechy) … increase and decrease; of what can come to be and pass away, coming to be and passing away; of what can be carried along, locomotion." Also 4.3:211ᵃ14–17: (local movement) "Of this kind of motion there are two species – locomotion on the one hand and, on the other, increase and diminution. For these too involve change: what was then in this place has now in turn changed to what is larger or smaller" (Oxford trans.). Aristotle's distinction between the quantitative increase and diminution of inanimate matter and the generation and decay of living organisms perhaps corresponds in some degree to the meaning which modern physics gives to the terms "entropy" and "metabolism." In the case of inanimate matter, entropy – the tendency of the particles of a closed system towards a state of increasing disorder – transposes the existent to an "after" which is always less incorrupt than the "before." In the case of living organisms, which are constituted of substances with little entropy, a new order is constantly created by metabolism, which tends in the opposite direction to what the principle of entropy would have permitted. We could therefore say that metabolism transposes the existent to an "after" which is more incorrupt than the "before." Nevertheless, every living individual, in spite of metabolism, tends finally towards a state of maximum entropy, which is death.

34 See *On Generation and Corruption* 2.10:336ᵃ15–33ᶜb16.

35 Ibid., 2.10:336ᵇ2–3: "the continuity of this movement is caused by the motion of the whole."

36 Ibid., 2.10:336ᵃ25–26 (Oxford trans.).

37 *Physics* 4.12:221ᵃ30–221ᵇ3 (Oxford trans.).

38 See Heidegger, *Sein und Zeit*, 2:1: Das mögliche Ganzsein des Daseins und Sein zum Tode, particularly the expressions on p. 245: "Das mit dem Tod gemeinte Enden bedeutet kein Zu-Ende-sein des Daseins, sondern ein *Sein zum Ende* dieses Seienden. Der Tod ist eine Weise zu sein, die das Dasein übernimmt, sobald es ist. 'Sobald ein Mensch zum Leben kommt, sogleich ist er alt genug zu sterben'" [The "ending" which we have in view when we speak of death, does not signify Dasein's Being-at-an-end but a *Being-towards-the-end* of this entity. Death is a way to be, which Dasein takes over as soon as it is. "As soon as man come to life, he is at once old enough to die" (Macquarrie-Robinson)]. And on p. 250: "Mit dem Tod steht sich das Dasein selbst in seinem *eigensten* Seinkönnen bevor" [With death, Dasein stands before itself in its own-most potentiality-for-being (Macquarrie-Robinson)].

[39] That is the sense of the following lines from George Seferis:
> Like the pines
> hold the form of the breeze
> though the breeze has gone, is absent
> so do words
> keep the form of the human person
> though the person has gone, is absent
> (*Three Secret Poems* [Athens, 1966], 33)

[40] See *On the Divine Names* 4.12 (PG 3:709bc).

[41] Ibid., 4.20 (PG 3:720bc).

[42] *Chapters on Theology* 5.98 (PG 90:1392a).

[43] *Centuries of Various Texts* 2.74 (PG 90:1248cd; Palmer-Sherrard-Ware). See also ibid. 3.56 (PG 90:1284c–85a): "Pleasure has been defined as desire realized .... Desire, on the other hand, is pleasure that is only potential .... Incensiveness is frenzy premeditated, and frenzy is incensiveness brought into action. Thus he who has subjected desire and incensiveness to the intelligence will find that his desire is changed into pleasure through his soul's unsullied union in grace with the divine, and that his incensiveness is changed into a pure fervour shielding his pleasure in the divine, and into a self-possessed frenzy in which the soul, ravished by longing, is totally rapt in ecstasy above the realm of created being" (Palmer-Sherrard-Ware).

[44] See *Various Texts* 4.33 (PG 90:1317c): "When God the Logos created human nature He did not make the senses susceptible either to pleasure or to pain; instead, He implanted in it a certain noetic capacity through which men could enjoy Him in an inexpressible way. By this capacity I mean the intellect's natural longing for God. But on his creation the first man, through an initial movement towards sensible objects, transferred this longing to his senses, and through them began to experience pleasure in a way which is contrary to nature" (Palmer-Sherrard-Ware).

[45] See *Other Chapters* 158 (PG 90:1437b): "Of the rational soul, the outer court is the senses, the nave is the intellect, and the bishop is the mind"; *Various Texts* 2.33 (PG 90:1233a): "The mind has the power to discriminate between the mental and the sensible, the transitory and the eternal"; *Centuries on Love* 3.92 (PG 90:1045b): "The mind has the authority and power to follow or resist whatever it wishes"; *To Thalassius* 25 (PG 90:332d): "The understanding of the word is a clear knowledge of the mind that has begotten it, since it manifests in itself the mind that subsists essentially, towards which it raises the mind that desires identity with God by grace"; *To Thalassius* 25 (PG 90:333cd): "Every mind that has become a lover of mystical theology has its head covered when praying or prophesying. That is to say, when it steps without dis-

cursive knowledge into the shrines of contemplation, or teaches or initiates others into theology, or if it has acquired some form of intellection, or has been initiated or initiates others into the Logos who is beyond intellection, it is ashamed of its head. It has subordinated him who is simple and far transcends any intellection to something that belongs to the realm of what has being and is knowable. It is necessary that it should be naked of all concepts and knowledge, and without eyes see the true God-Logos, knowing with clarity that with regard to God the supreme negations convey truth in the degree that they disclose the affirmation of the divine through the complete subtraction of beings."

[46] See Dionysius, *On the Divine Names* 4.15 (PG 3:713ab); ibid., 4.12 (709c): "Love for you came upon me like love for women" (cf. 2 Kgds 1:26); John Climacus, step 5.6.57: "I have watched impure souls mad for physical love but turning what they know of such love into a reason for penance and transferring that same capacity for love to the Lord. I have watched them master fear so as to drive themselves unsparingly toward the love of God" (trans. Luibheid-Russell, CWS) (cf. Yannaras, *Ê metaphysikê tou sômatos*, 157ff.); Gregory of Nyssa, *On the Making of Man* 13.5 (PG 44:168): "for it is through the senses that the union of mind with man takes place" (trans. Wilson, *NPNF*); ibid., 14.3 (PG 44:176): "Thus, neither is there perception without material substance, nor does the act of perception take place without the intellectual faculty" (trans. Wilson, *NPNF*).

[47] See Gregory of Nyssa, *On the Making of Man* 18.5 (PG 44:193).

[48] See E. Husserl, *Ideen zu einer reinen Phänomenologie und phänomenologischen Philosophie* 1, Husserliana, Band 3, 197: "Diejenige Zeit, die wesensmässig zum Erlebnis als solchem gehört, mit ihren Gegebenheitsmodis des Jetzt, Vorher, Nacher, des durch sie modal bestimmten Zugleich, Nacheinander usw., ist durch keinen Sonnenstand, durch keine Uhr, durch keine physischen Mittel zu messen und überhaupt nicht zu messen." See also 292, on the "Ursynthese des ursprünglichen Zeitbewusstseins."

[49] See E. Husserl, *Vorlesungen zur Phänomenologie des inneren Zeitbewusstseins* (Halle, 1928), ch. 2, §8, §14; also his *Ideen zu einer reinen Phänomenologie*, 1:§81, §113, §118.

[50] "Sin (*hamartia*), that is, a failure to attain, a falling away from what is fit, is what he refers to as falling short or going wide instead of hitting the target, to use a metaphor from archery. When we fail to attain the good and go against movement or order according to nature, we arrive at absolute non-existence, which is irrational and lacks substance in a manner contrary to nature" (Maximus the Confessor, *Scholia on the Divine Names* [PG 4:348c]).

[51] "The one nature has been shattered into thousands of fragments. And we who are of the same nature turn on each other like savage serpents" (Maximus the Confessor, *To Thalassius* (PG 90:256b). See also ibid., 397c: "The self-love of each person's will ... has turned nature from something most gentle into a savage beast, and changed the one essence into many contrary essences, not to put it more strongly, and cut it up into portions destructive of each other." Also ibid., 716b: "Having become estranged from nature, [man] uses every aspect of nature in a manner contrary to nature, corrupting nature's beauty by his abuse of it."

[52] "Take a beloved maiden ... her lover approaches from outside .... If indeed the maiden stretches out only her hand, covered in gold, through a small and narrow window and gives it to her lover, and he grasps it and understanding its exceeding beauty kisses it ... in consequence of this he feels the fire of passion all the more strongly .... And when a bridegroom sees the lifeless portrait of his bride made of pigments, he clings to it and gazes at it constantly and wishes to see her, his passion and desire inflamed for her. But when he sees his bride present in person, possessing the faultless form of her loveliness not in the form of the portrait but in her incomparable and inexpressible beauty, he embraces her and kisses her, and he can no longer bear to gaze at her portrait. Those who contemplate the power and wisdom of the Creator in the grandeur and beauty of the visible creation and ascend progressively from this to love and faith towards him and chaste fear. For when they are united essentially to God and are deemed worthy of his vision and participation in him, they no longer cleave passionately, or warmly or tentatively to the image of created things or to the shadow of what is visible" (Symeon the New Theologian, *Theological and Ethical Treatises* 4 [SC 129.70–74]).

[53] "For the weakness of the senses does not allow us to encounter the flame of things" (Isaac the Syrian, *Extant Ascetical Works*, logos 23 [ed. Spanos, 94]).

[54] "He himself, the cause of all things ... through the superabundance of his erotic goodness comes to be outside himself .... And through being carried away from his transcendence, he comes down to be in all things by an ecstatic suprasubstantial power which nevertheless leaves him not having gone out of himself" (Dionysius the Areopagite, *On the Divine Names* 4.17 (PG 3:712ab). See also Maximus the Confessor, *Scholia on the Divine Names* (PG 4:299c): "Do you see that when he says 'since he came as far as nature' you should understand our nature, since we do not properly speak of nature with regard to God. Observe that he says 'he came down as far as nature,' meaning he arrived at that which was less honorable, which he himself did not possess."

[55] "God, who is wholly uncontainable yet is wholly contained in the whole, is distinct from what has been created by him, and wholly but inseparably separate from them. The whole of him is in the whole entirely yet not at all. The whole of him is in the whole of visible creation and the whole of him is outside it. The whole of him is in what is visible and the whole of him is in what is invisible; The whole of him is present everywhere and the whole of him is wholly nowhere" (Symeon the New Theologian, *Gnostic and Theological Chapters* 25 [SC 51.79]).

[56] "For if man stands between mind and matter, and is a bond between the entire visible creation and the invisible, since the creator Word of God has been united to human nature, he is united through this to the whole of creation" (John Damascene, *On the Birthday of the Theotokos* 1 [SC 80.46]).

[57] "Following, therefore, the holy fathers, we all in harmony teach confession of one and the same Son our Lord Jesus Christ, the same perfect in Godhead and the same perfect in manhood, truly God and the same truly man, of a rational soul and body, consubstantial with the Father in respect of the Godhead, and the same consubstantial with us in respect of the manhood, like us in all things apart from sin, begotten from the Father before the ages in respect of the Godhead, and the same in the last days for us and for our salvation from the Virgin Mary the Theotokos in respect of the manhood, one and the same Christ, Son, Lord, Only-begotten, acknowledged in two natures without confusion, change, division, or separation (the difference of the natures being in no way destroyed by the union, but rather the distinctive character of each nature being preserved and coming together into one person and one hypostatis), not parted or divided into two persons, but one and the same Son, Only-begotten, God, Word, Lord, Jesus Christ" (*Definition of the Fourth Ecumenical Council* [*Chalcedon*], ed. I. Karmires, *Ta dogmatika kai symbolika mnêmeia tês Orthodoxou Katholikês Ekklêsias*, vol. 1 [Athens, 1960], 175; ET, Richard Price, *The Acts of the Council of Chalcedon* vol. 2 [Liverpool: Liverpool Univ. Press, 2005], 204).

[58] Maximus goes so far as to say that he finds no "natural difference of flesh and divinity after the union in the mystery" (*To Thalassius* 62 [PG 90:649a]).

[59] Maximus the Confessor, *Scholia on the Divine Names* (PG 4:313d).

[60] Gregory of Nyssa, *On the Inscriptions of the Psalms* 2.5 (PG 44:505a [crit. ed. J. Donough, vol. 5, 84.5]).

[61] Maximus, *Chapters on Theology* 1.51 (PG 90:1101c). See also Symeon the New Theologian, *Theological and Ethical Discourses* 1 (SC 122.182): The eighth day "has no beginning or end. For it is not something that is not now, will happen in the future, and will have a begin-

ning. No, it was before the ages and is now and will be for the ages of ages, and is said to have a beginning when it comes with certainty and is revealed to us finally as a day that never sets and becomes part of us without end."

62 "… the pleasure of women, which has no limit …" (Maximus the Confessor, *To Thalassius* 54 [PG 90:516c]).

PART THREE

Chapter One

[1] *Iliad* 23, 239.

[2] *De fuga et inventione* 112, ed. Starobinski-Safran (Paris: du Cerf, 1970), 184.

[3] *Laws* 10:895d4–5.

[4] *Phaedo* 78d1.

[5] *Metaphysics* 7:1029^{a}2–4 (Oxford trans.).

[6] Ibid., 7:1037^{a}6–7 (Oxford trans.).

[7] Ibid., 7:1028^{a}12–13 (Oxford trans., modified). Cf. 4:1017^{a}24–27: "some predicates indicate what the subject is, others its quality, others quantity, others relation, others activity or passivity, others its place, others its time" (Oxford trans.); 7:1029^{b}24–25: "There are compounds of substance with the other categories … quality, quantity, time, place, and motion" – "I mean the matter with something predicated of it" (2:995^{b}35) (Oxford trans.).

[8] "There are many senses in which a thing may be said to 'be,' but they are related to one central point, one definite kind of thing, and are not homonymous" (*Metaphysics* 3:1002^{a}33–34 [Oxford trans.]).

[9] "So, too, there are many senses in which a thing is said to be, but all refer to one starting-point; some things are said to be because they are substances, others because they are affections of substance, others because they are a process towards substance, or destructions or privations or qualities of substance, or productive or generative of substance, or of things which are relative to substance, or negations of some of these things or of substance itself" (*Metaphysics* 3:1003^{b}5–10 [Oxford trans.]).

[10] Ibid., 3:1003^{b}32.

[11] Ibid., 3:1003^{b}31. Cf. 4:1016^{b}8–9: "but the things that are primarily called one are those whose substance is one"; 10:1053^{b}25: "now being and unity are equivalent in meaning" (Oxford trans., modified).

[12] *Physics* 2:185^{b}7–8.

[13] *Metaphysics* 7:1035^{b}34–35.

[14] Ibid., 7:1034^{b}21.

[15] Ibid., 7:1028^{a}11–12.

[16] Ibid., 7:1028^{a}13–15.

[17] "For even the *logos* of man is not yet a declaratory *logos*, unless 'is' or 'will be' or 'was' or something of this sort is added" (*De Interpretatione* 5.17^{a}11–12).

[18] "The simple declaration is a meaningful utterance about whether something exists or does not exist" (ibid., 5:17^{a}23–24).

[19] "A single *logos* is declaratory either when it reveals a single thing or is one by a bond of union" (ibid., 5:17^{a}15–16).

[20] "Not every [*logos*] is declaratory, but only that in which there is truth or falsity" (ibid., 4:17^{a}2–3). Cf. John Damascene, *Dialectica* 64: On assertion and denial (ed. Kotter, 132); Heidegger, *Sein und Zeit*, 32ff.

[21] *Metaphysics* 7.12:1037^{b}11–12.

[22] Ibid., 7.12:1038^{a}8–9.

[23] *Categories* 5:2^{a}11–16 and *Metaphysics* 7.13:1038^{b}9–16.

[24] *Metaphysics* 7.12:1038^{a}19–20 (Oxford trans.).

[25] Ibid., 7.10:1034^{b}23.

[26] Ibid., 7.11:1037^{a}22–23.

[27] *Physics* 8.1:252^{a}13–14.

[28] Ibid., 2.9:200^{a}14–15.

[29] *Metaphysics* 7.11:1036^{a}28–29.

[30] Ibid., 8.2:1043^{a}19–20.

[31] *Topics* 6.6:143^{b}7–8 (*eidos* is both "form" and "species").

[32] *Metaphysics* 4.7:1012^{a}23–24.

[33] *De Interpretatione* 2:16^{a}27–28.

[34] *On Plants* 1.1:816^{a}14.

[35] On the conventional character of names in common speech, see Ferdinand de Saussure, *Course de linguistique générale* (Paris: Payot, 1969). Characteristic expressions are "La langue est une convention, et la nature du signe dont on est convenu est indifférente" (26); "La langue, c'est un système de signes où il n'y a d'essentiel que l'union du sense et de l'image acoustique, et où les deux parties du signe sont également psychiques" (32); "Tout moyen d'expression reçu dans une société repose en principe sur une habitude collective ou, ce qui revient au même, sur la convention" (100).

[36] *On the Soul* 3.2.426^{b}7.

[37] Ibid., 3.2:426^{a}27–30 (Oxford trans., except that the translation's "ratio" is left as *logos*).

[38] Ibid., 3.3:427^{a}19–22 (Oxford trans., very lightly modified).

[39] Cf. *Various Texts* 2.89 (PG 90:1253c) and *Mystagogy* 5 (PG 91:680b). See also *Various Chapters* 131 (PG 90:1432a): "Nor do thoughts (*logismoi*) belong to the irrational part of the soul, for there is no thought among irrational things. Nor do they belong to the intellective part, since thoughts do not exist among the angels. Being products of the rational (*logikês*) part itself, they ascend towards the mind from the senses, using the imagination as a ladder, and report to the mind what belongs to the senses. They also descend to the senses from the mind and propose what belongs to it."

[40] *On the Soul* 3.3:428ª23–24.

[41] For the distinction between *logos* and conventional *name* see Aristotle, *Prior Analytics* 1.35:48ª30: "for we shall often have phrases (*logoi*) to which no single name (*onoma*) is equivalent"; 1.39:49ᵇ5: "take a word (*onoma*) in preference to a phrase (*logos*)"; *Topics* 5.2:130ª39: "replaces words (*onomata*) by their definitions (*logoi*)"; *Physics* 1.1:184ᵇ10: "a name (*onoma*) ... means vaguely a sort of whole: its definition (*logos*) analyses this into particulars"; *Topics* 1.5:102ª2–5 "people whose rendering consists of a term (*onoma*) only, try it as they may, clearly do not render the definition (*orismos*), of the thing in question, because a definition is always a phrase (*logos*) of a certain kind" (Oxford trans.).

[42] See F. de Saussure, *Cours de Linguistique*, 21: "Le langage est un fait social"; 26: "Ce n'est pas le langage parlé qui est naturel à l'homme, mais la faculté de constituer une langue, c'est-à-dire un système de signes distincts correspondant à des idées distinctes."

[43] "Logic may be defined as the science which investigates the general principles of *valid* thought ... , it seeks to determine the conditions under which we are justified in passing from given Judgments to other Judgments that follow from them" (J. N. Keynes, *Studies and Exercises in Formal Logic* [London, 1906], introduction §1). "Logic is ... the examination of that part of reasoning which depends upon the manner in which inferences are formed .... It has so far nothing to do with the truth of the facts, opinions or presumptions, from which inference is derived but simply takes care that the inference shall certainly be true, if the premises be true" (Aug. de Morgan, *Formal Logic* (Elements of Logic) [London, 1947], ch. 1).

[44] This draws on Heidegger, *Holzwege* (Frankfurt: Klostermann, 1963), 25: "Van Goghs Gemälde ist die Eröffnung dessen, was das Zeug, das Paar Bauernschuhe, in Wahrheit *ist*. Dieses Seiende tritt in die Unverborgenheit seines Seins heraus. Die Unverborgenheit des Seienden nannten die Griechen *alêtheia* .... Im Werk der Kunst hat sich die Wahrheit des Seienden ins Werk gesetzt. 'Setzen' sagt hier: zum Stehen bringen. Ein Seiendes, ein Paar Bauernschuhe, kommt im Werk in das Lichte Seins

zu stehen. Das Sein des Seienden kommt in das Ständige seines Schei-
nens."

[45] This again draws on Heidegger, *Holzwege*, 9: "Mit dem angefer-
tigten Ding wird im Kunstwerk noch etwas anderes zusammengebracht.
Zusammenbringen heist griechisch *symballein*. Das Werk ist Symbol. –
Das Kunstwerk ist wohl ein angefertigtes Ding, aber es sagt noch etwas
anderes, als das blosse Ding selbst ist, *allo agoreuei*."

[46] Cf. Gregory of Nyssa's definition, already mentioned in an earlier
chapter: "Nothing concerning the body is in itself body, neither form,
nor color, nor weight, nor dimension, nor size, nor anything else connected with quantity. Each of these is *logos*. When they cohere with each
other and unite, they become body" (*On the Soul and Resurrection* [PG
46:124c]).

[47] *To Thalassius* 15 (PG 90:293d–96a).

[48] Maximus the Confessor, *Mystagogy* 1 (PG 91:665a).

[49] "For the origination and shaping of creation … the principle of the
origination of all things is the *logos* of God" (Ps.-Basil, *Against Eunomius* 5 [PG 29:736c]); "the omnipotent and perfectly holy Logos of
the Father himself who is present in all things and extends his power
everywhere, illuminating all things visible and invisible, containing and
enclosing them in himself" (Athanasius, *Contra Gentes* 42 [PG 25:84b;
trans. Thomson, OECT, except "Logos" substituted for "Word"]); "The
sun, as we know it, is one. It is a single illuminating light, acting upon the
essences and the qualities of the many and various things we perceive. It
renews them, nourishes them, protects them and perfects them. It establishes the differences between them and it unifies them. It warms them
and makes them fruitful. It makes them exist, grow, change, take root,
burst forth. It quickens them and gives them life. Each thing therefore
has, in its own way, a share of the one and the same sun and the one sun
contains within itself as a unity the causes of all the things which participate in it. All this holds all the more truly with respect to the Cause which
produced the sun and which produced everything else. The exemplars
of everything pre-exist as a transcendent unity within It. It brings forth
essences as an overflowing of essence. We give the name of 'exemplar'
to those *logoi* which pre-exist as a unity in God and which produce the
essences of beings. Theology calls them predefining, divine and good
acts of will which determine and create things and in accordance with
which the Transcendent One predefined and brought into being everything that is" (Dionysius the Areopagite, *Divine Names* 5.8 [PG 3:824bc;
Luibheid-Rorem, CWS, modified]).

Chapter Two

[1] These ideas have been set out at greater length in the first chapter of part 1 above, pp. 9–11.

[2] *Logische Untersuchungen*, 4th ed., 1:173–4.

[3] See Saussure, *Cours de linguistique générale*, 97ff.

[4] The acoustic image is identified with the *signifier* and the concept with the *signified*: "Nous proposons ... de remplacer *concept et image acoustique* respectivement par *signifié* et *significant*" (ibid., 99).

[5] "Sans remuer les lèvres ni la langue, nous pouvons nous parler à nous-mêmes ou nous réciter mentalement une pièce de vers. C'est parce que les mots de la langue sont pour nous des images acoustiques" (ibid., 98).

[6] "Le signe linguistique unit non une chose et un nom, mais un concept et une image acoustique .... Nous appelons *signe* la combinaison du concept et de l'image acoustique: mais dans l'usage courant ce terme désigne généralement l'image acoustique seule" (ibid., 98–99).

[7] "Le signe linguistique est arbitraire .... Le principe de l'arbitraire du signe n'est contesté par personne" (ibid., 100).

[8] "Positivism legitimizes only that which is said, branding the other – that which is not said, which is not put in words or expressed in language – as lacking reality or existence .... The tragedy of positivism is not that it has nothing to say but that it has nothing to be silent about" (Zisimos Lorentzatos, "O *Tractatus* tou Wittenstein kai 'o anax ou to manteion ... ,'" in *Dyo Keimena* [Athens: Ikaros, 1972], 41–42, 50).

[9] See Wolfgang Stegmüller, *Metaphysik-Wissenschaft-Skepsis* (Frankfurt and Vienna: Humboldt, 1954), 48–49.

[10] See ibid., 55.

[11] "Prise en elle-même la pensée est comme une nébuleuse où rien n'est nécessairement délimité ... rien n'est distinct avant l'apparition de la langue" (Saussure, *Cours de linguistique générale*, 155).

[12] See §3, pp. 8–15.

[13] [Etymologically "things" in Greek (*pragmata*) are closely connected with "acts" (*praxeis*) and with "what has been accomplished" (*pepragmena*). The personal reference is built into the word. It may also be noted that the Greek word for "reality" (*pragmakotês*) belongs to the same etymological group. Trans.]

[14] See pp. 87–89.

[15] "The word within a word, unable to speak a word" (T. S. Eliot, *Gerontion*).

[16] Cf. Gregory of Nyssa, *Against Eunomius* 2 (PG 45:980; ed. W. Jaeger, *Gregorii Nysseni Opera* 1:285): "There are times when merely by nodding we have made clear to those near us what is to be done, and

similarly a glance has indicated our inner wish, and a movement of the hand has either forbidden something to happen or has allowed it .... Beings enveloped in bodies often make known to those near them the secret movements of their mind even without uttering a word, and silence has in no way hindered what they have intended to do."

[17] "Mécanisme de la langue" (Saussure, *Cours de linguistique générale*, 176).

[18] "La langue comme pensée organisée dans la matière phonique" (ibid., 155).

[19] *Various Texts* 2.89 (PG 90:1253c).

[20] In *The Bald Primadonna* Ionescu gives a startlingly realistic account of the breakdown of language within the context of conventional human relations, and its final transformation into an unconnected succession of words which do not differ from inarticulate moans and groans.

[21] See further my *Orthos logos kai koinônikê praktikê* (Athens: Domos, 1984), 212ff., where these arguments are more fully developed.

[22] The way poetry works demonstrates the supreme realization of the transcendence of individualism within the context of the linguistic expression and service of the *common logos*: "Poetry is not for personal confessions, and although it makes them, it is not these that maintain it. It does not seek to express the personality of poets. Rather, it seeks to abolish it, as Eliot wrote. But in doing this, it expresses another *personality* which belongs to all; he who loses his life will find it, the Gospel says. So we should not expect from the poet the petty details of his daily life which we think he expresses, so as to get a feel for him. Even if they have been turned into poetry, these small happenings belong to you and me, and to those who have gone before us or will come after us. If it were not so, poetry would not exist" (G. Seferis, *Meres tou 1945–1951* [Athens: Ikaros, 1973], 168–69).

[23] In the theological tradition of the Christian East, "to name" manifests a personal energy and the realization of a relation. But the things named are named on the basis of the difference of the personal energy which they embody: "In accordance with the difference of the energies ... difference and the names are imposed" (Basil the Great, *Against Eunomius* 1.7 [PG 29:525a]); "The significance of names with regard to the essence comes from some energy or value" (Gregory of Nyssa, *On the Trinity* 8 [PG 32:696b]). The interpretation of the function of names and name-giving in the entire history of religion is also extremely interesting. G. van der Leeuw concludes that in every religion "der Name ist nicht eine Bezeichnung, sondern eine auf ein Wort gebrachte Wesenhaftigkeit" (*Phänomenologie der Religion* [1933], 129–41). Hans Bietenhard says: "Aussprechen oder Anrufen des Namens setz die in ihm enthaltene po-

tentielle Energie um in wirkende Kraft" ("Onoma," ThWNT, 5:242–43).
To bear a name signifies that you belong to a community and share in
a common relation. That is why for a child to take its place in society
it is given the name of its father (L. Lévy-Bruhl, *Die Seele der Primi-
tiven* [1930], 335). And to give something a name means to bring it into
the realm of communion and relation. Naming creates the possibility
of reference, summoning, and invoking, that is to say, the possibility
of relationship. According to Plato not everybody can become a name-
giver. Name-giving is not the product of arbitrary free will or choice
alone: "not every man is an artificer of names, but he only who looks to
the name which each thing by nature has, and is able to express the true
forms of things in letters and syllables" (*Cratylus* 390e1–4 [Hamilton-
Cairns]). The name refers to the formal uniqueness or essence: "so long
as the essence of the thing remains in possession of the name and appears in it" (ibid., 393d2–4 [Hamilton-Cairns]). Plato attributes these
views to Socrates, who argues against the opinion of Hermogenes that
the *correctness* of a name is only *convention* and *agreement* (see ibid.,
384d8). (On the significance of a *name* in ancient Greek philosophy, see
F. Heinimann, *Nomos und Physis*, Schweizerische Beiträge zur Alter-
tumswissenschaft 1 (1945), esp. 46–56, and W. Nestle, *Vom Mythos zum
Logos* (1940), esp. 197ff. and 271ff. In the Jewish tradition, knowledge
of a name implies some kind of power over the thing named: my giving
a name to something means that I bring it into the domain of my own
existence (see H. Bietenhard, "Onoma," ThWNT, 5:252). When Adam
gave names to all the animals of the earth (Gen 2:19–20), he manifested
his dominion over creation, his royal office. And every human being
bears a name which refers to his or her existential identity or person (see
M. Noth, *Die israelitischen Personennamen in Rahmen der gemeinsemi-
tischen Namengebung*, Beiträge zur Wissenschaft vom Alten und Neuen
Testament 3, no. 10 [1928], 66ff.). Having children is a blessing, because
the children will keep their father's name alive (cf. Gen 48:16). This
significance of the name makes the name of God unapproachable to the
Israelites. Both Jacob in his wrestling with God "at the ford of the Jab-
bok" (Gen 32:22–32), and Moses before the burning bush (Ex 3:13) ask
to know the name of God, which is the only assurance of the Theophany
(see F. Geisebrecht, *Die alttestamentliche Schätzung des Gottesnamens*
[1901], 17ff.). In the New Testament Christ declares that "I have come
in the name of my Father" (John 5:43). The revelation of God lies in
the disclosure of his Name: "I have manifested thy name to men" (John
17:6). The disciples do "mighty works in my name" (Mark 9:38–9;
Luke 9:41, 49). Christ's name is "the name which is above every name"

(Phil 2:9), "by which we must be saved" (Acts 4:12) (see Max Meinertz, *Theologie des Neuen Testaments*, 1:175–76, 2:75).

This brief reference to the function of the name in the field of religious traditions is merely indicative of a linguistic "semantics" which transcends the conventional meaning of names as *mere signs* for substituting the objects in the sentences of common speech. The sense of names as *mere signs* with a defined meaning (see Ludwig Wittgenstein, *Tractatus Logico-Philosophicus* 3.202, 3.203, 3.21, 3.22, 3.221, 3.23) represents a concept of language that is formally utilitarian. It presupposes the rejection of the distinction between essence and energy, which is an inability to regard language or experience it as a bearer and consequence of personal energy, as an existential fact revelatory of the person.

[24] Cf. Herodotus, *History* 2.930; Aeschylus, *Seven Against Thebes* 559; Plutarch, *Moralia* 117c.

[25] Cf. Euripides, *Medea* 1162; Plato, *Republic* 402b.

[26] Cf. Plato, *Philebus* 39b10–39c1: "pictures or images of what we previously opined or asserted" (Hamilton-Cairns).

[27] Cf. Plato, *Timaeus* 29abc: "If the world be indeed fair and the artificer good, it is manifest that he must have looked to that which is eternal ... and the world must therefore of necessity, if this is admitted, be a copy of something .... And in speaking of the copy and the original we may assume that words are akin to the matter which they describe; when they relate to the lasting and permanent and intelligible, they ought to be lasting and unalterable .... But when they express only the copy or likeness and not the eternal things themselves, they need only be likely and analogous to the former words" (Hamilton-Cairns). Cf. also 92c: "The world has received animals, mortal and immortal, and is fulfilled with them, and has become a visible animal containing the visible – the sensible God who is the image of the intellectual, the greatest and best ..." (Hamilton-Cairns).

[28] Specifically in *Notebooks 1914–1916* (ed. G. M. von Wright and G. E. M. Anscombe, Oxford: Blackwell, 1961) and in the *Tractatus Logico-Philosophicus*.

[29] "We picture facts to ourselves" (*Tractatus* 2.1; Pears-McGuinness).

[30] "What is the case – a fact – is the existence of states of affairs. A state of affairs (a state of things) is a combination of objects (things)" (ibid., 2 and 2.01).

[31] "The determinate way in which objects are connected in a state of affairs is the structure of the state of affairs" (ibid., 2.032). "Form is the possibility of structure" (ibid., 2.033). "Pictorial form is the possibility that things are related to one another in the same way as the elements of

the picture. *That* is how a picture is attached to reality; it reaches right out to it" (ibid., 2.151, 2.1511).

[32] Ibid., 2.2.

[33] "In a picture the elements of the picture are the representatives of objects" (ibid., 2.131).

[34] Ibid., 2.12.

[35] Ibid., 2.1511.

[36] Ibid., 2.182.

[37] Ibid., 2.19.

[38] "The world is the totality of facts, not of things" (ibid., 1.1).

[39] Ibid., 2.221.

[40] Ibid., 3.001.

[41] Ibid., 3.

[42] Cf. Maximus the Confessor, *To Thalassius* 13 (PG 90:293d–96a): "For when the things God has made are contemplated by us in accordance with nature, spiritually and with the necessary knowledge, they communicate to us in a hidden way the *logoi* by which they were brought into being and disclose the divine purpose in each creature."

[43] *Various Chapters* (PG 90:1425a).

[44] Cf. Methodius of Olympus: "having represented the beauty in his own mind by mental imaging" (*On Free Will* 22; ed. G. N. Bonwetsch, 205.13). Cf. also Clement of Alexandria: "Conceptions are the likeness and impressions of the subjects ... subjects are things by which the conceptions are impressed in us" (*Stromata* 8.8 [PG 9:588d]).

[45] *Antirrhetics* 3.34 (PG 99:405a).

[46] "... since it invites all things to itself (whence it is called 'beauty')" (Dionysius the Areopagite, *On the Divine Names* 4.7 [PG 3:701c]).

[47] I owe this observation to Christos Karouzos, "Oi arches tês aisthêtikês orasês ston 5on aiôna p. Ch." in his book *Archaia technê* ([Athens: Hermes, 1972], 43ff.), where the term "conscious view" is used for the art of the fifth century as distinct from the "unconscious view" expressed by archaic art.

[48] Karouzos, "Oi arches tês aisthêtikês orasês," 51.

[49] Cf. Gorgias, frag. 11 (17): "This vision has recorded images of the things that are visible in the mind" (Diels-Kranz, *Die Fragmente der Vorsokratiker*, 2.293). See also G. Rudberg, "Hellenisches Schauen," *Classica et Medievalia* 5 (1942), 162: "Die Hellenen besassen in hohem Grade die Gabe des Sehens, des Schauens. Sie waren ein Volk des Auges, mit feinem Sinn für das Geschaute verschiedener Art und auf verschiedener geistiger Höhe."

[50] Frag. 142 (Diels-Kranz, *Die Fragmente der Vorsokratiker*, 2.170.9). See also lines 10–14: "Zeus' name is a symbol and image in sound cre-

ative of essence so that those who first laid down the names for things through an excess of wisdom, just like excellent makers of statues, manifested their powers through names as if through images."

[51] The theme of Plato's *theoria* is vast and lies at the heart of Platonism. Here I can only offer the briefest of sketches and simply refer the reader to two basic handbooks: F. Boll, *Vita Contemplativa* (1922), and A.-J. Festugière, *Contemplation et vie contemplative selon Platon* (Paris: Vrin, 1967). Very much to the point is also the chapter called "Das Motiv des Schauens bei Plato" in Otfrid Becker, *Plotin und das Problem der geistigen Aneignung* (Berlin, 1940), 72–87.

[52] *Republic* 5:475e4: *tês alêtheias philotheamonas.*

[53] See ibid., 4:443e–44a.

[54] Ibid., 7:533d2.

[55] Ibid., 7:527de.

[56] Cf. *Symposium* 204c: "for the beloved is, in fact, beautiful, perfect, delicate and blessed, but the lover possesses a different idea, such as I have already described." And I. Sykoutris comments: "Here the word 'idea' has its primordial etymological meaning (from *eidon*, "I saw"). It is that which is presented to sight, a thing. But since sight is the faculty which leads us more deeply and more precisely than any of the other faculties into the nature of things (a perception characteristic of the Greek soul, which relies primarily on vision), 'idea' comes to mean the *nature of a thing*" (*Platônos Symposion*, Academy of Athens Publications 2 [Athens, 1949], 147).

[57] See *Symposium* 210a–11c.

[58] *Logikôs theôrein*: *Posterior Analytics* 1.21:82^{b}35–36.

[59] *Physiognomonics* 6:813^{a}30.

[60] "It is the soul by which primarily we live, perceive and think" (*On the Soul* 2.2.414^{a}12–13; Oxford trans.).

[61] *On Memory* 1:449^{b}17.

[62] *Posterior Analytics* 1.1:71^{a}1–2.

[63] Ibid., 1.3:72^{b}19–20.

[64] *Prior Analytics* 1.35:48^{a}30.

[65] *Metaphysics* 1:1072^{b}24.

[66] *Eudemian Ethics* 7:1249^{b}16ff. For further discussion, see my *Schediasma Eisagôgês stê Philosophia* 1:125–26; 2:23–29, 89–101; *Orthos logos kai koinônikê praktikê*, 205–10; *Protaseis kritikês ontologias*, 30.

[67] "For beauty on earth is not self-made, but ... sent by the hand and will of God" (Athenagoras, *Embassy on Behalf of the Christians* 34.1 [PG 6:968b]). "The beauties of the phenomenal world are representations (*apeikonismata*) of the invisible loveliness" (Dionysius the Areopagite, *On the Celestial Hierarchy* 1.3, SC 58 *bis*, 72 [PG 3:121c]).

[68] "I reverence [the matter] not as God but as brimming with divine energy and grace" (John Damascene, *Apologetic Discourse* 2.14 [PG 94:1300b; ed. Kotter, 105.17–20]).

[69] "If it should wish to understand the external beauty fully, it knows how to wonder at the Creator analogously from the creatures ... for in this way the mind becomes cognizant of the Creator from the wealth and beauty of creatures, and ascends to the contemplation of him" (Symeon the New Theologian, *Ethical Treatises* 1, *Or.* 6 [SC 129.138]).

[70] "it is impossible ever to be entirely satiated with the beauty of contemplation" (Symeon the New Theologian, *Ethical Treatises* 4 [SC 129.70]). And on 96 (no. 5: "All the *logoi* and all the explanation of them come to us rather through the vision and contemplation of them .... How can anyone speak of God and divine things or discuss them ... and say what the vision of God is like ... unless he has first been illuminated by the light of knowledge?" Cf. Dionysius the Areopagite, *On the Ecclesiastical Hierarchy* 4.3.1 (PG 3:473b): "When it fixes its attention on that fragrant and noetic beauty ... it moulds and fashions itself in imitation of the supreme beauty."

[71] Symeon the New Theologian, *Ethical Treatises* 4 [SC 129.68–70].

[72] "For the more frequently [the persons of Christ and the saints] are seen in iconic representation, the more are those who see them raised up to the remembrance and desire of the prototypes" (I. Karmiris, *Dogmatika kai Symbokika Mnêmeia* 1.239 [Mansi 13.373]). "For the honor of the image passes over to the archetype" (Basil, *On the Holy Spirit* 18.45 [PG 23:149c]). "An image is a likeness depicting an archetype, but having some difference from it; the image is not like the archetype in every way" (John Damascene, *On the Divine Images* 1.9 [PG 94:1240c; ed. Kotter, 83; trans. Louth]). See also 3.16–17.1337aff. (ed. Kotter, 125–26): "An image ... a likeness and pattern and impression of something, showing in itself what is depicted .... Every image makes manifest and demonstrates something hidden" (trans. Louth). See also Epiphanius, *Against Heresies* 72.10 (PG 42:396c): "Since an image is of something else not of itself ... and bears in itself the characteristics of the archetype, it presents otherness, but otherness as likeness."

[73] "These dissimilar similarities are to be fashioned from material things and applied to the intelligible and the intelligent in one mode for what is intelligent and in a different one for what is sensory" (Dionysius the Areopagite, *On the Celestial Hierarchy* 2.4, SC 58 *bis*, 81 [PG 3:141c]). See also 83 (144bc): "So, then, forms, even those drawn from the lowliest matter, can be used, not unfittingly, with regard to heavenly beings. Matter, after all, owes is subsistence to absolute beauty and keeps, throughout its earthly ranks, some echo of intelligible beauty. Using matter, one

may be lifted up to the immaterial archetypes. Of course one must be careful to use the similarities as dissimilarities, as discussed, to avoid one-to-one correspondences, to make the appropriate adjustments as one remembers the great divide between the intelligible and the perceptible" (trans. Luibheid-Rorem, CWS).

[74] The iconic portrayal but essential concealment of truths, which transcends the noematic content of the given in the common linguistic idiom of concepts, corresponds broadly to the fundamental demands of Wittgenstein's epistemological approach as expressed in the *Tractatus*: "[Philosophy] must set limits to what can be thought; and, in doing so, to what cannot be thought. It must set limits to what cannot be thought by working towards ('von innen') through what can be thought" (4.114). "[Philosophy] will signify what cannot be said, by presenting clearly what can be said" (4.115). "There are, indeed, things that cannot be put into words. They *make themselves manifest*. They are what is mystical ('das Mystische')" (6.522). "What we cannot speak about we must pass over in silence ('Wovon man nicht sprechen kann, darüber muss man schweigen')" (7; Pears-McGuinness).

[75] *On the Celestial Hierarchy* 2.2, SC 58 *bis*, 76–77 (PG 3:140ab; trans. Luibheid-Rorem, CWS, modified).

[76] "In this way, the wise men of God ... separate the 'Holy of Holies' from defilement by anything in the realm of the imperfect or the profane. They therefore honor the dissimilar shape so that the divine things remain inaccessible to the profane and so that all those with a real wish to see the sacred imagery may not dwell on the types as true. So true negations and the unlike comparisons with their last echoes offer due homage to the divine things" (*On the Celestial Hierarchy* 2.5, SC 58 *bis*, 84–85 [PG 3:145a; trans. Luibheid-Rorem, CWS]).

[77] "However, this divine ray can enlighten us only by being upliftingly concealed in a variety of sacred veils which the providence of the Father adapts to our nature as human beings" (*On the Celestial Hierarchy* 1.2, SC 58 *bis*, 72 [PG 3:121c; trans. Luibheid-Rorem, CWS]).

[78] The objectification of truth by the intellect is noted in patristic literature as the ultimate danger for the lover of truth. Maximus the Confessor writes, for example: "And when any mind that has become a lover of mystical theology prays or prophesies 'with his head covered' (1 Cor 11:4) (that is, enters without knowledge into the inner sanctuary of contemplation), or teaches and initiates others into theology, if he should keep any form of intellection while being initiated or initiating others into the Logos who is beyond intellection, he 'dishonors his head' (1 Cor 11:4), for he has subjected him who is simple and beyond any intellection to some being or something that is subject to knowledge. It is neces-

sary for him to see the true God Logos sightlessly and stripped of every concept and knowledge, knowing clearly that with God it is the supreme negations that are more likely to be true, in the degree that they initiate one into what belongs to the divine through the complete subtraction of beings" (*To Thalassius* 25 [PG 90:333cd]).

[79] *Kata athroan morphôsin* (*Scholia on the Divine Names* 1.5 [PG 4:201b]).

[80] "The mind (*nous*) of a reality is one thing and its *logos* is another; and different again is that which comes under the senses. The first is essence (*ousia*), the second is an accident (*symbebêkos*), the third the difference of the subject" (*Other Chapters* 112 [PG 90:1425ab]).

[81] *To Thalassius* 49 (PG 90:456b).

[82] "The standard and measure of beings is the *logos*" (*To Thalassius* 64 [PG 90:709b]).

[83] "Sense perception approaches the practical through the imagination" (*Other Chapters* 110 [PG 90:1425a]).

[84] "... imagination ... around which, the philosophers say, the senses gather things that are alike, its organ being the perception of the things imagined by it" (*Ambigua* 10 [PG 91:1116a]).

[85] "For the knowledge of sensory things is neither completely alien to the intellectual faculty nor is it confined solely to the operation of the senses. But since it is a middle term like a meeting of the mind with the senses and the senses with the mind, it is the means by which these are joined to each other, in the case of the senses as impressed formally by the shapes of sensory things, and in the case of the mind as translating the impressions into *logoi* of the forms" (*To Thalassius* 49 [PG 90:456b]).

[86] "Without the rational faculty, there is no scientific knowledge" (*Various Texts* 2.74 [PG 90:1248c]).

[87] "The senses are the atrium of the logical soul. The name is the understanding. The bishop is the mind. In the atrium, then, stands the mind circumscribed by inopportune thoughts. In the nave is the mind possessed of opportune thoughts. The mind deemed worthy to enter the holy sanctuary is possessed by neither of these" (*Other Chapters* 158 [PG 90:1437b]).

[88] "... the *logos* arrives at rational things (*logika*) through thought (*logismos*)" (*Other Chapters* 110 [PG 90:1425a]). "Thoughts neither belong to the irrational part of the soul, for there is no thought among irrational things, nor do they belong to the intellectual part, for we do not find them in the angels. Being products of the rational faculty, they ascend towards the mind from the senses, using the imagination as a ladder, and communicate to the mind what pertains to the senses. They also descend to

them from the mind submitting to the senses what pertains to the mind" (*Other Chapters* 131 [PG 90:1432a]).

[89] "For what is rational (*logikon*) by nature has a natural faculty and rational appetite which is also called the will of the intellective soul. It is in accordance with the faculty that we deliberate (*logizometha*) when we will something, and when we deliberate, we exercise the will. In willing, we seek and reflect and determine and judge and adopt a disposition" (*Disputation with Pyrrhus* [PG 91:293bc]).

[90] "An intellective being that moves intellectively in accordance with its own principle naturally apprehends with its intellect. Moreover, it will love what it apprehends and so in a passive manner, under the influence of the erotic ecstatic impulse, it will be drawn out of itself towards that which it loves; and this impulse will grow continually more urgent and intense. In this way it will not rest until it is entirely immersed in the total reality of what it loves, wholly and willingly encompassed by the wholeness of that reality, welcoming its saving embrace, and completely conformed to that which delineates it. So much will this be the case that it will now wish to be recognized not from itself but from what delineates it, like air made luminous by light or iron penetrated through and through by fire, or something else of this kind" (*Various Texts* 5.70 [PG 90:1377ab; Palmer-Sherrard-Ware, lightly modified]).

[91] Ibid., 5.84 (PG 90:1392a).

[92] *To Thalassius* 65 (PG 90:752a).

[93] Ibid., 60 (PG 90:621cd).

[94] Ibid. (PG 90:624a).

[95] *Ambigua* 10 (PG 91:1108c).

[96] *To Thalassius* 60 (PG 90:621cd).

[97] "There is a contemplative aspect of the soul … and an active aspect. The contemplative aspect he called *nous*, the active aspect *logos*" (*Mystagogia* 5 [PG 91:673d]).

[98] *To Thalassius* 60 (PG 90:621cd).

[99] Ibid. (PG 90:624a).

[100] Ibid. (PG 90:624a).

[101] *Ambigua* 10 (PG 91:1108c).

[102] *To Thalassius* 60 (PG 90:624a).

[103] Ibid. (PG 90:621c).

[104] "Having come to know that the soul lies between God and matter, and possesses powers that unify us with both, I mean the mind with God and the senses with matter" (*Ambigua* 10 [PG 91:1193d]).

[105] *Various Texts* 2.12 (PG 90:1225b).

Chapter Three

[1] Analogy, as a power and method of cognition, from Plato and Aristotle to Thomas Aquinas and the neo-Thomists, is such a vast theme that its systematic and historical examination would require a separate study. Here I shall confine myself simply to noting certain aspects of the theme which help us, positively or negatively, to approach the notion of hierarchy.

[2] *Republic* 6:508b12–18 (Hamilton-Cairns).

[3] Ibid., 10:596b6–10 (Hamilton-Cairns). And the creator of the world himself, as presented in the *Timaeus*, "looked to the eternal" and contemplated the pre-existing Ideas when he was about to create the things that constitute the world (see *Tim.* 29a3).

[4] Ibid., 6:508e1–2.

[5] Ibid., 6:509b6–10: "In like manner, then, you are to say that the objects of knowledge not only receive from the presence of the good their being known, but their very existence and essence is derived to them from it, thought the good itself is not essence but still transcends essence in dignity and surpassing power" (Hamilton-Cairns).

[6] Cf. ibid., 6:508d4–9.

[7] Ibid., 6:508a11–c2: "Neither vision itself nor its vehicle, which we call the eye, is identical with the sun. – Why, no. – But it is, I think, the most sunlike of all the instruments of the senses. – By far the most. – And does it not receive the power which it possesses as an influx, as it were, dispensed from the sun? – Certainly. – Is it not also true that the sun is not the power of sight, yet as being the cause of it is beheld by the power of sight? – That is so, he said. – This, then, you must understand that I meant by the offspring of the good which the good begot to stand in a proportion with itself. As the good is in the intelligible region to mind and the objects of mind, so the sun is in the visible world to vision and the objects of vision" (Hamilton-Cairns, modified).

[8] Ibid., 6:508c4–d9 (Hamilton-Cairns, lightly modified).

[9] *Gorgias* 465c1–3 (Hamilton-Cairns).

[10] *Sophist* 231a6–8 (Hamilton-Cairns).

[11] The theory of mathematical analogies is said to owe its origins to the Greek mathematician, Eudoxus of Cnidus (408–355 BC). See Arpád Szabó, *Anfäge der griechischen Mathematik* (Munich and Vienna: Oldenbourg, 1969), 143ff. At any rate, the concept of analogy is found in the earliest Greek philosophers (see Diels-Kranz, *Die fragmente der Vorsokratiker*, 3.43). Szabó (205, 219) notes on the sources of mathematical analogy: "The word itself (*analogia*) was not originally a term peculiar to grammar or linguistics, but was a mathematical expression. It is in-

deed quite clear that the word *analogia* developed from the mathematical use of the word *logos*. For in mathematics *logos* was the relation of two numbers or masses to each other (a : b), and the analogy expressed the coupling of the relations, that is to say, what from Cicero's time was rendered in Latin as *proportio* (a : b = c : d) .... Already in Plato analogy is no longer simply a mathematical expression. It seems that by this period the purely mathematical sense had already dropped out of the speech of educated people. Finally, one has the impression that in Aristotle analogy is a purely 'philosophical expression.'"

[12] *Nicomachean Ethics* 5.3:1131ᵇ5–12: "As the term A, then, is to B, so will C be to D, and therefore, *alternando*, as A is to C, B will be to D. Therefore also the whole is in the same ratio to the whole; and this coupling the distribution effects, and, if the terms are so combined, effects justly. The conjunction, then, of the term A with C and of B with D is what is just in distribution, and this species of the just is intermediate, and the unjust is what violates the proportion; for the proportion is intermediate and the just is proportional (*to gar analogon meson, to de dikaion analogon*)" (Oxford trans.).

[13] *Nicomachean Ethics* 5.3:1131ᵃ31: "For proportion (*analogia*) is equality of ratios (*logoi*)."

[14] Ibid., 5.5:113ᵃ16–24: "For it is not two doctors that associate for exchange, but a doctor and a farmer, or in general people who are different and unequal; but these must be equated. This is why things that are exchanged must be somehow commensurable. It is for this end that money has been introduced, and it becomes in a sense an intermediate; for it measures all things, and therefore the excess and the defect – how many shoes are equal to a house or to a given amount of food" (Oxford trans.).

[15] Ibid., 5.5:113ᵃ29–31.

[16] Ibid., 5.5:113ᵃ5–10.

[17] Ibid., 5.5:1133ᵇ4–5, 1133ᵃ32–33. Cf. my *Protaseis kritikês ontologias*, 107–9.

[18] *Poetics* 21:1457ᵇ6–25 (Oxford trans.).

[19] "Solche Metapher und Analogie bezeichnen und bewerten die Thomisten als *externa analogia proportionalitatis impropriae* um so von abzuheben die innere Entsprechung der eigentlichen Verhältnisgleichheit, nach der nicht bildlich, uneigentlich, sondern auf beiden Seiten eigentlich, streng begrifflich geredet werde" (G. Söhngen, "Analogie," in the *Handbuch theologischer Grundbegriffe* 1 [Munich: Kösel, 1962], 57). The *externa analogia proportionalitatis impropriae* is to be distinguished from the *interna analogia proportionalitatis propriae (dicta)*.

[20] *Metaphysics* 4.2:1003ᵃ33–34 (Oxford trans.).

²¹ "Those things are said in their own right to be that are indicated by the figures of predication; for the senses of 'being' are just as many as these figures. Since some predicates indicate what the subject is, others its quality, others quantity, others relation, others activity or passivity, others its place, others its time, 'being' has a meaning answering to each of these" (ibid., 5.7:1017ª23–27 [Oxford trans.]).

²² See *Physics* 1.7:191ª7–8: "The underlying nature can be known by analogy."

²³ *Metaphysics* 7.1:1028ª13–15 (Oxford trans., modified).

²⁴ Ibid., 4.2:1003ᵇ32 (Oxford trans.).

²⁵ Ibid., 9.1:1045ᵇ29–31 (Oxford trans., modified).

²⁶ See ibid., 12.6:1071ᵇ.

²⁷ Ibid., 3.8:1012ᵇ31.

²⁸ Ibid., 12.7:1072ª25–26 (Oxford trans., modified).

²⁹ See Söhngen, "Analogie," 53.

³⁰ According to Thomas Aquinas, "Ce que l'on nomme essence dans les autres êtres est en lui l'acte même d'exister" (Étienne Gilson, *La Philosophie au Moyen Age* [Paris: Payot, 1962], 532). "Nihil igitur est in Deum praeter essentiam eius" (Thomas Aquinas, *Summa contra Gentiles* 1:21).

³¹ "On peut suivre une deuxième (voie) et chercher à nommer Dieu d'après les analogies qui subsistent entre les choses et lui …. En ce sens, nous attribuerons à Dieu, mais en les portent à l'infini, toutes les perfections don't nous aurons trouvé quelque ombre dans la créature" (Gilson, *La Philosophie au Moyen Age*, 533).

³² "Vom (induktiven) Analogieschluss ist wohl zu unterscheiden der (deductive) Syllogismus mit analogem Mittelbegriff. Gibt es das, dann wäre solcher Mittelbegriff nicht empirisch-analog, sondern transzendental-analog, wie der Transzendentalbegriff des Seins (*ens*) und die darin beschlossenen fünf Transzendentalien: *res, aliquid, unum, verum, bonum*" (Söhngen, "Analogie," 56).

³³ "Le procédé analogique en général consiste en une extension du concept: un concept tiré des sujets donnés dans l'experience, et de soi representatif de la perfection telle qu'elle se trouve en ces sujets, est étendu à un sujet situé hors de mon expérience, me permet d'atteindre ce sujet, et simultanément devient representatif de la perfection telle qu'elle se trouve en lui. C'est de cette manière, que par le moyen de concepts tirés des créatures et représentatifs de perfections créées, la raison peut réellement atteindre le Créateur et connaître, encore que très imparfaitement, ses attributs essentiels" (J.-H. Nicolas, *Dieu connu comme inconnu* [Paris: Desclée de Brouwer, 1966], 273).

³⁴ See Thomas Aquinas, *De veritate* 10:6; *Summa Theologiae* 1:79.2–4.

[35] "Dieu contient virtuellement en soi l'être et les perfections de toutes les creatures" (Gilson, *La Philosophie au Moyen Age*, 533).

[36] "Deum ut est naturae principium et finis, Deum secundum quod est objectum beatudinis supernaturalis" (Thomas Aquinas, *Summa Theologiae* 1–2:62.1. Cf. 1:62.2.ad.1). See also M.-D. Chenu, *La théologie comme science au XIIIe siècle* (Paris: Vrin, 1969), 42: "Saint Thomas, lui, faisant prévaloir la considération de l'objet, s'engage ainsi dans une recherché qui d'une part ménagera le concept authentique de science, et qui surtout l'amènera à accepter l'objectivation de la connaissance de foi dans la théologie."

[37] See Thomas Aquinas, *Summa Theologiae* 1.44. Cf. Jacques Maritain, *Approches de Dieu* (Paris: Alsatia, 1953), 9–23; Nicolas, *Dieu connu comme inconnu*, 66: "Je ne puis, en effet, connaître Dieu qu'à partir des créatures et au moyen des concepts tirés des créatures. Ces concepts représentent les créatures, et donc ce que Dieu n'est pas. Mais ces mêmes créatures me contraignent d'affirmer Dieu comme leur cause." Gilson, *La Philosophie au Moyen Age*, 532: "Ce qui est par autrui ne peut avoir d'autre cause première que ce qui est par soi. Il faut donc qu'il y ait, comme cause première de toutes les existences de ce genre, un être en qui l'essence et l'existence ne fassent qu'un. C'est cet être que nous nommons Dieu." M.-D. Chenu, *La théologie au XIIe siècle* (Paris: Vrin, 1966), 309–11. Cf. the Greek neoscholastics who have introduced into Orthodox theology the Roman Catholic priority of the essence over the persons and the accompanying deterministic methodology, e.g., Zikos Rosis, *Systêma Dogmatikês* (Athens, 1903), 141–42: "Working back from effects to causes and from these as effects in turn to other causes *ad infinitum*, we would be left with an infinite series of causes, which cannot be conceived. Hence the human mind necessarily accepts a first or supreme creative cause of the world, which is not in turn the effect of another cause. This supreme cause is God"; P. N. Trembelas, *Dogmatikê*, vol. 1 (Athens: Zoe, 1959), 157–58: "In seeking the causes of movement in the universe we find ourselves faced with an incalculable series of movers, each of which takes its movement from another, and this series cannot be thought of as extending to infinity, but we are compelled to conceive of some First Mover which is the source of movement for all things."

[38] Gilson, *La Philosophie au Moyen Age*, 532. The truth of the person and the cognitive power of personal relationship are absent from the two limbs of Thomist epistemology, which are reason (*ratio*) and faith (*fides*). Thomists distinguish reason from faith – philosophy from theology – and demonstrate the need for their harmony. The distinction is conventional because in both cases the cognitive categories are common,

being the axioms (*principia*) both of reason and of faith. Reason relies on the *a priori* given powers and "principles" of the intellect, which can always be proved or verified objectively. Faith relies on an *a priori* given revelation, that is, on divine authority, which is formulated objectively by the Church's infallible magisterium. Consequently, the epistemological problem for the Thomists is the formal coincidence of the axioms of reason and faith in the affirmation of truth ("les considérer comme formant idéalement une seule verité totale"). Reason must confirm the axioms of faith by the givens of the intellect, by means of ascending syllogisms, and faith must verify its axioms, arriving at the givens of the intellect by descending syllogisms ("de remonter par la raison vers la révélation et de redescendre de la révélation vers la raison") (Gilson, *La philosophie au moyen age*, 528). See also Chenu, *La théologie comme science*, 85, 86, 91: "La foi comporte une capacité d'élaboration rationelle, de manifestation, de probation, selon le sens philosophique du mot *argumentum* ... La définition même de la foi s'ouvre désormais, comme sur un horizon homogène, à une expansion rationelle de qualité scientifique ...." See also Chenu, *Le Thomisme* (Paris: Vrin, 1942), 113; Nicolas, *Dieu connu comme inconnu*, 237ff.

[39] See A. Dempf, *Metaphysik des Mittelalters* (Munich and Berlin, 1930), 31ff.; Nikolaus M. Häring, "Die Erschaffung der Welt und ihr Schöpfer," in *Platonismus in der Philosophie des Mittelalters* (Darmstadt: Wiss. Buchges, 1969), 203ff.

[40] *On the Celestial Hierarchy* 2.4, SC 58 *bis*, 83 (PG 3:144c).

[41] In contrast to the Scholastics, the Greek Fathers do not seek to offer compelling objective arguments for the truth, which can then be imposed authoritatively. They seek to preserve the truth as a personal-moral possibility of existential perfection. Eastern theologians link the obligation to proclaim the truth and confess their faith both with the transmission and dissemination of the truth and with the attempt to *conceal* the truth, or rather, to transmit it through concealing it in types and symbols which permit the dynamic-personal reception and cognition of the truth "so that the divine things remain inaccessible to the profane and so that all those with a real wish to see the sacred imagery may not dwell on the types as true. So true negations and the unlike comparisons with their last echoes offer due homage to the divine things" (Dionysius the Areopagite, *On the Celestial Hierarchy* 2.5, SC 58 *bis*, 85 [PG 3:145a; trans. Luibheid-Rorem, CWS]).

[42] H. Denzinger, *Enchiridion Symbolorum*, 31st ed. (Freiburg: Herder, 1950), §432.

[43] "For example, in the case of a man or a city, anyone who wishes to tell other people about them speaks to them of what he has seen and heard.

Those who listen, not having seen the man or the city they are hearing about, cannot know that man or that city merely by a report in the same way as the narrator who has seen them. It is similar with the Jerusalem above and the invisible God who dwells there. Nobody can speak about the unapproachable glory of his countenance and about the energy and power of his all-holy Spirit, or light, unless he has first seen this light with the eyes of the soul and gained precise knowledge of the radiance and energy within himself .... Neither can he therefore say that he has arrived at knowledge of God simply by hearing about it. For how can he know what he has not seen?" (Symeon the New Theologian, *Ethical Treatises* 5 [SC 129.98.100]).

[44] "The Lord's initiates have passed from the flesh to the spirit, by the transformation of the senses which the Spirit has effected in them" (Maximus the Confessor, *Ambigua* 10 [PG 91:1128a]). "Holy Scripture has an intimate connection with knowledge" (Cyril of Alexandria, *Commentary on John* [PG 73:1044c]).

[45] "Knowledge unites man by experience with God" (Diadochus of Photice, *Gnostic Chapters*, ed. Weis-Liebersdorf [Teubner, 1912], 10.22). "Knowledge is life, since it is in travail with the whole power of the mystery ... by which we are assimilated to the living and life-giving Logos" (Cyril of Alexandria, *Commentary on John* [PG 74:485d]).

[46] "Our way of life is not predetermined and the free will of those benefiting from the gift of divine Light does not take away from such light its attribute of being a providential source of enlightenment. What actually happens is this. The dissimilarity of the sacred sights either makes the overflowing gift of light of the Father's goodness completely unpartaken and unbestowed, because of their resistance, or there is an unequal participation in these gifts in large or small amounts, in clarity or obscurity. And in the meantime the shining well-spring of all this continues to be single and simple, forever the same and forever overflowing" (Dionysius the Areopagite, *On the Celestial Hierarchy*, SC 58 *bis*, 133–34 [PG 3:260cd; trans. Luibheid-Rorem, CWS, modified]).

[47] See Isaac the Syrian, *Extant Ascetical Works*, Or. 49 (ed. Spanos, 203).

[48] "For knowledge unites the knower with the known, while ignorance is always the cause of change and of the inconsistency of the ignorant" ("knowledge unites the knowers with the known, while ignorance becomes the cause of the division of the ignorant. For the ignorant person has an unstable will divided among many things") (Dionysius the Areopagite, *On the Divine Names* 7.4 [PG 3:872cd; *Scholia* 888cd]).

[49] "Knowledge is the perfection of man as man" (Clement of Alexandria, *Stromata* 7.10 [PG 9:477c]). "The power of the Godhead spreads out

everywhere ... and manifests itself proportionately (*analogôs*) to every intelligent being .... To put it more clearly ... the rays of the sun pass easily through primary matter, since it is the most translucent of all, and through this they light up their own brilliance more resplendently. But as they encounter more opaque matter, they appear dimmer and more diffused, because this matter is less suited to the outpouring of light. This unsuitability becomes progressively greater until finally it halts completely the journey of light" (Dionysius the Areopagite, *On the Celestial Hierarchy* 13.3, SC 58 *bis*, 150–52 [PG 3:301ab; trans. Luibheid-Rorem, CWS, modified]).

[50] See Endre von Ivanka, *Plato Christianus* (Einsiedeln: Johannes-Verlag, 1964), 262–98: "Inwieweit ist Pseudo-Dionysius Neuplatoniker?"; R. Roques, *L'Univers Dionysien, Structure hiérarchique du monde selon le Pseudo-Denys* (Paris: Aubier, 1954); Vladimir Lossky, "La notion des 'analogies' chez le Pseudo-Denys l'Aréopagite," in *Archives d'histoire doctrinale et littéraire* 5 (1930), 279–309; Hugo Ball, *Byzantinisches Christentum* (Einsiedeln: Benziger, 1958), 167–211: "Die dionysische Hierarchie"; Vladimir Lossky, *La théologie mystique de l'Eglise d'Orient* (Paris: Aubier, 1944), 22–23 (ET, *The Mystical Theology of the Eastern Church* [London: James Clarke, 1957], 29–30).

[51] In my opinion hierarchy is a sacred order, a state of understanding, and an activity approximating as closely as possible to the divine. And it is raised up to the imitation of God in proportion to the illuminations divinely given to it" (Dionysius the Areopagite, *On the Celestial Hierarchy* 3.1, SC 58 *bis*, 87 [PG 3:164d; trans. Luibheid-Rorem, CWS, modified]).

[52] Ibid., 3.2, SC 58 *bis*, 89–90 (PG 3:165b).

[53] "Since the beauty befitting God is simple, good and teletarchic [i.e., the source of perfection], it has no admixture whatsoever of dissimilarity. It transmits to each, according to their merit, a share of his own light, and perfects them by a most divine rite in a fitting way, according to the form, precisely similar to himself, of those who are being perfected" (ibid., 3.1, SC 58 *bis*, 87 [PG 3:164d]).

[54] Ibid., 3.2, SC 58 *bis*, 88 (PG 3:165a).

[55] Ibid., 3.2, SC 58 *bis*, 89–90 (PG 3:165b).

[56] "The goal of hierarchy, then, is assimilation to God and union with him so far as is attainable, since it has him as its guide in all matters of sacred knowledge and energy, and gazes undeviatingly at his most divine beauty and is stamped with it so far as possible, and makes its devotees images of the divine" (ibid., 3.2, SC 58 *bis*, 87–8 [PG 3:165a]).

[57] "Perfection for each of those who have been allotted a share of hierarchy is to be raised up to the imitation of God in proportion to his own

capacity, and what is the most wonderful of all, to become a 'co-worker with God', as Scripture says, and exhibit the divine energy manifested in himself so far as possible" (ibid., 3.2, SC 58 *bis*, 90 [PG 3:165b]).

58 Ibid., 3.2, SC *bis*, 90 [PG 3:165b]).

59 Cf. Cyril of Alexandria, *Commentary on Isaiah* 5.2 (PG 70:785b); Basil the Great, *On the Holy Spirit* 75 (PG 32:209a); Maximus the Confessor, *Chapters on Theology* 5.94 (PG 90:1388d).

60 "For this is a property of the cause of all things and of the goodness that is beyond all things, to summon all beings to communion with it, as has been laid down proportionately (*analogôs*) for each being" (*On the Celestial Hierarchy* 4.1, SC 58 *bis*, 93 [PG 3:177c]).

61 "All inanimate things participate in being (for the being of all things is the deity that is above all things), living things participate in the power that fires life and transcends all life, and rational and intellectual things participate in that consummate and perfect wisdom that transcends all *logos* and mind" (ibid., 4.1, SC 58 *bis*, 93–94 [PG 3:177d]).

PART FOUR

Chapter One

1 *Einführung in die Metaphysik*, 14.

2 See *Was ist Metaphysik?* 33–42; *Einführung in die Metaphysik*, 13–15, 23–25, 25, 57ff.

3 See Heidegger, *Was ist Metaphysik?* 34: "die ursprüngliche Offenheit des Seienden als eines solchen: dass es Seiendes ist – und nicht Nichts." Cf. Sartre, *L'Être et le Néant*, 40: "L'être est *cela* et, en dehors de cela, *rien*."

4 See, for example, *Einführung in die Metaphysik*, 62; *Zur Seinsfrage*, 33, 38; *Was ist Metaphysik?* 35, 39.

5 See *Sein und Zeit*, 166ff., 346ff.; *Über den Humanismus*, 21: "Das Wort (Verfallen) meint nicht einen 'moralphilosophisch' verstandenen und zugleich säkularisierten Sündenfall des Menschen, sondern nennt ein wesenhaftes Verhältnis des Menschen zum Sein innerhalb des Bezugs des Seins zum Menschenwesen."

6 "Das Dasein ist von ihm selbst als eigentlichem Selbsteinkönnen zunächst immer schon abgefallen und an die 'Welt' verfallen. Die Verfallenheit an die 'Welt' meint das Aufgehen im Miteinandersein" (*Sein und Zeit*, 175). ["Dasein has, in the first instance, fallen away from itself as an authentic potentiality for Being its Self, and has fallen into

the 'world'. 'Fallenness' into the 'world' means an absorption in Being-with-one-another" (Macquarrie-Robinson).]

[7] See *Sein und Zeit*, 126ff., 175ff., 383. [Macquarrie-Robinson translate *Man* as "they."]

[8] "Das Man, das kein bestimmtes ist und das Alle, obzwar nicht als Summe, sind, schreibt die Seinart der Alltäglichkeit vor" (*Sein und Zeit*, 127. ["The 'they,' which is nothing definite, and which all are, though not as the sum, prescribes the kind of Being of everydayness" (Macquarrie-Robinson).]

[9] See *Über den Humanismus*, 8. The German word "öffentlich" means public or common in antithesis to "privat," which means private. Consequently, the "Diktatur der Öffentlichkeit" has the sense of the tyrannical privation of the possibility of "private Existenz." It means the totalitarian imposition of a mode of life which leaves no room for anything private or personal in the life of the individual.

[10] "In der Benutzung öffentlicher Verkehrsmittel, in der Verwendung des Nachrichtenwesens (Zeitung) ist jeder Andere wie der Andere .... In dieser Unauffälligkeit und Nichtfeststellbarkeit enfaltet das Man seine eigentliche Diktatur. Wir geniessen und vergnügen uns, wie *man* geniesst: wir lesen, sehen und urteilen über Literatur und Kunst wie *man* sieht und urteilt .... Die Öffentlichkeit verdunkelt alles und gibt das so Verdeckte als das Bekannte und jedem Zugängliche aus" (*Sein und Zeit*, 126–27). ["In utilizing public means of transport and in making use of information services such as the newspaper, every Other is like the next. ... In this inconspicuousness and unascertainability, the real dictatorship of the 'they' is unfolded. We take pleasure and enjoy ourselves as *they* take pleasure; we read, see, and judge about literature and art as *they* see and judge .... By publicness everything gets obscured, and what has thus been covered up gets passed off as something familiar and accessible to everyone" (Macquarrie-Robinson).]

[11] See his *One-Dimensional Man: Studies in the Ideology of Advanced Industrial Society* (Boston: Beacon Press, 1964).

[12] Cf. Aristotle, *Metaphysics* 4:2.1004^{b}27–28: "in the list of contraries one of the two columns is privative, and all contraries are referred to being and non-being, and to unity and plurality" (Oxford trans.).

[13] See, for example, Heidegger's comments on the ideological presuppositions of Western culture in his book *Nietzsche*, especially in the sections of vol. 2 titled "Der Nihilismus und der Mensch der abendländischen Geschichte" (80), "Der Nihilismus als Geschichte" (90), and "Die Herrschaft des Subjekts in der Neuzeit" (141).

[14] "Die 'Ontologie' gründet auf der Unterscheidung von Sein und Seiendem. Die 'Unterscheidung' wird gemässer durch den Namen 'Differenz'

bennant, worin sich anzeigt, dass Seiendes und Sein irgendwie aus-ein-
andergetragen, geschieden und gleichwohl aufeinander bezogen sind,
und zwar von sich aus, nicht erst auf Grund eines 'Aktes' der 'Unterscheidung'" (Heidegger, *Nietzsche*, vol. 2, 209).

[15] See *Sein und Zeit*, §65: "Die Zeitlichkeit als der ontologische Sinn der
Sorge" ["Temporality as the Ontological Meaning of Care"] and §76:
"Der existenziale Ursprung der Histoire aus der Geschichtlichkeit des
Daseins" ["The Existential Source of Historiology in Dasein's Histori-
cality"].

[16] See *Sein und Zeit*, 38; *Über den Humanismus*, 24.

[17] "die Achtung der Grenzen, die dem Denken als Denken gesetz sind"
(*Über den Humanismus*, 37).

[18] [The Greek for "individual" is *atomon*, the word that gives us "atom"
in English. The positive connotations which "individual" and "individuality" may be thought to have in English are lacking in the Greek *atomon*
and *atomikotês*, where the sense of "indivisible unit" is uppermost. Hence
atomikotês is often translated here as "atomic individuality." Trans.]

[19] *Disputation with Pyrrhus* (PG 91:301b). On the sense of *nous* ("mind")
and *noeros* ("intelligent"), see above, pp. 144 and 197–199.

[20] *On the Soul and Resurrection* (PG 46:101cd).

[21] *Homily* 80.3 *On the Gospel of John* (PG 59:477a).

[22] See pp. 25–28.

[23] "Anhypostatic nature, which is essence, can never exist. It must be
enhypostatic, which is a thing regarded as subsisting in itself" (Leontius
of Byzantium, *Against Nestorians and Eutychians* 1 [PG 86:1280a]).
"'Enhypostatic' refers to that which is common according to the essence, namely the species, subsisting in actual fact in individuals and not
simply conceptually in the mind" (Maximus the Confessor, *To Marinus*
[PG 91:149b]). "The enhypostatic sometimes means the essence, since
the essence is observed only in hypostases, and sometimes each of the
things that come together to combine as one hypostasis" (John Damascene, *On the Composite Nature* 6 [PG 95:120c]).

[24] "Energy is called a passion when it is contrary to nature. For energy is
movement in accordance with nature, passion movement contrary to nature" (Nemesius of Emesa, *On Human Nature* 16 [PG 40:673bc]). "The
passion of the power naturally underlying habit is the misused mode of
the natural energy. And the misuse of the energetic mode is the movement of the power towards what does not subsist naturally" (Maximus
the Confessor, *To Thalassius* 58 [PG 90:593a]). "The intellect functions
in accordance with nature when it keeps the passions under control …"
(Maximus the Confessor, *Chapters on Love* 4.45 [PG 90:1057c; Palmer-
Sherrard-Ware]).

25 "Spiritual freedom is release from the passions" (Thalassius, *On Love and Self-Control* 2.33, in *Philokalia*, vol. 2 [Athens: Astir, 1958], 213, trans. Palmer-Sherrard-Ware). See also Mark the Ascetic, *On the Spiritual Law* 32: "The law of freedom is studied by means of true knowledge, it is understood through the practice of the commandments, and is fulfilled through the mercy of Christ" (*Philokalia* 1:98 [Palmer-Sherrard-Ware]). See also Clement of Alexandria *Stromata* 2.23 (PG 8:1046a): "To restrain these [the passions] is freedom alone."

26 "the freedom – that is to say, the dispassion – of soul, which as a result of ascetic practice raises the aspirant to the contemplation of the spiritual essences of the created world and then inducts him into the divine darkness of theology" (Niketas Stethatos, *On the Practice of the Virtues* 1, in *Philokalia* 3:273 [Palmer-Sherrard-Ware]).

27 "One who has partaken of freedom knows the mysteries of the Father" (Kallistos Kataphygiotes, *On Divine Union and the Contemplative Life* 10, in *Philokalia* 5:8). See also Mark the Ascetic, *On the Spiritual Law* 30: "The law of freedom teaches the whole truth" (*Philokalia* 1:98). See also Isaac the Syrian, *Hom.* 35: "The more the mind is freed from the bonds of evil thoughts, the more radiant it becomes. And the more radiant it becomes, the lighter it becomes and is raised up from the conceptions of this age, which upholds the modes of grossness. And then the mind understands how to contemplate in God in his way and not in ours" (*Ascetic Works* [ed. Spanos, 154]).

28 "The commandments ... guard the frontiers of the freedom that has been given to us" (Mark the Ascetic, *On Holy Baptism* 4 [PG 65:992a]).

29 "He gave us his life-giving commandments as purgative medicines for our impassioned state. For what medicines are to a sick body, the commandments are to an impassioned soul" (Isaac the Syrian, *Ascetic Works*, *Letter* 4, [ed. Spanos, 367]). "He gave us his holy commandments, one might say, as tools ... so that we should be instruments ... with the commandments as tools, through which the craftsman Logos restores and renews those who are workers of his commandments" (Symeon the New Theologian, *Ethical Treatises* 1.12 [SC 122.282–83]).

30 "Justice ... the correct leadership of the soul and the moderation of the subject passions" (Theodoret of Cyrus, *On Providence* 6 [PG 83:648a]).

31 See Maximus the Confessor, *To Thalassius* 61: "the most unjust principle arising from pleasure ... for the destruction of most unjust pleasure" (PG 90:628d). "... that by suffering unjustly [Christ] might remove the principle of origin that dominates our nature tyrannically as a result of unjust pleasure" (PG 90:629b). See also *Various Texts* 1.47 and 46: "God became man that he might unite human nature to himself and stop it from acting evilly towards itself, or rather from being at strife and divided

against itself, and from having no rest because of the instability of its will and purpose." "The self-love and cleverness of men, alienating them from each other and perverting the law, have cut our single human nature into many fragments. They have so extended the insensibility which they introduced into our nature and which now dominates it, that our nature, divided in will and purpose, fights against itself" (PG 90:1196abc; Palmer-Sherrard-Ware).

[32] Cf. Isaac the Syrian, *Hom.* 62: "These are the works of justice: fasting, almsgiving, vigils, sanctification and the rest of what is accomplished by the body" (*Ascetic Works* [ed. Spanos, 254]). Cf. *Hom.* 23.91. See also Symeon the New Theologian, *Ethical Treatises, Hom.* 8 (SC 129.214).

[33] "Nobody can defeat the passions, except by contemplated sensible virtues" (Isaac the Syrian, *Hom.* 6.8, *Ascetical Works* [ed. Spanos, 269]). See also *Letter* 4.383: "If you want your heart to be a place of the mysteries of the new world, first enrich yourself with bodily works, fasting, vigils, liturgy, *askesis*, patience, purification of thoughts, and so on."

[34] "Do not despise matter, for it is not dishonorable. Nothing is dishonourable that has been made by God. This is a Manichaean opinion. The only thing which is dishonorable is that which does not take its cause from God, but is our own invention, through the arbitrary inclination and deflection of the will from that which is according to nature to that which is contrary to nature, which is sin" (John Damascene, *Apologetic Discourse* 1 [PG 94:1246c; ed. Kotter, 90]).

[35] "He who through love ... fixes his gaze on beauty ... refers himself through this beauty to the artificer and to the true beauty, for he has proved the luminous character of justice to be a holy symbol" (Clement of Alexandria, *Stromata* 7.2 [PG 9:416a]).

[36] In the words of the RSV: "For the creation waits with eager longing for the revealing of the sons of God; for the creation was subjected to futility, not of its own will but by the will of him who subjected it in hope; because the creation itself will be set free from its bondage to decay and obtain the glorious liberty of the children of God. We know that the whole of creation has been groaning in travail together until now" (Rom 8:19–22).

[37] John of Sinai, *Spiritual Ladder* 15.4 (Constantinople ed. [1883], 86).

[38] See, for example, Isaac the Syrian, *Hom.* 58: "Love knows no shame and therefore does not know how to give the form of beauty to its members. It is a natural property of love not to feel shame and to be oblivious to its appearance" (*Ascetic Works*, 236).

[39] Niketas Stethatos, *Gnostic Chapters* 3.91 (*Philokalia* 3:352).

[40] The whole passage from Niketas Stethatos (see note 39) is as follows: "He who has risen above the threats and promises of the laws, and has

entered into the life which is not subject to law, has himself become
the law of the Church and is not ruled by law. The life that is free is not
subject to law, and therefore transcends all natural necessity and change.
He who has attained such a life is as if liberated from the outer flesh, and
through his participation in the Spirit he becomes incandescent. Since
what is partial within him has been abolished (cf. 1 Cor 13:9–10), he is
united wholly with Christ, who transcends all nature" (Palmer-Sherrard-
Ware, modified).

[41] "When you have reached the end of the road of justice, then you will
cleave to freedom in all things" (Isaac the Syrian, *Ascetic Works*, Hom.
23.91).

[42] "Être libre c'est être condamné à être libre" (*L'Être et le Néant*, 174).

[43] See *L'Être et le Néant*, III 1, IV: "Le regard," 310ff. Some characteristic
expressions are "Le regard d'autrui comme condition nécessaire de mon
objectivité …" (328); "Autrui est d'abord pour moi l'être pour qui je suis
object, c'est-à-dire l'être *par qui* je gagne mon objectité …. Dans l'épreuve
du regard, en m'éprouvant comme objectité non-révélée, j'éprouve directement et avec mon être l'insaisissable subjectivité d'autrui" (329); "Si
l'on me regarde, en effet, j'ai conscience *d'être* objet" (330).

[44] *L'Être et le Néant*, 349.

[45] Isaac the Syrian; see note 38.

[46] Dionysius the Areopagite, *On the Divine Names* 4 (PG 3:709bc).

[47] "Il s'agit de mon être tel qu'il s'écrit dans et par la liberté d'autrui.
Tout se passe comme si j'avais une dimension d'être dont j'étais séparé
par un néant radical: et ce néant, c'est la liberté d'autrui" (Sartre, *L'Être
et le Néant*, 320).

[48] Ibid., 350.

[49] See Martin Heidegger, *Identität und Differenz* (Pfullingen: Neske,
1957), 70–71. Also idem, *Holzwege*, 201, 204, 239–40. Cf. James Rob-
inson, "Die deutsche Auseinandersetzung mit dem späteren Heidegger,"
in *Der spätere Heidegger und die Theologie*, Neuland in der Theologie,
vol. 1 (Zurich: Zwingli, 1964), 46, 91; Olivier Clément, "Dionysios et
le Ressuscité: Essai de réponse chrétienne à l'athéisme contemporain,"
in *Evangile et Revolution* (Paris: Centurion, 1968), 67ff.; Yannaras, *Ê
theologia tês apousias kai tês agnôsias tou Theou* (ET, *The Theology of
the Absence and Ignorance of God*), 13–43.

Chapter Two

[1] See Vladimir Lossky, *La Théologie mystique de l'Église d'Orient*, 109–
10 (ET, 114–15).

[2] "The Godhead, that is, the essence, is unfolded triadically and is known without division in three hypostases" (John Damascene, *On the Thrice-Holy Hymn* 2 [PG 95:25c]). "We see the Godhead celebrated in a sacred manner on the one hand as a monad or henad, because of its simplicity and unity and supernatural indivisibility ... and on the other as a triad, because of the trihypostatic manifestation of its supraessential fecundity" (Dionysius the Areopagite, *On the Divine Names* 4 [PG 3:589d–592a]).

[3] Duality is potentially multiplicity because it is generative of every number from the monad: "Number comes from the one and the indefinite dyad" (Aristotle, *Metaphysics* 13.7:1081a14). See also Lossky, *Théologie mystique*, 46 (ET, 47).

[4] See Maximus the Confessor, *Ambigua* (PG 91:1400d): "The monad is a triad, since it is perfect in the perfect hypostases, that is, in the mode of existence. And the triad is truly a monad by reason of the essence." See also 1034a: "To transcend the dyad and not stay fixed as a dyad and on the other hand to be defined as a triad and fix the movement of the monad as a triad ... are the same thing." And 1036bc: "the monad ... is truly a monad, for it is not the beginning of those things that are after it like the contraction of a distension ... but is the hypostatic reality of a co-essential triad, and the triad is truly a triad, not dissolved by number ... but the essential existence of a trihypostatic monad; for the triad is truly a monad for that is how it *is*, and the monad is truly a triad because that is how it *subsists*, since there is one Godhead which *is* as a monad and *subsists* as a triad." See also *Chapters on Theology* 2.4 (PG 90:1180a): "unconfused monad and undivided triad"; and 2.1 (1125a): "one God because one Godhead: a monad which is unoriginate and simple ... the same monad is also a triad, at the same time wholly a monad and wholly a triad: wholly a monad in its essence and wholly a triad in its hypostases."

[5] "A specific ... number is not to be attributed to the infinite Godhead, except the oneness (monad) of the essence and the threeness (triad) of the hypostases" (John Damascene, *On the Thrice-Holy Hymn* 5 [PG 95:32c]). "[God] transcends all number. For if God is said to be one, he transcends oneness .... And if he is hymned as a triad or as a monad, he is nevertheless neither a monad nor a triad, whether according to our concept of number or a different one" (Maximus the Confessor, *Scholia on the Divine Names* [PG 4:369d, 412bc]).

[6] "[Perichoresis is] the indwelling and abiding of the hypostases in each other. For these are undivided and inseparable from each other, since they mutually interpenetrate each other" (John Damascene, *On the Orthodox Faith* 1.14 [PG 94:860b]). "For they are united ... not so as to be confused but so as to cleave to each other. And they have this mutual indwelling without any compounding or confusion" (Cyril of Al-

exandria, *On the Trinity* 10 [PG 77:1144b]). "Neither are they divided in essence, nor are they separated in power, nor are they divorced in place, or energy, or will, for they have their indwelling and perichoresis inseparably in each other" (John Damascene, *Against the Jacobites* 78 [PG 94:1476b]).

[7] "From the wise contemplation of creation we gain insight into what pertains to the Holy Trinity, I mean to the Father, the Son and the Holy Spirit .... Indeed creation cries out aloud through the things that have been made in it, and proclaims, as it were, to those able spiritually to hear its own cause hymned in a threefold manner" (Maximus the Confessor, *To Thalassius* 13 [PG 90:296bc]) – see also above, pp. 89–92. "In Christ the mystery of the Trinity is hymned ... for the Father was well pleased and the Word came to dwelt among us and the divine Spirit overshadowed" (Andrew of Crete, *Canon on the Nativity* 6 [PG 97:1324c]).

[8] "Trinity ... is not just a name and an invented word, but a trinity in reality and truth" (Athanasius, *To Serapion* 1.28 [PG 26:596ab]). "To believe in one holy Trinity, not a trinity in name only, but having true being and subsistence" (Athanasius, *Synodal Letter* 5 [PG 26:801b]). "The Father, the Son and the Holy Spirit are one in all things, except in unbegottenness, begottenness and procession, and are divided only conceptually. For we acknowledge one God in the properties alone of fatherhood, sonship and procession, and ... we understand by this difference the perfection of the hypostasis, or the mode of existence" (John Damascene, *On the Orthodox Faith* 8 [PG 94:828–29; ed. Kotter, 29]). "... the mode of the begottenness and the procession are inaccessible to us" (John Damascene, *On the Orthodox Faith* 8 [PG 94:820; ed. Kotter, 24]).

[9] "The name 'father' belongs neither to the essence, nor to the energy, but to the relation and to how the Father stands with regard to the Son, or the Son with regard to the Father" (Maximus, *Ambigua* [PG 91:1265d]). "One should know that we do not say that the Father is from anybody. We say that he is the Father of the Son. And we do not say that the Son is a cause or a father. We say that he is from the Father and is the Son of the Father. And we say that the Holy Spirit is both from the Father and the Spirit of the Father. We do not say that the Spirit is *from* the Son. We call him the Spirit *of* the Son, and we confess that he was manifested by the Son and communicated by him to us" (John Damascene, *On the Orthodox Faith* 8 [PG 94:832ab; ed. Kotter, 30–31]). "The title of 'Father' does not represent the essence; it indicates the relation with the Son" (Gregory of Nyssa, *Against Eunomius* 2 [PG 43:473b; ed. Jaeger, 2:319]).

[10] The identification of the persons with the relations, the view that the persons are internal relations of the essence, is characteristic of Roman Catholic theology. See Thomas Aquinas, *Summa Theologiae* 1a, ques. 29, a.4. Cf. Nicolas, *Dieu connu comme inconnu*, 325: "La Forme divine … est subsistante, elle est Sujet, et c'est ce Sujet qui est commun aux trois Personnes, c'est-à-dire que les trois Personnes s'identifient avec lui, tout en se distinguant entre elles par l'opposition relative"; Juan-Miguel Garrigues, "L'energie divine et la grace chez Maxime le Confesseur," in *Istina* 3 (1974), 277: "Les noms des personnes trinitaires apparaissent comme les *relations* qui les distinguent entre elles dans l'essence sans faire nombre avec elle et donc sans altérer sa consubstantialité."

[11] "Everything that God has made he made by the energy of the Holy Spirit." "The Spirit being participated by the whole of creation and of his own agency creating all things and giving substance to them, and sanctifying them, and maintaining them in existence" (John Damascene, *On the Orthodox Faith* 86 [PG 94:1141; ed. Kotter, 194] and 8 [PG 94:821; ed. Kotter, 26]). "Supplying, as it were, through itself, illumination to every rational power in the search for truth … filling all things with its power … in essence simple, in powers various, wholly present in each and being wholly everywhere" (Basil the Great, *On the Holy Spirit* 22 [PG 32:108c; trans. Jackson, *NPNF*, modified]).

[12] "Having learned about the Spirit of God that accompanies the Logos and discloses his energy … an essential power, contemplated in itself in its particular hypostasis … that rests in the Logos and is disclosure of him" (John Damascene, *On the Orthodox Faith* 7 [PG 94:805; ed. Kotter, 16–17]). "In himself [the Spirit] shows the glory of the Onlybegotten, and in himself he bestows on true worshippers the knowledge of God" (Basil the Great, *On the Holy Spirit* 47 [PG 32:153b; trans. Jackson, *NPNF*, modified]). "It is not possible to arrive at a conception of the Son if one has not previously been enlightened by the Holy Spirit" (Ps.-Basil, *Letter* 38 [PG 32:329c]).

[13] "For when we receive gifts, the first thing that occurs to us is the giver, then we think of the sender, and then raise up our thoughts to the source and cause of these benefits" (Basil the Great, *On the Holy Spirit* 37 [PG 32:133d; trans. Jackson, *NPNF*, modified]). "Neither can the Father be conceived of without the Son, nor can the Son be comprehended without the Holy Spirit" (Gregory of Nyssa, *On the Holy Spirit, against the Macedonians* 12 [PG 45:1316b]). "So long as the Logos was not yet the Son, nobody as yet knew the Father" (Athanasius, *Against the Arians* 4.23 [PG 26:501d]). "For the Father is with the Son as the Father of the Son, and the Son is the true teacher about the Father" (Clement of Alexandria, *Stromata* 5.1 [PG 9:9a]).

[14] "Thus the way of the knowledge of God is from one Spirit through the one Son to the one Father, and conversely the natural goodness and the inherent holiness and the royal dignity extend from the Father through the Only-begotten to the Spirit" (Basil the Great, *On the Holy Spirit* 47 [PG 32:153bc]). "And he who grasps in thought the 'form,' so to speak, of the Son images 'the figure of his (the Father's) person' or 'hypostasis,' seeing the latter through the former, not seeing, however, in the copy any unbegottenness of the Father ... but discerning the unbegotten beauty in the Begotten .... Thus the person or 'hypostasis' of the Son becomes as it were the form and countenance by which the Father is made known, and the person or 'hypostasis' of the Father is made known in the form of the Son, although their observed individuality abides in each to serve as a clear differentiation of their persons or 'hypostases'" (Ps.-Basil, *Letter* 38 [PG 32:340b; trans. Deferrari, LCL]).

[15] John Damascene, *On the Orthodox Faith* 13 (PG 94:853c; ed. Kotter, 39).

[16] "The very cause of the universe ... in the superabundance of his erotic goodness is carried outside of himself ... and is, as it were, beguiled by goodness, love and eros, and is enticed away from his transcendent dwelling place and comes to abide within all things, and he does so by virtue of his supraessential and ecstatic capacity to remain nevertheless within himself" (Dionysius the Areopagite, *On the Divine Names* 4.13 (PG 3:712ab; trans. Luibheid-Rorem, CWS, modified]).

[17] "The will and energy of God is the creative and providential cause of all place and time and of every nature" (Irenaeus, *Frag.* 5 [PL 7:1232b]). "The gnostic knows ... through the created world the energy through which he adores the will of God" (Clement of Alexandria, *Stromata* 7.14 [PG 9:520c]). "... the *logoi* which pre-exist as a unity in God and which produce the essences of things. Theology calls them predefining, divine and good acts of will which determine and create that which is" (Dionysius the Areopagite, *On the Divine Names* 5.8 [PG 3:824c; trans. Luibheid-Rorem, CWS, modified]). "In the case of the Father, the Son and the Holy Spirit, we have knowledge of the identity of the essence from the identity of the energy and the will" (John Damascene, *On the Orthodox Faith* 58 [PG 94:1033c; ed. Kotter, 137]).

[18] "There is no necessity governing the divine nature" (Gregory of Nyssa, *Against Eunomius* 1 [PG 45:329a; ed. Jaeger, 1:101]). "With regard to God, creation is a work of the will, not something coeternal with God ... God simply by willing brought all things into existence from non-being" (John Damascene, *On the Orthodox Faith* 8 [PG 94:813; ed. Kotter, 21]). "Since our calling did not previously exist, but now has supervened, it

was preceded by will and … has occurred according to the good pleasure of the will" (Athanasius, *Against the Arians* 3.61 [PG 26:452a]).

[19] "[Selon Augustin, Dieu] contient éternellement en soi les modèles archetypes de tous les êtres possibles, leur formes intelligibles, leurs lois, leur poids, leur measures, leur nombres. Ces modèles éternels sont des Idées, incréées et consubstantielles à Dieu de la consubstantiabilité même du Verbe" (Gilson, *La Philosophie au Moyen Age*, 132). See also Thomas Aquinas, *Summa Theologiae* 1.44.3: "In divina sapientia sunt rationes omnium rerum, quas supra diximus ideas, id est formas exemplares in mente divina existentes." "Puisqu'elles subsistent dans l'intelligence de Dieu, les Idées participent nécessairement à ses attributs essentiels. Comme lui-même, elles sont éternelles, immuables et nécessaires" (Étienne Gilson, *Introduction à l'Étude de Saint Augustin* [Paris: Vrin, 1969], 109). See also Augustine, *De diversis questionibus* 83, ques. 46.1–2, vol. 40, col. 29–30; Étienne Gilson, *Le Thomisme* (Paris: Vrin, 1972), 146–48.

[20] "Dans l'explication de la Trinité, Augustin conçoit la nature divine avant les personnes. Sa formule de la Trinité sera: une seule nature divine subsistant en trois personnes, celles des Grecs au contraire disait: trois personnes ayant une même nature …. Saint Augustin au contraire, préludant au concept latin que les scolastiques lui ont emprunté, envisage avant tout la nature divine et poursuit jusqu'aux personnes pour atteindre la réalité complète. Deus, pour lui, ne signifie plus directement le Père, mais plus généralement la divinité" (E. Portalié, "Augustin (saint)," *Dictionnaire de Théologie Catholique*, vol. 1, col. 2268ff.).

[21] "Toute essence, ou quiddité, peut être conçue sans que l'on conçoive rien au sujet de son existence. Par example, je peux concevoir *homme* ou *phénix* et ignorer pourtant s'ils existent dans la nature. Il est donc clair que l'existence (esse) est autre chose (aliud) que l'essence ou quiddité" (Thomas Aquinas, *De ente et essentia*, ch. 4, ed. M.-D. Roland-Gosselin [Paris: Vrin, 1948], 34).

[22] For an interpretation of existence within the context of an objective-rationalist causality which bypasses the question concerning the *mode* of existence and confines the existential fact to an intellectual-aetiological combination of being and Being (*ens = rem habentem esse*) see Martin Heidegger, "Die Metaphysik als Geschichte des Seins," in *Nietzsche*, vol. 2 (Pfullingen: Neske, 1961), 416ff.; Gilson, *Le Thomisme,* 88–89, 186–87; Aimé Forest, *La structure métaphysique du concret selon saint Thomas d'Aquin* (Paris: Vrin, 1931); Jacques Maritain, *Court traité de l'existence et des existants* (Paris: Hartmann, 1947).

[23] "Les scolastiques opposent essentia et existentia: l'essence est la nature conceptuelle d'une chose; elle est conçue comme un pouvoir d'être;

l'existence au contraire est la pleine actualité, *ultima actualitas*" (R. Eucken, *Geschichte der philosophischen Terminologie*, cited by André Lalande, *Vocabulaire technique et critique de la Philosophie* [Paris: PUF, 1972], 318). See also Heidegger, *Über den Humanismus*, 18: "Die in ihrer Wesensherkunft verborgene Unterscheidung von essentia (Wesenheit) und existentia (Wirklichkeit) durchherrscht das Geschik der abendländischen und der gesamten europäisch bestimmten Geschichte."

[24] "La signification principale et directe *d'ens* (selon saint Thomas) n'est pas l'exister, mais la chose même qui existe. Le thomisme devient alors un 'chosisme' que l'on peut accuser de 'réifier' tous les concepts qu'il touche et de transformer en une mosaïque d'entités closes dans leurs propres essences le tissu vivant du réel" (Gilson, *Le Thomisme*, 187).

[25] St. Gregory Palamas writes in a famous passage: "When God was conversing with Moses, He did not say, 'I am the essence,' but 'I am the One Who is.' Thus it is not the One Who is who derives from the essence, but essence which derives from Him, for it is He who contains all being in Himself" (*Triads in Defence of the Holy Hesychasts* 3.2.12 [ed. Christou, 1:666; trans. Gendle, CWS]).

[26] See Gregory of Nyssa, *On the Hexaemeron* 7 (PG 44:69c), and *On the Soul and Resurrection* (PG 46:124c).

[27] "The one nature has been divided into a myriad fragments. And we who belong to this one nature are victims of one another like vicious serpents" (Maximus the Confessor, *To Thalassius*, intro. [PG 90:256b]). See also *To Thalassius* 40 (397c): "The self-love of each person's will … has made the mildest nature savage. And it has cut up the one essence into many opposing parts which, not to put it more strongly, are destructive of one another." See also Maximus the Confessor, *Various Texts* 1.46 (PG 90:1196ab): "The self-love and cleverness of men, alienating them from each other and perverting the law, have cut our single human nature into many fragments. They have so extended the insensibility which they introduced into our nature and which now dominates it, that our nature, divided in will and purpose, fights against itself" (Palmer-Sherrard-Ware).

[28] See pp. 240–41 above.

[29] *L'Être et le Néant*, 321: "S'il y a un Autre, quel qu'il soit, où qu'il soit, quels que soient ses rapports avec moi, sans même qu'il agisse autrement sur moi que par le pur surgissement de son être, j'ai un dehors, j'ai une *nature*; ma chûte originelle c'est l'existence de l'autre."

[30] "Tout se passe comme si j'avais une dimension d'être dont j'étais séparé par un néant radical: et ce néant, c'est la liberté d'autrui" (ibid., 320).

[31] *Huis clos*, at the end of the fifth scene: "L'enfer, c'est les Autres."

[32] *The Brothers Karamazov*, A.6.3: From the teachings and homilies of Staretz Zosima, 9. See also Isaac the Syrian, *Ascetic Works*, Hom. 84 (ed.

Spanos, 326): "But I say that those who are punished in Gehenna are scourged by the whip of love .... It is absurd for anyone to think that sinners in Gehenna are deprived of the love of God. Love is the product of the knowledge of truth, which is admittedly given to all in common. By its power, love works in a twofold manner, punishing sinners, as happens even in this life between friends, and giving joy to those who fulfil its obligations."

[33] "He is called Logos because he is related to the Father as the *logos* is to the mind; not only on account of his passionless generation, but also because of the union, and of his declaratory function. Perhaps, too, this relation might be compared to that between the definition and the thing defined, since this also is called *logos* ... and the Son is a concise demonstration ... of the Father's nature .... And if anyone should say that this name was given him because he exists in beings, he would not be wrong. For what exists unless it has by constituted by *logos*?" (Gregory of Nazianzus, *Or*. 30.20 [PG 36:129a; trans. Browne and Swallow, *NPNF*, modified]).

[34] "The great mystery of the Incarnation remains a mystery eternally. Not only is what is not yet seen of it greater than what has been revealed – for it is revealed merely to the extent that those saved by it can grasp it – but also even what is revealed still remains entirely hidden and is by no means known as it really is. What I have said should not appear paradoxical. For God is beyond being and transcends all beyond-beingness; and so, when he wished to come down to the level of being, he became being in a manner which transcends being. Thus, too, although transcending man, yet out of love for man he truly became man by taking on the substance of men; but the manner in which he became man always remains unrevealed, for he was made man in a way which transcends man" (Maximus the Confessor, *Various Texts* 1.12 [PG 90:1134b; Palmer-Sherrard-Ware]). "As for the love of Christ for humanity, the Word of God, I believe, uses this term to hint that the transcendent has put aside its own hiddenness and has revealed itself to us by becoming a human being. But he is hidden even after this revelation, or, if I may speak in a more divine fashion, is hidden even amid the revelation. For this mystery of Jesus remains hidden and can be drawn out by no word or mind. What is to be said of it remains unsayable; what is to be understood of it remains unknowable" (Dionysius the Areopagite, *Epistle* 3 [PG 3:1069b; trans. Luibheid-Rorem, CWS]). See also *On the Divine Names* 2.9 (PG 3:648a).

[35] "Christ accomplished the renewal of our nature in his own hypostasis. And we have clothed ourselves with him from water and the spirit, and he has united us to himself by an ineffable mystery and has made us members of his own body" (Isaac the Syrian, *Ascetic Works*, *Ep*. 4

[ed. Spanos, 387]). "For our Lord Jesus Christ came for this reason, to change and transform and renew human nature and to recreate this soul that had been overturned by passions through the transgression. He came to mingle human nature with his own spirit of the Godhead. A new mind and a new soul and new eyes, new ears, a new spiritual tongue, and, in a word, new humans – this was what he came to effect in those who believe in him" (Macarius of Egypt, *Spiritual Homilies*, Hom. 44.1 [ed. Dörries-Klostermann-Kroeger, 291; trans. Maloney, CWS]).

[36] "In his love for man God became man so that he might unite human nature to himself and stop it from acting evilly towards itself, or rather from being at strife and divided against itself, and from having no rest because of the instability of its will and purpose" (Maximus the Confessor, *Various Texts* 1.47 [PG 90:1196c; Palmer-Sherrard-Ware]).

[37] Christ "having joined what is earthly to what is heavenly, offered it up to God, saving … and deifying it not by identity of essence but in virtue of the Incarnation. Through his holy flesh which he took from us as the first fruits he also made us 'partakers of the divine nature'" (Maximus the Confessor, *Ep.* 11 [PG 91:468c]). See also *To Thalassius* 59 (PG 90:608a): "Grace in no way abrogates the power of nature, but rather when nature has been abrogated by the practice of what is contrary to nature, it renders it active again by the practice of what is in accordance with nature, initiating it into the understanding of divine things."

[38] [*Metanoia*, the Greek word for repentance, means etymologically a change of mind or outlook. Trans.]

[39] By "mystical life" I mean humanity's participation in the *mysteries* [in Western terms the *sacraments*] of the Church. And by a "mystery," in the Church's parlance, I mean the mystical, that is, living, experience of that space in which human freedom encounters the Grace of God, which is dynamically actualized divine love. Responding to the love of God is not simply an emotional or moral event. It is the mode of personal existence, the mystery of humanity's existential communion with God. Thus the primordial mystery is the very body of the Church: Human beings bring to the Church their free will, that is to say, their daily attempt, even if unsuccessful, to return to a mode of existence which is "in accordance with nature," to unity with other human beings, and to communion with God. And they find in the Church the grace-filled complement of their own ineffective efforts, the total fulfilment of their goal. In the space of the mystery, human effort encounters divine love. Personal ascetic discipline or personal failure and sin are made good by the power of God, by the life which his love bestows. By the practice of such a dialectic, the image of the "new man," the image of the citizen of the Kingdom, is gradually disclosed. The ethos of existential authenticity is revealed.

Human beings bring to the Church every phase of their natural life, of their fallenness and failure. And each such approach finds in the Church a corresponding acceptance, a corresponding mystery of the encounter of human freedom with divine Grace. Each of the Church's mysteries offers the possibility of the human being's dynamic and repeated approach and incorporation into her life-giving body, into her theanthropic nature, into her authentic ethos. It is an event that transforms a life which is "contrary to nature" into a life which "transcends nature," that transforms the corruptible time of atomic existence into the incorruptible time of personal relation.

[40] The passage in St. Maximus is as follows: "Nature does not contain the inner principles (*logoi*) of what is beyond nature any more than it contains the laws of what is contrary to nature. By what is beyond nature I mean the divine and inconceivable pleasure which God naturally produces in those found worthy of being united with him through grace. By what is contrary to nature I mean the indescribable pain brought about by the privation of such pleasure. This pain God naturally produces in the unworthy when he is united to them in a manner contrary to grace. For God is united with all men according to the underlying quality of their inner state; and, at the creation of each person, he provides each person with the capacity to perceive and sense him when he is united in one way or another with all men at the end of the ages" (*Various Texts* 4.20 [PG 90:1312c; Palmer-Sherrard-Ware]). See also *Centuries on Love* 1.71 (PG 90:976c): "It was on account of this that our Lord and God Jesus Christ, showing his love for us, suffered for the whole of mankind and gave to all men an equal hope of resurrection, although each man determines his own fitness for glory or punishment" (Palmer-Sherrard-Ware).

[41] *Metaphysics* 3:1005^{b}27–28. See also Thomas Aquinas, *Summa Theologiae* 1:45.1c: "idem autem est nihil, quod nullum ens."

[42] "Failing to attain movement or order in accordance with nature, we are carried towards non-existence, which is contrary to nature, irrational and utterly without substance" (Maximus the Confessor, *Scholia on the Divine Names* [PG 4:305b]. Cf. *Ambigua* [PG 91:1322a]).

Chapter Three

[1] Aristotle, *Poetics* 6:1450^{a}5–6 (Oxford trans.).

[2] See, for example, Plato, *Republic* 7:517bc; C. Ritter, *Die Kerngedanken der platonischen Philosophie* (Munich, 1931), 18ff., 55ff.; J. Stenzel, *Platon der Erzieher* (Leipzig, 1928), 249ff.

[3] See, for example, Plotinus, *Enneads* 1.8.3 and 1.8.5; Fr. Billicsich, *Das Problem der Theodizee im philosophischen Denken des Abendlandes,*

Philosophische Abhandlung der österreichischen Leo-Gesellschaft 1 (1936), 56–97.

[4] Cf. *Corpus Hermeticum* 5:4a, 6:2a. See also A. Festugière, *La révélation d'Hermès Trismégiste*, vol. 2 (1949) and vol. 4 (1954) (Paris: Gabalda).

[5] See Ugo Bianchi, ed., *Le origini dello gnosticismo* (The origins of Gnosticism), Colloquium of Messina 1966 (Leiden: Brill, 1972²).

[6] "... le rationalisme moral chrétien (du moyen age)" (Étienne Gilson, *L'Esprit de la Philosophie Médiéval*, 2nd ed. [Paris: Vrin, 1969], 310–11.

[7] Thomas Aquinas, *Summa Theologiae* 1a.2ae.64.1.ad.1m. "Ainsi nous voyons se déterminer la notion de vertu prise sous sa forme la plus parfaite; elle doit sa qualité de bien moral à la règle de la raison" (Étienne Gilson, *Le Thomisme, Introduction à la Philosophie de saint Thomas d'Aquin*, 6th ed. [Paris: Vrin, 1972], 327).

[8] "Bonum autem hominis est secundum rationem esse, et malum hominis est praeter rationem esse. Unde virtus humana, quae hominem facit donum et opus ipsius bonum reddit, intantum est contra naturam hominis, inquantum convenit rationi; vitium autem intantum est contra naturam hominis, inquantum est contra ordinem rationis" (Thomas Aquinas, *Summa Theologiae* 1a.2ae.71.2.resp.); "... définir la vertu et le bien moral comme ce qui s'accorde avec la raison. Inversement, le mal moral, le péché et le vice dont le péché découle, ne peuvent se concevoir que comme des manques de rationalité dans l'acte ou dans l'habitude" (Gilson, *L'Esprit de la Philosophie Médiévale*, 307).

[9] "La loi éternelle est la raison divine ou la volonté de Dieu, ordonnant de conserver l'ordre naturel et défendant de le troubler" (Gilson, *L'Esprit de la Philosophie Médiévale*, 314). "Unde ejusdem rationis est quod vitium et peccatum sit contra ordinem rationis humanae et quod sit contra legem aeternam" (Thomas Aquinas, *Summa Theologiae* 1a.2ae.71.2.ad.1m).

[10] "Désobéir à la raison, c'est désobéir à Dieu même .... Toute rectitude de la volonté humaine se mésure donc à son accord avec la volonté divine en même temps qu'à son accord avec la raison" (Gilson, *L'Esprit de la Philosophie Médiévale*, 308–9, 311). "Virtus est habitus in modum naturae, rationi consentaneus" (Thomas Aquinas, *Summa Theologiae* 1a.2ae.71.2.ad.1m).

[11] "Le Dieu créateur de l'Écriture s'affirme donc comme source et cause de toute legislation naturelle, morale et sociale" (Gilson, *L'Esprit de la Philosophie Médiévale*, 316).

[12] "La morale de Kant n'est peut-être qu'une morale chrétienne sans la métaphysique chrétienne qui la justifie" (Gilson, *L'Esprit de la Philosophie Médiévale*, 323).

[13] Kant, *Grundlegung zur Metaphysik der Sitten*, Akademie-Ausgabe, Abtlg. 1, Bd. 4, 421 ["Treated in such a way that the maxim of your will can always be at the same time a principle of valid universal law."]

[14] See Kant, *Kritik der reinen Vernunft*, 2:2.2: Von dem Ideal des höchsten Gutes. Also Heidegger, *Einführung in die Metaphysik*, 150–51: "Das Sollen tritt als Gegensatz zum Sein auf, sobald dieses sich als Idee bestimmt .... Für Kant, der Natur tritt, gleichfalls von der Vernunft und als Vernunft bestimmt, der kategorische Imperativ gegenüber."

[15] Nicolai Hartmann, *Ethik*, 4th ed. (Berlin, 1962), ch. 39, §F, 380.

[16] See Heidegger, *Über den Humanismus*, 41; *Sein und Zeit*, §§ 4, 5, 7c, 9, 10.

[17] Frag. 119 (ed. Diels-Kranz, *Die Fragmente der Vorsokratiker*, 1:177).

[18] *Iliad* 6.511.

[19] *Odyssey* 14.411.

[20] *Works and Days* 167.525.

[21] *History* 7.125; cf. 1.15.

[22] *Laws* 865e.

[23] *Anabasis of Alexander* 5.20.4.

[24] *Theogony* 66.

[25] Demetrakos, *Mega Lexikon tês Ellênikês Glôssês*, 4:3239.

[26] See Heidegger, *Über den Humanismus*, 39–41.

[27] "Dieses Denken is aber dann auch nicht erst Ethik, weil es Ontologie ist" (*Über den Humanismus*, 41).

[28] Albert Camus, *Le Mythe de Sisyphe* (Paris: Gallimard, 1946).

[29] See Sartre's very representative play, *L'engrénage* (Paris: Nagel, 1948).

[30] See Herbert Marcuse, "Existentialismus," in *Kultur und Gesellschaft*, 2 (Frankfurt: Suhrkamp, 1968), 49, 52.

[31] See Sartre, *L'Être et le Néant*, 642.

[32] Ibid., 561ff.

[33] See ibid., 30ff., 115ff. This ontological distinction (*en-soi, pour-soi*) also has its roots in Heidegger. See *Was ist Metaphysik?* 15: "Das Seiende, das in der Weise der Existenz ist, ist der Mensch. Der Mensch allein existiert. Der Fels ist aber er existiert nicht. Der Baum ist, aber er existiert nicht. Das Pferd ist, aber es existiert nicht. Der Engel ist aber er existiert nicht. Gott ist, aber er existiert nicht."

[34] "La liberté humaine précède l'essence de l'homme et la rend possible, l'essence de l'être humain est en suspens dans sa liberté" (Sartre, *L'Être et le Néant*, 61).

[35] See ibid., 587: "même les tenailles du bourreau ne nous dispensent pas d'être libres." See also Marcuse, "Existentialismus," 64.

[36] "Ce que nous appelons liberté est donc impossible à distinguer de *l'être* de la 'realité humaine.' L'homme n'est point *d'abord* pour être

libre *ensuite*, mail il n'y a pas de différence entre l'être de l'homme et son 'être-libre' " (Sartre, *L'Être et le Néant*, 61).

[37] Sartre, *L'existentialisme est un humanisme*, 57ff.

[38] "Für Camus ist der einzig angemessene Ausdruck, das absurde Leben zu leben, und das künstlerische Schaffen, das sich weigert das Konkrete zu begründen, und mit Bildern das ausfüllt, was keinen Sinn hat" (Marcuse, "Existentialismus," 51).

[39] See Ernst Bloch, *Das Prinzip Hoffnung* (Frankfurt, 1959); Herbert Marcuse, *One-dimensional Man* (Boston: Beacon Press, 1968); Roger Garaudy, *Marxisme du XXe siècle* (Paris: Union général d'editions, 1966); Garaudy, *Le grand tournant du Socialisme* (Paris: Gallimard, 1969); Garaudy, *Humanisme marxiste* (Paris: Éditions sociales, 1957). In the end even these humanist tendencies, which attempt to bring a humanist dimension to Marxism (or to draw from Marxism ways of making humanism topical and viable) do not free themselves from the characteristic polarization of Western thought between an absolute anthropocentric subjectivism on the one hand and an equally anthropocentric search for absolute objectivity on the other. Sartre illustrates this European schizophrenia nicely when after *L'Être et le Néant* he wrote his *Critique de la raison dialectique* to relate his existentialism both to Hegel's methodological principles (concerning (i) the dialectical form of the development of logic and historical evolution, and (ii) the correlation of what is true with what is the totality) and to Marx's principles concerning humanity's social nature, which is tied up with the historical evolution of productive work and the history of technology. This same imprisonment in perfect subjectivity along with a simultaneous attempt to achieve absolute objectivity (with the individual at the center in both cases) is perpetuated in the work of the "Frankfurt school" of Adorno and Horkheimer, which sought to bridge the gulf between subjective experience and that "socialization" of humanity which makes humanity simply a dependency of its social environment. The Frankfurt school relies on the principle of doubt, that is, on the critical function of intellection and generally of consciousness, on the ability of the subject to control critically the logical forms which can be attributed to historical evolution and to become conscious of the contradictions which the dialectics of historical "progress" create. The problem of the moral testing of personality within the context of the relations which shape historical "becoming" remains untouched – a despised problem of "metaphysical" thought which can only sustain subjective dogmatisms.

[40] See *Sein und Zeit*, §25–27, 35–38, 51–52, 59, 68c, 71, 73, 81: "Das Dasein ist von ihm selbst als eigentlichem Selbstseinkönnen zunächst immer schon abgefallen und an die 'Welt' verfallen" (175). "Das Nicht-

es-selbst-sein fungiert, (existenzial-ontologisch gesehen) als *positive* Möglichkeit des Seienden das besorgend in seiner Welt aufgeht" (176). "Im Verfallen dokumentiert sich ein *existenzialer Modus* des In-der-Welt-seins" (176). ["Dasein has, in the first instance, fallen away from itself as an authentic potentiality for Being its Self, and has fallen into the 'world'" (175). Macquarrie-Robinson note here: "While we shall follow English idioms by translating 'an die "Welt"' as 'into the "world"' in contexts such as this, the preposition 'into' is hardly the correct one. The idea is rather that of falling *at* the world or collapsing *against* it" (*Being and Time* [Oxford: Basil Blackwell, 1967], 220n1). "Not-Being-its-self functions as a *positive* possibility of that entity which, in its essential concern, is absorbed in a world" (176). "An *existential mode* of Being-in-the-world is documented in the phenomenon of falling" (176).]

41 "L'homme absurde entrevoit un univers brulant et glacé, transparent et limité, où rien n'est pas possible mais tout est donné, passé lequel c'est l'effondrement et le néant" (Albert Camus, *Le Myth de Sisyphe* [Paris, 1946], 83).

42 "La réalité humaine est avant tout son proper néant. Ce qu'elle nie ou néantit de soi comme pour-soi, ce ne peut-être que *soi*. Et, comme elle est constituée dans son sens par cette néantisation et cette présence en elle de ce qu'elle néantit à titre de néantisé, c'est le soi-comme *être-en-soi* manqué qui fait le sens de la réalité humaine" (Sartre, *L'Être et le Néant*, 132).

43 "Le Pour-soi ne peut jamais être que problématiquement son Futur, car il est séparé de lui par un Néant qu'il est: en un mot il est libre et sa liberté est à elle-même sa proper limite. Être libre c'est être condamné à être libre" (ibid., 174).

44 "You should know," says St. Maximus the Confessor, "that what is simply called evil is not evil in an absolute sense, but is evil in relation to one thing and not evil in relation to another. Similarly, what is simply called good is not good in an absolute sense, but good in relation to one thing and not good in relation to another" (*To Thalassius* 43 [PG 90:413b]).

45 Matt 19:17; Luke 18:19; Mark 10:18. "The first and chief good, the nature of which is goodness, is the divine" (Gregory of Nyssa, *On the Life of Moses* 7 [PG 44:301a; ed. H. Musurillo, 4.5–6]). "Only God is good by nature" (Maximus the Confessor, *Chapters on Love* 4.90 [PG 90:1069c]). "God is not good by participation in goodness, but is himself goodness. Man is good, however, by participation in goodness" (Ps.-Athanasius, *Dialogues on the Trinity* 1.12 [PG 28:1136b]).

46 "Calling thearchic existence goodness" (Dionysius the Areopagite, *On the Divine Names* 4.1 [PG 3:693b]). "Natural goodness … extends from the Father through the Only-begotten to the Spirit" (Basil the Great, *On*

the *Holy Spirit* 47 [PG 32:153b]). "The essence of goodness is the one triadic cause of beings, from which beings derive their being and well being through goodness" (Dionysius the Areopagite, *On the Ecclesiastical Hierarchy* 1.3 [PG 3:373c]).

[47] See Hippolytus, *Against Heresies* 1.19 (PG 16:3045c): "The nature of evil has not come about from God, nor does it have hypostasis in itself, but it has come about by being opposite to and consequential upon the good." Athanasius the Great, *Against the Pagans* 7 (PG 25:16a): "evil neither came from God nor was in God, nor did it exist in the beginning, nor has it any independent reality (*oute ousia tis*)" (trans. Thomson, OECT). Basil the Great, *Homilies* 9.5 (PG 31:341b): "You must not suppose God to be the cause of evil, nor must you imagine that evil has its own hypostasis, for wickedness is not a subsistent being like an animal." And *Homilies* 9.4 (PG 31:341b): "Evil is a privation of good." Maximus the Confessor, *Ambigua* (PG 91:1332a): "Evil, the being of which is characterized by non-existence." See also the *Scholia on the Divine Names* (PG 4:304d–5a): "Evil has no hypostasis but only a dependent existence (*parypostasis*), having come about on account of the good and not of itself. For we do evil not with an evil end in view, but under the impression that we are doing good, even though the outcome proves to be the opposite." John Damascene, *Dialogues against the Manichees* 1.13 (PG 94:1517a): "Evil is privation of being."

[48] "Evil is corruptible because corruption is the nature of evil, which does not possess any true existence whatsoever" (Maximus the Confessor, *Various Chapters* 3.57 [PG 90:1285c; Palmer-Sherrard-Ware]). "But when it turns from its course and is twisted away from what it naturally is, then we speak of the vice of the soul" (Athanasius, *Life of Antony* 20 [PG 26:873b; trans. Gregg, CWS]). "All evil naturally operates in a deficiency of or an excess of virtue" (Gregory of Nyssa, *Life of Moses* 288 [PG 44:420a; ed. Musurillo, 132; trans. Malherbe-Ferguson, CWS]). "Evil is the abuse of natural powers .... Evil is the dissolution of order, or *ataxia*" (John Damascene, *Against the Manichees* 1.14, 1.47 [PG 94:1517c, 1548d]).

[49] "Evil is properly speaking sin ... for it depends on our free will" (Basil the Great, *Homilies* 9.5 [PG 31:337d]). "Evil consists ... in the difference between our deliberate will and the divine will" (Maximus the Confessor, *Opuscula* [PG 91:56b]). "Since evil is outside of free choice, it has no nature; when all free choice comes into being in God, evil disappears completely" (Gregory of Nyssa, *On the Soul and Resurrection* [PG 46:101a]).

[50] In patristic literature even the demons, because they are personal existences of the spiritual world with a perverted will which opposes the

will of God and provokes the corruption of human freedom, are not evil
by nature but only in their exercise of free will. Cf. Maximus the Confessor, *Centuries on Love* 3.5 (PG 90:1020a): "Not even the demons are
evil by nature, but they have become evil through the misuse of their
natural powers" (Palmer-Sherrard-Ware). Ps.-Athanasius, *Questions to
Antiochus* (PG 28:604a): "Why is the essence of demons made different
to the essence of angels? There is no difference of essence, only of the
will." "Nor are the demons evil by nature .... They are called evil not
because of what they are (for they are from the good and have been allotted a good essence), but because of what they are not, because they
were unable (as Scripture says) to maintain their own position .... They
are not evil by nature, but through the lack of the angelic virtues" (Dionysius the Areopagite, *On the Divine Names* 4.23 [PG 3:724c–25b]).
"The demons are from the angels. For they have not cast off the angelic
gifts given to them, that is to say, they have not returned the good they
possess by nature, even though they do not wish to see the light that is
in them, having shut up powers they have that are capable of seeing the
good .... Note that the demons, too, are radiant, or rather they are lights
by essence like the rest of the angels. Hence in the Gospels: 'They saw
Satan like lightning'" (Maximus the Confessor, *Scholia on the Divine
Names* [PG 4:293a]).

[51] See Dionysius the Areopagite, *On Mystical Theology* 5 (PG 3:1045d–
48b): "neither is it [the Godhead] goodness." Maximus the Confessor,
Scholia on the Divine Names (PG 4:412bc): "[the Godhead] is neither
beautiful nor good, since these are in some sense passions, and, as it
were, relations and accidents."

[52] "There are two ways, one of life, the other of death ... the way of life
is this, first you must love God ... secondly, your neighbour as yourself"
(*Didache* 1.1.2; ed. Gebhardt-Harnack-Zahn [Leipzig, 1920]).

[53] "It is, therefore, not in outward shape or form that the distinguishing
characteristic of Christians consists. Many Christians believe that the
difference does lie in some external sign .... It is through the renewing
of the mind and the tranquillity experienced in our thoughts and the love
of the Lord and the love for heavenly things that every new creation of
Christians distinguishes them from the men of this world. For this reason
did the Lord come" (Macarius the Egyptian, *Spiritual Homilies* 5.4–5
[ed. Dörrie-Klostermann-Kroeger, 49–50; trans. Maloney, CWS]). "He
[God] does this so that they may prefer to be righteous in reality rather
than in appearance, discarding the cloak of hypocritical moral display
and genuinely pursuing a virtuous life in the way that the divine Logos
wishes them to. They will then live with reverence, revealing the state
of their soul to God rather than displaying the external appearance of a

moral life to their fellow-men" (Maximus the Confessor, *Various Texts* 1.74 [PG 90:1209b; Palmer-Sherrard-Ware]).

[54] "Repentance (*metanoia*) is to return from being contrary to nature to being in accordance with nature" (*Scholia on John Climacus* [PG 88:781bc]). "Repentance (*metanoia*) is great understanding (*synesis*)" (Hermas, *Shepherd* 4.2.2; ed. Lightfoot [London, 1898]).

[55] "Hence he who practises virtue for the sake of truth is not wounded by the darts of vainglory, but he who pursues the truth for the sake of virtue has the arrogance of vainglory as his companion" (*To Thalassius* 30 [PG 90:369a]).

[56] *Various Texts* 3.71 (PG 90:1292b; Palmer-Sherrard-Ware). See also 3.1 (1260b), where a biblical image is used to express both the priority of the *knowledge* of truth in relation to the *practice* of virtue and the interdependency of the two: "The person who combines spiritual knowledge with the practice of the virtues and practice of the virtues with spiritual knowledge is a throne and a footstool of God (cf. Isa 66:1) – a throne because of his spiritual knowledge and a footstool because of his ascetic practice" (Palmer-Sherrard-Ware).

[57] "Wisdom is a unity contemplated indivisibly in the various virtues which arise from it; and it is perceived in a single form in the operations of the virtues. Again, it appears as a simple unity when the virtues which issued from it are reintegrated with it. This happens when we, for whose sake wisdom has produced from itself each individual virtue, are drawn upwards towards it by means of each virtue" (*Various Texts* 3.44 [PG 90:1280ab; Palmer-Sherrard-Ware]).

[58] *Scholia on the Divine Names* (PG 4:348c).

[59] Ibid. (PG 4:305b).

[60] "The condemnation, then, for Adam's freely-chosen sin is the remodelling of nature towards passion, decay and death. Man did not originally possess this from God. He brought it about knowingly, having created sin freely through the transgression. Clearly, his being condemned to die is the product of this" (Maximus the Confessor, *To Thalassius* 42 [PG 90:408c]).

[61] Ibid., 42 (PG 90:405c).

[62] Cf. John 3:19: "And this is the judgement, that the light has come into the world, and men loved darkness rather than light."

[63] Maximus the Confessor, *To Thalassius* 29 (PG 90:364b). See also *Centuries on Love* 1.100 (PG 90:984a): "… (God's) goodness and wisdom and power, creative, preserving and judging beings."

[64] See Rev 20:14.

[65] *Spiritual Homilies* 1.2 (ed. Dörries-Klostermann-Kroeger, 1–2, lines 28–32; trans. Maloney, CWS).

Index

389

Moses 353
Mozart, Wolfgang Amadeus 58,
   115-16
mysteries 380-1

name 351-3, 355
nature 25, 44-5, 50, 52-4, 66-70,
   236, 300, 302, 306, 309
Nemesius of Emesa 369
Neoplatonism 15, 22
Nicholas of Cusa 21
Nicolas, J.-H. 311, 362-3
Nietzsche, Friedrich 225, 323
nothingness 133-5, 139, 142, 223-
   93, 272-4, 304

Oehler, Klaus 296
ontology 6-17, 28-30, 173-8, 267-
   72, 276-80
otherness 25-8, 105, 223, 232,
   234-6, 246, 249-51

Panofsky, Erwin 101
participation 60-2, 63-4, 67, 152,
   198-9, 203, 208
passions 237, 369-71
perichoresis 44, 253, 318, 373
Perse, Saint-John 83
person 5-6, 16-20, 25-70, 137,
   146, 232-4, 244, 309, 375;
   defined 53, 300
Philo of Alexandria 159
Philolaus of Croton 73
physics, modern 79-80
Pius XII, pope 321
place 106, 117-18
Plato 74-5, 92, 159, 189, 201-4,
   258, 278, 281, 296, 317, 322,
   323, 325, 338, 352, 353, 355,
   360

Plotinus 278, 296, 338-9, 340
Portalié, E. 377
praxis 85-6, 305
Proclus 322
Pythagoras 73

Régnon, Theodore de 298
regressus in infinitum 9
relation 5-8, 15-20, 34-5, 52-3,
   80-2, 83, 85, 93, 105, 112-18,
   124, 131-2, 149, 166, 226-7,
   235, 245, 259, 262, 276, 305,
   324, 375
repentance (*metanoia*) 270, 288,
   380, 388
Rodin, Auguste 58
Rosis, Zikos 363

Sabellius 15, 99
salvation 237, 260, 267-71
Sartre, Jean-Paul 6, 31, 32,
   48, 68-9, 108-13, 241, 243,
   247-8, 265, 266, 267, 384;
   Huis clos 379; *Le Diable et
   le Bon Dieu* 321, 336; *L'Être
   et le Néant* 108-9, 324, 334,
   339, 367, 372, 378-9, 384,
   385; *L'existentialisme est un
   humanisme* 303
Satan 387
Saussure, Ferdinand de 175, 295
scholasticism 9, 21, 98, 101, 103,
   208, 210-12, 225, 278-9, 298
Scotus, John Duns 21
Seferis, George 342, 351
shame 243-5
sign 175, 193, 350, 353
sin 290-3, 343, 388-9
Söhngen, G. 361-2
Son 374-5, 379, 381

Made in the USA